IAN LITTLE

Photo: Barry Supple

PUBLIC POLICY AND ECONOMIC DEVELOPMENT

Essays in Honour of Ian Little

Edited by

MAURICE SCOTT AND DEEPAK LAL

CLARENDON PRESS • OXFORD

1990

Oxford University Press, Walton Street, Oxford ox2 6or

Oxford New York Toronto
Delhi Bombay Calcutta Madras Karachi
Petaling Jaya Singapore Hong Kong Tokyo
Nairobi Dar es Salaam Cape Town
Melbourne Auckland

and associated companies in
Berlin Ibadan

Oxford is a trade mark of Oxford University Press

Published in the United States
by Oxford University Press, New York

British Library Cataloguing in Publication Data
Public policy and economic development: essays in
honour of Ian Little.
I. Scott, M. FG (Maurice FitzGerald)   II. Lal, Deepak
III. Little, I. M. D. (Ian Michael David)
330.9172'4
ISBN 0–19–828582–5

Library of Congress Cataloguing in Publication Data
Public policy and economic development: essays in honor of Ian Little/
edited by Maurice Scott and Deepak Lal.
p.   cm.
Bibliography: p.
Includes index.
1. Developing countries—Economic policy.   2. Developing
countries—Foreign economic relations.   3. Economic development.
4. Little, Ian Malcolm David.   I. Scott, Maurice FitzGerald.
II. Lal, Deepak.
HC59.7.P749   1989   89-16129
338.9'009172'6—dc20
ISBN 0–19–828582–5

Typeset by Asco Trade Typesetting Ltd, Hong Kong

Printed in Great Britain by Biddles Ltd
Guildford and King's Lynn

Preface

IAN LITTLE's practical introduction to public economic policy was his appointment as Deputy Director of the Economic Section of the Cabinet Office in Whitehall in 1953. His first visit to a developing country as an economist was to India in 1958. As this Preface is being written, he is masterminding a comparative study of macroeconomic policies in developing countries for the World Bank. Public Policy and Economic Development are two themes on which he has worked for over 30 years and on which he is still working, and so they are the right ones for a book of essays in his honour by his friends, colleagues, and pupils.

The public policy aspect of any field of economics is one that claims attention. Understanding more about how economies function can be fascinating, but perhaps not much more so than how a beehive functions. It is when better understanding points to better public policies that curiosity is reinforced by awareness of practical importance. While not comprehensive, a great many important policy questions are discussed in this book. Most of the essays provide the reader with a summing-up of a group of policy questions by an expert in that field. The aim, in keeping with Ian Little's own writings on these matters, has been to help and influence policy-makers, and the first requirement in doing so is that what is written should be understandable beyond the narrow circle of professional economists.

The first group of essays deals with macroeconomic issues, and the first of these, by Max Corden, with two problems which have confronted. and still confront, a great many countries. How can a country with a deficit in its balance of payments and with too high inflation reduce both at minimum cost in terms of employment and output? On whom will the inevitable costs fall and how does this affect the outcome? There are complex interactions between balance-of-payment and budgetary deficits, inflation, capital flight, and the real economy, depending in particular on how different prices and expectations respond to policy changes, all of which feature in Max Corden's analysis.

The chapter by David Bevan, Paul Collier, and Jan Gunning examines the effects of sudden changes in the values of exports or imports, due to exogenous causes such as an increase in commodity prices, on the economies of developing countries. Such changes are often reversed, but may nevertheless have serious effects, and confront governments with the problem of how to react. Should taxes, subsidies, current expenditure, or public investment be adjusted? The authors emphasize that the pre-shock control regime is at least as important in determining the outcome as the government's response. This is illustrated by the examples of the coffee boom in Kenya and the oil shocks in Indonesia and Nigeria.

Exchange rate policy is a crucial component of macroeconomic policy. Vijay Joshi's chapter begins by distinguishing between the *nominal* and the *real* exchange rate, and explains why it is important to set the latter at the right level. He then analyses the choice of exchange rate regimes in a world in which the major currencies are floating. Regimes range from permanently pegged rates to freely floating rates, with intermediate possibilities. The arguments for and against different regimes are given, each being judged by its effectiveness in achieving the right level of the real exchange rate at minimum sacrifice of the main objectives of economic policy.

A powerful cause of macroeconomic instability in some developing countries has been their dependence on exports of one or a few primary commodities whose prices fluctuate. David Newbery's chapter examines the costs of this instability and discusses how they can be reduced and, in particular, the role of publicly owned buffer stocks. He recommends that the latter should be operated differently from the way they generally have been hitherto. Instead of trying to maintain prices between an upper and lower band, one should mimic the behaviour of stabilizing private speculators. He concludes that borrowing and lending, futures markets and transactions in other financial instruments are likely to be less costly as a means of stabilizing consumption (which is the main objective to be borne in mind) than buffer stocks, whose past history is, indeed, not encouraging.

In many developing countries, industrialization has been seen both as a means of escape from the risks of relying on a few primary commodity exports and as the engine of growth and modernization. John Page describes the three main measures governments have taken to speed it up: protection from foreign competition, the allocation of subsidized credit, and direct public investment in industry. He shows how these have resulted in very varying rates of total factor productivity growth. Indeed, in some countries productivity appears to have fallen, and in many a larger share of growth has been due to input growth than to productivity growth as compared with the experience of developed countries, suggesting that expansion in the developing countries has been relatively inefficient. This, in turn, has been due to the way in which policies have reduced competitive pressures, whether from foreign or other domestic firms. Although, in recent years, many countries have accepted the need to reverse the anti-export bias of their policy regimes, fewer have actively promoted competition. There is still a widespread need to do this, to improve the working of capital markets and the performance of state enterprises, and to slim down and simplify the number and variety of often contradictory policy interventions whose net effect on particular industries is uncertain, but whose total cost is likely to be considerable.

To understand the emphasis on public enterprise in many developing countries after the Second World War, and especially in India, Sudhir Mulji recalls how the thinking at that time was influenced both by writers such as Keynes and Tawney and by the example of Soviet Five-Year Plans. These Plans were instructions which required a public sector to implement them. It was not, he argues, so much their design which was faulty as their execution. The need for enterprise autonomy was sacrificed to that for accountability to Parliament. He suggests that Japanese experience may point the way to a solution which still avoids private ownership.

A powerful justification for the import-substitution policies pursued by so many developing countries after the Second World War was export pessimism. Gerald Meier's chapter describes the three versions of pessimism to be found in the writings of Nurkse, Rosenstein-Rodan, and Mahalanobis, all influential in their day. However, the policies were often adopted initially as a means of coping with balance-of-payments problems, and because they appealed to both bureaucrats and the protected businesses. The outcome, once the easy stages of substitution had passed, was stagnation and an ever tighter foreign exchange constraint. Some countries, notably those in the Far East, passed on to an export-promotion phase which was much more successful (although trade liberalization has its own problems). The benefits have not just been those of a more efficient, static, resource allocation, but (as argued also in John Page's chapter) a faster rate of growth of productive efficiency. The question arises, however, as to whether similar gains can still be made by other countries, and the chapter concludes with an optimistic answer—export pessimism is still unjustifiable.

With significant exceptions, economists have long preached the virtues of freer trade, but governments have remained sinfully attached to protection. Why so? Increasingly, economists are attempting to provide theories which explain *government* behaviour, and not just the behaviour of private agents. The importance of the political aspects of economic policy is evident in many of the essays in this volume, but it is the next two chapters, by Anne Krueger and Jagdish Bhagwati, which give most attention to recent theories. Anne Krueger's is concerned with commercial policy, and, after a brief survey of relevant theory, the bulk of the chapter discusses the particular historical example of US policy with respect to sugar, perhaps the most important commodity exported by developing countries which has been subject to developed country protection. The lessons to be learned from this fascinating case are subtle: protection, once instituted, develops complexities and a life of its own, sustained by the interests of those whose human capital has been invested in mastering those complexities. The principal groups who attempt to manipulate protection for their own benefit are not always successful, nor do they perceive their own long-term interests clearly. Some of the simpler theories of the determinants of government behaviour omit these effects, yet they can be important.

Jagdish Bhagwati's chapter is concerned with policy towards foreign investment and its relation to commercial policy. It has long been noted that foreign firms may invest in a country in order to 'jump over the tariff wall'. There are, however, other interesting possibilities. The foreign firms may offer a politically powerful domestic firm (or trade union) what amounts to a share in the profits from its investment in return for political support in reducing the threat of protection against the foreign firm's exports. Or the government of foreign investing firms may persuade them to invest so as to reduce this threat. Jagdish Bhagwati has called this quid pro quo investment, and provides examples of it relating to Japanese investment in the USA.

The following chapter, by Deepak Lal, considers three aspects of capital flows to developing countries. First, some theoretical models of their determinants and effects on development are reviewed and explained. Then, subdividing capital flows, the determinants and effects of their different forms (official aid, direct investment by foreign enterprises, and portfolio capital and bank lending—recently very important in the debt crises of several countries) are discussed. Finally, some political as well as economic implications of the integration of capital markets world-wide are drawn.

A powerful way of influencing both trade and international capital flows is through taxation. Tax policy and tax reform must, however, pay attention to more general effects: on incentives, on the distribution of income, on production efficiency, and, of course, on the amount of revenue raised. Ehtisham Ahmad and Nicholas Stern show how theories of taxation can take account of all these effects, and how they can be used to organize and direct empirical work on policy, and their relation to tax reform and to shadow pricing (the subject of the following chapter). They then extend the theory to dynamic issues—effects on savings and investment—and discuss the effects of taxation on the pattern of production. In developing countries (unlike developed) much of the applied work has been on the structure of effective protection provided by tariffs and quotas to different industries, but this approach, they argue, is in principle less satisfactory than shadow pricing. There is no presumption that uniform rates of effective protection (or indirect taxation) are optimal, for example. Next, they discuss the taxation of agriculture, which is especially important in developing countries, and then the taxation of income and profits. They conclude with some guiding principles for tax policy.

The chapter on social cost-benefit analysis (SCBA) by Maurice Scott starts by defining what it is, and by explaining some terms commonly used in it. SCBA is mainly used to improve investment decisions in the public sector, while retaining, so far as possible, the advantages of decentralization of decisions. It is not easy, and is best regarded as a stage in the reform of the actual price system. Aid agencies, however, are likely to want to use it for a long time to come. Following these general points, Maurice Scott reviews a number of problems of shadow pricing: unequal weighting of benefits, the choice of numéraire, the rate of discount, the pricing of commodities (including the use of 'world' or 'border' prices), and the shadow wage of unskilled labour. He concludes with some suggestions for further reading.

The next two chapters are concerned with populations and their movements and employment. From a long-term perspective, Goran Ohlin's chapter discusses some of the most fundamental problems of all: what are the determinants of population change? How do we and should we regard it? He warns that we do not know the answers to these questions, and so should be cautious in viewing population growth as inevitably harmful to development, although family planning can still be seen as an essential ingredient in social policy. Population is starting to decline in Europe, and its *growth rate* is coming down elsewhere, although not in Africa. Substantial international migration was the norm in the past, and, despite restrictions, is still important and likely to be so, and may continue to drain talent from poor to rich countries.

The distinction between the 'formal' and the 'informal' sectors of employment in towns in developing countries has often been emphasized. In the 'formal' sector, wages are very much higher, and are maintained at such levels by institutional factors, such as minimum wage laws. The result, so it is alleged, is to restrict employment there and to create a prima-facie case for a wage subsidy, assuming that the distortion cannot be directly removed. Deepak Mazumdar's chapter challenges this view so far as *private* sector employment is concerned. While agreeing that wages are indeed much higher in large than in small firms, he points out that this phenomenon is not strictly dualistic, since there is a continuous gradation from larger to smaller firms. Furthermore, it has been observed in the absence of institutional explanations for it, for example in Japan. It can, he suggests, be mostly accounted for by the higher supply price of permanent than of temporary migrant workers, by the need of larger, more modern, firms for permanent workers with their acquired skills, and by other similar considerations. A case for favouring smaller firms could be made on equity grounds, but he heavily criticizes the methods and results of the actual policies adopted in India.

The last chapter is concerned not with current policies in developing countries, but with the impact on them of the colonial policies of the past. Angus Maddison considers some aspects of that impact, one measure being the net flow of payments for factor services and current transfers from particular colonies to the metropolitan countries, another being the number of expatriates in the colonies. He estimates that, between the two world wars, rather less than a sixth of Indonesian net domestic product took the form of income earned by the Dutch, of which about two-thirds was transferred to The Netherlands, the rest being spent in Indonesia. These fractions were large by comparison with those of other colonies. In India, for example, only about one-twentieth of NDP accrued to the British. The number of British people in India was also a much smaller proportion of the local population than that of Dutch people in Indonesia. Other comparisons are with Malaya, the Japanese colonies of Korea and Taiwan, and the US colony of the Philippines. In many colonies, expatriates came from other countries (e.g. from China and India) as well as from the metropolitan country. He concludes with some comments on the macroeconomic policies pursued by the colonial powers, and argues that these resulted in a more severe deflation in the 1930s in Indonesia, and possibly in other colonies, than in the independent countries of Latin America and China, who were able to default on their debts.

The volume concludes with a bibliography of Ian Little's published works. His contributions to nearly all the topics covered by the essays have been considerable, not only as an author but also as a promoter and editor of work by others. This can be seen from his joint volumes and from the three large projects he has led on industry and trade, on social cost-benefit analysis, and (currently) on macroeconomic policies in developing countries. His contributions to economics are wider still: welfare economics, fuel and power, business concentration, the behaviour of earnings per share, fiscal policy, and pricing policy for airports are some of the very diverse subjects he has written about.

Nor has his career been just that of an academic at Nuffield College, Oxford. He gave distinguished service in the Royal Air Force during the Second World War. He has worked for the British Civil Service, the Massachusetts Institute of Technology Centre for International Studies, the Overseas Development Institute, Investing in Success Equities Ltd. and General Funds Investment Trust Ltd., the Development Centre of the OECD, the Asian Development Bank, the British Airports Authority, and the World Bank. He has been Visiting Professor at the Universities of Boston, Columbia NY, and Princeton. No attempt will be made in this preface to summarize the first chapter in the book, by Francis Seton. It may be in order, however, for the editors to add some personal reflections and memories of their own.

Some who meet Ian are terrified by him. One of us can remember floods of tears shed by a secretary whom he chided for being late in Korea. Some find him difficult to talk to. When asked by one of us to explain his elliptical style of discourse (in which a correct conclusion is stated without explaining the intervening steps), he replied that he had been brought up to believe that other people one talked to were as clever as oneself and could work out the intervening steps just as easily. Yet the rewards of friendship and conversation are great. There is no one better to respond to an idea, probe an argument, or share in a joke. His intervention in a discussion is always attended, and can never be dismissed. Sometimes it shocks, and, anticipating this, one trembles slightly. Ian can attack hard, especially if he believes his opponent is talking or writing dangerous nonsense which could be influential. But he is the soul of politeness, kindness, and generosity, and, unlike some others of his eminence, would never try to browbeat or overawe an honest seeker after truth. Being one himself, his sympathies are clear.

M. FG. S.

D. L.

Contents

Notes on Contributors

EHTISHAM AHMAD is Director of the Development Economics Research Programme at the London School of Economics, and has worked for the World Bank and at Warwick University. In recent years he has undertaken research on fiscal reform in India, Pakistan, and Mexico, has collaborated with Nicholas Stern on *The Theory and Practice of Tax Reform in Developing Countries*, and has contributed to *The Theory of Taxation for Developing Countries*.

DAVID BEVAN is a Fellow of St John's College, Oxford, and a member of the Unit for the Study of African Economies, Institute of Economics and Statistics, Oxford University. He has collaborated with Paul Collier and Jan Gunning on *East African Lessons in Trade Liberalisation*, *Peasants and Governments: An Economic Analysis*, and *The Political Economy of Poverty, Equity and Growth in Nigeria and Indonesia*.

JAGDISH BHAGWATI is Arthur Lehman Professor of Economics and Professor of Political Science at Columbia University, New York. He was Ford International Professor of Economics at MIT and taught previously at the Delhi School of Economics and the Indian Statistical Institute. He has published extensively on development, aid, migration, and trade. His latest work is on *Protectionism*.

PAUL COLLIER is a Fellow of St Antony's College, Oxford, and is a member of the Unit for the Study of African Economies, Institute of Economics and Statistics, Oxford University. He has collaborated with David Bevan and Jan Gunning on the volumes noted above, as well as with Deepak Lal on *Poverty and Labour in Kenya*, and with S. Radwan and S. Wangwe on *Poverty and Labour in Rural Tanzania*.

W. MAX CORDEN is Professor of International Economics at the School of Advanced International Studies of the Johns Hopkins University. He has been Nuffield Reader in International Economics at Oxford University, Professor of Economics in the Research School of Pacific Studies of the Australian National University, and Senior Adviser in the Research Department of the International Monetary Fund. He is the author of *The Theory of Protection*, *Trade Policy and Economic Welfare*, *Inflation, Exchange Rates and the World Economy*, and *Protection, Trade and Growth*.

JAN WILLEM GUNNING is Professor of Economics and Director of ESI-VU at the Free University of Amsterdam. He is also a member of the Unit for the Study of African Economies, Institute of Economics and Statistics, Oxford University, and has collaborated with David Bevan and Paul Collier on the volumes noted above.

VIJAY JOSHI is Fellow of Merton College, Oxford, has been Economic Adviser in the Indian Ministry of Finance and Special Adviser to the Governor of the Reserve Bank of India, and has also worked for various international bodies including the World Bank. He has published widely on international economics and development and in particular in recent years on exchange rate and other macroeconomic policies.

ANNE O. KRUEGER is Arts and Sciences Professor of Economics at Duke University, North Carolina. She was formerly Vice-President, Economics and Research, World Bank. Her publications include *Foreign Trade Regimes and Economic Development, Liberalization Attempts and Consequences*, and *Alternative Trade Strategies and Employment in Developing Countries*. She has undertaken research on development policies in a number of countries including India, Korea, and Turkey.

DEEPAK LAL is Professor of Political Economy at University College London. He is the author of numerous articles and books on development, including *The Poverty of Development Economics* and *The Hindu Equilibrium*. He has advised a number of governments in developing countries and has worked for various international organizations including the World Bank.

ANGUS MADDISON is Professor of Economics at the University of Groningen and was formerly at the OEEC and OECD in Paris. He is the author of numerous books and articles on economic growth and development.

DIPAK MAZUMDAR is in the Studies and Training Design Division of the Economic Development Institute of the World Bank. He taught for many years at the London School of Economics and was Professor of Economics at the Unversity of Toronto. He has published on labour markets in developing countries, on the economies of South-East Asia, and on industrialization. He recently collaborated with Ian Little and John Page on *Small Manufacturing Enterprises: A Comparative Analysis of India and Other Economies*.

GERALD M. MEIER is Konosuke Matsushita Professor of International Economics and Policy Analysis at Stanford University. He previously taught at Williams College, Yale University, Oxford University, and was Professor of Economics at Wesleyan University. He has worked extensively as a consultant, including three World Bank missions to China. He has published numerous volumes on trade and development and has been General Editor of the *Economic Development Series* published by the Oxford University press.

SUDHIR MULJI is Chairman of the Great Eastern Shipping Company, for which he has worked for many years. He was recently invited to be Chairman and Managing Director of the State Trading Corporation of India—a Government of India undertaking—from which he resigned a year later due to ill health. He has been a Visiting Fellow of Nuffield College, Oxford and has collaborated with Ian Little in work on social cost-benefit analysis.

DAVID NEWBERY is Professor of Applied Economics and Director of the Department of Applied Economics at Cambridge University and a Fellow of Churchill College. He has worked for the World Bank and the International Monetary Fund, and has collaborated with J. E. Stiglitz on *The Theory of Commodity Price Stabilization: A Study in the Economics of Risk*, as well as with Maurice Scott and John MacArthur on *Project Appraisal in Practice* and with Nicholas Stern on *The Theory of Taxation for Developing Countries*.

GÖRAN OHLIN is Professor of Economics at Uppsala University and Assistant Secretary-General for Development Research and Policy Analysis at the United Nations, New York. He has worked for the Pearson Commission and was Executive Secretary of the Brandt Commission. From time to time he has worked on demographic issues in economic development, as in *Population Control and Economic Development* for the OECD Development Centre with which Ian Little was associated.

JOHN M. PAGE is Division Chief of Trade, Finance, and Industry Operations Latin America and the Caribbean in the World Bank, which he joined after spells at Oxford and Princeton Universities. He collaborated with Ian Little and Dipak Mazumdar on *Small Manufacturing Enterprises: A Comparative Analysis of India and Other Economies*.

MAURICE SCOTT is a Fellow of Nuffield College, Oxford. He collaborated with Ian Little and Tibor Scitovsky on *Industry and Trade in Some Developing Countries* for the OECD Development Centre, and then with Ian Little and others on studies of social cost-benefit analysis at Nuffield College. More recently he has worked on economic growth.

FRANCIS SETON is an Emeritus Fellow of Nuffield College, Oxford, and has worked as a consultant for the United Nations and the Governments of the

United Kingdom, Iran, Chile, and Indonesia. His publications include works on Chile, Indonesia, and the Soviet Union, as well as on value theory and inter-system comparisons, most recently *Cost, Use and Value*.

NICHOLAS STERN is Professor of Economics at the London School of Economics and Chairman of the Suntory-Toyota International Centre for Economics and Related Disciplines. He was formerly Professor of Economics at Warwick University and Director of the Development Economics Research Centre, and before that a Fellow of St Catherine's College, Oxford. He collaborated with Ian Little on work on social cost-benefit analysis, and edited jointly with David Newbery *The Theory of Taxation for Developing Countries*. He has also published extensively on other aspects of development and growth.

1

Ian Little—A salute *Inter Vivos*

FRANCIS SETON

THE title is intended to put the reader on notice not to expect an *éloge*. Happily Ian Little is still among us and likely to remain so for many years to come. *De mortuis nil nisi bonum* must be replaced by *de vivis nil nisi verum*, an injuction vastly more difficult to follow, even to the extent that *verum* may be granted an objective meaning in what can only be a personal impression rather than a biography.

Nor would it be proper, even in different circumstance, to treat Ian like a cardboard paragon. Indeed, no material is further removed from his character than cardboard. If one were to scour the physical world for more appropriate substances, one would probably be led to mercury rather than anything else. He certainly has its brilliance and vivacity, and also its outstanding *gravitas* in the councils of his profession and everywhere else. When I started my career at Nuffield College he first impinged on me as a somewhat austere, but benevolent, eminence, presiding invariably from the back-benches, whose views,—however modestly expressed—would command immediate acceptance for their lucidity and independence. He had no need to seek effects, to hedge about, manipulate the waverers, or lobby the influential. Nothing seemed more alien to him than showmanship, conformity, plodding exertion, or nail-biting discomposure. Yet, a sympathetic observer might be forgiven for suspecting behind this elegant insouciance a very genuine modesty, an almost self-denigrating diffidence, whose occasionally visible traces only added to his ineluctable charm. The directness, I fancied, sprang from a still deeper sense of intrinsic worth which elaboration and art could only diminish, a rock-bed of confidence built up by the collective ego-massage of Eton where he was nurtured and the unshakeable certainties of the Edwardian upper middle class into which he was born. Whatever this produces will triumph over natural modesty of the most paralysing sort to generate the leadership qualities of the English gentleman, and Ian was to me, as he still is, the embodiment of the English gentleman in the best sense of the word.

This does not mean that he is free from the defect of these virtues. He feels attracted to influence, power, even wealth, and cultivates those who possess them—dignitaries, business magnates, and stockbrokers—in preference to others, though it should be added that, if he did not do so, they would eagerly seek his company without any prompting from him. Given that this in no way clouds his objective judgement, which remains fair-minded and generous to a fault, this predilection is as innocent as it is aesthetically motivated, and does not result in authoritarian pretensions. As a latter-day specimen of Disraeli's heaven-born oligarchy his hegemony is based on consensus instilled by charm rather than coercive power of any kind. Unlike the murdered King of Denmark, he does not have an eye like Mars to threaten and command, but, like him, sports a station like the herald Mercury new lighted on a heaven-kissing hill.

With so much on offer from nature and nurture and his own inner direction, he may be forgiven for seeming remote and daunting on occasion, as if he made a point of eschewing those less well endowed than himself in intellect, spirit, or *savoir-faire*, as if he ignored them and put them calmly and dispassionately aside. He may indeed create the impression of backing success and not wasting much sympathy on failure, even if undeserved. In fact, however, his concern for the underendowed and underprivileged is highly unusual in one so far removed from their condition. Yet the mistaken impression persists, and it speaks volumes for Ian Little's personal magetism that it does nothing to dim the admiration and esteem he enjoys; for even the less favoured and disadvantaged, hurt and alienated as they may be by the breeziness and arrogance of the beau monde he is taken to represent, show him as little resentment as he shows envy towards those more favoured than himself, and are apt to feel comforted and flattered by any crumb of attention from him that may come their way. Indeed, experience might teach them to put greater reliance and trust on him than on the more fiery intercessions of professional tribunes.

He was indeed born into the Edwardian upper middle class. His mother descended from the distinguished family of Brassey whose ancestor had worked with Telford and built railways all over the world, thereby laying the foundation of the family fortune. His father was a brigadier-general who had commanded the 9th Lancers, with the authority and prestige of a great military family. His maternal grandfather had been master of the Heythrop Hunt for over 40 years, his mother delighted in horse-riding, his eldest brother in steeplechasing and racing, and one other brother, an enthusiastic polo player, had followed the family tradition in joining the 9th Lancers before becoming a doctor. Ian spent his childhood with four brothers, one sister and nine indoor retainers in the big country house of Dunsmore near Rugby, surrounded by the appurtenances of the landed gentry and their pursuits which, however, he does not appear to have shared to the full. It is unlikely that the atmosphere was particularly conducive to book-learning or other forms of intellectuality, and any proclivity towards such deviant behaviour may well have been firmly discouraged. Just as Philip of Macedon chided his son for playing the lyre too well, so a gentleman of the old school was under a subtle injunction to be ashamed of being too good at anything, and the model Etonian of those days was most probably an 'all-rounder', not to say a bonehead. It seems that Ian was not entirely happy at Eton where he went at the age of 13 after his early nurture by a governess and prep school at Farnborough, and showed comparatively little interest in the particular sports and pastimes which opened the way to success and popularity in that school. Yet there is little indication that he had any wish to change his life-style substantially on moving to New College a few years later. He became an enthusiastic card player and continued to hunt and to go racing—in fact confirmed the widespread impression of himself as an amiable playboy.

During the war he became a test pilot of exceptional daring. He began flight-training as a member of the famous Oxford University Air Squadron, which involved joining the Royal Air Force Volunteer Reserve and therefore active duty immediately after the outbreak of war. He was one of the four pilots selected to fly Cierva autogiros—those romantic, maverick craft which so spectacularly disappointed the exaggerated hopes placed on them, but were used during the war to calibrate the ring of radar stations without which the Battle of Britain could not have been won. Ian later volunteered to test-fly the tiny autogiro glider known as the Rotachute which was initially intended as a parachute-substitute. It took several crashes to prove that the original version was unstable. A modified, more controllable version, which Ian flew some fifty times, became the model for a larger project, the conversion of an ordinary jeep into an autogiro glider to be towed to the point of attack. This more ambitious so-called Rotabuggy programme ended abruptly after only one hair-raising, near-disastrous, flight. The Air Force Cross Ian was awarded, almost post-humously, was certainly richly deserved.

When the war was over Ian left the RAF and returned to Oxford to take a First in shortened (wartime) PPE (Philosophy, Politics, and Economics) in 1947. A Fellowship by examination at All Souls followed shortly thereafter and, although this triumph still did not convince everyone that he was a real academic at heart, his conversion to the committed intellectuality which informed his later life must be assumed to date from that period. He certainly struck up friendships with a number of bourgeois Labour intellectuals, especially Crosland and Dalton, though one particular undergraduate friendship, begun earlier and continued by correspondence throughout the war, may well have been more decisive than all the others in sowing the seeds of his academic bent. Contrary to superficial impressions, Ian is capable of great warmth and friendship, often lying unsuspected below his outward breeziness, and he is well able to absorb deep influences from those he respects.

Already in 1946 he had married Doreen (Dobs) Hennessey whom he had met at an air force camp during the war. From a background rather different from his own and a woman who combined personal sweetness with great courage and independence of mind, Dobs came to share his idiom and life-style and was always very closely identified with his background. They made a brilliant, hospitable couple, a magnet to all who aspired to elegance, dash, and good living, amused by snobbery rather than repelled by it, yet warm-hearted and generous to a fault. In keeping with changing times they replaced a love of racehorses by a penchant for fast cars, tennis, and lavish parties. Hidden below this enviable polish there always lay not only a genuine and almost unfashionable depth and kindliness, but also an inner restlessness which manifested itself in frequent moves from one country to another, from one house to another. They lived in North Oxford, Sutton Courteney, Clifden Hampden, Bagley Wood— wherever comfort and deeper aesthetic qualities combined to form a suitable ambience for their harmonious lives, before moving abroad—to Paris, Washington, and to their final home in La Garde Freinet on the French Riviera, where Dobs, after fighting and triumphing over afflictions which would have broken lesser spirits, was struck down by her fatal illness and had to be brought back to Oxford for medical treatment and her last days. She is sorely missed by all who knew her, and survived by a son and a daughter who has made Ian into the grandfather he has long wanted to be.

By the time the Ian–Dobs team began to make its impact on the social scene in Oxford Ian had firmly established himself in academia, first exchanging his All Souls Fellowship for a Tutorial Fellowship in succession to Anthony Crosland at Trinity, and finally establishing his permanent academic home at Nuffield College in 1952, where he was elected almost by acclamation, and stayed with occasional interruptions until his departure for Washington in 1976, serving the College outstandingly well as Investment Bursar. The Nuffield College bursarship in which Ian coxed and boxed with Sir Donald MacDougall for the first three years could indeed be described as a triumph of pragmatism. The timing was of course highly propitious, coinciding with a doubling of the FT index during 1958 and 1959, but the brilliant Ian–Donald team, advised (though not spoonfed) by Vickers da Costa, the brokers appointed by them on the basis of previous experience with private portfolios, managed to beat the index by a substantial margin, and in effect did for the College what Ian's ancestor, Thomas Brassey, had done for his family fortune. To some extent this success was due to the release of the College from the obligation to keep as much as one-third of its investments in the then low-yielding holdings of agricultural land, an obligation which ceased with its full independence from university tutelage in 1958. But the major part of the credit is due to the dynamism and acumen of the eagle-eyed duo who shifted a substantial portion of investments to Japan and, above all, concentrated on buying growth stocks, i.e. shares in companies whose profits had increased markedly over a period of years, regardless of the expansion or decline of the sector of industry in which they found themselves. In doing so they were doing no more than jumping on the most fashionable bandwagon of the time, but it took experience, discernment, and courage of a high order to do so. After Ian joined the board of the Vickers Trust 'Investing in Success' ('Insects' for short) of which Donald MacDougall was a founding director, he embarked on a statistical analysis of the hypothesis that past growth of earnings per share was an indicator of future growth—and found that it was not. This result was published in his 1962 article 'Higgledy Piggledy Growth' mentioned below. It seemed to cut the ground from under the College's policy and that of the Trust, much to the discomfiture of some of his associates. Academic interest had triumphed over self-interest and the pen was proved mightier than the profit and loss account. In any case, the growth bandwagon was slowing down. This did not prevent either the College or 'Insects' from continuing to be very successful investors. Unfortunately, however, Ian's next venture, the Unit Trust 'Oxcut', through which he hoped to do for other Oxford Colleges what he had done for Nuffield, was notably less successful and dogged by misfortune.

But quite apart from his success as Investment Bursar, his theoretical, quasi-philosophical, turn of mind did not prevent him for long from conquering a College intent on fulfilling its Founder's behest to forge links with the real world of business and politics. Through sheer force of intellect and personality he stood out against powerful influences which sought to reserve prestige and influence above all to worldliness, topical interests, and up-to-date knowledge of current affairs, and made his quiet voice heard above the hubbub of the market-place. He was helped in this by a curious blend of intellectual tastes which combined the most rarefied forms of abstract thinking with a down-to-earth pragmatism which the most beguiling siren-songs of logical construction could not tempt him to abandon. While he often aspired to be a 'meta-economist' in the sense in which Bertrand Russell was a meta-mathematician, he was never afraid to stand back and ask the all-important homely question: 'What does it all mean? How could it affect policy?'

It was indeed on policy rather than theory that he sought to exert his strongest influence, whether as Deputy Director of the Economic Section of the UK Treasury between 1953 and 1955, as a member of the board of the British Airports Authority, in the UN Commission for Development Planning, or in the World Bank which he served from 1976 to 1978. In between he had been a member of the MIT Mission to India and Vice-President of the OECD Development Centre.

Policy-making bodies and institutions rooted in a world of recalcitrant reality tend to resent incursions from abstract theoreticians whom they either fail to understand or are unable to put to practical use, and keep on hankering after mandarins. Curiously enough, Ian functions quite well as a mandarin—not a mandarin duck, to be sure, but a mandarin eagle whose swoops down to earth by their very depth only confirm the loftiness of his eyrie, not the distance of his fall.

What of this eyrie itself? It is distinguished by its height and the clear air around it, well above the clouds, conducive to undisturbed, razor-sharp logic, and out of reach of emotional turbulence. The disappointment Ian met with when his thesis, in its early stages, was disparaged and severely criticized by the most distinguished member of the profession, did little to discourage him, still less to cloud his judgement. He pursued his studies unswervingly, and when his first book (*A Critique of Welfare Economics*) appeared in 1950 he was rewarded by many accolades which amply made up for his earlier reverses. The book is still regarded as an outstanding work and a classic, although its strength lies less in any particular method or message that could be singled out as truly innovative than in the general thrust and depth of its critique. It was one of the first to launch a sustained attack on exclusive reliance on marginalism and 'first best' analysis, the traditional technology of economists, and thus intoned a chorus which many have since joined; it sought to put indifference analysis on a 'behavioural' footing, and put distributional ethics firmly on the order of the day for all who wished to be taken seriously in welfare economics. Its influence was, and still is, vast.

Influence is indeed the keyword that should be used to characterize Ian's work; for policy could hardly ever be the same after the appearance of *The Price of Fuel* or *Aid to Africa* in the 1950s and 1960s. He discards jargon and mechanical devices and makes a bee-line for home truths which may have been suspected before, but failed to be perceived or taken into consideration with sufficient clarity. The same realism is evident in the *Manual of Industrial Project Analysis in Developing Countries* which he wrote in 1968 with J. Mirrlees. Though partly rooted in a judicious adaptation of established economic theory, it succeeds in providing busy consultants and administrators with eclectic, almost rule-of-thumb, criteria which they should be able to apply without going through a course in economic principles. The international agencies concerned adopted it with alacrity, and the methodology served as the basis for the important series of industrial project evaluations which figured prominently in Ian Little's next co-operative work (with Tibor Scitovsky and Maurice Scott), the important study of the experience in industrialization gained by Brazil, India, Mexico, Pakistan, the Philippines, and Taiwan which appeared in 1970 under the title *Industry and Trade in Some Developing Countries*. This, one of the most significant works in development economics, again concentrates on a critique of policy, particularly the beguiling policy of import substitution and the fetish of industrialization at the expense of agriculture, whose damaging effects are traced with deep understanding and a battery of impressively marshalled facts and figures. Acute common sense and minute observation are again in the forefront, while formal analytical principles, leashed in like hounds, like famine, sword, and fire, crouch for occasional employment only. Ian, in spite of his superb logical mind, is no worshipper of consistency and unified principle for its own sake, and not afraid to indulge in eclecticism when the hurly-burly of the real world demands it. Who but Ian Little would have spent precious time in a painstaking and ultimately fruitless search for the causes of differential growth in stock-exchange-quoted firms, and then had the courage and discernment to make a virtue of this frustration by publishing his non-findings in 'Higgledy Piggledy Growth' as a valid insight into this chaos—which indeed it is?

Behind a mind so uncompromisingly self-reliant and nonconformist one might suspect a thinker of solitary and retiring disposition, isolated and inhospitable in his intellectual seclusion. Nothing could be further from the truth. Well over 50 per cent of Ian's work was written in collaboration with others—with research associates or colleagues—with none of whom he quarrelled. This betokens no lack of drive or originality; for even in those cases where his collaborators contributed the bulk of the writing, Ian was the moving spirit, or at least the 'entrepreneur' to whom the work owed its conception and its consummation, and his most path-breaking early work was certainly all his own. Nor can it be said that he is intellectually supine and easily defers to others. In fact, his determination to get his own way has on occasion bordered on uncompromising toughness—as when his intent to suppress a draft of what later became the famous *Manual of Industrial Project Analysis in Developing Countries*: Vol. ii, *Social Cost-Benefit Analysis*, that had been submitted by a consultant firm, met with powerful opposition within the OECD. It then took the threat of his resignation from the Vice-Presidency to gain his point, but gain it he did, thereby securing the academic authenticity of the *Manual*.

Yet this determination to stick to his guns is in no way the outcome of a rigid mind. Ian has often profoundly modified his convictions—never more radically than in the face of practical experience. Abandoning his early sympathy with direct comprehensive planning, as practised for example in India, he became a powerful advocate of indirect controls to guide the economy. Disillusioned with exclusive reliance on fiscal policy, which he favoured as the most flexible and predictable instrument of control in the late 1950s, he was gradually converted to a larger armoury of selective controls, although it would certainly be wrong to describe him as a 'monetarist' even now. He also became wary of the traditional Keynesian prescriptions as a panacea for economic ills and would now probably fit most neatly into the post-Keynesian 'revisionist' camp which recognizes Keynesian 'fine tuning' as potentially effective only in the presence of an incomes policy so rigid as to be ruled out on political grounds. His early sympathies for Labour ideology which he conceived on moral as well as economic grounds have now been replaced by a total rejection of Labour policies—even to the extent of favouring tactical voting to keep Labour at bay, although he still rejects other party affiliations of any kind. He is in fact as politically uncommitted and eclectic in his views as a critical spirit is almost bound to be, without losing an ounce of his concern for his fellow-men, the Third World, or the poor and disadvantaged wherever they may be.

On retiring from his Oxford Chair in Development Economics in 1976 Ian wrote another major survey which was published six years later. He is now engaged on a comparative study of macroeconomic policies in Third World countries, having completed his investigation of small manufacturing enterprises in the Indian and similar economies. Development economists of his calibre, it seems, far from dying, never really retire; they do not even fade away.

In surveying Ian's academic and intellectual achievements it behoves a commentator to find failings as well as merit, lest he be accused of hyperbole and his encomium lose much of its credibility. Besides, the man would barely be tolerable if, with so many undoubted virtues, he had no defects at all. Given that one must specify defects, then, mention may be made of one failing, if failing it be, which springs from the very richness of Ian's endowment, the effortless superiority of his mind, which robs him of some of the spur of intellectual ambition, the urge which makes many of the less well endowed attempt the impossible, beat at locked doors with bleeding fists, or venture out ill-equipped into uncharted seas. Ian always knows what he is about, what can be done, and what is worth attempting, and his reach never exceeds his grasp. He does not look for the philosopher's stone, and values soundness of judgement above fantasy and speculation. It is this, of course, which makes his prescriptions uniquely reliable and his advice trusted, weighty, and always influential. It is this also, however, which might make one feel that he does not use his endowment to the full and leaves some creative potential deliberately underutilized. He can, however, be said to make the fullest use of his potential in a different sense: he is constantly aware of his own comparative advantage and deliberately eschews lines or aspects of enquiry in which he feels he does not enjoy this strength. The same lack of intellectual ambition which keeps his feet so firmly on the ground shields him from the blandishments of speculative construction and shaky generalization which so often lure the reckless out of their depth, and the same inurement to effortless superiority which lies at the basis of this lack deters him from further delving into lines of thought as soon as he perceives diminishing returns setting in. He gets bored with such pursuits, abandons them, and quickly turns to the tilling of other fields where the soil is less exhausted. Hence the multiplicity of his interests within economics, his versatility in the subjects covered and the methods used, but also his lack of revolutionary fervour and his distrust of boldness and radical innovation.

For the rest, his defects, if there be any, are self-confessed and not necessarily unwelcome. Thus Ian modestly disclaims some useful skills such as proficiency in languages and mathematics—the latter sometimes used as a bolt-hole by economists frustrated by the disorderliness and lack of system in descriptive and policy-oriented studies, a disorderliness which Ian always welcomes as a challenge. Ian certainly does not despise mathematics, and often has recourse to past masters of the art who are willing recruits and welcome the direction he gives to their efforts; but this does nothing to diminish his confidence in himself as 'perhaps the last reasonably successful economist of the century without mathematics'— surely a great distinction in itself.

He also on occasion confesses to a lack of 'inner direction', by which he understands a presumed inability to choose his own subject unprompted by others. He believes he does his best work when commissioned by inter-national institutions, research institutes, or stung into action by individual colleagues. To the extent that this self-appraisal is correct, it points to a degree of 'demand-orientatedness' which many would account a strength rather than a weakness. It has certainly led to Ian being constantly 'in demand' and his work exerting a far greater influence than would other-wise have been the case.

In the non-professional realm of art Ian has always shown great appre-ciation and discrimination in the visual arts, particularly in modern paint-ing and his somewhat idiosyncratic type of architecture, but confesses to a total lack of musical appreciation. It is all the more creditable that he should have shown so much courtesy and tolerance to those of his col-leagues who have sought to fill the College air with music, and that he and Dobs should have paid them the compliment of regular attendance at Col-lege concerts, thus demonstrating a total lack of that arrogance which moves lesser men to believe that any form of skill or appreciation they happen to lack must be of little account. Tolerance and respect for other people's intellectual or artistic interests, even if not shared by oneself, are indeed hallmarks of a civilized mind, and Ian possesses them to a high degree.

It may well be an appropriate summary to describe Ian Little as the last 'gentleman economist' of the era; for like the gentlemen farmers of old he eschews hidebound professionalism, is suspicious and largely innocent of much of fashionable technology, yet makes a hundred blades of grass grow where none grew before. May he long continue to sow, and to serve his country, profession, and his college and University as outstandingly as he has done in the past.

2

Macroeconomic Adjustment in Developing Countries

W. MAX CORDEN

BEGINNING with *A Critique of Welfare Economics*, the famous book that first established his reputation, Ian Little has shown a striking ability to assess ideas on important subjects critically with a high degree of sophistication combined with common sense, and to integrate and present these in a way that makes them accessible to students and the economics profession at large. This is certainly true of his monumental *Economic Development*.

This book deals with many of the issues discussed in the present chapter written in his honour. One chapter of the book reviews the Latin American 'structuralism versus monetarism' debate and there is also an extended discussion of the influence of International Monetary Fund programmes. But he was left dissatisfied by the state of thinking and by empirical research in this field. In a passage important from the point of view of his subsequent interests and initiatives he wrote: 'This past neglect [of analysis of the International Monetary Fund role] is an aspect of the more general absence of studies of actual and desirable year-to-year macroeconomic management in LDCs, which is the other side of the coin of excessive emphasis on five year plans and long-run structural change' (Little, 1982, p. 316).

It was these thoughts that led him to initiate a World Bank comparative countries project on 'Macroeconomic Policies, Crises and Long-Term Growth'.[1] Essentially this project is concerned with three issues, firstly how countries got into macroeconomic crises or how they averted potential crises in the face of various shocks, secondly how they dealt with them, i.e., how they 'adjusted', and thirdly how the adjustment affected longer-term growth. It is, of course, hoped that some results useful for policy will

This chapter was written while the author was on leave from the Australian National University as Senior Adviser in the Research Dept. of the IMF. The views expressed do not necessarily represent those of the Fund. I am indebted to valuable comments from Mario Blejer, Guillermo Calvo, Anthony Lanyi, Juan Carlos de Pablo, and Sarath Rajapatirana.

[1] The countries included in the project are Argentina, Brazil, Chile, Colombia, Costa Rica, Mexico, Cameroon, Côte d'Ivoire, Kenya, Morocco, Nigeria, Turkey, India, Indonesia, Pakistan, Sri Lanka, and Thailand. Various consultants to the Bank are doing these country studies. The director of the project is Sarath Rajapatirana from the World Bank and, apart from Ian Little, the other principal authors are Richard Cooper and myself.

come out of this and that much can be learnt from the comparison of the experiences of a variety of developing countries in three continents.

The present chapter deals with the second of these topics. It is not concerned with how balance-of-payments or inflation difficulties arose but rather how, given that there is an adjustment problem for whatever reason, countries have to or can deal with them. Hence it is concerned with the short-run adjustment problem.

The macroeconomic adjustment problem usually has two parts to it, the improvement of the current account and the reduction of inflation. Both aspects are dealt with here, and it is shown how they are related. The first aspect can be—indeed, must be—analysed with the help of standard balance-of-payments theory. This theory—using the concepts of expenditure reduction (or reduction of 'absorption') and 'switching'—is so well known that it hardly needs to be expounded here. It will only be used as a starting-point for introducing some simple concepts of adjustment costs, emphasizing particularly distributive effects.

But this standard analysis does not allow for inflation. Another body of literature is concerned with inflation, with anti-inflationary policies, and with the relationship between budget deficits and inflation. Since many developing countries, notably in Latin America, often face both a current account problem and inflation rates that are unacceptably high there is a need to show how the two parts of the adjustment problem interact.

Another matter to be dealt with here is so-called capital flight, i.e. the export of private capital when at the same time the government is borrowing abroad. This is not allowed for in the standard balance-of-payments adjustment theory but needs also to be related to it.

The chapter will not deal with one important matter that is certainly relevant to the subject, namely the particular methodology of the International Monetary Fund, especially financial programming methods and the use of the Polak model which focuses on monetary and credit aggregates in monitoring adjustment. This is a large subject of its own and has been discussed extensively elsewhere, notably in Khan and Knight (1981) and IMF (1987).

1. The Current Account Problem and Adjustment Costs

1.1. Expenditure Reduction and Switching

A small open economy has a current account deficit which needs to be removed. The less foreign credits are available the more speedily this has to be done. The standard analysis is that total real expenditure by government and the private sector combined on consumption and investment has to fall. This is 'expenditure adjustment' which reduces demand for both tradables and non-tradables. In addition there has to be a real devaluation which shifts both the pattern of domestic demand from tradables towards non-tradables and the output pattern from non-tradables towards tradables. This is a 'switching' policy which ensures that the process of attaining 'external balance' takes place while 'internal balance'—overall employment—is being maintained.[2]

If the policy instrument to bring about switching is to be exchange rate adjustment it is necessary that a real devaluation really does take place as a result of nominal devaluation. If wages rise when the prices of imports and the cost of living rise, or if there has not been an adequate expenditure reduction so that the devaluation-induced rise in demand for non-tradables creates excess demand and then some inflation of non-tradables prices (or, more broadly, of prices of home-produced goods), a real devaluation will not be achieved. It is common that initially a nominal devaluation does bring about real devaluation, but that its effects are gradually eroded at least to a partial extent. A great deal hinges on whether monetary policies are accommodating or not. Experiences have greatly varied among developing countries.[3]

An interesting question is whether a nominal devaluation could bring about some expenditure reduction automatically. This is possible, especially through the reduction in real balances that a general rise in the price level would yield. Here two other examples are given, though there can be no presumption that the expenditure reduction would necessarily be sufficient.

A devaluation raises the domestic currency prices of imported capital goods. If credit in nominal terms to the private sector (and also to the public sector) were kept constant investment in real terms would decline. The value of capital goods imports measured in domestic currency might stay constant, but imports in real terms would have fallen.

In the second example a devaluation raises export income in domestic currency and some of the higher incomes are likely to go to the government. In the case of revenue from Indonesian oil almost all of it goes to the

---

[2] There is a diagrammatic exposition of the standard analysis in ch. 1 of Corden (1985) which also contains references to the origins of these ideas. The basic theory originated with Meade (1951), the concept of 'switching' with Johnson (1958), and the formal dependent-economy model with Salter (1959). The concern in this paper with sectoral (distributional) effects of adjustment expands on my discussion in ch. 2 of Corden (1985).

[3] Edwards (1987) analyses 18 Latin American devaluation episodes and shows in each case what happened to the real exchange rate in each of 3 years after the devaluation. He calculates for each episode an 'effectiveness index' and shows that, when there was stepwise devaluation, in most cases the real exchange rate effect was quickly eroded, sometimes completely after 3 years. On the other hand, when there was a 'crawling peg' the real exchange rate did stay down, this result being obtained by frequent nominal depreciations. See also Connolly and Taylor (1976) for earlier evidence. Warr (1984) showed that the Indonesian devaluation of 1978 had quite a prolonged relative price effect. Broadly, the relative price of tradables rose about 23% shortly after the devaluation and this effect was gradually eroded until by the time of the March 1983 devaluation about a quarter of the initial effect remained.

government because of revenue-sharing and production contracts with foreign oil companies. In various African countries high export taxes transfer significant parts of increased export incomes in domestic currency terms to the government. If the extra government revenue resulting from devaluation is not spent, the fiscal, and hence current account situation will improve.

More generally, devaluation redistributes incomes from producers of non-tradables to producers of tradables, and the latter could conceivably have higher propensities to save so that a current account improvement could result from devaluation. In the example just given the government is the principal recipient of incomes from a major export and it has been assumed to have a high propensity to save.

A particularly important matter in highly indebted countries is that devaluation raises the domestic currency value of the government's foreign debt service. This will worsen the fiscal deficit, an effect which can—and sometimes has—offset the beneficial effects on the fiscal situation of higher revenues from export taxes or from the profits of government-owned export corporations. The unifying concept here is that debt service can be regarded as a tradable import and the government could be a net importer or exporter of tradables.

In general one can hardly rely on a devaluation to generate automatically the necessary reduction in real expenditure, though it is possible, and its effects on real expenditure must always be considered.[4]

The need for real expenditure reduction imposes an inevitable cost. This can be called the *primary adjustment cost*. It arises even when there is adequate switching or real factor prices are flexible so that internal balance continues to be maintained. A *secondary adjustment cost* arises when failure of switching mechanisms or rigidity of real wages, for example, lead to a decline in overall employment or underutilization of capacity. The primary adjustment cost is really the minimal cost. It is unavoidable. The secondary adjustment cost reflects inefficiency in adjustment. The aim of good adjustment policies should be to make this cost as low as possible.

1.2. The Costs of Adjustment

We begin with the primary adjustment cost. Here one can make a distinction between a *present cost* and a *future cost*, broadly the distinction between cutting consumption and cutting gross investment. A number of

---

[4] It is a well-known proposition that a devaluation may be deflationary for the kinds of reasons (and others) discussed here. See Diaz-Alejandro (1965) and Krugman and Taylor (1978). The concern has usually been that it may reduce real expenditures too much, rather than too little. In any case, explicit expenditure policy, whether fiscal or monetary, is always available to supplement, or alternatively compensate for the expenditure-reducing effects of devaluation.

policies which are often part of a country's adjustment programme can be looked at here. A primary cost is inevitable and all the policies have their problems. In all cases we now assume that adequate devaluation switches the pattern of demand sufficiently towards home-produced goods for over-all employment to be maintained even though expenditure is reduced.

(i) Wages of public sector employees are cut. Hence their consumption is likely to fall, though they are also likely to reduce the savings they were previously making, and in the short run they may even dissave. The extent of the reduction of consumption is likely to depend on whether or not the employees believe the wage cuts to be temporary or long-term. The current account will improve to the extent of the budgetary improvement minus the decline in private savings.

(ii) Budgetary subsidies for food or other products are cut, so that their prices rise. This also represents a fall in real income of the private sector and, as above, will lead to both a fall in consumption and in savings, with the current account improvement equal to the budgetary improvement minus the fall in private savings. Food consumption might be maintained, so that the higher cost of food to the general public would compel them to reduce consumption of other products. A policy of reducing food subsidies is likely to be highly unpopular and particularly difficult to implement, as experiences in Egypt, Sri Lanka, and Zambia, among others, bear out.

(iii) Subsidies to government corporations which are making losses are cut. In many of the countries studied in the World Bank project mentioned earlier, losses of such 'parastatal' corporations have been a major cause of fiscal problems. When their losses have to be reduced because subsidies can no longer be financed, the corporations are compelled to raise prices to consumers. This has much the same effect as cuts in food subsidies: real incomes of consumers fall and they have to reduce consumption, choosing no doubt both to reduce consumption of the products supplied by the corporations and of other products. The corporations are also likely to reduce gross investment, perhaps allowing their capital to run down, in which case there is a future cost. In addition, their customers may be other producers, whose costs thus rise. These adverse effects may be moderated by improvements in productivity that are induced by the more difficult situations in which the corporations find themselves.

(iv) Government gross investment is reduced. Possibly the infrastructure will be allowed to deteriorate. Possibly big development schemes will be slowed up or abandoned. One would normally expect this to lead to some future cost, though some investments—notably big schemes—may have been quite unsound, with a low or even zero social marginal product. Conceivably the prospective marginal product of an investment project may be negative: investments may involve commitments to future expenditures

—whether further investment or current expenditures—that could be better utilized.

(v) Net lending to the private sector is reduced so private investment, whether in fixed capital equipment, in building and construction, or on consumer durables, falls. In all the previous cases the current account improvement is brought about by a reduction in the budget deficit; in this case it is brought about by an improvement in the private sector net financial balance. Whether the reduction in investment actually imposes a cost depends on whether the investment that is forgone would have been efficient; this is discussed further below.

Just running through these cases—which do not exhaust the possibilities—is a reminder that adjustment is unlikely to be easy politically. It will be easier to impose a future rather than a current cost so that the natural tendency will be to cut investment first.

Adjustment is likely to be relatively easy if the current account crisis had been caused by an expenditure increase to which the system had not yet fully adapted. One might explain the relative success of Mexican adjustment from 1982 in these terms. There may have been a recent and large rise in public investment, or in some other category of expenditure. Perhaps there had been a public investment 'binge' because of excessive optimism about future prospects induced by a recent discovery of vast oil reserves combined with a rise in the terms of trade (the Mexican case). Perhaps a populist government has recently increased subsidies or allowed public corporations to get into large deficit. Perhaps a new regime has embarked on a military expenditure boom. If all this is fairly new it may not be too difficult to reverse.

But another possibility is that the crisis was caused by a more fundamental change, say a terms-of-trade deterioration relative to a level that had been much higher for a fairly long period. The expenditure levels may be long established, and have been sustained by high private incomes and high tax revenues resulting from the earlier prolonged favourable terms of trade. People believe they have property rights in their high real incomes and in the expectation that these will continue. Then the matter of cutting expenditures is decidedly more difficult. This is the heart of recent problems in several African countries. On the other hand—as shown in Balassa (1984)—some countries in Asia, such as Korea and Thailand, have managed to adjust quite well to steep deterioration of their terms of trade.

In thinking about the future cost it is really necessary to be more precise about what gave rise to the need for adjustment. If the terms of trade have deteriorated and this is expected to be lasting, an adjustment cost, whether present or future, is certainly inevitable. On the other hand, the pre-existing situation may have been one where there was a current account deficit and the need for adjustment arose because the country's reserves were running out or the availability of new foreign finance had declined or ceased. In this initial situation a future cost was actually being incurred every year: reserves were declining or foreign debt was increasing. If adjustment consisted of reducing consumption a present cost would be replacing a future cost, while if adjustment consisted of cutting domestic investment one form of future cost would be replacing another.

The net future cost may be positive or negative when investment is cut. It will be positive if the marginal social product of domestic investment that would have been financed by foreign borrowing would have exceeded the rate of interest that would have been paid. If funds had been unwisely used, the social product being below the interest cost, the reduced availability of foreign funds would yield a net gain, being a blessing in disguise.

All this has concerned the primary adjustment cost. In addition, there are various sources of secondary adjustment cost, one being real wage inflexibility, at least in the short run. An adjustment programme may well give rise to unemployment as a result of real wage rigidity, so that a serious secondary adjustment cost will be imposed. Real wage resistance or wage indexation imposed by public policy is a problem in a few developing countries, notably Brazil.[5]

The best example concerns public sector wages. When the government has to cut its expenditures, frequently the wage bill has to be reduced. The government may have to choose between cutting the nominal wage rates of its employees and reducing public employment. If nominal wage rates could be reduced sufficiently it would not be necessary to reduce public employment. On the other hand, if wages were rigid, because of real wage resistance, unemployment might be inevitable. Normally public employees dimissed from their jobs (or potential entrants into the public labour force) cannot move readily into the other fields, notably export industries, where profitability has improved as a result of devaluation. Rigidity of public sector wages which compels the public sector work-force to be reduced will then be a direct cause of unemployment. Of course, if time for adjustment is allowed either unemployment or reduced wage rates would lead to a desirable transfer of labour to industries producing tradables.

---

[5] Real wage rigidity is clearly not a problem in Argentina and Mexico where in recent years there have been sharp declines in real wages (notably in Mexico after the 1982 crisis), nor in India, Pakistan, or Indonesia. It is noteworthy that Argentina and Mexico are countries with strong trade unions in sectors of their economies. Wage rigidity in Brazil and (at times) in Chile has resulted not from direct trade-union action but from wage indexation arrangements imposed or endorsed by the government. The broad question of the behaviour of nominal and real wages in response to shocks in developing countries is a very important one. The World Bank project initiated by Ian Little mentioned at the beginning of this chapter should shed some light on this. Preliminary evidence suggests a great variety of situations. Private sector wages may generally be quite flexible downwards, but public sector nominal wages appear to be more rigid.

In addition, devaluation will have raised the cost of living, so that, if public sector wages were fully indexed to the cost of living, nominal wage rates would actually rise. The fall in employment for any given required cut in the public sector nominal wage would then have to be even greater.

In the private sector real wage rates are also likely to fall as the result of an adjustment programme. The devaluation will have raised the cost of imports, and reduced subsidies and higher indirect taxes will further raise the cost of living. If an adjustment programme of expenditure reduction and devaluation would initially reduce real wages, wage indexation, whether formal or informal, designed to restore real wage rates will then in due course lead to an increase in the nominal wage level that will reduce the competitiveness of import-competing and export industries and negate —perhaps only partially—the effects of the initial nominal devaluation.

Another source of secondary adjustment cost is the imposition of import restrictions to deal with the current account problem. This is, regrettably, very common and creates a familiar distortion cost which could be avoided by devaluing instead.[6]

1.3. *Factoral Income Redistribution Effects: need for Sectoral Cost-Benefit Analysis*

The well-known two-instruments two-targets policy analysis expounded here provides the basis for the standard adjustment package: a combination of expenditure reduction and nominal devaluation. The matter of particular interest here concerns the sectoral or factoral distributional effects of the devaluation. We assume now that it does lead to a real devaluation.

We have already noted that expenditure reduction will have various adverse effects on different sectors, depending on the nature of the adjustment. There will be losers and no gainers from that part of the policy package. The losers will be in the future when investment is cut. Real devaluation, on the other hand, is a relative price change and will yield both gainers and losers. Export producers will gain. Urban workers, whether private or public employees, are likely to lose owing to the higher prices of imports. In general, profits of producers of non-tradables are likely to fall and those of producers of tradables to rise.

One must then combine the net effects on various sectoral incomes of the expenditure reduction and of the devaluation combined. An analysis of this kind—a kind of *sectoral cost-benefit analysis*—is of particular importance because it gives to the policy-makers insights into where the principal political and economic resistances to an adjustment package may be encountered.

---

[6] The choice between import restrictions and devaluation as a switching device when the current account has to be improved is an important issue discussed in detail in Corden (1987).

For example, real wages of public employees may fall both because public expenditure, and hence their nominal wages, have been cut and because their cost of living has risen because of higher prices of imports. They may also be consumers of exportables the prices of which will also have risen, unless kept down by price controls. For others there may be offsetting effects. Peasants producing export crops may lose through reduced subsidies, say, for fertilizer or through higher prices for electricity supplied by a public corporation which has been forced to reduce its losses. On the other hand they will gain from higher domestic currency incomes for their crops, this being partially offset by higher costs of imported inputs.

Contrary to one's first expectations, some manufacturing industries that produce potentially tradable products may lose as a result of devaluation. Many developing countries have manufacturing sectors which are protected by quantitative import restrictions and the domestic prices of which would not be raised by devaluation. Instead, the profits of importers who hold the scarce import licences will be squeezed. While the manufactured products are potentially import-competing, quantitative restrictions have actually turned them into non-tradables, their prices depending on domestic demand and supply conditions. Only if the premium on import licences disappeared completely would prices to customers or users be raised by devaluation.

Demand for these protected products will decline as a result of the general expenditure reduction, and their costs will increase both because the costs of imported inputs rise as a direct result of devaluation and because in due course the cost of labour may rise as export industries, whether urban or rural, expand. In Argentina, Brazil, and Mexico, large parts of manufacturing industries producing consumer goods would fall into this category, and to a lesser extent this is also true for Indonesia.

The crucial point about short-term adjustment is that there are bound to be losers, leading to political resistance. This will often prevent orderly implementation of adjustment measures, and may also cause the present cost to be reduced at the expense of a future cost, i.e. for investment rather than consumption to be cut. If a country cannot obtain sufficient foreign credits it will have no choice but to make an expenditure reduction, if not a devaluation. But the particular choice of measures will be affected by the varying strength of interest groups. Often enough net investment ceases completely and the capital stock is actually run down through failure to maintain it adequately.[7]

[7] For developing countries with debt-service problems and hence serious adjustment needs there was a big fall in the investment ratio after 1981. For the three years 1979–81 the ratio of gross capital formation to gross domestic product averaged over 25% for them, but for the period 1983–6 it was down to 19%. (These figures refer to a large group of countries defined by the IMF as 'countries with recent debt-servicing problems' and are calculated from *World Economic Outlook* (IMF, 1987).

Normally, the urban population in a developing country is politically stronger than the rural population and is more likely to succeed in protecting its interests and perhaps shifting the burden of adjustment as far as possible towards the rural sector. More generally the poor, even though more numerous, usually have the least political muscle. It is not surprising that rural roads, water supply, or electrification tend to suffer more than urban facilities, public sector salaries, or expenditures on the military.

Adjustment may be 'disorderly'. It may be unplanned, chaotic, one unplanned crisis measure following upon another. One could fill pages describing such episodes. One aim of International Monetary Fund programmes, at least ideally, is to ensure that the inevitable adjustment is orderly rather than disorderly. The loss of efficiency that results from disorderly adjustment could be counted as part of the secondary adjustment cost, i.e. the cost that good management and flexible pricing could conceivably avoid. Disorderly adjustment is certainly not inevitable, as the experiences of various Asian countries, notably Thailand, Singapore, and Korea have shown. A description of a successful orthodox adjustment experience—Korea 1981–4—can be found in Aghevli and Marquez-Ruarte (1985).

1.4. Structural Rigidities: Low Import or Export Elasticities

Structural rigidities mean that in the short run some supply and substitution elasticities are very low and possibly even zero.

The general insight of Latin American structuralism was that some import or export elasticities may indeed be very low, at least in the short run, and this then compels most of the short-run adjustment to take place either at very high social cost or in parts of the economy where elasticities are relatively high, if there are such. Furthermore, when these elasticities are low and the adjustment has to be quick, real devaluation, and hence the domestic redistributive effects, may need to be high. Considerable factoral redistribution may then be required, presenting both political difficulties and sometimes the problem of real wage resistance.

A typical situation is 'import starvation'. The country has become highly dependent on particular imports for which there are no domestic substitutes, at least in the short run. Import restrictions may already have eliminated less essential imports and all those for which local production, though high-cost, is at all possible. The imports that remain are either essentials, such as medical supplies, petroleum, spare parts for transport vehicles, and so on, or basic components or materials for local manufacturing industry. Ian Little has called this situation 'import starvation' and he makes the point that 'such a country may always be hovering on the point of crisis' (Little, 1982, p. 317).

Reducing imports further would cause unemployment and output losses in local manufacturing industry. This is an unplanned consequence of a

long-term policy of import substitution which has kept exports down to a
level where only the most essential imports could be financed. As Ian Little
has pointed out, a major reform of the trading regime designed to foster
exports is really needed. This reform should have taken place before the
balance-of-payments problem arose. But here we confine ourselves to the
short-term problem.

If imports cannot be reduced much the real devaluation will have to
expand exports—and rather quickly—if major problems are to be
avoided. A greater real devaluation will be needed to attain a given current
account outcome than if the domestic price elasticity of demand for imports had been higher. Hence the factoral redistribution effects—with all
their problems—will be greater.

2.   The Adjustment Problem with Capital Flight

In most developing countries with balance-of-payments adjustment problems there is a fiscal deficit and this is the essential cause of the current
account deficit. The current account deficit is definitionally equal to the
sum of the fiscal deficit minus the excess of private savings over private
domestic investment. The fiscal deficit should be defined as the 'public
sector borrowing requirement' and the public sector should be broadly
defined to include all branches of government as well as government-owned
or controlled corporations, these sometimes being called 'parastatals'.
Sometimes there is considerable ambiguity as to what is public and what
is private. This is particularly so when supposedly private borrowing is
guaranteed explicitly or implicitly by the government.

The usual situation is that the fiscal deficit is financed partly by borrowing abroad, whether or not on concessional terms, and partly from the
excess of domestic private savings over domestic investment. The mechanism in most developing countries by which domestic savings are channelled
to the government is not through a capital market (which hardly exists) but
through the banking system. Private savers deposit their funds with the
banks and the government borrows from the banks.

The simplest situation is one where there is little or no international
capital mobility, so that private savers cannot send their money abroad
because of exchange controls and, similarly, foreign funds do not flow
directly to the private sector (though they may do so indirectly through
government borrowing abroad, the funds then being passed on by the government). In this simple case government borrowing abroad plus the reduction in foreign exchange reserves is equal to the current account deficit.
An adjustment problem arises when reserves run out or new borrowing
becomes very difficult or costly. In practice what is required, above all, is a
decline in the fiscal deficit.

Let us now consider the case where the private sector is open to the world capital market, as it is in many developing countries now. Local investors and banks do not have faith in the government, or at least in the exchange rate, so that the excess of private savings over domestic investment is sent abroad rather than being kept in local currency available to be lent to the government. This is often called capital flight, and has been an important phenomenon in Argentina and Mexico (Cuddington, 1986). It might just as well be described as prudent portfolio diversification by local private investors, or as reflecting an anticipated devaluation combined with a domestic interest rate that is too low. At the same time, the government borrows abroad to finance its deficit. The private sector is lending abroad and the government is borrowing abroad. When the country's own citizens are declining to finance its fiscal deficit foreign borrowing by the government has to be greater than otherwise.

We now suppose, again, that there is an adjustment problem: the government's foreign borrowing has to be reduced possibly because foreign funds have dried up. In principle there are now two ways of dealing with this problem. The first is to reduce the fiscal deficit, and hence the current account deficit, associating this with real devaluation to maintain internal balance. The second is to divert domestic private savings from going abroad and to induce them or force them to finance the fiscal deficit instead—in other words, to reverse capital flight. In that case the fiscal and hence current account deficits may not need to be reduced at all.

Certain remedies are available for capital flight. The remedy that is often tried but in many cases cannot be enforced, or that is administratively very costly to enforce, is the imposition of exchange controls. Operating through the market and providing appropriate inducements may be better. Given the domestic interest rate, a major reason for capital flight is often the expectation of devaluation. Timely exchange rate adjustment or the introduction of a floating rate, are then possible solutions. Even better, an end might be put to the domestic policies—usually inflationary policies—that gave rise to the expectation of devaluation in the first place. Furthermore, the expectation may have been created that in case of fiscal difficulties the government might default on loans from local banks or on bonds sold to domestic residents. Even if it did not default it might sharply increase tax rates on interest income.

Interest rate policy is crucial. For any set of expectations, other than the certainty of default, there is, in principle, some after-tax interest rate that should attract domestic funds to finance the budget deficit rather than going abroad. One might then argue that the problem always comes down to the relationship between the domestic interest rate and the various expectations just discussed. For example, a country wtih high international capital mobility is Indonesia. In 1981 and 1982 it faced substantial capital outflow and this was reversed with a 20 per cent devaluation and a rise in nominal interest rates in 1983.

If expectations cannot be changed a very large rise in the interest rate may be needed if it is desired to finance the budget deficit with domestic (or, indeed, foreign) private savings. But there is likely to be some limit to the rise in the interest rate that is useful: the higher the real rate of interest that the government offers the greater will be its future expected debt-service burden and hence the more the market will allow for the possibility of default or of inflationary financing. A reduction in the non-interest fiscal deficit may thus be unavoidable.

When foreign borrowing is replaced by local financing of a budget deficit this can be called 'adjustment' from a national point of view. Presumably domestic savings could indefinitely finance part or even all of the fiscal deficit. On the other hand, it is just a change in the pattern of financing of the fiscal deficit. Furthermore, solving the immediate problem by reversing capital flight may not be optimal: it may be much better for the country, especially its long-term prospects, if the fiscal deficit is reduced, with local savers financing more private investment at home and perhaps also fruitfully investing abroad to some extent. Some private investment abroad may sometimes be optimal from a national point of view—for example, when the funds would otherwise finance wasteful public spending or private investment in highly protected industries.

In any case, some reduction in the fiscal deficit may be inevitable. Local private savings may not be enough to finance the whole of the deficit as well as existing private investment. This must be so if there is a current account deficit; in that case the excess of private savings over private investment falls short of the fiscal deficit and if we rule out any crowding out of domestic private investment there will still have to be some decline in the fiscal deficit if foreign borrowing is to cease completely.

3. Reducing Inflation

Countries that have high rates of inflation usually also have current account problems, but this association is not essential. We now consider a country that has high inflation but does not have a current account problem. The aim here is to isolate the inflation problem by assuming away the current account problem discussed so far. The government wants to reduce inflation because of the various dislocations it causes. The country's inflation rate is higher than that of its trading partners, so that the exchange rate will have to depreciate steadily—possibly with a 'trotting peg'—to avoid continuing real appreciation.

The inflation problem has in recent years certainly been a major one for some developing countries, though experience has greatly varied. In 1986 the average inflation rate of all developing countries was 29 per cent, but the Asian average was only 7.9 per cent, while the Western hemisphere average was 86.5 per cent. In 1985 the latter was 149 per cent, a figure much influenced by the Brazilian annual inflation rate of that year of 235 per cent.[8]

We start now with a situation where either the current account has to stay in balance or where there is a given inflow of new foreign funds per annum—whether obtained by public or by private borrowing—which cannot be increased but also does not for the time being need to be reduced. Assuming no structural or other real changes at home or abroad (aside from those that result from the disinflation process to be discussed here) the real exchange rate should stay constant and, with domestic inflation exceeding foreign inflation, continuous nominal depreciation will ensure this.

Adjustment now refers to anti-inflationary policy. There is an *inflation adjustment problem* and it will have some *inflation adjustment costs*. It will now be shown that the problem has two quite distinct parts, namely the 'inflation tax replacement problem' and the 'price adjustment problem'.

3.1. The Inflation Tax Replacement Problem

Presumably inflation will be fed and financed by monetary expansion. In most developing countries such monetary expansion is explained by the need to finance a fiscal deficit: monetization of the deficit is normally the essential cause of prolonged inflation. Holders of money balances have to save to obtain increases in nominal money supply sufficient to keep their real money balances at desired levels. These savings in effect finance partially or wholly the government's dissavings, i.e. the fiscal deficit. The reduction of real balances owing to inflation is the inflation tax.

Of course the demand for real balances will increase because of real growth of the economy. It may also increase because the advanced, monetized sector is expanding relative to the subsistence (or less monetized) sector. To that extent a growing supply of money that finances a fiscal deficit need not lead to inflation. Furthermore, growth in the money supply need not inevitably be caused by a fiscal deficit: it can also result from expansion of credit to the private sector. In addition, if inflationary expectations accelerated, the demand for real balances would fall, so that even a given growth in the money supply would lead to increasing inflation. Nevertheless, taking all this into account, it remains true that when

---

[8] The Brazilian figure refers to the GDP deflator. The aggregative figures come from *World Economic Outlook* (IMF, 1987) and refer to consumer prices.

inflation is high a principal explanation is usually a monetized budget deficit.[9]

Given then that the fiscal deficit is the principal cause of monetary expansion, and monetary expansion is the cause of inflation, government expenditure has to fall or other sources of taxation have to be found if inflation is to be reduced. That is the 'inflation tax replacement problem'.

The cost or distortion that high inflation imposes even in a steady state where the economy has fully adjusted to inflation is well known: money holdings (which normally bear little or no interest) yield negative returns so that people will economize on the use of money to the general inconvenience of private and business affairs. In addition, high inflation inevitably leads to distortions in relative prices. At the same time, alternative taxes also have familiar distortion costs—on incentives and on the patterns of consumption and of resource use—and, in addition, they have collection and compliance costs. Similarly, cutting government expenditure involves costs and political obstacles as discussed earlier.

The inflation tax is likely to be very inefficient, at least when inflation is high, and thus more costly than, say, a value added tax or even a revenue tariff. High inflation—which is inevitably not at a constant predictable rate—creates so much 'noise' in the economic system that it is liable to disrupt all normal economic activity. It is not difficult to explain the political popularity of programmes that succeed in getting high inflation under control. It is thus possible that in an overall or economy-wide sense (leaving aside distributional effects) there may be a net gain, and hence, no inflation adjustment cost at all, when the inflation tax is replaced by a well-constructed set of explicit taxes. This could also be true when government expenditure is cut, rather than taxes being raised.

Another relatively happy thought is that the actual fiscal deficit expressed as a proportion of gross national product is likely to be much greater than the deficit which has to be eliminated if inflation financing is to end. There are two reasons for this.

Firstly, inflation usually leads to reduced tax revenue—i.e. in revenue from explicit taxes measured in real terms—even with given tax rates. This is explained by the inevitable lags in tax collections. Nominal tax collections lag behind nominal government expenditures which frequently adjust more rapidly to inflation. Cutting the rate of inflation would boost real tax

---

[9] It is well known from the theory of hyperinflation that if inflationary expectations exceed the actual rate of inflation the latter will accelerate, essentially because the demand for real balances relative to GDP is falling. As the inflation tax *rate* rises the *base* of the tax actually falls. Hence the revenue from the inflation tax (expressed as a proportion of GDP) would fall if the monetized budget deficit increased beyond a certain point: sufficient private savings to finance the budget deficit at an initial rate of inflation could not be generated, this leading to a dynamic monetary disequilibrium, i.e. hyperinflation.

revenues. This 'Olivera–Tanzi effect' can be very important.[10] Secondly, a part of the deficit is likely to be bond-financed and this does not need to be reduced or eliminated in order to reduce the money growth rate. In fact, as will be discussed below, this part of the deficit will itself decline owing to a reduced nominal interest bill when inflationary expectations decline.

While a shift from the inflation tax to, say, a value added tax or a simple excise tax may yield a net overall gain through reducing distortions, there will be important sectoral redistribution effects, just as in the case of devaluation. A 'sectoral cost-benefit analysis' is again appropriate. Inflation taxes money-holders—especially those not smart enough to get into interest-bearing or real assets as much as possible—while alternative taxes are quite likely to bear heavily on more specific groups, who may strongly resist imposition of the new taxes. If taxes cannot be increased government expenditure will have to be reduced, leading again to sectoral resistance. Usually, ordinary people will gain from a reduction of inflation because their accumulated savings in the form of bank deposits will not be taxed so much, while they will lose through the price-raising effects of higher commodity taxes.

3.2. The Price Adjustment Problem

So far we have been concerned with the budgetary problem that an anti-inflationary policy presents. Quite distinct is the 'price adjustment problem'. Let us assume for the moment that the country is in a steady-state inflation where all prices are fully adjusted to expected inflation, notably the nominal interest rate, the nominal exchange rate, and the nominal wage. Actual inflation is equal to expected inflation. The real interest rate, the real exchange rate, and the real wage are not raised or reduced just because there is inflation.

An anti-inflationary programme—requiring a reduction in the fiscal deficit and leading to a reduction in the money growth rate—is then embarked upon. The problem is that product prices may fail to respond in reasonable time and, in addition, major distortions in relative prices can result. Hence big overall costs and factoral redistribution effects can be imposed. These costs are not inevitable. It appears that when Indonesia reduced inflation after the end of the Soekarno era in 1966 the transition to low inflation was surprisingly smooth (with the growth rate rapidly rising). But there have certainly been problems in Argentina, Brazil, and Chile.

---

[10] See Olivera (1967) and Tanzi (1977). This effect was particularly noticeable in Argentina in 1985 when there was a drastic reduction in the rate of inflation as a result of the Austral Plan. The monthly inflation rate was about 20% in 1984, 31% in June 1985, and 6% in July 1985, falling further after that. Between 1984 and 1985 revenue rose by about 5% of GDP, and a significant part of the increase was probably explained by this effect (though some taxes also increased).

One can give a few examples of the kinds of problems that can arise and have arisen.

(i) Agents in product markets are surprised by the anti-inflationary policy, do not expect the programme to last, and hence continue to raise prices on the basis of the initially expected rate of inflation. In Latin America this has been called 'inertial inflation', i.e. inflation that is not quickly responsive to demand contraction. Hence, given the policy of monetary restraint, the real money supply falls, the real interest rate rises, and the economy contracts. The anti-inflationary policy has a classic deflationary effect.

With a floating exchange rate and international capital mobility this would lead to incipient capital inflow and thus real appreciation, the rate of depreciation falling behind the rate of domestic price inflation. Hence the relative prices of tradables to non-tradables would be lowered and there would be a particularly adverse effect on tradable-goods industries. If intervention by the central bank ensured sufficient depreciation to prevent the real exchange rate from appreciating to the full extent (so as to maintain the competitiveness of tradables) there would be some actual capital inflow in response to the higher interest rate, which would tend to increase the money supply and so moderate the anti-inflationary policy.

This kind of experience—both real appreciation and capital inflow associated with anti-inflation stabilization programmes—can be found in the recent histories (1977–82) of Argentina, Chile, and Uruguay.[11]

The implication is that if the 'inertia' is to be overcome, the policy shift must be widely understood and credible, something that is not easy to attain when inflation has been long-lasting and previous attempts to slow it up have failed. The fact that an anti-inflationary policy is likely to involve a short but painful period of deflation because of the slowness of expectations to adjust leads to the expectations that such a policy once begun would not be sustained for political reasons. This very expectation is then the cause of the adverse deflationary effect. This does not mean that continued 'inertial inflation' is inevitable, but only that a difficult transition period must be allowed for, and that the firmness of the orthodox anti-inflationary programme must be clearly established.

(ii) The rate of increase of wages fails to adjust to the lower rate of money growth as rapidly as do product prices. Hence real wages rise. Nominal wages in industrial countries and in the formal sectors of some developing countries tend to be somewhat inflexible, possibly because of explicit or implicit contracts. When there is inflation, inflexibility or inertia refers to the rate of increase rather than the absolute level of prices and wages. On the other hand, product prices may be quite flexible. Tradable-

[11] See the references in fn. 12.

goods prices will be heavily influenced by the rate of depreciation, and this depreciation rate may decline rapidly because of lower money growth and, even more, because of expectations of lower money growth in the future. The policy implication is that the anti-inflationary policy must be well understood and believed by agents in the labour market. In some countries the role of trade unions, especially in the public sector, is crucial.

In a few countries there is formal wage indexation, as there has been in Brazil and Chile at various times. This is inevitably lagged, wages in the current period being adjusted to price changes in a previous period. This means that when the rate of price inflation declines, the decline in the rate of nominal wage growth will lag behind and so real wages will rise. Such real wage increases squeeze profits and are likely to increase unemployment. The policy implication is that if indexation itself cannot be ended, the indexation formula should be adjusted to prevent real wages from rising.

(iii) Firms may have locked themselves into incurring debts with nominal interest rates adjusted to the initially expected rate of inflation. While the loans may be fairly short-term, a sudden decline in the rate of inflation could have a radical short-term effect in redistributing wealth from debtors to creditors and thus in causing bankruptcies. In addition, high inflation tends to benefit the financial sector, and a successful reduction of inflation can have a severely adverse effect. This was observed in Brazil during the short period when the 'Cruzado Plan' was successful.

In considering these costs of reducing inflation it must be remembered that the starting-point is never a well-adjusted steady-state inflation. Relative prices are always distorted when there is high inflation (say above 50 per cent per annum). A good reason for wishing to reduce or even eliminate inflation is that the distortions caused by inflation are often so high. Normally there are institutional rigidities and various controls which prevent some prices, but not others, from adjusting adequately to the rate of growth of nominal demand. The motivation for controls is usually a misplaced effort to control inflation not at the source but by tackling some of the symptoms. Hence some nominal interest rates are controlled, leading to negative real rates, some product prices may be controlled, leading to shortages and distortions in resource allocation, and frequently the exchange rate is not depreciated sufficiently to compensate for the excess of domestic over foreign inflation, leading to a squeeze on the profitability of industries producing tradables and to a current account deficit.

Against the distortions caused by inflation must be set the costs of an anti-inflationary programme. As we have seen an anti-inflationary programme which faces 'inertia' and is initially not fully credible will have price adjustment costs. The latter costs—which are likely to be temporary— must then be weighed against the costs created by the existing distortions caused by inflation which will eventually be ended. Essentially there is a trade-off to be made between the possibly high short-term costs of an anti-inflationary programme and the long-term benefits—some of which may also be felt immediately—of reducing the rate of inflation.

3.3. Exchange Rate and Heterodox Policies: minimizing Inflation Adjustment Cost

Two particular approaches to the problem of minimizing the part of the inflation adjustment cost that is caused by the 'price adjustment problem' have been tried.

One approach has been to fix the nominal exchange rate—or at least to have a pre-announced movement of the exchange rate on the basis of some kind of scale (called 'tablita' in Argentina).[12] The exchange rate is maintained by exchange market intervention and in an indirect way prices of tradable goods will then be somewhat controlled, depending on inflation abroad. When import-competing goods are only imperfect substitutes for imports the control is inevitably imperfect.

The problem is that if domestic credit continues to expand faster than the exchange rate depreciates, prices of non-tradables will rise faster than those of tradables—the real exchange rate will appreciate—with the usual adverse resource allocation effects. It is crucial that the exchange rate policy be associated with orthodox credit-restraint policies. Furthermore, with some wage inflexibility, nominal wages in the tradable sector may not adjust sufficiently fast, causing a cost-price squeeze in tradables, and hence unemployment.

A second, broader approach is the so-called 'heterodox approach' (Dornbusch and Simonsen, 1987; Blejer, 1987). It really embraces the first as a special case. It has been tried in 1985–6 in Israel, Argentina, and Brazil, with considerable success in the first case and none in the last.

This time many prices—product prices, wages, the exchange rate, the nominal interest rate—are controlled or at least are made subject to various predetermined scales. In theory, at least, this does not replace but only supplements the 'orthodox' policy of monetary restraint through reducing the fiscal deficit. The idea is that for a transitional period controls take the place of market expectations in determining prices and wages, given the difficulty discussed above of getting expectations to adapt to the anti-inflation programme. It is, of course, crucial that the heterodox policies be regarded as complements to, and not substitutes for the essential orthodox policy of monetary restraint.

---

[12] This was tried in Argentina, Chile and Uruguay in the 1970s. There is now a large literature analysing these episodes. For a detailed description of the Chilean episode, see Edwards and Edwards (1987) and for overviews of all three 'Southern Cone' experiences, see Corbo and de Melo (1985) and Corbo *et al.* (1986)

The central problem is the familiar one of getting relative prices right. If relative prices were initially in reasonable equilibrium, with no notable shortages or excess demands, and if there were no changes in demand and supply conditions, in the terms of trade, and so on, it would be simplest to freeze all prices and wages. In practice comprehensive enforcement is difficult, so that some relative prices will change in unplanned directions. Leaving this aside, there are usually some underlying shifts in demand and supply that require relative price changes. One would surely expect a shift from inflation tax to explicit taxes or a reduction in government expenditures to change equilibrium relative prices.

Furthermore, one cannot assume that in the initial high inflation situation relative prices were in 'equilibrium'. It may be necessary to make some once-and-for-all price and wage changes before the whole set is frozen or set on some kind of automatic pilot for a temporary period, and these preparatory reforms are not easy. Usually price determination is something that is best left to the market rather than to central controllers. Controlling prices is likely to lead to shortages for particular products, making the programme both unpopular and inefficient.

In both the Brazilian and Argentinian stabilization attempts, prices of public sector enterprises were frozen or prevented from rising sufficiently while wages continued to increase. The increased subsidies needed to keep the enterprises afloat then militated against the policy of monetary restraint which was the key 'orthodox' element of the anti-inflationary programme without which the 'heterodox' element could achieve very little. In fact, the fundamental cause of the breakdown of the Brazilian Cruzado Plan of 1986 was a failure to pursue the orthodox part of the package so that the Cruzado Plan broke down after about nine months. In addition, very unwisely, real wages were allowed to increase and the anti-inflationary programme came to be associated with a consumption boom.

The heterodox approach might work for a brief period, as it seems to have in Israel, until expectations adjust so that controls can be removed. But it may be difficult to convince people that prices will not rise again when controls are removed since they may attribute the short-term decline in inflation more to the price and wage controls than to the decline in the money growth rate.

4. Two Adjustment Problems: Current Account and Inflation

We have seen that a current account problem is likely to be caused by a fiscal deficit. In principle it could also be attributable to an excess of private investment over savings, but in most cases the correct focus is on the consolidated budget deficit, broadly interpreted to include the deficits of all public agencies.[13] In addition, in most developing countries where there is serious and prolonged inflation the explanation is continued monetary expansion resulting from monetization of a fiscal deficit. Thus a fiscal deficit can cause both a current account and an inflation problem, and there have been plenty of cases where these two problems have coexisted. It is then necessary to combine the analyses of the two adjustment problems.

4.1.   The Financing of the Fiscal Deficit

Let us now assume that the fiscal deficit is financed in two parts. Partly it is financed by borrowing abroad. And partly it is financed by money creation, which produces inflation, and hence leads to saving by the private sector designed to restore real balances. At this stage we assume that there is no domestic borrowing by the government, other than from the central bank. Furthermore, there has not been any domestic borrowing in the past so that the government and central bank combined have no indebtedness in domestic currency. The whole of the public sector's interest bill is debt service on the accumulated foreign debt denominated in foreign currency. The complication of domestic debt will be introduced later.

A reduction in the current account deficit requires reduced foreign borrowing. Unless there is increased inflationary financing, the fiscal deficit must be reduced appropriately either by government expenditure being cut or taxes being increased. This is familiar. To avoid unemployment the reduction in the fiscal deficit has to be associated with real devaluation. If there is some degree of real wage rigidity or other factors giving rise to frictions some unemployment may be unavoidable.

A reduction in inflation requires the money-financed fiscal deficit to be reduced. Unless there is to be more foreign borrowing and hence a worse current account, this also requires cuts in government spending or increased taxes. This time, because of the price adjustment problem, leading to a temporary decline in the real money supply and possibly a temporary rise in real wages, there may also be temporary unemployment. The conclusion is that a reduction in government spending or rise in tax rates could both improve the current account and reduce inflation. How much one objective rather than the other is achieved depends on which of the two forms of financing is reduced more.

The implications for the exchange rate are interesting. The improvement of the current account requires real devaluation if employment is to be maintained. At the same time the reduction in inflation requires a reduced

---

[13] From 1977 to 1981 Chile's public sector was practically in balance (with an average deficit of only 0.5% of GDP), but there was a large current account deficit—rising to 14% of GDP in 1981—financed by private borrowing abroad. This is a notable exception to the generalization here. By contrast in 1981 Brazil had a public sector deficit which was 11.5% of GDP and a current account deficit of 6.6%.

rate of nominal depreciation to maintain a given real rate. When a reduction in the deficit leads to improvements on both fronts various desirable time-paths of the nominal exchange rate can then be envisaged. At first, as domestic inflation is reduced the rate of depreciation might continue as before, until the desired real depreciation is attained, and then the rate of depreciation would decline in line with the decline in the rate of monetary expansion.

It also follows that either objective—current account improvement or reduced inflation—can be achieved at the expense of worsening the situation with respect to the other. Suppose the fiscal deficit is given. A shift from money financing to foreign borrowing will reduce inflation and worsen the current account, and a shift from foreign borrowing to money financing will increase inflation but improve the current account. It is a shift of the latter kind that took place in the 1980s in a number of heavily indebted countries—notably Argentina, Brazil, Mexico, and Turkey—which had no choice but to improve their current account positions but were unable to bring about sufficient fiscal contraction. Hence the rapid acceleration in the rate of inflation in these countries can be explained essentially by the need to improve the current account.

4.2. *Borrowing Domestically: The Four Parts of the Fiscal Deficit*

Finally, government debt denominated in domestic currency can be introduced.[14] This leads to complications which cannot be ignored but do not really alter the main messages presented so far. Thus this discussion could be regarded as an extended footnote. One part of government expenditure consists now of interest payments on domestic debt. And the deficit will be financed partly by issuing more of such debt.

Just to simplify, it will first be assumed that the whole of the deficit is financed in this way. There is no foreign borrowing or use of reserves and no money-financing, and no inflation or inflationary expectations. Initially there is internal balance. Furthermore, owing to effective exchange controls, there is no international capital mobility. Therefore the domestic and foreign interest rates are not related. It can be shown that the whole of a fiscal deficit financed by domestic borrowing will—given the assumptions—be financed by crowding out domestic investment.

Domestic borrowing raises the domestic interest rate and thus crowds out some domestic private investment in the first instance. In addition,

---

[14] The term 'government' is used here to include the central bank. Hence domestic borrowing refers to borrowing by the government from the private sector or, conceivably, the sale of bonds by the central bank in the open market while at the same time it is buying bonds from the government. The main point is that the budget deficit is financed domestically without the money supply being increased. When a fiscal deficit is money-financed it is actually financed by borrowing from the central bank, which then creates the extra money; this process is *not* defined as domestic borrowing here.

with a constant real money supply and an unchanged exchange rate it would raise aggregate domestic demand both for imports and for home-produced goods. It must be remembered that, in the absence of foreign borrowing by the government and with no change in reserves, and with no international capital mobility, the current account cannot change. Hence the exchange rate must depreciate to divert all the extra expenditure towards home-produced goods. But, since there was initially internal balance, this must lead to excess demand for home-produced goods, so prices rise and, with a given nominal money supply, the real money supply will fall and the interest rate will rise further, crowding out domestic investment further.

Finally, real expenditure will be back where it started, the increase that resulted from the fiscal deficit being offset by the reduction of private investment. If the higher interest rate generated more domestic savings, there will have been some crowding out of domestic consumption as well as investment.

If the domestic and foreign capital markets are linked, the higher domestic interest rate will attract capital inflow, which will appreciate the exchange rate and produce a current account deficit. For this purpose capital mobility does not have to be perfect nor domestic and foreign bonds perfect substitutes. The capital inflow will also moderate the rise in the domestic interest rate and hence the decline in domestic investment. In this quite realistic case the fiscal deficit will be financed partly by a reduction in domestic investment and partly by foreign borrowing carried out this time by the private sector in the capital market rather than directly by the government.

Putting all this into reverse one can start again with the familiar balance-of-payments adjustment problem: the country has a current account deficit that has to be reduced. The fiscal deficit is financed partly by the government borrowing abroad and partly by borrowing domestically. For the moment we assume no inflationary financing. To achieve a given current account improvement the fiscal deficit would then need to be reduced more when domestic financing is reduced because in that case part of the effect would be a fall in the domestic interest rate which would increse domestic investment. If such an increase in investment is not desired, direct foreign borrowing by the government should be reduced first. The more integrated in the world market is the local capital market—so that the domestic interest rate can change very little—the less difference does it make which form of borrowing is reduced.

Inflation must now be brought back into the picture. Inflation generates inflationary expectations, and inflationary expectations raise the nominal interest rate. As is well known the effects depend on the length of maturities of bonds and whether or not they are floating rate bonds. In any case the effect of an increase in inflationary expectations is to raise the interest bill on the domestic-currency denominated debt. This refers only to expectations about domestic inflation since foreign inflation and expectations are given.

Holding all other elements of government expenditure and tax revenue constant, the net effect will be to increase the fiscal deficit. One part of the deficit can thus be directly attributed to inflationary expectations. If the real interest rate is 4 per cent and inflationary expectations are 46 per cent, so that the nominal interest rate is 50 per cent, no less than 92 per cent of the interest bill on domestic debt bill be attributable to inflationary expectations. This part can be called the 'domestic-inflation-caused deficit'. Financing this part of the deficit with domestic bonds will simply maintain constant the expected real value of these bonds held by the public.

This part of the deficit will decline if money-financing of the rest of the deficit declines provided reduced money-financing also leads to a decline in inflationary expectations. Thus, if inflation is to be reduced to a given extent without any deterioration in the current account, the proportion of the fiscal deficit that must be eliminated by cutting non-interest spending or raising taxes is less than might appear at first sight because there will be some endogenous reduction in the deficit.

To summarize, the total nominal fiscal deficit can be classified as follows:

(i) First, there is the *money-financed deficit*. To the extent that it causes or increases inflation, it is matched by private savings to restore real balances and hence does not affect the current account. As noted earlier, it is likely that some of the increase in the money supply does not generate inflation because the demand for money is expanding for other reasons, for example general growth of the economy.

(ii) Second, there is the *domestic-inflation-caused deficit*, just discussed. This is caused by inflationary expectations which raise the domestic interest rate and hence debt service: it would disappear if inflation were not expected and is thus essentially endogenous.

(iii) Third, there is the *foreign-borrowing-financed deficit* which deteriorates the current account and appreciates the real exchange rate.[15]

(iv) Finally, there is the *domestic-bond-financed real deficit* which is the part of the deficit financed with domestic currency denominated bonds less the part attributable to inflationary expectations. This will both crowd out domestic investment and deteriorate the current account, crowding out being relatively less the more integrated is the domestic capital market in the world market.

---

[15] This part of the deficit could be divided into two parts. One part is attributable to inflationary expectations abroad (which raise the nominal interest rate) and the remaining part is the foreign-financed *real* deficit. The first part will simply restore the real value of the foreign debt or, at least, will be expected to do so on the basis of inflationary expectations.

5. Conclusion

No simple conclusion emerges from an analytical paper of this kind, other than that adjustment is likely to be difficult. But a few themes and distinctions that have emerged can be underlined, apart from the obvious concern with expenditure reduction and switching to deal with a current account problem and the key role of the fiscal deficit both for this problem and for reducing inflation.

The distinction has been made between the primary adjustment cost and the secondary adjustment cost, the latter resulting from unemployment and output losses caused by failure to devalue sufficiently, by real wage resistance, or by the inappropriate use of import restrictions. Structural rigidities (i.e. low price elasticities) raise adjustment costs. Present and future costs have also been distinguished.

Adjustment is difficult because, inevitably, there are losers and factoral income redistribution effects of devaluation are important in determining who the losers are from expenditure reduction and devaluation combined. There is a need for what has been called here 'sectoral cost-benefit analysis' to understand and anticipate the political and pressure group obstacles to adjustment.

Capital flight has been related to the adjustment problem and various ways of reversing it have been noted.

A fiscal deficit can be monetized and so give rise to inflation. Unavoidably, the fiscal deficit must be reduced if the rate of inflation is to be cut. The problem of reducing inflation—yielding inflation adjustment costs— has been decomposed into two parts, namely the inflation tax replacement problem and the price adjustment problem, the latter having several facets. Policies of predetermining the nominal exchange rate according to a scale ('tablita'), or 'heterodox' policies which regulate many prices as well as wages, are meant to overcome the latter problem (especially 'inertia') but have their difficulties.

Finally it has been shown that the nominal fiscal deficit has various components, notably the money-financed deficit, which is likely to create inflation, and the part financed by foreign borrowing. If real government expenditure and taxes are kept unchanged, raising the proportion financed by the first will reduce the current account deficit at the cost of increasing inflation, while raising the proportion of the second will reduce inflation at the cost of worsening the current account. Reducing real government expenditure or increasing non-inflation taxes can help with both problems.

References

Aghevli, Bijan B., and Marquez-Ruarte, Jorge (1985), *A Case of Successful Adjustment: Korea's Experience during 1980–84*, Occasional Paper, 39, (Washington, DC: IMF).

Balassa, Bela (1984), 'Adjustment Policies in Developing Countries: A Reassessment', *World Development*, 12/9, pp. 955–72.

Blejer, Mario I. (1987), 'Transitional Strategies and Fiscal Policies in Recent Hyper-Stabilization Experiences' (Washington, DC: IMF), unpublished.

Connolly, M., and Taylor, D. (1976), 'Testing the Monetary Approach to Devaluation in Developing Countries,' *Journal of Political Economy*, 84/4, pp. 849–59.

Corbo, Vittorio, and de Melo, J. (1985), 'Liberalization with Stabilization in the Southern Cone: Overview and Summary', *World Development*, 13 (Aug.).

——de Melo, V., and Tybout, J. (1986), 'What Went Wrong with the Recent Reforms in the Southern Cone', *Economic Development and Cultural Change*, 34 (Apr.).

Corden, W. Max (1985), *Inflation, Exchange Rates, and the World Economy: Lectures in International Monetary Economics*, 3rd edn. (Oxford: OUP).

——(1987), *Protection and Liberalization: A Review of Analytical Issues*, Occasional Paper, 54 (Washington, DC: IMF).

Cuddington, John T. (1986), 'Capital Flight: Estimates, Issues, and Explanations', Princeton Studies in International Finance, 58 (Princeton: Princeton University).

Diaz-Alejandro, C. P. (1965), *Exchange Rate Devaluation in a Semi-Industrialized Country*, (Cambridge, Mass.: MIT Press).

Dornbusch, Rudiger, and Simonsen, Mario Henrique (1987), 'Inflation Stabilization with Incomes Policy Support' (Discussion: Mario Brodersohn, Michael Bruno, and G. G. Johnson) (New York: Group of Thirty).

Edwards, Sebastian (1987), *Exchange Controls, Devaluations and Real Exchange Rates: The Latin American Experience*, NBER Working Paper, 2348 (Cambridge, Mass.: National Bureau of Economic Research).

——and Edwards, Alejandra Cox (1987), *Monetarism and Liberalization: The Chilean Experiment* (Cambridge, Mass.: Ballinger Publishing Co.).

IMF (1987), *Theoretical Aspects of the Design of Fund Supported Adjustment Programs*, Occasional Paper, 55 (Washington, DC: IMF).

——(1987) *World Economic Outlook* (Washington, DC: IMF).

Johnson, H. G. (1958), 'Towards a General Theory of the Balance of Payments', in H. G. Johnson, *International Trade and Economic Growth* (London: Allen & Unwin).

Khan, Mohsin S., and Knight, Malcolm D. (1981) 'Stabilization Programs in Developing Countries: A Formal Framework', *Staff Papers*, 28/1 (Washington, DC: IMF).

Krugman, P. R., and Taylor, L. (1978), 'Contractionary Effects of Devaluation'. *Journal of International Economics*, 8/3, pp. 445–56.

Little, Ian M. D. (1982), *Economic Development: Theory, Policy, and International Relations* (New York: Basic Books).

Meade, J. E. (1951), *The Balance of Payments* (London: OUP).

Olivera, Julio H. G. (1967), 'Money, Prices and Fiscal Lags: A Note on the Dynamics of Inflation', *Banco Nazionale del Lavoro Quarterly Review*, 22.

Salter, W. E. G. (1959), 'Internal and External Balance: The Role of Price and Expenditure Effects', *Economic Record*, 35 (Aug), pp. 226–38.

Tanzi, Vito, (1977) 'Inflation, Lags in Collection, and the Real Value of Tax Revenue,' *Staff Papers*, 24/1 (Washington, DC: IMF), pp. 154–67.

Warr, Peter G. (1984), 'Exchange Rate Protection in Indonesia' *Bulletin of Indonesian Economic Studies*, 20/2 (Canberra: Australian National University).

3

Economic Policy in Countries Prone to Temporary Trade Shocks

DAVID BEVAN, PAUL COLLIER, AND JAN GUNNING

1. Introduction

The economies of many developing countries are 'small', 'open', and experience spasmodic external shocks. By 'small' we mean that the country is not able to influence its external terms of trade but must accept the prevailing world market prices for its imports and exports. By 'open' we mean that international trade forms a substantial component of GDP. In the past decade, economists have developed a model of how small open economies are affected by external shocks, the theory being termed 'Dutch Disease' (after the supposed effects of the discovery of natural gas in The Netherlands in the 1960s). We provide a brief summary of this in Section 2.1. However, this theory focuses upon the effects of a permanent change in the terms of trade, whereas the more relevant phenomenon for many developing countries is that of temporary trade booms and slumps which may last for only a few years. The extension of 'Dutch Disease' theory to temporary shocks is more recent; it forms the focus of the present review. The key elements of the theory are outlined in Section 2.2. Asymmetries between booms and slumps are discussed in 2.3. Section 3 considers government policies, and Section 4 describes three examples of temporary trade shocks, a coffee boom in Kenya and the oil shocks in Indonesia and Nigeria.

2. Optimal Responses in the Absence of Government

2.1. The Theory of Permanent Trade Shocks

When a country experiences a boom, the effects always depend on government policies, policies either adopted in response to the shock or already part of the pre-shock control regime. But it is useful first to consider the hypothetical situation when there is no government. The terms of trade gain then necessarily accrues entirely to private agents. If they see the shock as a permanent one, they must decide how to adjust their expenditures to the change in permanent income. These expenditures may include investment, but the distinction between consumption and investment is not an essential one in the case of a permanent shock. If there are no market imperfections the effects of the responses by private agents to the increase in their permanent income depend on two characteristics of the economy: factor mobility and tradability.

First, consider factor mobility. At one extreme all production factors (labour, capital, land) are completely specialized; they are, in the economist's jargon, sector-specific. In this case a boom cannot affect resource allocation, for any producer who would want to expand production would have to attract factors by bidding them away from other uses and this is impossible if all factors are fully specialized. At the other extreme, if all factors are fully mobile then, for example, labour employed in the textile industry can costlessly and instantaneously move to, say, the oil sector. In practice one finds situations between these extremes: all sectors have specific factors (e.g. the machines used in the textile sector), but there also exist mobile factors (e.g. unskilled labour) which can be used in more than one, perhaps in all, sectors. This has important implications for the way a boom affects an economy. For if a production factor, say labour, is mobile between all sectors, then the booming sector can expand at the expense of other sectors by bidding away this factor.[1] Part of the benefits of the boom are then transferred to labour, through an increase in wages. Hence factor mobility (or the lack thereof) affects the consequences of a boom, both for production and for income distribution.

Now consider tradability. Tradable goods and services are (or can be) traded internationally. For a small, price-taking country the domestic price of a tradable is determined by the world price. An increase in the domestic demand for a tradable therefore has no effect on its price: the market will be cleared through an increase in imports (or a decrease in the volume of exports). By definition, such changes are impossible for non-tradables. For these goods domestic prices are not tied to world prices and a shift in demand triggers a price change: e.g. the price rises until demand falls (and domestic production increases) sufficiently for the market to clear. We must now distinguish between the booming sector (X), non-booming tradables (M), and non-tradables (N). To the extent the boom income is spent on non-tradables it will lead to price changes; typically (but not necessarily) the relative price of non-tradables rises.[2] This has the usual income and subsitution effects on demand. In addition, producers of non-tradables now have an incentive (provided they use mobile factors) to increase production. The net effect is ambiguous, except for the M-sector: the non-booming tradable sector suffers from a boom. For it cannot benefit through a price increase (since the price for its output is determined in the world

---

[1] Provided, of course, that there is at least some factor substitutability, so that production can expand when labour use increases, but other factors are kept constant.

[2] If those who lose from the boom have a strong preference for non-tradables (relative to those who gain), then it is possible that the boom reduces the relative price of non-tradables.

market), but it must lose through an increase in its costs (in this case through an induced wage increase).

Clearly, there are many possible outcomes, depending upon the combination of factor mobility and tradability characteristics of the economy.[3] These need not be considered as given once we take the government into account: one way in which governments affect the consequences of trade shocks is through the effects of government policies on the tradability of goods and the mobility of factors.

2.2.   The Theory of Temporary Trade Shocks

The contraction of the non-boom tradables sector, discussed above, is commonly referred to as 'Dutch Disease'. Whether or not it is Dutch, as described above it is certainly not a disease: if the windfall is permanent, the resource reallocation out of the sector is optimal. The implication that the reallocation may be undesirable, which is a common theme of the literature, rests upon the recognition that windfalls are usually only temporary. It is indeed likely to be suboptimal to respond to a temporary windfall as if it were permanent for resource reallocations will have to be reversed. There may well be asymmetries in the costs of such reallocations: for example, once an industrial sector is wiped out by 'Dutch Disease' it may be difficult to rebuild. However, if the windfall is only temporary, at least some private agents in the economy are likely to recognize it as such. They will then treat some of their current income as 'transient' and have a high savings rate out of it. This change in savings behaviour forms the core of the theory of temporary trade shocks (Bevan *et al.*, 1987, 1989*a*), which is an extension of the theory of 'Dutch Disease'. Without such an extension, the theory depends upon the rather special circumstance in which a windfall is actually temporary but is mistaken for being permanent by all private agents.

By contrast, the theory of temporary trade shocks considers the case in which private agents fully recognize that the windfall is temporary. They therefore increase their consumption only by that amount which is sustainable if the rest of the windfall is saved. Although individually private agents can save by means of domestic financial assets, these must be offset by other agents incurring liabilities. Hence, in aggregate, the country can only increase its savings either by adding to its capital stock or by acquiring foreign financial assets (or repaying foreign debts). Most developing countries are normally capital-scarce, so that the return upon capital within the economy is above the world deposit rate of interest. It is therefore unlikely to be the best policy for the windfall savings to be permanently held

---

[3] Surveys of the various models may be found in Corden and Neary (1982), Corden (1984), and Neary and van Wijnbergen (1986).

abroad. Consider, however, the case in which all the windfall savings are used to finance domestic capital formation.

The demand for capital goods then increases relative to consumer goods (since there is an unusually high savings rate and these savings are used to buy capital goods). Recall that the theory of permanent shocks imposes a disaggregation into tradable and non-tradable goods consequent upon the exogenous change in the pattern of supply (the foreign exchange windfall only increases the supply of tradable goods). Analogously, this change in the pattern of demand imposes a disaggregation into capital and consumer goods. Combining the two disaggregations there are therefore four distinct groups of goods. However, tradable capital goods and tradable consumer goods have a constant relative price since both prices are set on the world market and are exogenous to the home country. Because of this, they can for some purposes be treated as a single aggregate. The distinction between capital and consumer goods is central, however, for non-tradables. Although the change in the pattern of supply will raise the price of all non-tradables relative to tradables, as discussed above, the change in the pattern of demand will raise the price of non-tradable capital goods relative to non-tradable consumer goods. Hence, the effects of a temporary trade boom will be most pronounced in the sector which produces non-tradable capital goods, the construction industry being the most obvious example: a temporary trade boom will generate large profits in the construction industry.

So far we have argued that although for the typical developing country it is inappropriate to hold windfall savings permanently in the form of foreign financial assets, if savings are used only for domestic capital formation then the price of non-tradable capital goods will be bid up. If the windfall is large but brief it is likely to be efficient to spread the investment boom over a longer period than the savings boom by means of temporarily holding foreign financial assets. The gain from such a strategy is that the purchase of non-tradable capital goods can thereby be deferred to a time when their resource cost is lower. Since in the long term the return on domestic capital is above the world interest rate, deferring investment also has a cost: the optimal foreign asset path in response to a windfall therefore moderates rather than eliminates the temporary surge in investment which would otherwise occur.

2.3. *Asymmetries between Booms and Slumps*

So far we have discussed only positive trade shocks. Statistically, these appear to be more common than negative shocks because the path of the typical commodity price tends to have some short sharp peaks whereas the troughs are long and shallow. However, in the 1980s many developing countries have suffered sharp negative foreign exchange shocks, partly through a sudden deterioration in their terms of trade and partly through the sudden burden of debt service repayments as world interest rates rose and further borrowing became difficult. To some extent the analysis of trade booms carries over directly to slumps; however, there are some important asymmetries.

First, in foreign financial markets, whereas with a temporary boom it is always possible to accumulate assets and then run them down, during a temporary slump it may not be possible to borrow because of a poor credit rating. Second, whereas during a temporary boom it is always possible to add to the domestic capital stock through imports of tradable capital goods, during a temporary slump the existing capital stock probably cannot be exported in any significant quantity, for capital once in place has a low resale value. The rate of decumulation of the capital stock depends upon the rate of depreciation. The above asymmetries have been quantitative, in that although there is a reversal of sign of the response between booms and slumps (adding to assets versus running them down) the magnitude of that response will vary depending upon the sign of the shock. We now consider a more radical asymmetry in which there need not even be a reversal in the sign of the response. Permanent shocks, whether positive or negative, can give rise to a temporary increase in investment. This is because in either case there is a change in the relative price of tradable and non-tradable goods and hence a shift in the optimal allocation of resources. Since capital once installed tends to be specific to that sector, investment becomes the means by which capital can be added to the sector in which there is an incentive to expand output. Hence, a large change in relative prices in either direction creates a premium upon resource mobility, and thereby an incentive to increase investment. To the extent that the shock is temporary rather than permanent, the incentive to reallocate resources is reduced (since at some point the reallocation will have to be reversed). A temporary positive shock therefore stimulates investment both through this mobility premium effect and through the windfall savings effect discussed earlier. A temporary negative shock has the mobility premium effect stimulating investment while transient dissaving reduces it so that the net effect is ambiguous (see Besley and Collier (1989) for a formal analysis). These asymmetries are sufficiently important to require a distinct theory for negative trade shocks, and in the following discussion we confine ourselves to the case of windfalls.

3. Government Policies

The part played by government in determining the overall response to the trade shock is considered here from four distinct perspectives, two normative and two positive. Section 3.1 examines what tax and expenditure choices may be appropriate when the shock initially accrues to the private sector and when the private sector is itself capable of responding optimally. Section 3.2 poses the same question, but relaxes the assumption of optimal private response. Section 3.3 is concerned with public responses in the case where a windfall accrues directly to the government. Finally in Section 3.4 the nature of the control regime itself is examined, and its possible effects in distorting private responses and hampering public attempts at management.

3.1. Government Taxation and Spending in Response to a Private Windfall

Since a well-managed private windfall requires no custodial intervention from government, it might appear that a relatively passive or *laissez-faire* public response would be appropriate. Matters are more complicated than this, however, for three different sets of reasons. These involve, respectively, the long-run level of public expenditure and taxation, the marginal cost of public funds, and the nature and composition of public expenditure. The first relates to the new long-run equilibrium following adjustment to the shock, the others tend to affect the trajectory of adjustment to this equilibrium. Each is considered in turn.

Permanent national income is higher following the boom, so that tax revenue will rise at existing tax rates. There is no equivalent mechanism ensuring an automatic rise in public expenditure, so a passive response will generate an arbitrary fall in the public sector deficit. However, it is plausible to assume that the elasticity of desired public expenditure with respect to permanent national income is positive, so that there should be discretionary increases in planned public expenditure. If this elasticity differs from the corresponding elasticity of tax revenue at existing rates, some change in the level and/or structure of tax rates will also be necessary. In effect, the size and shape of the public sector will automatically change, but there is no reason to suppose that these automatic changes will correspond to what is wanted.

We do not consider this question of long-run design further here. The properties of the short-run adjustment path will be compounded from the changes required to implement the new long-run equilibrium and those of a purely transitional nature. In the rest of this section we concentrate on the latter.

One reason for supposing that the appropriate short-run fiscal response should differ from the long-run response is that the marginal cost of public funds may temporarily drop during the boom (see, for example, the round table discussion in Neary and van Wijnbergen, (1986). The usual argument is that the windfall is rather like an economic rent, so that it can be taxed away with minimal incentive effects. Whether this is so depends on the type of income instability involved, and the informational content attributed to the increment in income.

When income is in any case volatile, the increment may carry no informational content at all. This is to say, it is perceived as being generated by a known stochastic process, and does not cause individuals to revise their perceptions of that process. Call this the case of unrevised inclusive expectations. Second, the increment may be viewed as generated by a special one-off event, not allowed for in the prior perception of the underlying stochastic process, and not relevant to later perceptions in view of its unrepeatable singularity. Call this the case of unrevised exclusive expectations. Finally, the increment may be viewed as not only generated by the underlying stochastic process, but throwing some light on that process. In other words, individuals have incomplete knowledge of this process, or believe that it is non-stationary, and so revise their expectations in the light of events. Call this the case of revised inclusive expectations.

These three cases provide a full characterization of the possibilities.[4] In each case perceptions may or may not be rational, in the sense that the revision—or lack of it—is appropriate to the underlying process. Such marginal or incremental expectations may be rational without necessarily requiring that expectations are rational on average. They have different implications for the marginal cost of public funds.

The principal determinant of the marginal cost of public funds is the dead-weight cost of the tax system, reflecting disincentive effects. The marginal cost will be low when these disincentive effects are small because the relevant private substitution elasticities are low. The question, therefore, is whether these elasticities are likely to be low in respect of incremental income. For the unrevised exclusive case, this does appear to be likely. The increment is truly a windfall in this case; it was anticipated neither in fact nor probabilistically; and it has no implications for future supply decisions. If the windfall could be gathered with no increase in current labour supply, it would then be pure profit or rental income, and taxation of it would have no incentive effects.

Now suppose that one of the inclusive cases holds. Taxation of the incremental income at an enhanced rate now lowers mean expected net income, unless it is accompanied by correspondingly reduced taxation during periods of low income. No general conclusions can be drawn about the implications of either approach for the level of the marginal cost of public funds. In principle this could rise or fall, depending on the nature of preferences, the form of the distribution, and the structure of taxes. Hence there

---

[4] The taxonomy might suggest a fourth possibility, that of revised exclusive expectations. But this is an 'empty box' since if the increment was believed to be a unique event (exclusive) it could not sensibly be held to induce a revision of opinion about the 'normal' stochastic process.

does not appear to be any general presumption in favour of a high effective tax rate on the increment in cases where this is perceived to be part of the normal ups and downs of economic life.

This discussion may be summarized as follows. If a windfall is commonly perceived as both temporary and once for all, then there are powerful arguments that a high proportion of the incremental income should be taxed at source. If it were perceived as unusual, but part of the normal pattern, these arguments do not go through.

Finally, appropriate fiscal response may be influenced by the nature and composition of public expenditure, particularly by the allocation between tradable and non-tradable goods on the one hand, and that between capital and consumption goods on the other. The sharp movement in the relative price of non-tradable goods will imply some shift in the optimal allocation of public expenditure between tradable and non-tradable goods, more markedly in the short run than in the long run.

It may also have implications for the level of government spending, as opposed to its allocation. For example, if most public services are non-tradable, these will become relatively more expensive during the windfall, and contraction of public expenditure might be desirable. Expenditure on goods from the non-tradable sector during this period will be relatively inefficient from the government's point of view. In the worst case the rise in non-tradable prices reflects real increases in resource costs, so there is a social loss arising from excessively bunched spending. But even if the price rises constitute pure transfers to factor owners, there is no reason to suppose that the government would value these unintended transfers high enough to match the marginal cost of public funds.

The flow of current government services can be sustained in two quite different ways. The government may simply purchase part of current final output and then supply this in the form of public services. Alternatively, it may create and operate capital facilities which generate output directly (as with government-owned factories) or in co-operation with privately owned factors (as with much infrastructure).

Assume, for simplicity, that the government wishes to increase the flow of public services in line with changes in permanent national income. Then if public services constitute only purchases of final output, public expenditure will also rise in line with permanent national income. However, to the extent that public services are provided by public capital, the actual pattern of incremental expenditure will exhibit an early peak followed by a decline. As a polar case, suppose that the government's main activity was building infrastructure with very low maintenance costs and depreciation rates. Then virtually all the incremental government expenditure would occur as a short surge of capital expenditure very soon after the windfall.

While intertemporal considerations indicate that a stable deficit is unlikely to be optimal during a windfall, this discussion demonstrates that even the direction of change is ambiguous. Consider the following polar cases. In the first, the windfall is external to expectations, so it is optimal for the government to obtain a large share of it as incremental revenue. Meanwhile public expenditure exclusively takes the form of purchases of final output. In these circumstances, expenditure rises in line with government permanent income which increases relative to permanent national income following the boom. During the boom, the government runs a large surplus and has the task of lending this to the private sector and attempting to ensure that it is all invested in private capital.

In the second polar case, the windfall is internal to expectations, so the government's revenue rises only proportionately. Meanwhile public expenditure exclusively takes the form of infrastructure investment. (Non-tradable goods are ignored.) Public services are planned to rise proportionately to permanent national income. Hence the government undertakes a massive capital expenditure programme equal to the sum of its windfall tax income and the present value of taxes on incremental permanent national income. In consequence, the budget goes heavily into deficit during the boom.

A realistic pattern would lie somewhere between these extremes; but it does not appear possible to sign the transitional budget changes.

3.2. Stabilizing Taxation

So far, we have assumed that the private sector responds optimally. Deferring considerations of the control regime itself, there are two principal reasons why this may not hold. The first involves market imperfections that constrain private choices, the second involves faulty private perceptions of events.

If private sector agents' spending decisions are constrained not by their permanent income but by, for example, their marketable assets and current income, then the government has to correct for these constraints. Its fiscal stance must be chosen in such a way that the paths of private sector current assets and disposable income permit spending decisions which are appropriate to the underlying permanent incomes. This problem is likely to be acute in the case of a long-lived windfall, for example the discovery of oil reserves. It may then be necessary for the government to run a large deficit to generate a sufficient relaxation of private sector current constraints to enable the sector to increase spending appropriately. In the case of a very short-lived windfall, this complication is likely to be much less serious, and will be ignored here.

Both public and private sectors may misunderstand what is happening during the windfall. For example either or both may get the duration of the windfall, and hence its magnitude, wrong. For concreteness, suppose that the government gets it right, while the private sector is over-optimistic. The private sector is likely to attempt to consume too high a proportion of the windfall, and the government must attempt to prevent this. Ideally the government would raise a forced loan returning the money when the windfall was clearly over or, equivalently, temporarily raise taxes, subsequently to lower them. However, all this is predicated on two assumptions, that the government has more accurate perceptions than the private sector of the underlying instability and that it is capable of exercising the required custodial function. Even if the first assumption holds, the obvious response is to disseminate the superior information rather than to act on the assumed ignorance of private agents. In any case, the second assumption requires substantiation.

3.3. Public Windfalls

Sometimes trade windfalls automatically accrue to the government without any tax decision because it owns the asset (e.g. oil). The government then faces a difficult problem of how to pass the benefits on to the population.[5] This is particularly marked in the oil states of the Middle East. If it is administratively impossible to make direct transfers to the population, the government can either subsidize private consumption or purchase goods and services on behalf of the population. In the case of subsidies, private agents benefit partly by lower prices and partly by higher factor incomes consequent upon the increased demand. Two special cases are revealing: that in which the subsidy is on non-tradables and is just sufficient to keep their relative price to consumers unaltered by the boom-cum-subsidy; and that in which the subsidy is on tradables and is just sufficient to keep their relative price to producers unaltered by the boom-cum-subsidy. In the former case, since consumer prices are unaffected by the trade shock the only transmission mechanism is via factor incomes. In the latter case, since producer prices are unaltered, the only transmission mechanism is via lower consumer prices.

If instead of subsidies the government purchases goods and services, the effects upon the population depend partly upon whether they are desired and partly upon whether they are tradable or non-tradable. If the goods are both undesired and tradable, such as armaments, then the windfall yields no benefits to the population. If they are undesired but non-tradable, such as pyramids, then the population gains because the government must purchase the factor services of its population in order to build the pyramids. Factor services will only be willingly supplied if the government offers incomes higher than those available in other activities. If the goods are both desired and non-tradable, like roads or schools, then the

---

[5] This section has benefited from discussions with A. Al-Yousof.

population gains both through higher factor incomes and through the benefits directly provided by the expenditures.

3.4. The Pre-Shock Control Regime

The government responses to trade shocks discussed so far (changes in public spending, including subsidies, and in taxation) are often assumed to be chosen in the context of a particularly simple control regime: one in which the government does not intervene in any market, except indirectly through its fiscal policies. This is convenient, but unrealistic. An analysis of shocks must take the set of controls in force at the time of a boom into account.

Interventions in goods markets may affect the tradability of goods and hence the consequences of a boom. If, for example, the government has imposed price control, increased demand for non-tradables cannot be accommodated through relative price increases. Private agents will be unable to realize their demand for non-tradables and will spend correspondingly more on tradables. When these adjustments are completed, the boom is reflected in an increase in the volume of imports while domestic prices have remained constant at their controlled levels, much as if the boom affected an economy in which all goods are tradable. The only difference is a welfare loss: agents have not been free in the allocation of their extra income between goods. Hence price control makes non-tradables behave as tradables in the process of adjustment to a boom. If price control applied to all goods and services (and were fully effective) then the boom would virtually bypass the economy. For the spending of the boom income would not lead to any relative price changes. There would therefore be no change in resource allocation: in every sector output would remain constant. Similarly, the boom's effect on income distribution would be extremely simple. Gains would be limited to the boom's initial benificiaries, the owners of the factors specific to the booming sector. Clearly, this example is extreme, but it illustrates that predictions of the effects of a boom which ignore the pre-shock control regime, may be very misleading.

While price control makes non-tradables similar to tradables, trade policy may make a good which can in principle be imported non-tradable (in the technical sense that the market is not cleared by changes in imports or exports, but by changes in the domestic price). Quantitative restrictions (QRs) on imports have this effect: provided the constraints are binding, the link between domestic and world prices is lost. Importables then become non-tradable in the economic sense of the word. Hence when the spending of the extra income generated by the boom raises domestic demand for an importable protected by QRs, this does not cause an increase in imports, but a price rise. Obviously, this changes the impact of a boom. Resource allocation is affected because domestic producers of the imported good now have an incentive to expand production. In many countries manufacturing is a sector producing tradables and is protected by QRs. The effect of a boom on the output of the industrial sector, which declines according to the standard 'Dutch Disease' model, may therefore be positive. Hence trade policy may dramatically change the consequences of a shock. This also applies to a boom's distributional effects. There now are more goods for which the price is determined endogenously. This may have the effect of eroding the gains of the boom's initial beneficiaries. Conversely, as increased demand for importables is now reflected in price increases, the rents earned by those with access to import licences increase.

The adjustment process may also be affected by government interventions in factor markets. Wage controls, for example, effectively reduce factor mobility. If the relative price of non-tradables increases as a result of a boom then the product wage falls, both in the booming sector and in the sectors producing non-tradables (or tradables protected by QRs)[6] and labour demand therefore increases. But labour, while potentially mobile, will not actually move out of other sectors if the wage is prevented (by controls) from rising.

When the trade shock is a temporary one, interventions in goods and factor markets may affect both the rate of savings out of windfall income and the efficiency of the transformation of these savings into real capital formation. In addition, we have to consider controls in financial markets.

First, if import controls apply to capital goods, domestic investment has to cope with a more steeply sloping supply curve, just as if it required more non-tradable goods. This affects the choice between domestic investment and foreign asset acquisition. In the previous section there was only one reason for (temporarily) acquiring foreign assets: to the extent that domestic investment requires non-tradables, an attempt to convert a windfall gain very quickly into domestic real assets may be inefficient, because the price of non-tradables would be pushed up. This argument is now reinforced because QRs make imported capital goods similar to non-tradables. This strengthens the case for foreign asset acquisition (without which the permanent income increase which the boom may potentially bequeath will not be fully realized).

Secondly, trade liberalization is a customary government response to a boom. If the boom is recognized as temporary, private agents will also see the liberalization as temporary. In that case the pre-shock control regime affects the consumption–investment choice. The existence of QRs implies an unsatisfied demand for imports. It may therefore be rational to use the opportunity of the temporary trade liberalization to increase the purchases

---

[6] The product wage falls if the nominal wage falls relative to the price the employer receives for the good he produces.

of imported consumer goods (in particular of consumer durables), at the expense of investment.

Thirdly, the pre-boom control regime often includes foreign exchange control which makes foreign asset acquisition by private agents illegal. This control (while it restricts private agents' asset choices to domestic real and domestic financial assets) does not affect their response to a temporary shock in the (unlikely) event that the public sector acts as a custodian for the private sector's savings. If private agents could hold domestic financial assets (e.g. bank deposits) and get the same return on them as on foreign assets, then they would be able to hold foreign financial assets indirectly, via the banking system. The central bank would then issue fiat money, backed by the increase in its foreign exchange reserves. Once private agents spent their temporary extra holdings of fiat money on capital goods, the central bank's extra foreign assets would be run down. In practice foreign exchange controls are unlikely to be so harmless. In a situation of financial repression banks will be able to increase their advances by more than the increase in fiat money and to that extent the control has an inflationary potential. In addition, for the control to be harmless, the monetary authority must realize that part of the foreign assets it holds will later be claimed by private agents. Clearly, it is informationally demanding to decide which part of the reserves are in fact only held in trust for private agents. Hence the public sector may, intentionally or by accident, pre-empt the use of the foreign assets.

4.   Examples of Temporary Shocks

4.1.   Kenya[7]

A severe frost in Brazil in 1976 caused a rise in coffee prices, yielding a windfall gain to other coffee-exporting countries. The shock was well understood to be temporary, and was substantial: the cumulative terms of trade gain to Kenya over 1976–9 was equivalent to 24 per cent of 1975 gross domestic product. Most of the affected countries either already had, or rapidly installed, substantial export taxes on coffee, so the government was a direct beneficiary of the boom. Kenya provides an interesting exception, because the government initially chose to allow the entire windfall to accrue to the private sector, in the first instance preponderantly the peasant farmers themselves. Of course, the rapid rise in private incomes inevitably led to increased yield from existing taxes, so government revenue also rose, albeit with a lag. Kenya was also at this stage a fairly heavily controlled economy, with foreign exchange controls, import controls, and monetary controls all in operation.

[7] This discussion draws on our research on the Coffee Boom, reported in Bevan *et al.* (1987, 1989*a*, and 1989*b*).

In the context of this chapter, the combination of circumstances just outlined naturally prompts three questions. How well did the private sector handle the boom? How well did the public sector do so? What part did the system of controls play in redirecting or distorting the outcomes?

The successful transformation of temporary windfall income into permanent income requires both that a high proportion of the windfall be saved and that these savings be appropriately invested. Our calculations suggest that the private agents did indeed save around 70 per cent of the windfall; they correctly perceived its temporary nature and reacted accordingly. We do not know whether these savings would have been transformed efficiently into domestic real assets in the absence of controls but the existence of controls restricted private agents' asset choice, and their freedom to choose an extended period for investment. Since non-tradable capital goods were in inelastic supply, the accelerated rate of investment forced by exchange controls induced a very substantial rise in the relative price of those goods. Similarly, attempts to increase consumption were constrained by import controls, temporarily raising the relative price of import substitutes.

The existence of controls made these relative price changes much more substantial than they otherwise would have been. The relative price changes were associated with two important effects. First, they were the vehicle for powerful redistributions within Kenya; our calculations suggest that a very large part of the total gain ended up in urban rather than in rural hands. Second, they tended both to reduce the total quantity of, and to distort the sectoral allocation of, the increment in real investment. Part of the windfall was dissipated in higher resource costs of capital than would have occurred had the asset formation been phased more evenly, part was dissipated by being allocated to sectors whose temporarily high output prices were inappropriate signals of relative long-run scarcities. These difficulties were compounded by the inadequacy of a financially repressed banking system to allocate investible resources efficiently.

The conclusions on the private sector performance are therefore mixed. The basic response was right, but execution was faulty, partly because choices were inefficiently restricted by the control regime, partly because the distorted price and other signals induced by the controls were very hard to interpret.

Government revenue rose by nearly 50 per cent between 1976/7 and 1977/8. This reflected the general growth in incomes and, in particular, the import liberalization following the boom. Once again, it was clearly perceived as temporary, and the government decided it would be appropriate temporarily to increase its capital expenditure massively. Given the heavy pressure on the non-tradable capital goods sector, this timing was unfortunate. More ominously, there appeared to be a ratchet effect at work, and expenditure continued to grow as a share of GDP until 1980/1. During this period the share of government capital formation in GDP fell back below its pre-boom level, so all of the increase was ultimately in consumption expenditure. What is more, this increase was larger than the increase in revenue, despite considerable efforts to increase this as the boom receded. Even though the diagnosis was reasonably accurate, the coffee boom induced a loss of expenditure control, a large cumulative budget deficit, and extensive foreign borrowing by a government whose previous fiscal record had been relatively conservative. Far from acting efficiently in a custodial role the Kenyan government appears to have handled the boom far less astutely than private agents did.

4.2.   Indonesia[8]

Indonesia during the oil shocks offers examples of exceptional public sector responses to trade shocks. The windfall income accrued largely to the public sector (unlike the coffee boom in Kenya),[9] and it was decided to keep part of it outside the budget, in a secret account with the central bank. Nevertheless, government oil revenues as listed in the budget rose enormously, from 5 per cent of GDP in 1972/3 to 10 per cent in 1976/7 and (after a slight decline) to 15 per cent in 1980/1. Thereafter, oil revenue declined, to 12.4 per cent of GDP in 1983/4.

The hoarding of part of the oil money in a secret account (to make it immune from lobbying for expenditure increases) is an unusual way of preventing the loss of fiscal control. But Indonesia is also unusual in the way public expenditure was adjusted to the increase (and to the subsequent decline) in budgetary oil revenue.

First, expenditures rose roughly in line with revenues, the budget deficit (conventionally defined)[10] rising from 2.5 per cent of GDP in 1972/3 to 4.8 per cent in 1976/7. Second, and more remarkably, ratchet effects were overcome: expenditures fell (relative to GDP) during the slumps. Third, there is little evidence of spending on 'pyramids'. An important use of the oil money was the fertilizer subsidy, through which the boom contributed to the rice yield increases of the 1970s. The agricultural sector also benefited from major public investments in the rehabilitation and extension of irrigation canals and in the reclamation of swamp land. The share in development expenditure of agriculture and irrigation rose to 16 percent in 1977/8, and of education to 12 per cent. Fourth, both oil booms led to trade liberalization, which was reversed (but only partly, in sharp contrast to Nigeria) during the slumps. Fifth, foreign assets were acquired throughout the 1970s; foreign reserves rose from $0.6 billion at the end of 1972 to $5.4

---

[8] This discussion draws on Bevan *et al.* (1989).

[9] In 1974 the government take of the net operating income of the oil companies was raised to 85%. In part because of uncertainties about the finances of Pertamina (the state oil company) it is not clear how high the government's share of the windfall was.

[10] The Indonesian balanced budget principle applies to a budget in which aid is included with revenue.

billion in 1980. These reserves were used to cushion the impact of the slump in the early 1980s. Finally, when oil prices fell there were large devaluations, in 1978 and again in 1983.

One reason for the Indonesian response is that a strong commitment to 'balanced' budgets was part of the pre-boom control regime (a result of the memory of the hyperinflation of the Soekarno years, which was deemed to have been caused by budget deficits). The large share of agriculture in public expenditure (offsetting the 'Dutch Disease' effect on non-booming tradables) was partly the result of the government's sensitivity to rice short-ages (the regime had been shaken by rice riots in 1972). The decision not to invest all savings domestically but to hold a substantial part as foreign assets was, and this is perhaps most remarkable about the Indonesian case, based in part on an awareness of the possibility of 'Dutch Disease' prob-lems.

4.3. Nigeria[11]

Nigeria experienced the same oil windfalls as Indonesia and they consti-tuted a similar magnitude as a percentage of GDP. However, both policies and outcomes differed to a remarkable extent. Policies differed both in terms of the pre-boom control regime and in terms of responses to the boom. Whereas in Indonesia there was a commitment to convertibility, in Nigeria there were foreign exchange controls. Whereas the Indonesian Government accumulated secret foreign assets, the Nigerian Government used the improved collateral provided by its oil wealth to borrow. The counterpart of this borrowing was a large increase in public expenditure relative to revenue so that the budget moved from surplus prior to the windfall to heavy deficit during and after it. In combination these policies amplified both the boom and the post-boom recession in Nigeria relative to Indonesia.

As in Indonesia, the Nigerian Government had a very high investment rate out of the windfall, but a rather different type of investment. As we have seen, the Indonesian government placed a high priority upon invest-ments in agriculture. These were, in terms of our discussion of Section 3.3, desired non-tradables, so that they benefited the population both directly and through the factor incomes which government expenditure generated. In Nigeria a mere 2 per cent of the budget was spent on agricul-ture. The incremental capital/output ratio (ICOR) rose to double digits during the boom, implying that much investment was unproductive. Since much of this was imported equipment (for example, new steel mills) in terms of Section 3.3 much government expenditure took the form of un-desired tradables and so had neither direct nor indirect beneficial effects upon the population. There was also a rapid expansion in public sector

---

[11] This discussion is based on Bevan *et al.* (1989).

employment. Some of this was, of course, for the delivery of useful services. However, there are good grounds for believing that the administration became heavily overstaffed. Overstaffing is, in effect, the purchase of a useless non-tradable. The population benefited from the windfall only to the extent that its labour services were sold for a higher income.

Once the boom was over, the Nigerian Government was slow to change policies. It continued to borrow abroad until locked out of the world capital market. Thereafter, it resorted to increasingly drastic import restrictions. By the mid 1980s private consumption per head was lower than it had been before the oil windfall. Eventually, in 1986, there ʼwas a large and abrupt policy change, including a huge devaluation. The mismanagement of the temporary trade boom had given rise to a government-inflicted domestic shock which the Indonesian economy had avoided.

5. Conclusion

Countries prone to temporary trade shocks face some unavoidable economic fluctuations. As discussed, it is desirable for the investment rate to fluctuate in response to such shocks so that the economy achieves the maximum permanent gain from them. Government policy mistakes can interfere with this process to such an extent that virtually the entire windfall is dissipated (as in Nigeria). One type of error is for the government to respond to the temporary windfall by excessive and irreversible increases in its own expenditure. Both the Kenyan and Nigerian Governments appear to have made this mistake not so much by design as through a loss of control over spending decisions. The Indonesian government was fortunate already to have in place rather longer-term rules on the limitation of public expenditure. In many ways, a more fundamental matter than the response to the shock is the policy stance prior to the shock. Exchange convertibility and freedom from price controls and from quota restrictions upon imports create an environment in which private agents are not impeded from making the most efficient long-term use of windfall opportunities. Of course, if their expectations happen to be wrong then they will still make errors. But on the evidence we have reviewed above, government policy-makers also appear capable of such errors. There seems, however, to be little case for the government taking upon itself a difficult task at which it is liable to fail.

References

Besley, T. J., and Collier, P. (1989), 'Import Compression and Trade Policy', in R. Kanbur (ed.) *Trade and Development in Sub-Saharan Africa*, (London, Centre for Economic Policy Research).

Bevan, D. L., Collier, P., and Gunning, J. W. (1987), 'Consequences of a Commodity Boom in a Controlled Economy: Accumulation and Redistribution in Kenya, 1975–83', *World Bank Economic Review*, 1, pp. 489–513.

——(1988), *Poverty, Equity and Growth in Nigeria and Indonesia, 1950–86* (New York, OUP for World Bank).

——(1989a), *Controlled Open Economies* (Oxford: OUP).

——(1989b), *Peasants and Governments* (Oxford: OUP).

Corden, W. M. (1984), 'Booming sector and Dutch Disease economics: survey and consolidation', *Oxford Economic Papers*, 36, pp. 359–80.

——and Neary, J. P. (1982), 'Booming sector and de-industrialisation in a small open economy', *Economic Journal*, 92, pp. 825–48.

Neary, J. P., and van Wijnbergen, S. (eds.) (1986), *Natural Resources and the Macroeconomy* (Oxford: Blackwell).

4

Exchange Rate Regimes in Developing Countries

VIJAY JOSHI

THE purpose of this chapter is to set out the issues involved in the choice of exchange rate regime in developing countries. Two assumptions which we believe to be realistic are made in the course of the analysis. *First*, we assume that the major currencies of the world will continue to float against one another (though there may be some zones of stability like the European Monetary System). While there is a sporting chance that some scheme to moderate the swings in their exchange rates will be successfully introduced and implemented, we think it unlikely that the industrial countries will return to anything resembling fixed rates. *Second*, we assume that most developing countries will continue to maintain some controls on capital movements even if they move towards liberalizing trade. Again, whatever one's views about the wisdom of maintaining capital controls, this assumption is surely a realistic prediction of how governments of developing countries will act in the near future.[1]

The author would like to record his intellectual debt to John Williamson's writings on the subject of this chapter. These are listed in the bibliography.

[1] There is now wide agreement that trade restrictions are an extremely inefficient method of managing the balance of payments. Ian Little played a leading role in destroying the protectionist orthodoxy of the 1950s and 1960s (see Little *et al.*, 1970). The wisdom of maintaining capital controls, however, is a much more controversial matter. The case for capital controls in developing countries is that, even if they cannot prevent a slow seepage of capital, they do give policy-makers an extra degree of freedom by insulating the country from sudden, destabilizing movements of funds. Such movements seem to afflict even the thickest of foreign exchange markets and can play havoc with internal and external balance. The case against capital controls is that (a) they are not feasible, (b) they lead to misallocation of capital, and (c) they reduce the discipline on governments exercised by free capital movements. The infeasibility argument is overstated; several developing countries including Brazil, Korea, and Peru have successfully implemented capital controls. The prime requirement for the successful operation of capital controls seems to be the maintenance of a realistic real exchange rate. The welfare losses from misallocation of capital are uncertain, while capital controls clearly do not prevent a country from securing welfare gains by drawing on foreign capital to supplement domestic savings. As for discipline on governments, its value may be limited if capital movements lead to misalignment of the exchange rate. Moreover, some developing countries (e.g. Argentina and Chile) have had unfortunate experiences with capital market liberalization and it would appear that the dynamics of such liberalization are not yet well understood. We incline to the view that it would be rash of developing countries to eliminate capital controls entirely. For a balanced assessment of capital controls see Cuddington (1986). [See also Chapter 11, below, Eds.]

1. Recent Evolution of Exchange Rate Regimes

Table 4.1 presents the IMF's classification of exchange rate regimes in 1987. Using the same classification, Table 4.2 gives a summary picture of the quanitiative importance of various exchange rate regimes in developing countries since 1973.

Under the adjustable peg arrangements prevailing in the quarter century prior to 1971, most currencies, including those of developing countries, were pegged to the US dollar though changes in the value of the pegs occurred from time to time. In the case of developing countries, it is worth noting that (*a*) while some currencies were directly pegged to the US dollar, the currencies of most ex-French colonies and many ex-British colonies were pegged to the French franc and pound sterling respectively (which currencies were of course themselves pegged to the US dollar) and (*b*) the currencies of many Latin American countries were pegged to the US dollar but sometimes in a 'crawling' fashion. As Table 4.2 shows, when the major currencies began floating in 1973, most developing countries maintained their existing exchange rate arrangements. By 1976, however, there had been significant changes as many countries reacted to the costs of single-currency pegging in the new environment. There was a sizeable switch from single-currency pegging to multi-currency pegging. This tendency has continued up to the present day; in addition, there has been a large increase in the number of currencies which the IMF classifies as 'managed floaters' and 'independent floaters'.

The following comments on the IMF's classification should be kept in mind:

(i) The classification relates only to exchange rate arrangements in the major currency market. It is compatible with dual exchange markets and with trade and capital controls. In fact, there are very few (perhaps half a dozen) developing countries which have maintained complete freedom of trade and capital movements on a sustained basis.

(ii) The countries which 'peg' do not necessarily have permanently fixed pegs. The latter description does apply to the member countries of the Communauté Financière Africaine which peg to the French franc and to some mini-states in Central America which peg to the US dollar. These two together constitute roughly half of the 53 countries classified as single-currency peggers in 1987. The remaining single-currency peggers and all the composite-currency peggers should be regarded as following an adjustable peg regime.

(iii) The 'flexible arrangements' category requires careful interpretation. Under the category 'limited flexibility against a single currency' the IMF includes four oil-exporting countries which are formally pegged to the

TABLE 4.1. Exchange rate arrangements as of 30 June 1987[a]

Pegged					Flexibility limited vis-à-vis a single currency or group of currencies		More Flexible		
Single currency			Currency composite						
US dollar	French franc	Other	SDR	Other	Single currency[b]	Co-operative arrangements[c]	Adjusted according to a set of indicators	Managed floating	Independently floating
Afghanistan[d]	Benin	Bhutan (Indian rupee)	Burma	Algeria[d]	Bahrain[e]	Belgium[e]	Brazil	Argentina	Australia
Antigua and Barbuda	Burkina Faso	Kiribati (Australian dollar)	Burundi	Austria	Qatar[e]	Denmark	Chile[d]	China	Bolivia
The Bahamas[d]	Cameroon	Lesotho[d] (South African rand)	Iran, Islamic Republic of	Bangladesh[d]	Saudi Arabia[e]	France	Colombia	Costa Rica[d]	Canada
Barbados	Central African Republic	Swaziland (South African rand)	Jordan	Botswana	United Arab Emirates[e]	Germany, Federal Republic of	Madagascar	Dominican Republic[d]	The Gambia
Belize	Chad	Tonga (Australian dollar)	Kenya[f]	Cape Verde		Ireland	Portugal	Ecuador	Ghana
Djibouti	Comoros		Libya[g]	Cyprus		Italy		Egypt[d]	Guinea
Dominica	Congo		Rwanda	Fiji		Luxembourg[d]		Greece	Japan
El Salvador	Côte d'Ivoire		São Tomé and Principe	Finland[f]		Netherlands		Guinea-Bissau	Lebanon
Ethiopia	Equatorial Guinea		Seychelles	Hungary				Iceland	Maldives
Grenada	Gabon		Vanuatu	Israel				India[h]	New Zealand
Guatemala[d]	Mali			Kuwait				Indonesia	Nigeria[d]
Guyana[d]	Niger			Malawi				Jamaica	Philippines
Haiti	Senegal			Malaysia[f]				Korea	Sierra Leone
Honduras	Togo			Malta				Mauritania	Somalia[d]
Iraq				Mauritius				Mexico[d,i]	South Africa[d]
Lao People's Democratic Republic[d]				Nepal				Morocco	United Kingdom
Liberia				Norway				Pakistan	United States
Mozambique				Papua New Guinea				Peru[d]	Uruguay
Nicaragua[d]				Poland				Spain	Zaïre
Oman				Romania				Sri Lanka	
Panama				Singapore				Tunisia	
Paraguay[d]				Solomon Islands				Turkey[k]	
St Kitts and Nevis				Sudan[d]				Western Samoa	
St Lucia				Sweden[l]				Yugoslavia	
St Vincent				Tanzania					
Surinam				Thailand					
Syrian Arab Republic[d]				Zimbabwe					
Trinidad and Tobago									
Uganda									
Venezuela[d]									
Vietnam[d]									
Yemen Arab Republic									
Yemen, People's Democratic Republic of									
Zambia									

[a] No current information is available relating to Democratic Kampuchea.

[b] In all cases listed in this column, the US dollar was the currency against which exchange rates showed limited flexibility.

[c] This category consists of countries participating in the exchange rate mechanism of the European Monetary System. In each case, the exchange rate is maintained within a margin of 2.25% around the bilateral central rates against other participating currencies, with the exception of Italy, in which case the exchange rate is maintained within a margin of 6%.

[d] Member maintains dual exchange markets involving multiple exchange arrangements. The arrangement shown is that maintained in the major market.

[e] Exchange rates are determined on the basis of a fixed relationship to the SDR, within margins of up to ±7.25%. However, because of the maintenance of a relatively stable relationship with the US dollar, these margins are not always observed.

[f] The exchange rate is maintained within margins of ±2.25%.

[g] The exchange rate is maintained within margins of ±7.5%.

[h] The exchange rate is maintained within margins of ±5 percent on either side of a weighted composite of the currencies of the main trading partners.

[i] As of 30 June 1987 the spread between the two exchange rates was less than 1%.

[j] Member maintains a system of advance announcement of exchange rates.

[k] The Central Bank establishes its selling rate daily and the buying rate is set at $\frac{1}{2}$% below the selling rate. Commercial banks must use the Central Bank's selling rate, but are free to set their own buying rate.

[l] The exchange rate is maintained within margins of ±1.5%.

Source: IMF *Annual Report 1987.*

TABLE 4.2 Developing countries: Exchange rate regimes in selected years (No. of countries)

	1973	1976	1982	1987
Pegged to a single currency	86	67	56	53
of which:				
US dollar	54	46	38	34
French franc	17	13	13	14
Pound sterling	11	3	1	—
Other	4	5	4	5
Pegged to a composite	—	25	34	37
of which:				
SDR	—	11	15	10
Other	—	14	19	27
Flexible arrangements	11	15	35	42
of which:				
Limited flexibility against single currency	—	2	10	4
Adjusted according to a set of indicators	8	6	4	4
Managed floating	—	4	16	22
Independent floating	3	3	5	12
TOTAL	97	107	125	132

Source: Annual Reports of the IMF.

SDR with wide margins round the peg but which, in practice, maintain an informal peg with the US dollar. It would be more informative to think of these currencies as being pegged to the US dollar. A flexible rate 'adjusted according to a set of indicators' is what is usually called a (rule-based) crawling peg. 'Managed floating' in the IMF's classification does not have its usual meaning of a market-determined exchange rate. It means an exchange rate which is administered but whose level or rate of change the government does not commit itself to defending and which may there-fore be changed frequently. In our analysis, we use the term 'discretionary crawling peg' to describe this category. 'Independent floating' means a market-determined rate (with or without government intervention in the market), i.e. it covers what we normally mean by both clean and managed floating. Note that this category includes not only the major industrial countries but also countries like Ghana and Nigeria which have recently instituted exchange auctions. Many of the developing countries classified as 'independent floaters' continue to have capital controls.

2. Criteria for Evaluation of Exchange Rate Regimes

Exchange rate regimes must clearly be judged by their comparative effec-tiveness in helping to achieve the desired mix of domestic macroeconomic and microeconomic objectives subject to the requirement of maintaining external balance. Bearing this general proposition in mind, we employ the following three criteria of evaluation corresponding to three policy targets:

(i) The *External Balance* Criterion: How do the various exchange rate regimes perform with regard to securing external balance by achieving appropriate changes in the country's international price competitiveness?

(ii) The *Internal Balance* Criterion: How do the various exchange rate regimes compare in helping or hindering macroeconomic policy in securing domestic macroeconomic objectives, here taken to include high employment, price stability, and a sustainable rate of growth?

(iii) The *Efficiency* Criterion: How do the various exchange rate regimes affect real income through their impact on the efficiency of microeconomic resource allocation?

Since exchange rate regimes affect all three targets simultaneously and there are trade-offs between these targets, the criteria are not independent of each other and their separation is for convenience only. The test of performance in terms of each target must take into account not only how well an exchange rate regime fulfils that particular target but the cost incurred in terms of other targets of doing so.

2.1. Terminology and concepts

In thinking about the choice of exchange rate regimes, it is useful to make a few distinctions and clarifications.

We begin with the concept of *external balance*. What does this target imply? It is clearly desirable that many developing countries should run current account deficits. But how large should the deficit aimed at be? In principle this is a very complicated problem. The appropriate current account deficit cannot be determined without simultaneously solving for the appropriate capital inflow, the appropriate level of trade restrictions, and the appropriate values of the internal balance variables. In practice, policy-makers would have to (*a*) make a realistic projection of the capital inflow, (*b*) decide what level of trade restrictions they were aiming for (it would obviously be desirable in most cases to reduce restrictions much below their current levels), and (*c*) decide what inflation/employment mix they were aiming for supported by the appropriate domestic expenditure policy. On this basis, they can guess the appropriate current account deficit and how it changes in response to various shocks. No doubt they could only do this in a very approximate way, but that should suffice since what matters is not fine tuning but avoiding gross mistakes.

Exchange rate regimes affect external balance through their effect on international price competitiveness. An indicator of the latter is the *real exchange rate*, which is quite different from the *nominal exchange rate*. The nominal exchange rate is just the exchange rate as ordinarily understood, so many units of domestic currency per unit of foreign currency. The real exchange rate is affected both by the nominal exchange rate and by cost–price relationships between the home country and foreign countries. It is usually defined as the domestic price of tradables relative to the foreign price of tradables measured in a common currency (i.e. deflated by the nominal exchange rate).[2,3] In a world in which the exchange rates of many countries are changing frequently and in a non-uniform manner 'the' nominal exchange rate and 'the' real exchange rate can only meaningfully be defined against an average of other currencies. The average nominal exchange rate and real exchange rate of a currency are commonly referred to in current usage as the *nominal effective exchange rate* and the *real effective exchange rate* respectively. What the weights in these indexes should be is of course a large question which is briefly discussed later. It is also useful to introduce the notion of an *appropriate* real exchange rate, which is that real exchange rate which (along with appropriate trade restrictions and appropriate monetary and fiscal policies) produces the appropriate (or target) current balance.

Internal balance is also a difficult concept to define because it involves the question of trade-offs between inflation and unemployment. Recent experience suggests that the possibility of a *long-run* trade-off between the two should be looked at with considerable suspicion. But a short-run trade-off clearly exists and policy-makers may wish to exploit it to achieve their long-run inflation targets.

3. Fixed and Floating Rates: General Considerations

Before investigating the suitability of different regimes for developing countries, we consider the choice between the polar cases of floating ex-

---

[2] Of the readily available price indexes, the wholesale price index is probably the most suitable for comparing the domestic and foreign prices of tradables. Indexes such as the consumer price index and the GDP deflator cover non-tradables and services as well as tradables.

[3] Two mechanisms of substitution in demand and/or supply are involved in altering the current account of the balance of payments: (i) substitution between domestic and foreign tradables, and (ii) substitution between domestic tradables and non-tradables. The definition of the real exchange rate in the text focuses directly on mechanism (i). Another alternative is to define the real exchange rate as the relative price of tradables and non-tradables in the home market, thus focusing directly on mechanism (ii). This latter definition is more suitable if the law of one price holds so that prices of domestic and foreign tradables *cannot* differ. Yet other definitions of the real exchange rate focus on the cost relationships underlying mechanisms (i) and (ii). For example, the real exchange rate can be defined as (*a*) the ratio of domestic unit labour costs and foreign unit labour costs measured in a common currency or as (*b*) the ratio of an index of domestic wages and an index of domestic prices of tradable goods. There is no perfect indicator of international competitiveness and policy-makers should, if possible, examine several indicators. The discussion in the text follows the usual definition of the real exchange rate (viz. the relative price of domestic and foreign tradables in a common currency) but could be adapted for other definitions without making any essential difference.

change rates and fixed exchange rates at a rather general level.[4] This is useful because the basic arguments for and against fixity or flexibility crop up again and again even when considering intermediate regimes. We shall also make some reference to the experience of industrial countries.

It should be clear to begin with that in principle both freely floating and permanently fixed exchange rates are capable of securing balance-of-payments adjustment but the mechanisms involved are radically different. The real exchange rate changes in both cases, but while with a floating exchange rate that comes about through a change in the nominal exchange rate, with a fixed exchange rate it comes about through a change in the domestic price level.

3.1. *Floating Exchange Rates*

The classic argument in favour of a floating exchange rate is that exchange rate variation will take care of external balance without any sacrifice of internal balance. National policy-makers could choose their own preferred rate of inflation, or if an inflation/unemployment trade-off exists, their preferred mix between the two, without being constrained by external considerations. If there is a change in the external real environment calling for payments adjustment, this would also take place automatically. Consider two cases: (*a*) the home economy has a higher inflation rate than its trading partners; (*b*) the home economy suffers a terms of trade deterioration, say due to a higher price of imported oil. In both cases the nominal exchange rate would depreciate. In case (*a*) this would prevent an undersirable appreciation of the real exchange rate, in case (*b*) it would promote a desirable depreciation of the real exchange rate; in both cases the change in the real exchange rate would be achieved without the domestic price level (which, in effect, means thousands of money wages and prices) having to fall or grow more slowly. Policy-makers would have more autonomy, particularly in the conduct of monetary policy. Since the government would not have to intervene in the exchange market to maintain the exchange rate, it could control the money supply to secure domestic objectives.

Opponents of floating exchange rates have, however, advanced a number of counter-arguments to the case for a floating exchange rate.

(i) Take first the external balance criterion. Three objections have been made:

    (*a*) It is sometimes contended that trade elasticities are very low, particularly in the short run, and perhaps even in the long run. This

---

[4] For a classic discussion of fixed and floating exchange rates see Friedman (1953). For modern discussions of the choice between these exchange rate regimes see Corden (1985), Williamson (1983, 1985), IMF (1984). The 'optimum currency area literature' is also relevant to the topic. For a useful summary see Tower and Willett (1976).

would lead to slow balance-of-payments adjustment and to large movements in the exchange rate which would threaten internal balance. Note, however, that while this is generally put forward as an objection to a floating rate, it really questions the efficacy of all relative price changes or changes in the real exchange rate to affect trade flows. So it is really an objection to the price system in general, including one with a fixed exchange rate.[5]

(*b*) It has been contended that adjustment to incipient balance-of-payments deficits would be problematic because a depreciation of the nominal exchange rate would not be translated into the required depreciation of the real exchange rate if there is real wage resistance. This raises the unpleasant possibility of a depreciation–inflation spiral if the money supply is accommodating (and, as explained below, a floating exchange rate is thought to make monetary irresponsibility more likely).

(*c*) Another criticism of a floating exchange rate is that it may move too little, too much, or in a perverse direction for reasons which are quite distinct from low trade elasticities. Even if the foreign exchange market acts efficiently and rationally with full knowledge of long-run equilibrium, the exchange rate can 'overshoot' as a consequence of different speeds of adjustment in goods and assets markets. *A fortiori* if the market is not guided by fundamentals, there can be bandwagon effects and speculation can be destabilizing leading to misalignment of the exchange rate for substantial periods. Such misalignment can hamper adjustment of the current account instead of promoting it.

(ii) There are two criticisms of a floating exchange rate on the internal balance criterion.

(*a*) It is alleged that a floating rate regime would reduce anti-inflationary discipline. It may well liberate monetary policy from the external constraint but this should be counted as a cost, not a benefit.

---

[5] Low elasticities are often put forward as an objection not only to floating the exchange rate but also to discretionary adjustment of the exchange rate. As argued above, this objection applies equally to a fixed exchange rate since all exchange rate regimes rely on changes in the *real* exchange rate (i.e. changes in the appropriate relative prices) to change export and import volumes. Elasticity pessimists are therefore naturally led in the direction of managing the balance of payments by direct controls in domestic markets and in foreign trade. Theory suggests and experience confirms that such methods are extremely inefficient and should be avoided. Evidence also suggests that trade elasticities *are* sufficiently high, particularly in the long run and particularly from the viewpoint of an individual developing country. Considerations of space prevent us from discussing these issues. We proceed on the basis that changes in the real exchange rate are necessary for balance-of-payments adjustment and superior to trade interventions (except when the latter are levied on genuine terms of trade or second-best grounds). Whether the necessary changes in the real exchange rate should be achieved by fixed or variable nominal exchange rates is an entirely separate issue, which is central to our concern and which we do discuss at some length.

Since no visible balance-of-payments deficits emerge, the political will to resist money supply increases would be blunted.

(b) The second criticism follows from the mobility of capital and the possibility of destabilizing capital flows. It is contended that capital mobility dilutes the insulation properties of a floating exchange rate. If capital flows lead to exchange rate misalignment, internal balance is adversely affected and the task of macroeconomic management is made much more complicated.

(iii) On the criterion of microeconomic efficiency, the case against a floating exchange rate goes back to the behaviour of capital flows. If capital movements are not substantially stabilizing, the exchange rate (and therefore the price level) will exhibit a great deal of volatility in the face of random shocks. This will reduce the usefulness of domestic money, act as a disincentive to trade and investment, promote unnecessary and wasteful resource movements, and increase protectionist pressures.

The major industrial countries have had floating currencies since 1973 and their experience has underlined one of the above criticisms as being of particular importance. (Of course floating has been managed, but most people would agree that the difficulties with clean floating would be as great if not greater than those experienced with managed floating.) The problem which has most impressed observers is not low trade elasticities (measured elasticities have been adequately high, at least in the long run), or the inflationary bias of floating rates (industrial countries have successfully reduced inflation since 1979), or the microeconomic costs of short-term volatility (exchange rates have been volatile but econometric estimates have failed to pick up adverse effects on trade, perhaps because firms have been able to see beyond very short-term changes). The most important shortcoming of the system has turned out to be its tendency to produce medium-term misalignment of exchange rates, as exemplified by the phenomenal rise of the US dollar in the first half of the 1980s. Partly as a consequence of this, serious current account imbalances have persisted for long periods and there have been substantial adverse effects on domestic variables. The lesson from the industrial countries' experience with floating surely is that one would be unwise to put much faith in the ability of foreign exchange markets with unrestricted freedom of capital movement to guide exchange rates to their appropriate levels.

3.2. Fixed Exchange Rates

The case for fixed exchange rates is that external balance and internal balance are reconciled by movements in the internal price level. Pegging a country's exchange rate to the currency of a large country with a stable price level provides an anchor against inflation in the sense that in the long run the domestic inflation rate cannot exceed that of the stable peg-country. There are a number of forces which tend to produce this result: (*a*) there is a tendency for the prices of tradable goods to be equalized over time by arbitrage, (*b*) balance-of-payments deficits (surpluses) reduce (increase) domestic monetary growth putting downward (upward) pressure on the prices of tradable and non-tradable goods, and (*c*) the credible expectations generated by the above mechanism act as a check on the inflationary behaviour of workers and the government. The mechanism which keeps home inflation in line with the rest of the world also guides the real exchange rate to the level necessary to preserve external balance. The complete and guaranteed stability of the exchange rate has another important benefit in that it is very likely to lead to equilibrating capital movements. This means that any sudden movements in domestic prices and wages are unlikely to be necessary: large disequilibria in the balance of payments would be prevented by stabilizing capital flows. A fixed exchange rate also brings efficiency benefits. Under this regime, temporary and reversible shocks—e.g. a bad harvest or a cyclical downturn in commodity prices—change the stock of foreign exchange reserves, not the exchange rate. Consequently, the price level is likely to be more stable than with a floating exchange rate. This promotes trade, investment, and the use of money and prevents wasteful movements of resources.

The case against a fixed exchange rate is conveniently grouped under the following headings:

(i) *External Balance*: Balance-of-payments adjustment may be very slow if it has to be achieved by variations in the domestic price level, and money wages and prices in modern economies are notoriously sluggish, particularly in a downward direction.

(ii) *Internal Balance*: The downward inflexibility of money wages and prices would imply a very painful adjustment to balance-of-payments deficits since the burden would, in the short and medium run, be borne by a fall in output and employment. There is no guarantee that the harshness of this process would be significantly softened by equilibrating movements of capital, since output decline may have adverse effects on the expected rate of profit.

(iii) *Internal Balance*: The necessary equalization of domestic and foreign inflation in the long run is a cost, not a benefit. This is of course patently clear if the rest of the world is exporting inflation to the home country. It may even be true if the home country is inflating faster than the rest of the world *if* there is a trade-off between inflation and unemployment. In these cases, the loss of monetary independence clearly imposes a substantial long-run cost. Note that if capital movements are free, monetary policy cannot be used as an instrument even for purposes of short-term stabilization. With capital controls, policy-makers have some leeway in this regard but equilibrating capital movements may be discouraged.

(iv) *Efficiency*: A fixed exchange rate is stable but it may nevertheless result in instability of profit incentives since it makes domestic output and employment less stable. Moreover, the slowness of the adjustment process increases the temptation on governments to impose trade restrictions. Trade restrictions reduce efficiency quite directly; the possibility of trade restrictions does so indirectly by adding to uncertainty.

4. Alternative Exchange Rate Regimes for Developing Countries

We now turn to investigating the suitability of different exchange rate regimes for developing countries.[6] We consider the following options based largely but not wholly on the IMF's classification:

1. Independent floating
2. Single-currency pegging
3. Multi-currency pegging
4. Adjustable peg
5. Crawling peg: (*a*) Rule-based crawling peg and (*b*) Discretionary crawling peg

4.1. Independent floating

Independent floating refers to a regime in which the exchange rate is market-determined, with or without government intervention. A crucial distinction is that between independent floating without and with capital controls.

Independent floating without capital controls is most unlikely to be suitable for developing countries. The case for a floating exchange rate relies very heavily on the presence of stabilizing speculative activity which (*a*) irons out unnecessary exchange rate fluctuations in the face of random, reversible shocks, and (*b*) guides the exchange rate to the appropriate level when changes in the real exchange rate are necessary. The experience of industrial countries does not inspire confidence in the ability of even the most sophisticated of financial markets to avoid unnecessary exchange rate volatility and misalignment. But this failure is likely to be even more complete in developing countries whose financial and forward markets are rudimentary but which are likely to suffer frequent shocks because many of them have large agricultural and primary export sectors. Another problem with independent floating in some developing countries is likely to arise

---

[6] For further reading on this topic, see Bird (1982), Black (1976), Joshi (1979, 1984), Wickham (1985), Williamson (1981, 1982, 1987). Many other references are cited in these papers. For empirical evidence on the performance of exchange rate regimes see Williamson (1981), IMF *Annual Reports* (1981 onwards), and IMF *World Economic Outlook* (1981 onwards).

from their extreme openness in trade. This would imply that exchange rate changes would feed directly and substantially into the price level. Two consequences could follow: (*a*) the large and visible changes in the cost of living caused by exchange rate changes could erode the money illusion which is necessary for nominal exchange rate changes to be translated into changes in the real exchange rate, and (*b*) if the exchange rate and consequently the domestic price level are unstable, there would be a strong disincentive to the use of domestic money. The above arguments suggest that independent floating without capital controls, if adopted by a developing country, could lead to a highly unstable exchange rate with extremely undesirable consequences for macroeconomic balance, microeconomic efficiency, and the integrity of domestic money itself.

It is not surprising then that there are practically no cases of developing countries which have floated successfully and independently on a sustained basis without capital controls. Until recent troubles, Lebanon was a long-standing exception but it has a highly sophisticated banking system. Most of the other examples of developing countries currently listed by the IMF as independent floaters are of countries which have introduced foreign exchange auctions in the context of IMF stabilization programmes with capital controls still in place. These countries have all previously had grossly overvalued currencies and highly distorted economies with severe import controls and flourishing parallel markets. The performance of the auctions has been mixed. The Zambian and Ugandan auctions have collapsed because the exchange rate rapidly sank to unacceptable levels. In some other countries such as Ghana and Nigeria the auctions are still surviving and have shown some positive features. The exchange rate has shown a great deal of volatility (as indeed one would expect since the capital market is so restricted) but the availability of imports has been unfrozen compared to what was previously the case. The government has benefited from the exchange rate being depoliticized and the auctions have provided some indication of a realistic price for foreign exchange. Nevertheless, these positive features are only in comparison with the previous highly distorted system. The mildly encouraging results of some of these experiments cannot be elevated into a case for independent floating with capital controls as a normal regime for developing countries.

Having rejected independent floating as a desirable option for developing countries, we now consider the opposite exteme of fixed exchange rates. In this case, we immediately come up against a difficulty. Given the mutuality of the exchange rate relationship, how can any country whose trade is diversified fix its exchange rate if its trading partners are floating against one another? Clearly, the traditional developing-country practice of pegging to one currency does not fix the *effective* exchange rate. It is in answer to this problem that the technique of *multi-currency pegging* was devised. We therefore consider single-currency pegging and multi-currency pegging separately.

4.2 Single-currency pegging

Though many countries have switched away from single-currency pegging, this arrangement is still the practice in about twenty countries with strong historical links to a metropolitan power, namely the ex-French colonies which are members of the Franc Zone and some small Central American countries such as Panama.

Single-currency pegging offers important benefits, particularly when a large proportion of trade is with the peg-country. The microeconomic efficiency benefit comes from exchange rate stability and certainty. The consequential reduction in the variability of the price level underpins the liquidity of domestic money. The stability in the value of the currency in which trade is invoiced and prices are quoted promotes trade and capital flows. But these benefits are reduced as trade diversification takes place. In that case if the peg-currency is floating, the bilateral nominal and real exchange rates of the home currency against all other currencies will be changing constantly. So a great deal of price and exchange rate instability and risk would remain. Of course, exchange rate risk can, in principle, be eliminated by complete forward markets. But forward cover only comes with a cost, forward markets are thin for contracts longer than 3 months, and the involvement of developing countries in forward markets is quite perfunctory; and, even if forward markets reduce risk, the cost of instability remains. If random exchange rate fluctuations cause variations in the relative profitability of different lines of production (say tradable and non-tradable goods), there are costly but avoidable resource shifts between industries. Of course producers can be expected to learn and to see beyond day-to-day or month-to-month exchange rate variations, but exchange rate misalignments between major currencies have often been of quite long duration.

On the *macroeconomic* front, the benefit of single-currency pegging arises from the anti-inflationary discipline provided by the peg, assuming of course that the peg-country has a low and stable rate of inflation. Note that this benefit would be present in the long run *even if* trade were diversified and the peg-currency floated, if we make the further assumption that in the long run the exchange rates of major currencies move more or less in line with purchasing power parity. But in the short and medium run, experience suggests that such correspondence with purchasing power parity is very far from being fulfilled. In such a case the average rate and stability of inflation in the developing country would be dictated to a considerable extent by countries other than the peg-country. However, this may not matter very much: if we consider a typical developing country as having pronounced inflationary propensities but trading with much-less-inflationary major industrial countries, a single-currency peg is probably a perfectly good anchor against inflation.

A single-currency peg does not, however, look so good if we consider other aspects of external and internal balance. Two cases can be considered: (*a*) where the trade of the developing country is heavily concentrated with the peg-country, and (*b*) where the trade of the developing country is diversified. In case (*a*) the case against a single-currency peg is basically exactly the same as that against fixed exchange rates considered in an earlier section. If costs and prices in the developing country are rising faster than those in the peg-country, or if there are real changes which require a depreciation of the real exchange rate in the developing country, the adjustment has to come about by a fall in the level or growth of money wages and prices which could have adverse transitional effects on employment and output. On the other hand, if integration between the developing country and the peg-country is very close, equilibrating movements of capital (and perhaps even of labour) could ease the pain of adjustment very considerably. In addition, if the peg-country is highly open (so that its marginal propensity to import is high), the effect of domestic demand restriction on employment would be rather muted. Moreover, a long historical exchange rate link with the peg-country may itself contribute to wage/price flexibility. In case (*b*) the problem takes on a rather different character. Suppose the peg-currency appreciates against other major currencies (and more so than would be indicated by differential rates of inflation). It then follows that the developing country's real effective exchange rate would appreciate for reasons which have nothing to do with underlying cost/price trends or any genuine need to adjust. This would lead to a quite unnecessary deterioration in the developing country's balance of trade, employment, and output position. If the peg-currency depreciates with respect to other currencies, this could have the opposite effects (balance-of-trade surplus and inflation). It is not at all plausible to expect equilibrating factor movements between the peg-country and the developing country in such a case. What we are saying, in effect, is that for a developing country with diversified trade, single-currency pegging is like having a floating rate which is moving without any reference to the country's situation or needs.

It may be useful at this stage to refer to the experience of developing countries which have practised single-currency pegging. The following points may be noted:

(i) It has been confirmed by various studies that the real effective exchange rates of single-currency peggers have been volatile in comparison with multi-currency peggers and the volatility of the former is positively related to the degree of trade diversification (see Brodsky and Sampson, 1984).

(ii) The expectation that *permanent* single-currency pegging would lead to low long-run inflation rates appears to be reasonably well borne out. It has been shown that the franc-pegging CFA countries and the dollar-pegging Central American countries have had lower inflation rates than other countries in the region (see Connolly, 1983). The word *permanent* is rather important, however.

(iii) Some high-inflation countries which have attempted to bring down their rates of inflation by having fixed single-currency pegs ended up in crisis. The dramatic illustration here is the Chilean case. Chile pegged its exchange rate to the US dollar in 1980 as part of a stabilization-cum-liberalization programme. But contrary to 'international monetarist' doctrine, inflation was slow to come down. Two reasons stand out:

> (*a*) The fixing of the exchange rate was accompanied by internal and external capital market liberalization. Nominal interest rates in Chile rose to high levels; combined with a pre-announced fixed exchange rate they implied a very high real rate of return to foreign capital. Consequently, there were massive capital inflows which had an expansionary effect on the money supply.

> (*b*) Wage indexation based on *past* inflation continued during the programme. This made it difficult to bring down the rate of inflation quickly. As a consequence, the real exchange rate appreciated, the current account deficit grew massively, and the fixed exchange rate had to be abandoned in 1982.

The recent Israeli stabilization programme (which included fixing the exchange rate) appears to have been successful but it is significant that the Israeli package included an abrogation of indexation arrangements.

(iv) Another point worth emphasizing about the Chilean case is that not only did Chile peg its exchange rate to the US which had a much lower rate of inflation, but the US dollar was itself appreciating strongly in the early 1980s against other currencies. Consequently, Chile's nominal effective exchange rate rose, constituting an *additional* reason for the rise in its real effective exchange rate quite apart from stubbornly high inflation in Chile. This tendency for dollar-pegging countries having to accept large appreciations in their real effective exchange rates was seen in many Central American countries in the first half of the 1980s. In several cases, e.g. the Dominican Republic and Guatemala, the exchange rate had to be devalued massively after a period of recession and exchange restriction. The depreciation of the dollar since 1985 has created the opposite range of problems for dollar-peggers such as Hong Kong and Taiwan. They have experienced large real effective depreciations which have led to growing current account surpluses disturbing their own macroeconomic balance and causing considerable resentment in their trading partners.

4.3. *Multi-Currency Pegging*

The object of multi-currency pegging is to eliminate the effects of third-currency fluctuations by pegging the nominal effective exchange rate or in other words by pegging the home currency to a suitable average of foreign exchange rates. To take a very simple example, suppose that the exchange rate of the home country is designated in terms of the US dollar and the chosen weights in the effective exchange rate index or 'basket' are 50 per cent for the US and 50 per cent for Germany. Then, if the US dollar depreciates against the DM by 10 per cent, the fixed multi-currency peg requires that the home currency be upvalued in terms of the US dollar by 5 per cent. Evidently, by its very construction, multi-currency pegging reduces the instability of the nominal effective exchange rate as compared with single-currency pegging and, therefore, if the weights in the exchange rate index have been correctly chosen, reduces the impact of third-currency exchange rate movements on the home economy.

It follows, of course, that the choice of weights is a matter of some importance. There is a large and complex literature on this subject in which theoretical sophistication has vastly outrun practical applicability. We do not propose to review it here.[7] The appropriate weights clearly depend on which variable policy-makers wish to stabilize. Third-currency fluctuations (which deviate from purchasing power parity) would affect the domestic price of tradables, the terms of trade, the distribution of income, the balance of trade (hence the level of output and employment) etc., and the set of weights which would stabilize one of these variables would be quite different from that which would stabilize another. It follows that it is impossible for a developing country by its choice of peg to shield itself from all the real effects of exchange rate fluctuations. We take the view that the primary object of a multi-currency peg is to offset the effects of third-currency fluctuations on internal and external balance. For a small country, this requires stabilizing the price of tradables (and consequently the price of tradables relative to non-tradables). This points to using bilateral trade shares of partner countries as the appropriate weights. For a large country, the relevant object of stabilization for internal and external balance is the balance of trade which points to the use of elasticity-based weights, i.e. weighting each foreign currency in proportion to the impact that a change in its exchange rate would have on the home country's balance of trade. In practice, however, estimation of elasticities is too complicted; so it is again

---

[7] The interested reader may wish to refer to the masterly survey by John Williamson (1982).

difficult to do better than using bilateral trade shares as the weights (with some modification to give adequate importance to competitor countries whose bilateral trade shares are small but changes in whose exchange rates do matter for the home country's trade balance due to cross-price effects).

Multi-currency pegging is an attempt to mimic a fixed exchange rate in a world of floating exchange rates. In evaluating it, therefore, it is worth separating two issues: (*a*) whether multi-currency pegging secures the benefits of fixed exchange rate better than single-currency pegging does, and (*b*) the merits and demerits of fixing the exchange rate as such.

Concerning question (*a*), on the macroeconomic front a comparison between a multi-currency peg and a single-currency peg is favourable to the former. With a single-currency peg, third-currency fluctuations (unrelated to purchasing power parity) take on the character of macroeconomic shocks: a multi-currency peg goes some way to insulating the economy from unnecessary variations in output, balance of trade, and inflation that would ensue with a single-currency peg. As for microeconomic efficiency, the comparison is a little more ambiguous. With a single-currency peg, the exchange rate of the home currency against one currency (or one currency-area) is stable though it is changing against all other currencies. With a multi-currency peg, the home currency's exchange rate against every currency is constantly changing though the average exchange rate is constant. It is arguable that, though both regimes involve uncertainty, traders and investors will find the former regime less uncertain. This is obviously true for short-term exchange risk within the period of trade contracts if the peg-currency is also the currency of invoicing (given the lack of suitable opportunities for forward cover). It may also be true that even beyond the typical contract period, when price instability rather than currency risk is the object of concern, traders would be comforted more by the stability of the incentive to export to and import from at least one currency area than by the stability of the average incentive to export and import combined with instability of the incentive with respect to every currency area.

The other advantages and disadvantages of multi-currency pegging simply follow from the fact that it is a fixed exchange rate system.[8] (Multi-currency pegging shares these characteristics with single-currency pegging, though the latter suffers the additional complication of being subject to random short- and medium-run variations in the effective exchange rate.)

---

[8] It will be noticed from Table 4.1 that multi-currency peggers can be subdivided into those that peg to the SDR and those that peg to their own tailor-made composites. We cannot see any merit in pegging to the SDR (except perhaps that it makes it easier to calculate how the exchange rate should be changed in terms of the *numéraire* currency—say the dollar—to maintain the peg). It is only by fluke that the weights in the SDR would correspond to the appropriate weights from the country's point of view and until the SDR can perform the functions of a currency of invoicing and trading, there is no compensating microeconomic benefit either.

Since the fixed exchange rate regime was analysed in Section 3, further discussion is unnecessary at this point.

A large number of developing countries are pegged to multi-currency composites (see Table 4.1) but they should really be classified as following an *adjustable* multi-currency peg. Some brief remarks on their experience are given in the appropriate section below. Here, it may be worth speculating on why developing countries do not seem to go in for *permanent* multi-currency pegging. We suggest that this is probably because the disadvantages of fixity can only be endured by single-currency peggers who are likely to be small countries with historically strong links with a metropolitan power and therefore benefit from financial integration.

4.4. Intermediate Options

Given the disadvantages of both permanently fixed and independently floating exchange rates, it is not surprising that developing countries have tried various intermediate regimes in an effort to combine the advantages of the two systems. These have been of two basic types: adjustable peg and crawling peg. Under the *adjustable peg* system, the country undertakes an obligation to defend the peg but reserves the right to alter the exchange rate to correct a fundamental disequilibrium. The adjustable peg could be combined with narrow or wide bands, the band giving the limits within which the authorities may vary the exchange rate around the announced peg. Under the *crawling peg* regime, the country undertakes an obligation to defend the peg but either commits itself to moving the peg in small steps in accordance with a pre-announced rule—the *rule-based crawling peg*—or reserves the right to change the peg in steps which are small but discretionary in size and timing—the *discretionary crawling peg*.[9]

4.5. Adjustable peg

This was the exchange rate regime which operated from the end of the Second World War until 1973 for all countries including the industrial countries. The rationale of the system was to secure the advantages of nominal exchange rate stability (avoidance of unnecessary exchange rate changes in response to temporary shocks, provision of anti-inflationary discipline) while avoiding the disadvantages of a misaligned rate in the face of prolonged or permanent disequilbria. Industrial-country adjustable pegging broke down because, in practice, exchange rates were changed very infrequently and this was incompatible with (*a*) large differences in rates of inflation and (*b*) greatly increased mobility of capital. Point (*b*) reinforced

---

[9] We could, in principle, distinguish another regime which resembles a discretionary crawling peg in that the government is prepared to change the peg frequently but with the minor difference that the changes do not have to be 'small'. In what follows, we subsume this case under the 'discretionary crawling peg' category.

point (*a*) in that an exchange rate which was unrealistic was open to a speculative attack which the authorities were incapable of resisting by intervention. By 1973, the mobility of capital had increased to the point where the system became unworkable. It is sometimes asserted that the adjustable peg would have been workable if only exchange rate changes had been much more frequent. Whether or not this is true, it must be said that *very* frequent exchange rate changes are not consonant with the adjustable peg. The spirit of the adjustable peg is to emphasize the financial discipline aspect of exchange rate stability, exchange rate changes being allowed only in the case of 'fundamental' disequilibrium.

A very large number of developing countries which are formally listed by the IMF as having pegged currencies and some which are formally listed as being 'managed floaters' are in effect on an adjustable peg. A question that immediately arises is how the developing countries can operate an adjustable peg system if the industrial countries cannot do so. The answer is, of course, that most developing countries have controls on trade and capital movements.

In discussing the adjustable peg, we must note the difference between a single-currency adjustable peg and a multi-currency adjustable peg. The relevant considerations in choosing between these two versions follow directly from our previous discussion. With a single-currency adjustable peg, there is an *extra* reason why fundamental disequilibrium may arise, namely medium-term misalignments between major currencies; with the multi-currency version this factor is offset on a continuous basis. In our view, abandonment of the idea of permanent pegging strengthens the case for a multi-currency peg. After all, if a single-currency peg is going to be adjusted from time to time to offset third-currency fluctuations, there is in any case a dilution of the microeconomic benefits which might follow from exchange rate stability against the peg-currency.

The adjustable peg is supposed to combine the advantages of fixed and flexible exchange rate regimes but in many developing countries, even more so than in industrial countries,it has often ended up with the disadvantages of both. On the one hand, the fact of past devaluations and the possibility of future devaluations erode the benefits of a fixed exchange rate in the following ways:

(i) They weaken the monetary resolve of the government and increase the rigidity of money wages.
(ii) They reduce the incentive for equilibrating capital movements.
(iii) They dilute the microeconomic benefits of exchange rate certainty.

On the other hand, the fixity of the exchange rate for prolonged periods means that the government is tempted to manage balance-of-payments disequilibria by international borrowing and trade restrictions. Trade restric-

tions of increasing severity combined with excess monetary expansion lead
to a further worsening of international competitiveness. When the exchange rate becomes grossly overvalued, capital controls lose their effectiveness and there are large outflows of capital. Finally, when devaluation
does come about in the middle of a crisis, it has to be large and that very
fact provokes a neutralizing response in domestic money wages and prices.

Many developing countries have played out the above scenario of
inflation-cum-overvaluation buttressed by import restrictions followed by a
maxi-devaluation followed by a repetition of the same cycle. Perhaps the
most dramatic instances are provided by various African countries such as
Tanzania, Uganda, Zambia, Ghana, and Zaïre. These countries were
pegged either to the US dollar or to multi-currency composites but
allowed their exchange rates to get enormously overvalued which finally
led to severe crises. (On the other hand, Kenya, Malawi, and Mauritius
avoided these problems by fairly frequent adjustments in the exchange
rate.) Perhaps the most important disservice done by pegging regimes in
African countries was to encourage the already present general distrust of
the price mechanism. (It is easy to forget that a fixed exchange rate regime
also relies on the price mechanism and cannot work if the adjustment of
the internal price level is prevented by trade restrictions.) Distrust of the
price mechanism is particularly prevalent in primary producing countries
where it is felt that relative prices do not matter since substitution possibilities for primary products are limited both in supply and demand. But there
is now a lot of evidence that an increase in production costs of primary
products due to domestic inflation squeezes profitability if the exchange
rate is fixed and leads to reduction in exportable supplies. As far as international demand is concerned, the elasticities of demand are often high for
individual developing countries even if they are low for developing countries as a whole.[10] While it is true that many non-market policies are important for the promotion of exports, prevention of exchange rate overvaluation is a crucial necessary condition. These remarks apply even more
strongly in the case of manufactured products.

4.6.   Crawling Peg

In a formal sense, only four developing countries (Brazil, Chile, Colombia,
Madagascar) are listed as being rule-based crawling peggers by the IMF in
1987, though several other Latin American countries and South Korea

---

[10] If *overall* demand for a primary product is inelastic, a single developing country may
increase exports by a real devaluation but only at the expense of other countries and there is a
danger of competitive devaluations to nobody's benefit. In such cases, there is obviously a
case for country quotas and export taxes. See Williamson (1987). Even in such cases, however, nominal devaluation may be required to maintain the existing real exchange rate if
domestic costs get out of line.

have been rule-based crawling peggers in the past. Table 4.1 does indicate, however, that many developing countries are currently practising a discretionary crawl ('managed floating' in the Table). Rule-based crawling has generally taken the form of adjusting the nominal exchange rate in line with purchasing power parity, i.e. by an amount sufficient to offset the differential between home and world (trading-partner) inflation. (Hereafter, this is labelled PPP-crawling.)

The crawling peg, like the adjustable peg, involves a choice between pegging to a single currency and pegging to a multi-currency composite. Again, the presumption must be that pegging to a multi-currency composite is better. On the question of microeconomic efficiency, it is arguable that a crawling peg is superior to a fixed exchange rate and the adjustable peg since it stabilizes the profitability of trading in real terms. As far as internal and external balance are concerned, the advantage of a PPP-based crawling peg is that corrective changes in the nominal exchange rate are carried out frequently and automatically and real exchange rate misalignments arising out of differential rates of inflation are not allowed to build up. It allows a country to have a different inflation rate from its trading partners. If the home inflation rate is low, it allows higher foreign inflation to be repelled by exchange rate appreciation. If, to take the relevant case for many developing countries, home inflation is high, it does not have to fall in line with the lower foreign inflation rate; exchange rate depreciation avoids the painful process of domestic disinflation accompanied by recession and output decline. This consideration is clearly of great importance in countries which have a history of rapid inflation and therefore have labour market mechanisms and indexation mechanisms which are geared to inflation.

The obverse of this advantage is that the country does not have an external anchor against inflation. This does not mean that a crawling peg has a tendency to *accelerate* inflation; nevertheless it does mean that the exchange rate is passive and ratifies any inflation that exists. Therefore, under this regime, control of inflation has to be achieved by domestic monetary policy.[11]

Of course, there is no reason why, in principle, the formula underlying the crawling peg should not have a measure of anti-inflationary discipline built into it. For example, the formula may specify that the home currency would depreciate somewhat less than the difference between domestic and

---

[11] The target rate of inflation constrains the trend growth of money supply. Note that with freedom of capital movements, monetary policy for *short-run* stabilization is also tightly constrained since asset market equilibrium requires that the domestic interest rate must equal the foreign interest rate plus the expected rate of exchange rate depreciation. With capital controls, policy-makers have some freedom of manœuvre in the conduct of monetary policy for short-run stabilization.

foreign inflation. But such external anti-inflationary discipline is bought at the expense of deliberate overvaluation of the real exchange rate. The more the PPP formula is overridden in this manner, the more the system begins to approximate a fixed exchange rate system. The danger in this approach should of course be evident from the Chilean example where the nominal exchange rate was fixed starting from a position of high inflation. In fact, the approach of pre-announced devaluations at a decelerating rate (sometimes called an 'active crawl') which was followed in Argentina and Uruguay at the end of the 1970s suffered broadly the same fate as the Chilean experiment.

A further objection to the PPP-based crawling peg needs some discussion. A PPP-based rule is not suitable if the *appropriate* real exchange rate changes are due to permanent real shocks. For example, a terms-of-trade deterioration, caused by a higher price for imported oil, may call for increased competitiveness to improve the non-oil current account. A PPP-based rule would not lead to a sufficient depreciation of the exchange rate. In fact, one can even imagine situations where a PPP-based rule would lead to exchange rate changes in the wrong direction. Suppose that discovery of a tradable natural resource calls for an appreciation of the real exchange rate. A PPP-based rule would not produce that result. Without such a rule, required real appreciation could come about naturally as the result of a once-for-all rise in the domestic price level following from the balance-of-payments surplus caused by the tradable resource being exported. But under a PPP-based rule, such a rise in domestic prices would signal a depreciation of the exchange rate. Indeed, if this leads to a wage–price spiral, blind adherence to the rule would lead to an even further depreciation. Thus, in the presence of real shocks, it may be necessary for the PPP rule to be overridden; if the real shock is large,it might even be optimal to have a large exchange rate change outside the PPP-determined formula.

These considerations take us in the direction of a discretionary crawling peg. But ideally the discretion should be limited—it should really be a *modified PPP crawl*. The presence of complete discretion often leads bureaucracies in the direction of inertia or bending to special interests. It is therefore essential to have a *framework* for making decisions about the exchange rate. A modified PPP crawl starts with the presumption that the nominal exchange rate should be altered with regularity to keep the real exchange rate constant and that departures from this rule require specific justification in terms of (*a*) compensating for mistakes in the initial level of the real exchange rate (i.e. compensating for mistakes made before the exchange regime is put into effect), (*b*) responding to real shocks, and (*c*) deliberate non-compensation for anti-inflationary purposes though, as seen earlier, this can be dangerous.

Experience with the crawling peg has been reasonably satisfactory with respect to maintaining real competitiveness. Several Latin American countries (Chile, Colombia, Brazil, Uruguay, Argentina, Peru) have practised a PPP crawl and many other countries (particularly exporters of manufactures) are currently on a discretionary crawling peg. The Latin American countries of course have had rapid inflation and the evidence is that, while the crawling peg cannot be blamed for causing their inflations, it is part of the process of keeping it going. That simply underlines the fact that with a PPP crawl, control of inflation has to be achieved by domestic monetary policies. Indeed there are now several low-inflation countries which practise discretionary crawling. This category includes India. In recent years, the Indian Government, while formally maintaining a peg to a multi-currency composite with undisclosed weights, has in fact followed a policy of discretionary crawling to maintain export competitiveness. Indian inflation is not much higher than that in industrial countries, an outcome attributable principally to conservative monetary policies.

5. Concluding Remarks

Which exchange rate regime should developing countries adopt? Single-currency pegging is feasible and desirable only in a country that satisfies some or all of the following criteria: (*a*) extreme openness: this implies that the internal price level is largely determined by world prices, so that it is very difficult for exchange rate variation to have much leverage; (*b*) financial integration with a low-inflation major country: this would impose anti-inflationary discipline and ensure that capital movements ease the process of balance-of-payments adjustment; (*c*) downward flexibility of the level or growth of money wages: this would ensure that deficits can be corrected by credit restriction without creating excessive losses in output and employment; and (*d*) a long tradition of a fixed exchange rate: this is important because it is likely to mean that policy-makers would find it difficult to abandon the fixed exchange rate regime simply because it was politically expedient in the short run.

Even if these criteria are satisfied, a single-currency pegger is likely to suffer macroeconomic disturbances due to instability of the effective exchange rate if its trade is diversified and if major currencies are floating. This problem can be eased by pegging to a multi-currency composite. But this technique is likely to erode both the microeconomic advantages of single-currency pegging and perhaps more significantly the tradition of an unalterable link with a major currency which may be important in fostering an anti-inflationary ethos.

Most developing countries in the 1980s do not satisfy the preconditions of a successful fixed exchange rate regime. Many of them have trade unions which make money wages downwardly inflexible at least in some sectors. Most of them are not financially integrated with major countries and can no longer draw on a long tradition of fixed exchange rates (with freedom of trade and capital movements) and price stability. Few of them are so open as to have their internal prices completely determined by external prices. Governments of such countries would not be willing to follow the full logic of fixed exchange rate policies and quite rightly so. Independent floating, however, is not feasible in developing countries. Given the lack of development of financial markets, it is likely to be very unstable. Hence, some form of pegged but variable exchange rates is obviously the relevant alternative. That leaves two questions: (*a*) what the form of the exchange rate peg should be, and (*b*) what arrangements should govern variations in the value of the peg.

As far as the form of the peg is concerned, once the idea of a permanently fixed exchange rate is abandoned, the balance of advantage shifts from a single-currency to a multi-currency peg. On the question of arrangements for exchange rate variation, experience has shown that the adjustable peg is not suitable. It leaves too much discretion in the hands of governments; without explicit rules and a framework for exchange rate variation, governments tend to postpone adjustment and impose trade controls.

Given the propensity of governments to postpone adjustment and their reluctance to adjust solely by credit restriction and demand management, the best compromise between rules and discretion is a *modified PPP crawl*, namely (*a*) a rule that the nominal exchange rate should be adjusted regularly to compensate for the difference between domestic and foreign inflation with (*b*) the proviso that the above normal rule can be overridden if a clear case can be made for a larger or smaller exchange rate adjustment to make up for past misalignment of the real exchange rate or in response to permanent real shocks (e.g. a terms-of-trade deterioration, or domestic trade liberalization, or a natural resource discovery, or an increase in the debt-service burden due to higher world interest rates). This implies of course that domestic inflation has to be handled by domestic means, not by fixing the exchange rate. But in the final analysis, this should not be seen as a drawback of the above system relative to fixed exchange rates. A fixed exchange rate cannot be a fundamental solution to inflation, since a government which is determined to follow inflationary policies will simply abandon the exchange rate. Nation-states are built upon the principle of self-determination which includes the right to follow irresponsible policies. In such a world, only freely chosen but responsible monetary behaviour by the government can be a reliable anchor against inflation.

References

Bird, G. (1982), *The International Monetary System and the Less Developed Countries* (London: Macmillan).

Black, S. W. (1976), *Exchange Policies for Less Developed Countries in a World of Floating Rates*, Princeton Essays in International Economics, 119.

Brodsky, D., and Sampson, G. (1984), 'The Sources of Exchange Rate Instability in Developing Countries: Dollar, French Franc and SDR Pegging Countries', *Weltwirtschaftliches Archiv*, 120.

Connolly, M. B. (1983), 'Optimum Currency Pegs for Latin America', *Journal of Money, Credit and Banking*, 15.

Corden, W. M. (1985), *Inflation, Exchange Rates and the World Economy*, 3rd edn. (Oxford: OUP).

Cuddington, J. (1986), *Capital Flight: Estimates, Issues and Explanations*, Princeton Studies in International Economics, 58.

Friedman, M. (1953), 'The Case for Flexible Exchange Rates', in *Essays in Positive Economics* (Chicago: Univ. of Chicago Press).

IMF (1981 onwards), *Annual Reports*.

——(1981 onwards), *World Economic Outlook*.

——(1984), *The Exchange Rate System: Lessons of the Past and Options for the Future*, Occasional Paper, 30 (Washington, DC: IMF).

Joshi, V. (1979), 'Exchange Rates, International Liquidity and Economic Development', *World Economy*, 2.

——(1984), 'The Nominal and Real Exchange Rate of the Indian Rupee', *Reserve Bank of India Occasional Papers*, 5/1.

Little, I., Scitovsky, T., and Scott, M. (1970), *Industry and Trade in Some Developing Countries* (Oxford: OUP).

Tower, E., and Willett, T. (1976), *The Theory of Optimum Currency Areas and Exchange Rate Flexibility*, Princeton Special Papers in International Economics, 11.

Wickham, P. (1985), 'The Choice of Exchange Rate Regime in Developing Countries', *Staff Papers*, 32. (Washington. DC: IMF).

Williamson, J. (ed.) (1981), *Exchange Rate Rules* (London: Macmillan Press Ltd.)

——(1982), 'A Survey of the Literature on the Optimal Peg', *Journal of Development Economics*, 11.

——(1983), *The Open Economy and the World Economy* (New York: Basic Books).

——(1985), *The Exchange Rate System* (Washington. DC: Institute of International Economics).

——(1987) 'Exchange Rate Policy for Developing Countries', *Journal of Foreign Exchange and International Finance*, 1.

5

Commodity Price Stabilization

DAVID M. NEWBERY

1. Introduction

In 1976, inspired by the success of OPEC in raising the price of oil, the United Nations Conference on Trade and Development (UNCTAD) passed a resolution calling for an Integrated Programme for Commodities (IPC) as part of the more ambitious establishment of a New International Order. The developed countries confined their discussions to the problems of primary commodities and supported the negotiation of international commodity agreements, and agreed in principle on the need for a Common Fund to finance international commodity stocks (see Little, 1982, ch. 17 and Gordon-Ashworth, 1984, pp. 42–6). The IPC was always intended to be more than just a solution to the problem of commodity price instability, and its prime aim, at least as perceived by the developing countries, was undoubtably to raise commodity prices to levels which were 'remunerative and just to producers and equitable to consumers'.

Since then the world has experienced the second and third oil shocks, the OPEC cartel has come under increasing pressure, oil prices have fallen in real terms to almost their pre-1974 levels, and the Tin Agreement has collapsed spectacularly. In 1985 the 33-commodity purchasing power index (which excludes energy) stood at 56 per cent of its 1974 peak, and at its lowest point in four decades, 80 per cent below its previous trough, and less than half its 1951 level.[1] The world is suffering from a debt crisis, much of which can be attributed to the dramatic commodity price fluctuations of the past decade. If anything there is an even keener awareness of the desirability of more orderly and stable commodity markets, but a greater scepticism that these markets can be stabilized, either by commodity agreements and buffer stocks, or by cartel action and supply controls.

What are the costs of commodity price instability? What are the benefits from price stabilization? How can prices most efficiently be stabilized? How can the costs of the risks facing primary producers best be alleviated? Why have commodity agreements such a disappointing record? What, if

I am indebted to Maurice Scott and David Hirshleifer for helpful comments on earlier drafts, even when I have not always followed their advice.

[1] The index is published in *Commodity Trade and Price Trends*, World Bank, (1986, Table 21), which gives the list of commodities. Their price is deflated by the manufacturing unit value price index to give a measure of purchasing power over manufactured goods.

anything, could be achieved by international co-operation to reduce the problem of commodity price instability? What have we learned from the past decade? What do we still need to know? These questions seem as pertinent now as they were 10 years ago when the the World Bank and the US Agency for International Development requested Joseph Stiglitz and myself to prepare a report on UNCTAD's proposals for commodity price stabilization.[2] In this chapter I shall discuss these questions, and show how far they can be answered with the techniques of applied welfare economics to which Ian Little contributed so much.

1.1. The Magnitude of Commodity Price Instability

In our original research, Stiglitz and I were asked to concentrate our attention on six of the 'core' commodities identifed by UNCTAD as suitable for buffer stock price stabilization. The common feature of these six was that they were agricultural commodities primarily produced by developing countries. I shall continue to have agricultural commodities in mind in this chapter, though much of the theory also applies to minerals and to temperate agricultural goods.[3] Table 5.1 updates some of the measures of price instability given in Table 20.6 of Newbery and Stiglitz (1981) (with the addition of tea, not in the earlier table). The first summary measure given for the two time-periods is the standard deviation of percentage deviations from the 5-year centred moving average of the real commodity price, and, like a coefficient of variation, is a dimensionless measure of volatility or instability. The commodity prices are deflated by an index of purchasing power, the manufacturing unit value index, but the measure of instability is virtually unchanged if it is measured in nominal dollar prices. The second measure is the standard deviation of the annual change in the price level divided by the average of the current and previous price. It is a dimensionless measure of the uncertainty of the real commodity price, but again the uncertainty of the nominal price is almost exactly the same.[4] The table allows the variability of commodity prices in the two time-periods to be compared, and the asterisks indicate changes which are statistically significant, using an F test.

The table shows that the variability of coffee, tea, and possibly cotton (depending on the measure of instability chosen) appear to have increased

[2] The report was subsequently transformed into *The Theory of Commodity Price Stabilization*, Newbery and Stiglitz (1981), and the present chapter draws heavily on that source, where more extensive defences of the position advanced here are to be found.

[3] Ghosh *et al.* (1987), on the other hand, are primarily concerned with the world copper market, though the area of overlap is considerable.

[4] The table corresponds to Table 20.6 of Newbery and Stiglitz. The measures of the variability in prices in Table 20.6 differ slightly from those here in that the deviations are there divided by the mean price, not the (centred) current price, as here. The present figures are a better measure of medium-run volatility or short-run uncertainty.

TABLE 5.1. Measures of price instability for primary commodities, 1950–1984 (%)

	5-yr moving average		Price change	
	1950–69	1970–86	1950–69	1970–86
	(1)	(2)	(3)	(4)
Cocoa	21	22	25	28
Coffee	12	24*	16	35**
Tea	7	19**	11	23**
Sugar	35	38	39	47
Cotton	6	13**	13	19*
Jute	20	12*	22	18
Rubber	16	18	24	23
Agriculture (Index)[a]	9	12	12	18

Notes: [a] Index of purchasing power of all agricultural commodities.
Prices are deflated by manufacturing unit value to give the real prices, p_t.
If M_t is the 5-year centred moving average real price, then Cols. (1) and (2) are the standard deviations of $(p_t - M_t)/M_t$. Cols. (3) and (4) are the SDs of $2(p_t - p_{t-1})/(p_t + p_{t-1})$.
* is a change in CV which is statistically significant at the 5% level.
** is a change in the variability significant at the 1% level.

Source: Commodity Trade and Price Trends, 1986, World Bank (1986), updated by the 1987 CRB Commodity Yearbook, Commodity Research Board.

in the second period, whilst that of jute may have fallen. (In the case of coffee and tea there was a sharp but short-lived increase in prices in 1977, and for tea another increase in 1982–3.) The final line in the table gives the volatility of an index of agricultural prices, predominantly food and beverages. This also shows some sign of increased volatility recently, though the increase is not statistically significant. Not surprisingly, as it is a portfolio of the underlying commodities, its volatility is lower. If individual commodities were roughly equally risky, as measured by the coefficient of variation (CV), and if their risks were uncorrelated, then the CV of a portfolio of n equally represented commodities would $1/\sqrt{n}$ that of each commodity. The index has 21 members, and might therefore have a CV 22 per cent that of each commodity, say 4.5 per cent for the commodities of Table 5.1 (over the full period). Instead, the volatility of the index is over twice as high,[5] suggesting that agricultural commodity prices are correlated—most noticeably at the major peaks and troughs, which are often caused by similar exogenous factors.

[5] The ratio the volatility of the index to the root mean squared values of the individual commodities is about the same over each time period.

2. The Costs of Price Instability and the Benefits of Stabilization

Commodity price instability affects producers, processors, those who store the commodity (stockholders), and consumers, though for 'core' commodities in the IPC I shall argue that the costs of instability are much larger for the producers and stockholders than for consumers. The costs to the consumers are in any case similar in nature to (though quantitatively different from) those facing producers, and for both reasons it makes sense to concentrate on the costs to producers and stockholders. The costs can be subdivided into costs of *price risk*, costs of *income risk*, costs of *misperception*, and *macroeconomic costs*. The first three costs would arise even if all markets cleared continuously and competitively, and lend themselves to the standard techniques of microeconomic analysis and welfare economics. The last raises larger issues which are best dealt with separately.

Agricultural markets are often held up as exemplars of perfect competition, as the commodities are homogeneous, can be traded over the telephone sight unseen (as on futures markets), and are typically produced and consumed by large numbers of individually insignificant agents. On the face of it, it would seem reasonable to start from the assumption that these goods are marketed under competitive conditions. It would, however, be potentially misleading not to query this assumption, for it has been argued that a characteristic of the more successful commodity agreements is that they applied to commodities with a high country concentration, that is, a small number of countries produce a large fraction of total supply (Gordon-Ashworth, 1984, p. 274). Newbery (1984*a*) lists eight agricultural commodities in which a single country is responsible for more than 50 per cent of world trade, including the two core commodities jute and rubber. Five other core commodities are produced by countries responsible for between 25 and 50 per cent of world trade. This potential for market power at the country level has implications for price stabilization which will be studied below, but for the moment it remains true that each producer (farmer) will be a price-taker even if the government intervenes. It is therefore reasonable to model the individual's behaviour as competitive.

2.1. The Costs of Price Risk and the Benefits of Arbitrage

The simplest approach to the study of commodity price stabilization starts with supply and demand schedules whose positions fluctuate, causing the market clearing price to fluctuate. In Fig. 5.1 supply will be either high or low depending on rainfall, demand is unaffected by weather, and the unstabilized market price will thus be either low in good years or high in bad years. If the commodity could be costlessly stored, and if bad years always followed good, and vice versa, then the price could be perfectly stabilized at a level at which demand was equal to average supply. In good years the

David M. Newbery

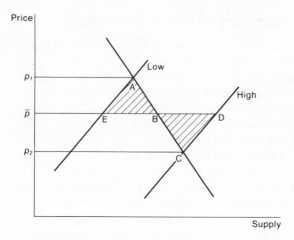

Fig. 5.1   Simple surplus analysis of price stabilization

excess would be placed in store, and in bad years the shortfall would be taken out of store. A crude measure of the benefits of price stabilization is then given by comparing the average consumer and producer surpluses (the area between the demand schedule and the price line or the supply schedule and the price line respectively) before and after stabilization. Massell (1969, 1970), who popularized this approach, showed that with linear demand and supply schedules, and additive shocks to supply (which causes supply to vary by a fixed additive amount independent of price, so that the supply schedule shifts sideways and remains parallel), as in Fig. 5.1, consumers would lose from price stabilization, but producers would gain more, and so on balance society would be better off (in the sense that the gainers could compensate the losers).

In bad years (of low supply) consumers benefit from price stabilization at $\bar{p}$ by the area $p_1AB\bar{p}$, but in good years they lose by an area $p_2CB\bar{p}$, which is larger. Producers lose in bad years by $p_1AE\bar{p}$ (since they only produce $\bar{p}$ E instead of p_1A), but in good years they gain by $\bar{p} DCp_2$, which is larger. The net gain of price stabilization, adding producer and consumer surplus in low years is area EAB, and in high years is BDC, so the total gain is their sum.

The source of the net benefits is the equalization of marginal values of the same good in different years. If storage is costless, as assumed here, then the act of transferring the good from the low-value state to a high-value state generates *arbitrage* gains, similar to the gains from trade across space. Whilst there is no doubt about these arbitrage gains, most of the other conclusions which have been drawn from the linear model of Fig. 5.1 are misleading. First, the linear additive model implies that the price which equates average supply to demand is the average price, and this has confusingly suggested that price stabilization means stabilizing the price at the mean price. In general this is not true, and the price which balances average supply and demand may be above or below the mean price, depending on the shape of the supply and demand schedules, and the nature of risk. Whether stabilization transfers income from consumers to producers (as here), or vice versa, or whether both gain also depends on these factors, and the source of the risk, i.e. whether the supply schedule is stochastic (because of weather) or demand shifts (due to income or price fluctuations elsewhere). The answers to many of these questions will be prejudged by the functional forms chosen for econometric estimation—whether linear or log-linear, for example.

The other obvious difficulty with this analysis is that storage is never costless, and there is no guarantee that each good year will be followed by one bad year. Faced with the problem of determining the efficient level of arbitrage or storage, the standard welfare economics answer is to ask what a competitive market would achieve, appealing to the theorem which claims that competitive equilibrium is Pareto-efficient. As we shall see below, the theorem requires *market completeness*, i.e. that all goods can be traded, both now and in the future, and all risks can be insured. Nevertheless, under assumptions to be discussed below, a competitive market in storage, supplemented, as is almost invariably the case in practice, by a futures market on which the price risks of storage can be hedged, provides a good bench-mark for efficient arbitrage.

First, consider the actions of a risk-neutral stockholder in the absence of a futures market. (The effect of introducing a futures market will be discussed once the spot market equilibrium has been clarified.) The stockholder has rational expectations and can forecast the future market-clearing spot price. He can compare the costs of buying the crop, holding it, and selling it at the future market-clearing spot price, and will continue to place the crop into store until the current price has risen, and the future price has fallen, enough to eliminate any excess profit on the storage. Storage will thus arbitrage the current price to the present discounted value of the expected future price, less storage costs. If, for example, storage costs per unit of crop per time-period are c, the rate of interest is r, and price at date t is p_t, then, provided that positive stocks are held, storage will drive the current price p_t up to

$$p_t + rp_t + c = Ep_{t+1} \qquad (5.1)$$

Here E is the expectations operator, so the Ep_{t+1} is the expected spot price at date $t+1$. The left-hand side is the cost of buying and holding the stock for one period, and if $\beta = (1+r)^{-1}$ is the discount factor, then (5.1) can be rewritten as

David M. Newbery

$$p_t = \beta E p_{t+1} - c, \qquad (5.2)$$

which shows more clearly the forces determining the current spot price (and jointly determining the futures price and the expected future spot price).

Several important conclusions can be drawn from this arbitrage model. First, if the current supply is smaller than some critical amount, then the current price will be too high to make storage profitable. After the existing carry-over from last year has been sold, it is not possible to depress the current price any further, and the arbitrage relation (5.2) will remain an inequality. Thus storage can prevent current prices falling too far (at least, until all available storage has ben filled) but is powerless to prevent prices rising in times of severe shortage. Storage has an asymmetrical effect on prices, and accounts for the appearance of commodity price time-series, with their long flattish bottoms and sharp upward spikes. Second, it is possible to characterize the nature of the storage rule in terms of the amount that needs to be stored (Newbery and Stiglitz, 1982a). Very roughly, about one-half of the current supply (current harvest plus last period carry-over) in excess of some specified amount should be placed in store to achieve the competitive arbitrage equilibrium.[6] (The figure of one-half arises because a unit of commodity placed in store raises the current price by some amount and reduces the price next year by a comparable amount, thus having roughly twice the effect on the price difference as it has on the current price. The exact figure will depend on the shape of the demand schedules in each year and is further modified by interest and carrying costs and the probability of carry-overs lasting more than one year.) Third, the extent of price stabilization which is profitable depends on the interest and carrying costs—the lower these are the smaller will be the resulting co-efficient of variation of the price and the smaller will be the variability in consumption from year to year (assuming the major source of fluctuation lies on the supply side).

This last point can be illustrated from some very interesting evidence on wheat from medieval England in McCloskey and Nash (1984). They studied the pattern of price movements of wheat over the season, for the arbitrage relation implies that after the harvest the price must rise at a rate equal to the total cost of carrying grain. They found the rate of increase to be between 2 and 3 per cent per month, and conclude that the rate of interest might have been as high as 30 per cent per year in medieval Eng-

---

[6] The specified amount below which storage is unprofitable depends on the nature of the risk, the shape of the demand schedule, the elasticity of supply, and the storage costs, as explained in Newbery and Stiglitz (1982a). As a very rough approximation it may be similar to the average harvest, or possibly somewhat higher.

land. Consequently, carry-over costs were high, possibly 40 per cent, and carry-overs were small (less than 5 per cent). The coefficient of variation of prices was high (between 20 and 43 per cent, compared with comparable figures of 16 to 34 per cent in the nineteenth century). More dramatically, the incidence of famine was high, for low carry-overs meant an increased risk from a poor harvest, and even more from two poor seasons in a row. When the rate of interest fell in the sixteenth century, carry-overs increased and the risk of famine fell.

If there is a futures market then it is no longer necessary to assume that the stockholder has rational expectations and is risk-neutral in order to characterize the storage rule. Using the theory of expected utility set out below, suppose the stockholder's income is y, where

$$y = (\beta p_{t+1} - p_t - c)s + \beta(p^f - p_{t+1})z,$$

and where s is the quantity to be stored, z is the level of futures sales, p^f is the futures price for delivery next period when the spot price is p_{t+1}. If the stockholder chooses s, z to maximize expected utility, $EU(y)$, then the condition for storage to be profitable will be the same as equation (5.2) with Ep_{t+1} replaced by p^f. The stockholder storage decision is now guided by observed market signals—he continues to store until movements in the current and futures price signal—that it is no longer profitable. Equation (5.2) will continue to hold if the futures price is an unbiased estimator of the future spot price, which requires that speculators have rational expectations and can compute the impact of storage on the future spot price, and also that they are effectively risk-neutral (i.e. that the risks they face in the futures market are uncorrelated with other asset prices and can thus be diversified).

2.2. The Magnitude of the Arbitrage Benefits

If the coefficient of variation (CV) of prices is reduced by storage to a fraction α of its original value, σ_p, then the total arbitrage gains from this reduction as a fraction of expenditure on the commodity are approximately $0.5(1 - \alpha^2)\sigma_p$, where ε is the elasticity of demand (Newbery and Stiglitz, 1981, pp. 255–8). (This provides the justification for measuring commodity price instability by the CV or its equivalent, as in Table 5.1.) It is interesting to gain some feel for the likely arbitrage benefits of reducing commodity price instability by, say, one-half. The first point to note is that this generates three-quarters of the maximum possible gains—in other words the benefits of reducing instability even a modest amount are initially quite large, then rapidly decrease, whereas the costs of further reducing price fluctuations are likely to steadily increase. If we take an optimistically large

TABLE 5.2. Arbitrage benefits[a] of halving price instability, 1950–1984 (%)

	5-yr moving average		Price change	
	1950–69	1970–86	1950–69	1970–86
	(1)	(2)	(3)	(4)
Cocoa	1.6	1.8	2.3	2.8
Coffee	0.5	2.2**	0.9	4.6**
Tea	0.2	1.3**	0.4	2.0**
Sugar	4.5	5.5	5.6	8.1
Cotton	0.1	0.7**	0.6	1.3*
Jute	1.5	0.5**	1.8	1.3
Rubber	1.0	1.2	2.2	2.0
Agriculture (Index)[b]	0.3	0.6	0.6	1.1

Notes: [a] Benefits are a percentage of total expenditure on the commodity.
[b] Index of purchasing power of all agriculture commodities.
* is a change in benefits which is statistically significant at the 5% level.
** is a change in benefits which is statistically significant at the 1% level.

Source: Commodity Trade and Price Trends, 1986, World Bank (1986), updated by the *1987 CRB Commodity Yearbook*, Commodity Research Board.

value for the demand elasticity of unity, then Table 5.2 shows the benefits for the commodities of Table 5.1.

The first point to note about the results is that most of the gains are quite small (and ignore the costs of achieving them—they are gross gains, not net benefits). Second, they are more sensitive to the time-period than the measures of price instability (naturally, as they involve squares of the CVs), though one should interpret this to mean that the potential benefits are measured with considerable error. Third, cost-effective storage requires some residual price variability to pay for the costs of storage, so there is a limit below which the price variability should not fall. Finally, the benefits depend on how prices are to be stabilized—about the centred moving average, or by reducing the annual fluctuations. In both cases the assumption is that storage or arbitrage is feasible—which would not be true if the commodity price followed a random walk. Without modelling the dynamics of price determination with storage, one cannot tell whether halving the price variability is remotely feasible, let alone cost-effective.

2.3. The Case for International Buffer Stocks

If the market is willing and able to arbitrage price risks by private storage, then what is the case for international buffer-stock schemes of the type advocated by UNCTAD? The standard argument for public intervention is that some market failure prevents the market achieving an efficient allocation, and that the proposed policy will on balance reduce the inefficiency.[7] If commodity markets are competitive, wherein lies the market failure? If we accept that markets are competitive and there are no macroeconomic market failures, then the failure lies in the incompleteness of the market structure. Specifically, the first theorem of welfare economics requires that all goods can be traded, where a commodity is distinguished not only by its physical characteristics, such as a Brazilian Santos 4 Unwashed Arabica, its place of delivery (New York), and its date of delivery (August 1987), but also the *state of the world* in which it is delivered, where each state of the world is a unique description of all relevant economic factors (e.g. weather in Guatemala). Clearly the market structure is not complete, and there is not a complete set of risk, insurance, or contingency markets. What does this imply for the efficiency of market equilibrium?

First, one of the main functions of markets is to provide agents with information about the value of their inputs and outputs, so that they can make efficient production decisions (even though they may not need to trade on the markets to obtain the inputs or sell the intermediate outputs). Futures markets and insurance markets reveal information about future prices and the size of various risks relevant for producers. In the absence of this information the producers may make systematic mistakes, discussed below as *misperception costs*. We can avoid this issue by assuming that agents have rational expectations, loosely, that they use the information they have efficiently and do not make avoidable or systematic mistakes (Muth 1961). Second, risk or insurance markets allow agents to avoid the risk inherent in agricultural production (and storage). If they cannot trade risk, then the costs of the unavoidable risk will be higher than if it were pooled, or shared, and transferred to those best able to bear it. At this point it can be objected that it is unreasonable to compare the market outcome with an idealized complete market world in which risks are efficiently traded, for this is to ignore the very real costs of operating insurance markets. The objection is well taken, and instead the appropriate bench-mark against which to test market outcomes is that of *constrained Pareto efficiency*. An equilibrium is constrained Pareto-efficient if there is no feasible intervention on the *existing* set of markets which could make everyone better off.

If the market structure is incomplete then the actions of the individual agents affect the risks facing other agents in ways they cannot insure against. Thus the combined decisions of large numbers of small stockholders to store will affect the price distribution and hence the risks facing producers. Consider a simple example. Suppose the demand schedule facing

---

[7] Note the qualification, for it is not enough to argue that the market fails, as public intervention might be more costly than the benefits it achieves. The Common Agricultural Policy of the EC is a pertinent example.

producers is unit-elastic, and that all producers face the same perfectly correlated risk. If there is no storage, when output is high, prices will be low but revenue and producer income will be the same as if output were low and prices high. Producers thus face no risk. Storage will reduce price fluctuations but not output variations[8] and will destabilize producer income. Risk in the absence of a complete set of insurance markets acts like a public good or externality, collectively generated by a large number of individually insignificant actions and collectively affecting a large number of agents. As with public goods and externalities, there is a presumption of market failure, and so it is the case with incomplete markets.[9] One possible case for international buffer stocks is therefore that the market undertakes too little storage, because it fails to take account of the improved risk-sharing offered by storage. This is a delicate argument, because whether the competitive market undertakes too little or too much storage hinges on such hard-to-measure features as the elasticity of the demand schedule, its degree of non-linearity, the source of the fluctuations, and the alternative risk-sharing institutions available to the participants. In any case, the size of the risk benefits from such market intervention are likely to be small, as the next section argues in more detail.

2.4. The Cost of Income Risk and the Availability of Risk-Reducing Alternatives

In a way it is odd that the producing countries have placed so much emphasis on the undesirability of *price* fluctuations, for producers are not so much interested in the price at which they sell their crop as the income they derive. Similarly, one would expect them to be more concerned with fluctuations in income rather than price. As the unit elastic demand case discussed above showed, the two are not the same. It is also worth pointing out that the surplus approach of Massell and others does not measure the costs of income risk at all, thereby totally undermining the case for policy intervention (for, as argued above, private storage will appropriate all the arbitrage gains to be had, but will not necessarily lead to an efficient allocation of risk).

We need, therefore, to be able to measure the costs of risk and the benefit of risk reduction.[10] The first obvious question to ask is how costly self-insurance is for farmers, assuming no alternative insurance possibilities are available. The standard method of measuring the cost of risk is to offer the farmer a choice between the risky wealth from farming, and a perfectly certain wealth whose value is somewhat less than the average or expected

---

[8] Assuming that supply decisions are taken before the price is known.

[9] The argument is presented more technically in Newbery and Stiglitz (1982*b*) and the analogy with public goods is taken further in Newbery (1989).

[10] This discussion follows that in Newbery (1989). See also Newbery (1987*a*).

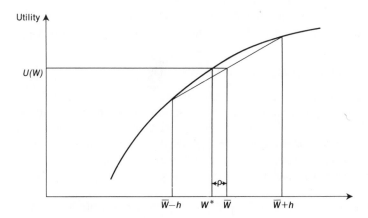

Fig. 5.2 The value of risky income

value of the risky wealth. The difference between this average value and the level of certain wealth which the farmer considers exactly as valuable is the *risk premium* associated with the risky choice, and the ratio of this premium to the certainty equivalent wealth is the proportional risk premium—a useful dimensionless measure of the relative cost of bearing the risk. Fig. 5.2 shows the risk premium ρ associated with an equal chance of receiving an amount $\bar{W} + h$ or $\bar{W} - h$. If W^* is the certainty equivalent wealth then $\rho = \bar{W} - W^*$. If $U(W)$ is the utility produced by receiving W, and $EU(W)$ is the expected utility, then ρ is equivalently defined by the equation

$$U(EW - \rho) = EU(W) = U(W^*). \tag{5.3}$$

An approximate value for ρ can be found expanding $U(W)$ as a Taylor expansion about its mean value $\bar{W}$:

$$EU(\bar{W}) \approx U(\bar{W}) + E(W - \bar{W})U'(\bar{W}) + E(W - \bar{W})^2 U''(\bar{W})/2. \tag{5.4}$$

(Primes refer to derivatives, and again E is the expectations operator.) The left-hand side of (5.3) can also be expressed as a Taylor expansion about $\bar{W}$:

$$U(\bar{W} - \rho) \approx U(\bar{W}) - \rho U'(\bar{W}). \tag{5.5}$$

Equate the right-hand sides of (5.4) and (5.5) to obtain

$$\rho \approx A \operatorname{Var}(W)/2, \tag{5.6}$$

where A is the coefficient of absolute risk aversion:

$$A = -U''(W)/U'(W). \tag{5.7}$$

The proportional risk premium $\rho/\overline{W}$ can be expressed in terms of the coefficient of relative risk aversion, R, and the coefficient of variation (CV) of W, σ:

$$\rho/\overline{W} \approx R\rho^2/2, \ R \equiv -WU''(W)/U'(W) = AW. \tag{5.8}$$

As shown, these expressions for the risk premium are approximate, with the accuracy of the approximation depending on the shape of the utility function and the nature of the risk. In certain cases these formulas are completely accurate, for example if W is normally distributed and the utility function exhibits constant absolute risk-aversion. (See Newbery and Stiglitz, 1981, ch. 6.) Equation (5.8) is the most useful as it is dimensionless.

In principle, to find the cost of risk, all we need are attitudes to risk, measured by R, and a measure of the riskiness of wealth, σ. In practice, neither is easy to measure, for two closely related reasons. First, the model discussed above is static, with a single moment of uncertainty which is resolved at the end of the period. In practice, producers face a sequence of risky outcomes. The theory can be extended to deal with intertemporal choices by noting that utility depends ultimately on the time-path of consumption, so that what we are really interested in is the variability in real consumption over time. If income fluctuates from year to year about a stable trend, then individuals could even out their consumption fluctuations by lending or borrowing. At any moment, the counterpart of the variability in wealth would be the variability of present discounted income. If successive years' incomes were statistically independent, then this variability would be very much less than that in income. The problem lies in relating the observed variability in income (or revenue, in the case of commodities) to the effect of the variability on consumption, which will depend on the degree of access to lending and borrowing, the rate of interest, the agent's expectations about future income, etc.—all hard to observe.

Second, the theory relates risk-aversion to attitudes to variations in *wealth*—i.e. present discounted income—since that is what constrains the time-path of consumption. Observations on attitudes to risk by Binswanger (1981) suggest that individuals appear to treat each risky event or lottery independently, rather than calculating the effect of a particular risky choice on the underlying riskiness of total wealth. One way of interpreting the evidence is that although individuals appear to behave in a systematic and predictable way, it is hard to believe that their behaviour reveals their underlying level of well-being according to the conventional theory of revealed preference (see Newbery and Stiglitz, 1981, ch. 7). What is therefore being measured is apparently closer to a measure of attitudes to variability in income rather than wealth, and to that extent appears more commensurate to the observed variability, that of income.

The point may be clarified as follows. Let P be the coefficient of *partial risk-aversion*, defined as $-YU''(W + Y)/U'(W + Y)$, where Y is the certainty equivalent of the risky prospect, say income over the period. Then $P = YR/(W + Y)$, where R is the normal coefficient of relative risk-aversion. Binswanger (1981) found that P was fairly stable across radically different-sized prospects (varying by a factor of 1000) and across peasants of varying wealth (CV 109 per cent). If one maintains the (untested) hypothesis that the values of the alternatives are weighted by their probabilities, then one must reject the assumption of the Expected Utility Hypothesis that prospects are valued by their impact on terminal wealth (see Quizon *et al.* 1984 for a more complete explanation). If P is a useful summary measure of risk-aversion (i.e. is moderately stable across prospects and agents), then R will be very sensitive to the size of the prospect relative to wealth, Y/W.

If, despite these reservations, we are prepared to accept the empirical evidence, then a value for P (defined over fluctuations in current income) of between 1 and 2 is defensible. The variability in the export revenue obtained from individual primary commodities by developing countries was typically between 20–25 per cent for representative countries for cocoa, coffee, cotton, jute, and rubber for the period 1951–75, (Newbery and Stiglitz, 1981, Table 20.5). The variability of an individual farmer's revenue from any one of these crops would typically be higher, since some smoothing takes place in the process of aggregation, but typically farmers receive income from more than one crop, and so their total farm revenue will be less variable than the variability of any one component. Then again, incomes will be more variable than revenue because the production costs will be less variable than revenue, but consumption will be less variable than income for the reasons set out above. As a compromise, suppose that a typical CV of income is 30 per cent. The cost of risk will be, taking a high value of $P = 2$, 9 per cent—a farmer would on this argument be indifferent between his original risky income, and a certain income 91 per cent of its average value.

Now a cost of risk of 9 per cent of average income is quite large, but it assumes that the farmer has no alternative but to bear all the risk. In practice, there are a whole variety of ways in which this cost can be reduced using existing institutions, and indeed a large part of the reason for the existence of at least some of these institutions is that their risk-reducing benefits make them cost-effective. The main point to note about the formula for the cost of risk is that the cost goes up as the square of the risk, so quite small reductions in risk have a relatively large impact on the cost. For example, if the risk is shared equally between two parties, so that each bears half the risk, then the cost to each is only one-quarter of the original cost (assuming equal degrees of risk-aversion) and the total cost of risk has been halved. Share contracts, in which the landlord receives a set fraction (frequently about one-half) of the total harvest, provides just such an example of a risk-sharing and hence cost-reducing action.

Some indirect evidence that the 9 per cent may be an overestimate comes from McCloskey's (1986) study of the medieval open-field system. He argues that the average cost of subdividing holdings into strips, as in the open field system, was about 10 per cent of the average yield of the consolidated strips (achieved after enclosure). The benefit was the considerable reduction in risk allowed by holding a portfolio of differently located strips. McCloskey calculates that the CV falls from 44 to 34.7 per cent as the number of strips increases from one to five, and the risk of disaster (famine level yields) falls from once in 9.3 years to once in 13.4 years (even allowing for the higher average return of the consolidated strip). The alternative of storing grain to reduce consumption fluctuations was even more expensive, as noted above, and so farmers were willing to pay a risk premium of 10 per cent of potential average income to reduce their risk. It seems unlikely that most producers of primary commodities would be so vulnerable to fluctuations in their receipts from the commodity, since none of the ones considered is a food crop, like the medieval grains studied by McCloskey, and hence is unlikely to constitute their sole crop.

Futures markets play a similar risk-reducing role, and are particularly relevant in the present context, for they provide a partial response to the problem of market incompleteness, just as the stock exchange also provides a partial response. Both go some way towards completing the market structure, and both can be remarkably effective at reducing the costs of incompleteness, even if they do not eliminate it. They therefore merit further (if brief) attention.

2.5. Futures markets for risk reduction

Futures markets offer price insurance, whereas agents want income insurance. In some cases the two are synonymous, for if the only source of income risk is price risk, then futures markets allow this to be insured. For example, if the only source of risk is the fluctuating demand facing the producer, and his production is completely certain, then he can sell his entire future output by means of a futures contract for a currently known and certain price. A stockholder who buys grain now to sell later in the season can hedge his purchase by an offsetting futures sale now. Farmers, however, typically face production risk as well as price risk and cannot therefore perfectly insure their income. Nevertheless, if they have access to an *unbiased* futures market (that is, one in which the futures price is an unbiased predictor of the future spot price), they may be able to reduce their income risk substantially, the exact amount depending on the elasticity of market demand and the correlation between their own output and the spot price. For example, if the elasticity of market demand is 0.5, and the CV of output is 20 per cent, and if the sole source of risk lies on the supply side, with all farmers experiencing perfectly correlated risk, then an optimal trade on an unbiased futures market will reduce the cost of risk to one-quarter of its unhedged value (Newbery and Stiglitz, 1981, p. 187, where the formulas lying behind such calculations are derived and presented). In more realistic examples, both prices and outputs are risky and imperfectly correlated, so the benefits of futures trading will be lower, but if one takes the five crops mentioned above, and examines the leading producer of each commodity to determine the relevant risk and correlation coefficients (given in Newbery and Stiglitz, 1981, Table 20.4, p. 291), then optimal trades on unbiased futures markets would reduce the cost of risk by between one-half and three-quarters. Whilst there is still considerable dispute as to whether or not futures markets are biased, the consensus appears to be that it is difficult to reject the hypothesis that the market is unbiased—if only because of the size of the underlying volatility.[11]

Another way to judge the risk-reducing effectiveness of futures markets is to compare them to the standard proposal for commodity price stabilization—that of operating a buffer stock in order to stabilize the price. Again, price stabilization is an imperfect method of reducing income risk, but because it provides price insurance (compulsory rather than optional) it is easy to compare with futures markets. The answer is clear— futures markets offer better income insurance than perfect price stabilization unless the correlation between price and output is very low (typically less than about 20 per cent—see Newbery and Stiglitz (1981), p. 187 for the formula and illustrative calculations). If the correlation is very low, then neither price stabilization nor futures markets are very helpful in reducing risk, and the relative advantage of price stabilization is very small, and almost certainly offset by various disadvantages (Newbery, 1983). Intuitively, the reason for the superiority of futures markets over price stabilization is that with a futures market the farmer is free to choose the optimal amount of harvest to hedge, whilst price stabilization gives him no choice, and may actually increase his income risk. It is also worth remarking that perfect costless price stabilization is only feasible within a single country, not at the level of the whole world, where storage costs alone make it infeasible. (Within a single country the government can operate a marketing board offering a guaranteed price, and match local supply to demand by importing or exporting. Effectively the government absorbs all the price risk. See Newbery, 1983.)

At this point it might be argued that the main benefit of a futures market is not its price insurance role, but its price discovery role, and this function

---

[11] But see Chang (1985) for a study of the grain market which relates the size and direction of the bias to whether aggregate hedging is long or short, as models of futures markets, such as Newbery (1983), would predict.

is a non-appropriable public good (Grossman and Stiglitz, 1980). This point has been mentioned above and brings us to the third microeconomic cost arising from unstable prices—that of misperception.

2.6. Costs of Misperception

Producers have to take many important investment and production decisions before the price of the final product is known. In the case of the four tree crops distinguished in Table 5.1 there may be a gestation period of several years after planting before any crop can be harvested, and the tree may continue to bear for 15–30 years thereafter. Even for annual crops like cotton and jute the planting decision is taken 5–9 months before the harvest. Suppose, as in a competitive market, that the value of the commodity is the market-clearing price at harvest. If there were no uncertainty, then efficiency in resource use would be ensured by the (competitive) producer maximizing profits given the prices of inputs and of future (alternative) outputs. But what is the appropriate bench-mark when the future output price is uncertain? It is clearly unreasonable to require the producer to forecast perfectly the price, and it is unreasonable if the post-market price turns out to be unexpectedly low to complain that the producer produced too much, or spent too much on production.

The answer is implicit in the theory of choice under uncertainty, briefly discussed above. The farmer is assumed to have beliefs about the joint probability distributions of post-harvest prices and his own output, so that he can determine the probability distribution of revenue. He then chooses inputs and the scale of operations (and perhaps decides on his futures market trades) to maximize the expected utility of wealth. If he held rational expectations about the revenue distribution, he would not make systematic or avoidable mistakes. Given the information available to him at the moment of decision, he would not be able to do any better. If, on the other hand, he held myopic expectations, always believing next year's price to be the same as last year's, then he would in general be systematically and predictably wrong. If a large number of producers acted thus, the result might be a cobweb, or an endogenously generated cyclical fluctuation in output and prices.

One of the arguments for international commodity schemes is that they might provide better information about future prices, and, since they would control or at least influence these prices in a predictable way, they would reduce the costs of myopic decision-making, or of misperceptions about market prospects. One can calculate the benefits of providing unbiased price information, at least if it is possible to describe the way in which agents make price forecasts in the absence of futures markets. I know of few explicit calculations of the likely magnitude of such gains, though Newbery and Stiglitz (1981, pp. 143–8) calculate their magnitude for an agricultural market in which initially producers make naïve forecasts. If prices in such a market are stabilized then this naïve forecasting rule will yield correct decisions, but not if the market is stochastic and output is correlated with price. The results suggest that the gains from improved information are small compared to the gains from price stabilization (which themselves are not large, as argued above). They may be only a few per cent of the stabilization gains, though they have a much larger effect on the distribution of income between producers and consumers.

Of course, this begs the question, which is what is the least-cost method of reducing misperception costs. The standard answer is that futures markets, which already exist for most primary commodities, do an excellent job of eliminating *avoidable* errors, and give agents incentives to collect market-relevant information, which is to a considerable extent revealed as they make use of it for profitable speculation. One must be rather sceptical that an international agency, motivated by complex political factors, would do such an impartial and effective job. It might be argued that small farmers do not trade on futures markets, but this does not prevent them using the published futures prices as a source of information (which is certainly very common in developed countries). In any case, there are alternative methods of disseminating information such as price forecasts—the US Department of Agriculture disseminates large quantities of information about likely levels of production of major crops, and other institutions peform similar informative roles.

3. Alleviating the Costs of Commodity Price Instability

The arbitrage benefits of price stabilization can only be realized by storage, whilst the other costs of price instability can be dealt with in a variety of ways, of which storage is often the least cost-effective. Misperception costs require better information and better decision-making on the part of agents, both of the which are facilitated by futures markets, for it is easier to judge the profitability of a crop which has already been sold forward (even if notionally) for a known price. Even if farmers cannot trade directly on futures markets, they can make forward contracts with middlemen or marketing boards, who in turn can hedge their forward contracts on futures markets. It might be argued that tree crops last for 20 years, whilst the longest futures contracts are for 24 months, and are typically for shorter periods. As far as providing information about the future, though, futures markets are not the only source, and the World Bank, amongst others, publishes long-term price forecasts. There is a case for trying to improve this information, but one must be rather sceptical about prospects of any dramatic improvement.

This leaves the costs of income risk to be dealt with, and here again futures markets can be quite effective over their admittedly limited time-horizon. Again, they are not the only solution. Income risk is costly because it leads to variations in consumption, with consequent variations in the marginal utility of consumption. The obvious remedy is to even out consumption by lending and borrowing, and, just like evening out price fluctuations by storage, the extent to which this is effective depends on the rate of interest. There is, however, one potential advantage that capital markets have over storage, for it is possible to hold negative stocks of money, i.e. to borrow. The ability to lend and borrow dramatically reduces the cost of risk—Newbery and Stiglitz (1981, pp. 201–4) show that if the income received fluctuates around a known stable level, then the cost can be reduced to approximately the rate of interest times the cost implied by matching consumption to income each year. Even if agents cannot borrow, but are able to lend and hence accumulate reserves (rather as buffer stocks cannot borrow) they can still reduce the costs of income fluctuations considerably by gradually building up a reserve of wealth upon which to call.

The existence of the credit market may explain why there is little call for futures markets stretching very far into the future. The main demand for futures trading comes from stockholders or shippers, who face very severe price risk—quite small falls in future prices lead to very dramatic decreases in their profits, which are a very small fraction of the value of the underlying stock. Since it is unusual to carry over stocks for more than 15 months or so, there is little call for more distant futures markets—and of course a stockholder can in any case construct a sequence of futures transactions to cover longer periods of storage.[12] The only demand for longer-term price insurance therefore comes from producers making investment decisions, and they can either even out their consumption fluctuations more effectively through the credit market, or they can issue shares in the plantations, or they can diversify in other ways. Given all these options, they would be willing to pay only a very small premium for the option of a longer-term futures contract, which would be insufficient to cover the costs of establishing the contract.

3.1. Institutional Alternatives to Price Stabilization

The success of futures markets in offering income insurance (and also of commodity price stabilization schemes) depends on how well income

---

[12] If the farmer sells a series of one-period futures, and if the price for a futures contract at date t (for delivery at date $t + 1$) moves closely with the spot price at t (as will typically be the case for continuously stocked commodities) then the sequence of n futures contracts will be equivalent to one n-period futures contract, abstracting from transactions costs. The thinness of distant futures markets suggests that it may even be cheaper to roll over a series of very liquid short-term futures contracts than to buy a smaller number of less liquid distant contracts. See Gilbert and Powell (1987).

fluctuations are correlated with price fluctuations. In those cases where the correlation is poor, one natural solution is to set up a domestic marketing board which attempts to stabilize revenue, rather than price. Specifically, if the normal or trend level of revenue is $\bar{R}$, and if actual production in a given year is Q, then the marketing board could set the price at $p = \bar{R}/Q$. Provided each farmer's output were reasonably well correlated with total output, this would offer income insurance. Moreover, this system of insurance is evidently attractive since it would still be in the interest of each farmer to produce the efficient level of output, as his own production would not affect the price he received. (Some systems of crop insurance guarantee a minimum return per acre, regardless of the farmer's effort. In such cases the farmer often has no incentive to care for the crop.) This proposal raises two obvious questions—if it is so attractive why don't private insurance companies offer such contracts, and second, if they don't, why don't governments offer instead? The answers are that we do observe such contracts offered by the private sector, and there are government schemes of this kind, but the schemes are vulnerable to arbitrage in some cases, and hence would not be viable.

As an example of a privately supplied income insurance scheme similar to that proposed, consider the so-called flexible cash rent contract which is beginning to appear in areas of predominant share-cropping in the US. Share contracts have already been cited as a risk-sharing and hence cost-reducing response to risk, but they appear to have the disadvantage that by not rewarding the tenant with the full value of his marginal product, he will be encouraged to slack unless carefully monitored. Share-cropping is very prevalent in the Midwest of the United States, and recently contracts have emerged in which the rent payable is determined by average yields in the local agro-climatic zone (DeBraal and Wunderlich, 1983, p. 138, and refs. there given). If the weather is bad and yields are low, then rent is low and the tenant keeps a larger amount than under a fixed-rent tenancy; conversely if conditions are good. If on the other hand the tenant is idle or incompetent, then his rent is not thereby reduced, as it would under standard share-tenancy contracts. (Though a landlord suspecting such behaviour would be unlikely to renew the contract, so there are incentives for efficiency even under traditional share-cropping.) One reason why such schemes are not more prevalent is that they require accurate, timely, public, and credible information on yields for well-defined zones, and this information is only likely to be obtained by public agencies.

As examples of a government response with almost exactly this form, both the European Community's STABEX, and the Compensatory Financing Facility of the IMF, operate by lending the shortfall on export earnings on favourable terms to commodity exporters. The main problem with the pricing aspect of the proposal is that it may give unreasonable incentives to farmers or others to store commodities when domestic output is high and hence the market board price is low.

4. Macroeconomic Costs of Price Instability

The microeconomic benefits of additional public price stabilization are small, and most of them can be achieved as well in other ways. Macro-economic disturbances are almost invariably more costly than market distortions—a shortfall in potential GDP of 5 per cent is not unusual and is arguably as costly as all the typical trade and monopoly distortions. Most microeconomic distortions are about little triangles of deadweight loss, whilst their macro counterpart of lost or forgone output is exactly what it seems.[13] The most serious defence of international commodity agreements is therefore that they reduce the macroeconomic costs of commodity price instability, and their leading proponent in the past was Kaldor (1976). Briefly, his argument was that whereas primary commodity markets cleared by price adjustments, markets in manufactured goods had sticky prices and adjusted by quantity and consequent income variations, in a Keynesian way. In addition countries were specialized, so that the develop-ing countries relied on primary commodities, whilst the developed coun-tries concentrated on manufactured exports. If commodity prices fell, then so did the incomes of the developing countries, who were then forced to reduce their imports of manufactured goods. This fall in demand for the exports of developed countries precipitated a recession—the adjustment took place not by a change in relative prices with all markets clearing, but by an income adjustment and a loss of output. If, on the other hand, com-modity prices rose (the key example here being the first oil shock), then the developed countries would be faced with an inflationary rise in import prices and deterioration in their balance of payments. They would respond by tight monetary and fiscal policy, which would again create unemploy-ment. If primary commodity prices were kept stable, then the developed countries could maintain full employment, average demand for primary commodities would be higher, their average terms of trade would be better, and the developed countries would find it profitable to pay for the full costs of running the required stabilization schemes.

Table 5.3 gives some relevant facts, and shows that, if petroleum is ex-cluded, primary commodities have fallen from over half the export value of developing countries to about one-quarter, not so very different from that

---

[13] One might claim that the increased leisure offsets, and this might be plausible if reduced employment were uniformly spread across all workers, and if the labour market cleared like the coffee market. Neither is the case, and the hidden costs of prolonged unemployment—increased morbidity and mortality, depression, crime, etc.—argue in the opposite direction.

TABLE 5.3. Shares of primary and manufactured goods in world trade, 1970–1983 (%)

	1970	1980	1983
Exports from developing countries			
Primary commodities	55.9	27.2	26.5
Petroleum	19.2	40.2	33.7
Total commodities	75.1	67.4	60.2
Manufactures	24.9	32.6	39.8
Exports from industrial market economies			
Primary commodities	22.4	19.9	18.2
Petroleum	3.5	7.4	8.6
Total commodities	25.9	27.3	26.8
Manufactures	74.1	72.7	73.2
Imports by industrial market economies			
Primary commodities	21.1	17.7	18.0
Petroleum	7.6	18.8	20.3
Total commodities	28.7	36.5	38.3
Manufactures	71.3	63.5	61.7
Imports by industrial market economies			
Primary commodities	30.3	19.8	18.8
Petroleum	9.9	27.7	22.8
Total commodities	40.2	47.5	41.6
Manufactures	59.8	52.5	58.4

Source: *Commodity Trade and Price Trends*, *1986*, World Bank (1986).

of developed countries. Oil is clearly in a category by itself, and is a major import and export for developing countries, and a large import for developed countries.

If Kaldor's argument applies at all, it is likely to apply to oil, and one could argue that the poor macroeconomic performance of the world economy since 1973 was due to the succession of oil shocks. It is certainly plausible to argue that the 1975 recession in many developed countries was caused by the counter-inflationary policies adopted after the cost-push inflation of the first oil shock. One might go further and argue that at least some of the dislocations in the 1980s resulted from the austerity programmes forced on debt-burdened developing countries whose export revenue from oil sales fell with the subsequent decline in oil prices—Mexico springs to mind here. It is possible that if oil prices had been stabilized about a sustainable real price trend[14] then neither adverse macro shock

[14] One would expect that the market-clearing price path of an exhaustible resource like oil would increase over time in real terms, reflecting its exhaustibility. See Newbery (1981).

would have occurred. It is also clear that it would have been difficult to achieve this stability, since the first shock reflected a fundamental change in market structure (from competitive to cartelized) and the subsequent price fall reflected the inconsistency of expectations about sustainable price, supply and demand levels.

The oil price shock contains a rather different message about the macro costs of price instability, and that is the difficulty of predicting the equilibrium level of prices around which to stabilize prices, or even on which to base long-run decisions. The 1974 oil price shock was widely interpreted as a fundamental change in the equilibrium price level of oil, not as a temporary departure from an existing trend. As such it required adjustment, rather than stabilization, and most of the macro costs arose from the need to restructure economies. A new branch of macroeconomics—that of the booming sector or 'Dutch Disease'—has developed in response, well expounded and illustrated in Neary and van Wijnbergen, (1986). This literature deals with the need to readjust in response either to the unexpected discovery of a natural resource like oil, or to a change in the equilibrium level of an important traded good, like oil. If an economy suddenly discovers oil, then its exports increase, displacing other manufactured exports, appreciating the real exchange rate, and requiring a shift of resources out of manufacturing into services. This process of adjustment may be painful if labour is immobile and real wages sticky, and the result may be a contraction of manufacturing, a rise in unemployment, and little corresponding expansion of the non-traded sector. The same story holds if the price of oil changes sharply *and is expected to remain at its new level*, at least for countries which are importing or exporting oil.

The main point to note is that stabilizing the price of oil is irrelevant in both cases. In the discovery case, the effect arises from a real windfall, whatever the price of oil (assuming the windfall to be sufficiently valuable). In the price shock case, the presumption is that the price is adjusting to a new equilibrium—if the price change were believed to be temporary there would be no need to restructure the economy, and conventional international borrowing and lending (which took place on a massive scale after the first oil shock) would allow economies to weather the temporary trade imbalance.[15]

Although on the face of it the lessons of the oil shocks and of the 'Dutch Disease' do not appear relevant to commodity price stabilization, I would argue that many of the macro costs of price fluctuations in developing countries arise from the difficulty of distinguishing between the needs of stabilization and of structural adjustment—in other words from the dif-

---

[15] This is not to deny that there may be an important role for strategic oil stocks to play, but their role is primarily one of countervailing cartel power, not the conventional price stabilization story.

ficulty in distinguishing between price changes which are temporary and those which are more long term, and signal some more deep-seated change in external circumstances. This may explain the problems caused by the coffee booms in East Africa, discussed below, and certainly the problems of the phosphate boom in Morocco. It is also worth pointing out that oil plays a disproportionate role in world trade. The largest non-oil primary exports (average 1981–3) from developing countries were coffee and sugar, each accounting for less than 9 per cent of the value of oil exports from developing countries. Doubling the price of oil causes a dramatically greater macroeconomic shock than doubling the price of any other primary commodity. Standard arguments of the kind illustrated above suggest that the cost of disturbances goes up as the square of the size of the disturbance, meaning that small shocks as essentially trivial. (This justifies the earlier remark that the consumer costs of 'core' commodity price instability are negligible, as they collectively account for less than 2 per cent of consumption.)

The other line of defence of the macro importance of non-oil primary commodities is that although most of the time their price fluctuations are not synchronized, so that each commodity has a small impact on the world economy, periodically, as in 1974, or 1980, prices all move together, and their collective impact is then of prime importance in precipitating a recession or depression. The problem with this argument is that if such events are infrequent and hard to predict, it will be immensely costly to store the required level of stocks to deal with them. Sharp price rises (such as the 1974 peak) can only be prevented by not stocking out, and there are serious problems of speculative attack on commodity stocks which attempt to hold down prices in the face of high demand (Salant, 1983; Newbery, 1984a). Very large stocks would be needed to deal with the price peaks. Price falls, such as those of the early 1980s, have adverse effects on the developing countries if they have to cut their import levels. There are simpler ways of dealing with such problems than buying up their exports at above market-clearing prices, and, if the political will is lacking for these alternatives, it is hard to be very enthusiastic about the prospects for the alternative buffer-stock schemes.

If the macroeconomic argument at the world level is either irrelevant or infeasible, then are there serious macroeconomic costs at the exporting country level, and if so, what can be done to alleviate them? The answer here is more positive. Individual countries are often highly dependent on single commodities for their export revenue. Ghosh *et al.* list 18 developing countries with concentration ratios above 40 per cent for a single non-oil export (Ghosh *et al.*, 1987, Table 1.7). The commodities are usually coffee, copper, or sugar. Coffee booms in Colombia (Edwards, 1986), Kenya, and Tanzania (Bevan *et al.*, forthcoming) have all been argued to have created major macroeconomic shocks, as has the phosphate boom in Morocco. The story varies, but often has the following features. A sharp increase in export prices for a major export improves the balance of payments, and often the fiscal balance, especially where the commodity is subject to an export tax, sold through a marketing board, or produced by a company subject to rent or profits taxes (as with many minerals). The government then typically increases public expenditure, and finds it difficult subsequently to reduce this expenditure once the price falls. The problem would not arise if the government made realistic estimates of its permanent income, but governments have notoriously short time-horizons, whilst future commodity prices are hard to predict. In the euphoria surrounding the success of OPEC, who would be surprised if Morocco genuinely believed that the price of phosphates was merely making a step change adjustment to its new long-run level?

The solution appears to be that adopted by Papua New Guinea, which operates a very conservative budgetary fund for smoothing government revenues from its copper and gold mines. Soon after the government renegotiated the Bougainville Copper agreement towards a resource rent tax which implied much larger fluctuations in government revenue than a system of royalties, it established a Mineral Resources Stabilization Fund. Under the rules of the Fund, the budget could only receive a level of transfer from the Fund which was sustainable in real terms for at least five years (Garnaut and Clunies Ross, 1983, p. 241).

The alternative of trying to prevent commodity prices ever experiencing sharp upward movements by holding international stocks appears to be extraordinarily inefficient by comparison. A better alternative is the IMF Compensatory Financing Facility, various IMF loans and programmes, and World Bank structural adjustment loans. Whilst the attendant austerity measures may be perceived as very bad news by the countries concerned, the message is that if the country had been more prudent in the first place the painful readjustment would have been avoided, thus providing an incentive for the country to avoid debt crises. The argument that lending and borrowing are remarkably effective methods of reducing the costs of income fluctuations continues to hold at the country level, and the costs of being put in a position in which the country cannot borrow any more are obviously high.

5.   The Management of Buffer Stocks and Commodity Agreements

The Common Fund proposed by UNCTAD in 1976 finally reached its target of two-thirds of capital subscription promised at the end of July 1987, so buffer stocks would still appear to be on the agenda, despite their apparent lack of success. What lessons does history and theory provide which might enable them to operate more successfully in the future? The question resolves into two parts—how to operate a buffer stock, and what rules should govern interventions on futures markets.

In the past most buffer stocks have defined upper and lower intervention prices, which they have defended. This 'band-width' rule may work for currencies, because the authorities can go negative in money, but this is not possible for commodities, and so one should seriously question the appropriateness of the currency model. If one asks what the optimal buffer-stock rule is, then, ignoring the impact on the distribution of risk for the moment, the answer is to mimic the competitive storage rule described above. The effect of arbitraging the spot and expected future price (or, if there is a futures market, the currently quoted futures price for future delivery) will be to choose a level of storage which depends on current supplies in a way quite different from the band-width rule. As described above, competitive arbitrage involves deciding what level of stocks to hold, and thus requires the manager to look at existing stocks as well as the current harvest. The band-width rule involves deciding what *additions* or *withdrawals* to make to the existing stocks. The effect of arbitraging prices on the size of the carry-over differs dramatically between the two rules. The key feature of the competitive rule is that only about one-half of the excess of the current supply (carry-over plus harvest) is placed in store, so that if the current harvest is equal to the critical level above which storage is profitable (which will typically be about equal to the average harvest), then only about half the current stock will be stored for a second year. This has a powerful stabilizing effect on the size of total stocks, so that there is no danger of the accumulation of commodity mountains so characteristic of the CAP. Newbery and Stiglitz (1982) found that a carefully designed band-width rule might achieve about the same degree of price stabilization as competitive storage, but because of the higher costs its net benefits were only about two-thirds as high. Anything other than a very carefully designed band-width rule (with strict upper limits on the maximum amount of stock ever carried) would achieve lower and probably negative net benefits.

The second problem with the band-width rule is that it is vulnerable to speculative attack (Salant, 1983). If the manager is committed to defend the upper price by selling from stock, then there comes a point when speculators will realize that the stock is inadequate to the task, at which point they will buy it all and then resell at a profit. The same phenomenon is familiar as a speculative run on the currency, and merely transfers profits from the buffer fund or producers to the speculators. The competitive storage rule, being profit-guided, does not suffer from this problem, for if the stockholder expects to make more profit by holding than selling, then he will not sell to defend the (indefensible) price.

There is another reason for urging buffer-stock managers to adopt something closer to the competitive rule, rather than the favoured band-width rule. As noted at the very beginning of this chapter, many core commodity markets are relatively concentrated, and can potentially be manipulated by dominant producers or cartels. If we ask how much storage a dominant producer will undertake, the answer is relatively simple, for instead of arbitraging price, as in equation (5.2), he will arbitrage marginal revenue. If the demand schedule is linear, then a monopolist will wish to undertake more stabilization than the competitive market; if of constant elasticity he will wish to undertake less. A dominant producer who does not monopolize the market will either wish to do more storage than the competitive amount, in which case he will be the sole stockholder, or he will wish to do less, in which case the arbitrage will be undertaken by competitive stockholders (Newbery, 1984b). If however, instead of confronting a competitive storage sector, the dominant producer or cartel faces a buffer stock operating a band-width rule, then the dominant producer has a greater incentive to speculate against the stock than competitive speculators, greatly restricting the extent to which the buffer stock can operate (Newbery, 1984a). Again, the competitive rule is not vulnerable to such manipulation.

Gilbert (1987), summarizing the historical experience with buffer stocks, concluded that buffer stocks were substantially more expensive than their advocates tended to suppose, and that many had suffered from underfunding (though this may of course have limited the extent to which they used resources inefficiently; see also Bhaskar *et al.*, 1978).

The other alternative is that the international commodity agency might intervene in futures markets to stabilize the price, much as McKinnon (1967) argued, The problem is exemplified by the activities of the buffer manager of the International Tin Agreement, who took very large and essentially uncovered long forward positions which did not appear on the balance sheet as futures market transactions, and which avoided the limits placed upon him by the rules of the Agreement. As a result his creditworthiness was not transparent, and the Agreement eventually went spectacularly insolvent. The conclusion drawn by Anderson and Gilbert (1988) was that it was not forward or futures trading *per se* which caused the problem, so much as forward trading in the absence of public scrutiny. The practical question is whether the gains from futures trading by buffer managers are greater than the costs, including the costs of scrutiny and ensuring compliance with the agreed rules. It is difficult to see how to avoid the costs of speculative attack if the buffer manager moves the price out of line with 'fundamentals', and it is hard to see the benefits if he merely follows these same fundamentals, unless one believes that speculative markets are prone to 'bubbles', which can be pricked by astute and far-sighted buffer managers. But this remains an open question.

Of course, it remains open to individual countries to hedge their primary exports on futures markets, though Gilbert (1987) points out that this requires access to credit to finance margin calls—and if the country had access to credit it could even out its export revenue by lending and borrowing. He suggests various instruments based on combinations of put-and-call options, which are essentially self-financing and which remove the extreme and therefore costly components of price fluctuations. Alternatively the country might issue commodity-indexed bonds, which would be cheap to service if the commodity price fell and the country was less well placed to service its debt. Indeed, the recent spate of financial innovations has highlighted the variety of specific instruments or contracts that can be designed to deal with particular types of risk. Perhaps the major role for public policy lies in policing these security markets, collecting the information needed for them to operate at low cost, and validating the credit-worthiness of developing countries, so that they are free to trade in the instruments.

References

Anderson, R. W., and Gilbert, C. L. (1988). 'Commodity agreements and commodity markets: lessons from Tin', *Economic Journal*, 98 (Mar.), pp. 1–15.

Bevan, D. L., Collier, P., and Gunning, J. W. (forthcoming), *Trade Shocks in Controlled Economies*, Oxford: OUP World Bank.

Bhaskar, K. N., Gilbert, C. L., and Perlman, R. A. (1978), 'Stabilization of the international copper market: a simulation study', *Resources Policy*, 4, pp. 13–24.

Binswanger, H. P. (1981), 'Attitudes towards risk: theoretical implications of an experiment in rural India', *Economic Journal*, 91 (Dec.), pp. 867–90.

Chang, E. C. (1985), 'Returns to speculators and the theory of normal backwardation', *Journal of Finance*, 40 (Mar.).

DeBraal, J. P., and Wunderlich, G. (1983), *Rents and Rental Practices in U.S. Agriculture*, Farm Foundation and Economic Research Service (US Department of Agriculture).

Edwards, S. (1986), 'A commodity export boom and the real exchange rate: the money-inflation link', in Neary and van Wijnbergen (1986), ch. 7.

Garnaut, R., and Clunies Ross, A. (1983), *Taxation of Mineral Rents* (Oxford: Clarendon Press).

Ghosh, S., Gilbert, C. L., and Hughes Hallett, A. J. (1987), *Stabilizing Speculative Commodity Markets* (Oxford: Clarendon Press).

Gilbert, C. L., and Powell, A. (1987), 'The management of developing country commodity risks: a new role for public policy', (Oxford Institute of Economics and Statistics, presented to the Academic Panel of the Bank of England, 13 July 1987), mimeo.

Gordon-Ashworth, F. (1984), *International Commodity Control* (Beckenham: Croom Helm).

Grossman, S., and Stiglitz, J. E. (1980), 'On the impossibility of informationally efficient markets', *American Economic Review*, 70, pp. 393–409.

Kaldor, N. (1976), 'Inflation and recession in the world economy', *Economic Journal*, 86, pp. 703–14.

Little, I. M. D. (1982), *Economic Development—Theory, Policy, and International Relations* (New York: Basic Books).

McCloskey, D. N. (1986), 'The Open Fields of England: Rent, Risk, and the Rate of Interest, 1300–1815' (Univ. of Iowa, presented at the AEA meeting, Dec. 1986), mimeo.

McCloskey, D. N., and Nash, J. (1984), 'Corn at Interest: the Extent and Cost of Grain Storage in Medieval England', *American Economic Review*, 74, pp. 174–88.

McKinnon, R. I. (1967), 'Futures markets, buffer stocks and income stability for primary producers', *Journal of Political Economy*, 75, pp. 844–61.

Massell, B. F., (1969), 'Price Stabilization and Welfare', *Quarterly Journal of Economics*, 83, pp. 284–98.

——(1970), 'Some Welfare Implications of International Price Stabilization', *Journal of Political Economy*, 78, pp. 404–17.

Muth, John (1961), 'Rational Expectations and the Theory of Price Movements', *Econometrica*, 29 (July), pp. 315–35.

Neary, J. P., and van Wijnbergen S. (1986), *Natural Resources and the Macroeconomy* (Oxford: Blackwell for Centre of Economic Policy Research).

Newbery, D. M. G. (1981), 'Oil Prices, Cartels and the Problem of Dynamic Inconsistency', *Economic Journal*, 91 (Sept.), pp. 617–46.

——(1983), 'Futures Trading, Risk Reduction and Price Stabilization', in M. E. Streit (ed.), *Futures Markets* (Oxford: Blackwell), ch. 9, pp. 211–35.

——(1984a), 'Commodity Price Stabilization in Imperfectly Competitive Markets', in G. G. Storey, A. Schmitz, and A. H. Sarris (eds.) *International Agricultural Trade* (Boulder: Westview), ch. 11, pp. 261–84.

——(1984b), 'Commodity Price Stabilization in Imperfect or Cartelized Markets', *Econometrica*, 52 (May), pp. 563–78.

——(1987a), 'Agricultural Institutions for Insurance and Stabilization', mimeo, Cambridge, 15 May; forthcoming, in P. Bardhan (ed.), *The Economic Theory of Agrarian Institutions*, (Oxford: OUP).

——(1989), 'Missing Markets, Consequences and Remedies', mimeo, Cambridge, 15 May; in F. H. Hahn (ed.), *The Economic Theory of Information, Games, and Missing Markets* (Oxford: OUP).

——and Stiglitz, J.E. (1981), *The Theory of Commodity Price Stabilization* (Oxford: OUP).

——(1982a), 'Optimal Commodity Stock-Piling Rules', *Oxford Economic Papers*, 34/3, pp. 403–27.

——(1982b), 'The Choice of Techniques and the Optimality of Market Equilibrium with Rational Expectations', *Journal of Political Economy*, 90/2, pp. 223–46.

Quizon, J. B., Binswanger, H. P., and Machina, M. J. (1984), 'Attitudes toward risk: further remarks', *Economic Journal*, 94 (Mar.), pp. 144–8.

Salant, S. W. (1983), 'The vulnerability of price stabilization schemes to speculative attack', *Journal of Political Economy*, 91, pp. 1–38.

World Bank (1986), *Commodity Trade and Price Trends*, 1986 (Baltimore: Johns Hopkins Univ. Press for World Bank).

6

The Pursuit of Industrial Growth:
Policy Initiatives and Economic Consequences

JOHN M. PAGE, JR.

1. The Pursuit of Industrial Growth

During the period following the Second World War rapid industrialization was viewed as a prerequisite for modernization and structural change in most, if not all, developing countries. The huge differences in the role and importance of industry in developing countries, as opposed to its place in advanced economies, was seen as, perhaps, the principal manifestation of economic backwardness and colonial dependence. Kwame Nkrumah, for example, wrote:

Industry rather than agriculture is the means by which rapid improvement in Africa's living standards is possible. There are, however, imperial specialists and apologists who urge the developing countries to concentrate on agriculture and to leave industrialization for some later time when their populations are well fed. The world's economic development, however, shows that is is only with advanced industrialization that it has been possible to raise the nutritional level of the people by raising their levels of income (Nkrumah, 1963).

A major objective of development strategy was, therefore, to accelerate the process of industrial growth in order to increase the share of industrial output to 15–20 per cent of national income, levels comparable with those of Europe and North America. Industrial policy in the developing countries primarily consisted of government interventions designed to achieve rapid expansion of manufacturing industry, both directly through public investment and the allocation of credit and indirectly through incentives for private industrial investment.

The legacy of colonial rule had left many politicians and economists in the developing countries with a profound suspicion of the ability of markets to generate sufficient levels of industrial investment and to allocate it to priority sectors. Decentralized economic decisions were regarded as likely to perpetuate both a pre-modern productive structure and an unde-

My intellectual debt to Kemal Dervis and Mieko Nishimizu is apparent from both the empirical results and the policy analyses offered in this chapter. I am grateful to Barbara Mierau for providing her unpublished data on Chile. The views and interpretations in this chapter are strictly those of the author and should not be attributed to the World Bank, to any of its affiliated organizations, or to any individual acting on their behalf.

sirable distribution of income. These factors gave rise to a major emphasis on economic planning and the role of the state in guiding industrial growth. Between 1940 and 1965, 77 of the 90 low- and middle-income countries published one or more development plans, most of which set targets for industrial investment and output growth and many of which attempted to guide the sectoral composition of industrial output.

In the pursuit of industrial growth public authorities used three principal instruments to accelerate and guide the growth of industry—trade and regulatory regimes designed to shield industrial producers from competition, directed allocation of subsidized credit through the commercial and development banking system, and direct public investment in industrial activities. Government interventions in the trade policy regime created the opportunity for profitable industrial investments largely by creating noncontested domestic markets through restrictions on international trade, and then by limiting entry through industrial licensing in order to regulate the size, timing, composition, and location of investments. Attempts to balance the interests of consumers with the promotion of industrial investments frequently took the form of producer price controls, intended to limit the extent to which the potential rents inherent in the quota regime were actually realized.

A key characteristic of industrial investment, as opposed for example to traditional commerce or agriculture, was the potential to generate high returns from longer gestation projects. Thus, an important challenge for public policy during the initial phase of industrialization was to encourage long-term investments. In most developing economies, however, lack of experience, political instability, and the rudimentary nature of financial markets militated against long-term investments. Domestic term financing needs of industry were often met by directing that the commercial banks allocate a portion of their loan portfolio to specific types of borrowers and activities. Given the high dependence of investment on imported capital goods, there was a basic need for long-term foreign exchange credit, and it was to overcome this obstacle that special industrial development banks (development finance companies) were established in a wide range of countries. Coupled with regulations which restricted interest rates below market-clearing levels, these 'directed credit' mechanisms became powerful instruments for affecting the allocation of investments within the industrial sector.

Public ownership of the industrial sector expanded rapidly in many developing countries in the 1950s and 1960s. In the low-income countries of Africa the rapid expansion of the public sector reflected a widespread view of the need for the state to act as entrepreneur. Public authorities regarded it as unlikely that indigenous entrepreneurs would respond with sufficient vigour to the opportunities for industrial investment created by even a highly protective trade regime. In the absence of state investment, it was argued, industrial development would remain in the hands of foreign investors.

In much of Asia and Latin America, however, there was little concern over lack of entrepreneurship. Public enterprises were seen more conventionally as a mechanism for guiding investment into key sectors (usually intermediate and capital goods) in which private investment was regarded as insufficient or undesirable. In other sectors, across a wide range of countries, public ownership was regarded as a mechanism for balancing the interests of consumers with the desire for expanded industrial production by moderating the impact of import restrictions on prices. Thus in sectors with economies of scale public enterprises were often granted domestic monopolies and prohibition of imports, coupled with administrative limits on output prices.

2. Investment, Productivity Change, and Industrial Growth

On the supply side economic growth is determined by the rate of expansion of productive inputs and by the efficiency with which inputs are combined and utilized—total factor productivity change. The early industrialization efforts of the developing economies focused primarily on mobilization of resources for industry (primarily through increased investment) with little attention directed toward improvements in productivity. In part this was due to models of economic growth in which productivity change was treated as a predetermined variable. And in part it was due to the absence of empirial evidence on the magnitude of rates of productivity change and its role in the development process.

Over the past 15 years a substantial body of literature has accumulated at the macro level about the relative contributions of total factor productivity (TFP) change and factor input growth to economic growth in a number of countries. Chenery and his associates recently pulled together these estimates for 30 economies, 18 developed, and 12 developing countries (Chenery, 1986). They found that, broadly, economies can be classified into three groups distinguished by the rate of TFP growth and by the relative contribution of TFP change to growth of value added. The developed countries other than Japan are characterized by low rates of both factor accumulation (labour and capital) and TFP growth, but the latter accounts for about one-half or more of GDP growth. Chenery's group of 'typical developing economies' exhibits somewhat faster growth rates of both factor inputs and TFP than the developed economies, but TFP change accounts for less than 20 per cent of output growth. The third group— rapidly growing middle-income economies, including Hong Kong, Israel, Taiwan, Korea, Spain, and Japan (which passed from middle income to developed during the period under evaluation)—had very rapid rates of factor input, TFP, and GDP growth. As in the case of the 'typical developing economies', however, TFP growth played a relatively less prominant role in output growth than in the developed countries.

Nishimizu and Page have recently assembled data on factor input, TFP, and total output growth for industrial activities at the ISIC two-digit level for eighteen countries (14 LDCs) (Nishimizu and Page, 1987). The estimation period varies from country to country but falls within the years 1956 to 1982, the period of early industrial development for the LDCs, and the measurement methodologies are reasonably comparable among countries. These results provide a first survey of the productivity and growth performance of the industrial sector in developing countries, and are summarized in Fig. 6.1. This figure shows the relationship between TFP growth and total factor input growth in a graph in which the 45°- lines provide the level of total output growth. The three rays from the origin show the combinations of TFP growth and total factor input growth that give the share of TFP growth indicated.

For the industrial sector as a whole in these economies productivity change contributed between 10 and 30 per cent to total output growth; although Yugoslavia's share was below 10 per cent and in three countries— India, the Philippines, and Zambia—average total factor productivity growth, and hence its contribution to output growth, in industry was negative. More rapid rates of output growth appear to be associated, as in Chenery's macroeconomic data, with a lower relative contribution of TFP growth to output growth. Among the developing countries in the sample, Hungary, Chile, Argentina, and Egypt combined relatively low rates of industrial growth with TFP contributions in the range of 20–30 per cent. Korea was the only LDC which combined both a high share of TFP growth with a high rate of output growth.

The authors' analysis of the variance in rates of productivity change among industries and countries reveals several significant phenomena. As income per capita rises, differentials in TFP growth rates among individual (two-digit) industries decrease markedly.[1] And, although significant inter-country variations in productivity performance arise within well-defined industries, sharing a largely common technology and rate of technological change, differences among industry-specific rates of TFP growth are not significant within individual countries.[2] In short there is greater variability

[1] There is a significant positive rank correlation between level of per capita income and the standard deviation of productivity distributions within the industrial sectors of countries in the sample.

[2] A two-way analysis of variance among countries and industries indicates that while it is not possible to reject the hypothesis that all industrial TFP growth rates are drawn from the same distribution within each country it is possible to reject the hypothesis that country-specific TFP growth rates are drawn from the same distribution within each industry.

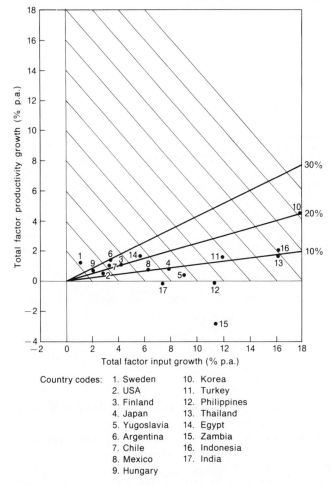

Fig. 6.1 Relationship between total factor productivity growth and total factor input growth by country

among countries in TFP performance than among industries within individual economies.

An obvious explanation for these inter-country variations in industrial TFP change rests on the infant industry argument. Infant industry considerations should imply that average TFP growth rates for industry decline as industrial development proceeds, thus facilitating the process of catching up by less industrially developed countries. Fig 6.2 summarizes this relationship for countries in the Nishimizu and Page sample by plotting the averge annual rate of TFP growth in the industrial sector of each country against its per capita income. The most striking feature of the figure is the

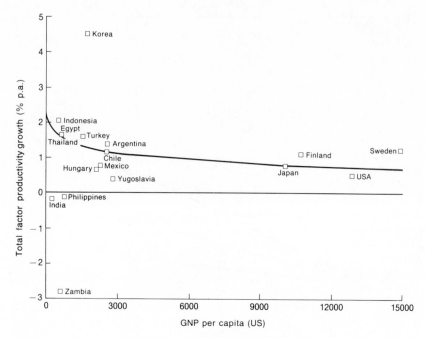

Fig. 6.2   Relationship between total factor productivity growth and GNP per capita

extreme difference in variance between the TFP performance of the four high-income countries and all others.

In the industrially advanced economies the rate of TFP growth appears to be on the order of 1 per cent per year and independent of the level of per capita income. It is more difficult to find regularities among developing countries. In the income range up to $3,000 per capita the relationship may be curvelinear with low-income countries associated with low or negative rates of industrial productivity change and with the middle-income countries showing higher rates of TFP change on average than the advanced industrial economies. No significant statistical relationship exists, however, between income and productivity growth for the sample as a whole.

Strictly interpreted, these results suggest that the infant industry argument may have little or no empirical validity. The industrial sector as a whole in the developing countries of the sample did not experience more rapid rates of productivity change than those of the developed economies. The presence in the sample of three economies in which industrial productivity change was on average negative during the period provides a problem for the interpretation of the data, however. It is unlikely that these negative rates of productivity growth can be interpreted as reflecting underlying patterns of structural change.[3] If these three outlying countries are excluded, a significant statistical relationship emerges relating rising per capita incomes to declining rates of industrial productivity change. This relationship is shown by the dashed line in the figure and indicates a decline of approximately 2 percentage points in the average rate of industrial TFP growth as incomes rise from $300 to $10,000 per capita. Similar results are recorded in a wide range of individual industries, both when negative observations are included and excluded. There is thus some support here for the infant industry argument.

The empirical findings of both Chenery and Nishimizu and Page seem to indiciate that productivity growth and factor accumulation play different roles in mature, industrialized economies from those in developing countries. For developed countries the rate of productivity change appears to approximate the long-run rate of technlogical change. Its relative contribution to growth is substantial, and there is surprisingly little inter-country and inter-industry variation in productivity performance. In the developing countries, on the other hand, substantially higher TFP growth rates are observed, accompanied by very large inter-industry and inter-country variability. TFP change provides a smaller relative contribution to total output growth in virtually all industrializing countries and in several it actually appears to have reduced the rate of output growth.

Differences in productivity performance between LDCs and developed economies taken as groups undoubtedly reflect aspects of the process of structural transformation. In well-functioning market economies differentials in levels and rates of productivity change tend to be minimized by the movement of resources out of lagging into leading industries. In economies at earlier stages of market development, however, productivity differentials can persist due to rigidities in factor mobility. The higher rates of productivity change encountered in the LDCs, both on average and for individual industries, reflect the realization of productivity gains arising from mastery of technology (gains in technical efficiency) added on to the gains from technical change.[4]

Within the group of developing countries, however, the extreme variability of both average and industry-specific rates of productivity change—as well as in their relative contributions to total output growth—point to policy-based as opposed to structural explanations (although measurement error may also be part of the explanation). Patterns of industrial output growth based primarily on factor accumulation have been characterized as extensive growth, while those based on a balance of accu-

[3] Industrial growth in the presence of rising real unit costs of production is sustainable only under policy regimes which countervail international market signals.

[4] Westphal (1982) presents a thorough discussion of technological mastery in developing countries. Nishimizu and Page (1982) provide an analytical framework integrating total factor productivity change, technical progress, and technical efficiency.

mulation and productivity change have been termed intensive. Both highly intensive and extensive growth patterns are observed among the developing countries, which strongly suggests that policies designed to promote industrial growth through rapid factor accumulation may have affected productivity performance, and, hence, altered both the rate and costs of industrial growth.

3.   Industrial Policy 1950–1980: Competition, Financial Repression, Public Investment, and the Costs of Extensive Growth

Since the main avenues for rapid industrial growth available to the newly industrializing countries were believed to be processing primary materials for export and producing local substitutes for imported manufactures, trade policy quicky emerged as a powerful instrument of industrial policy. During the first phase of industrialization the entire industrial sector was treated as an infant. High protective barriers to international competition were created by means of tariffs, quantitative trade restrictions, and exchange rate management, and relatively little attention was given to the costs of generalized protection. In the developing world industrial and trade policies became, for the most part, synonomous.[5]

The infant industry argument, which had successfully guided trade policy in the United States and Japan in the nineteenth century was applied to the industrial sector as a whole. The costs of industrial promotion, when considered, were assessed primarily within the framework of the orthodox applied welfare economics of trade policy and industrial organization. Comparative static analyses of the welfare costs of protection and regulation invariably resulted in very modest estimates of the allocative costs of industrial policy interventions, and led to a certain complacency about allocative inefficiency.[6] Implicitly policy-makers traded off the static costs of protection against the expected dynamic gains to be derived from infant industry development, and the judgement within the LDCs was clearly in favour of the latter. This is not altogether surprising in that there was almost no formal attention in the economic literature to the possibility that policy interventions could result in changes in total factor productivity and hence changes in the position of the marginal cost curve as well as in movements along it.[7]

---

[5] A tendency reinforced when Little *et al.* chose to title their seminal book *Industry and Trade in Some Developing Countries*.

[6] For a review of partial equilibrium measures of allocative inefficiency see Leamer and Stern (1970), ch. 8.

[7] This type of economic behaviour has come to be called 'rent-seeking'. Two distinct literatures have evolved in this field. Tollison (1987) reviews the literature as applied to developed countries. Examples from the development literature include Krueger (1974), Bhagwati *et al.* (1984), and Martin and Page (1983).

Starting in the mid 1960s a number of countries emerged from the first phase of industrialization, and their situation changed significantly. In countries such as Brazil, Mexico, Turkey, India, and Korea the size and degree of diversification of the industrial sector made it difficult to consider the industrial sector as a whole as an infant industry. Yet numerous studies carried out in the 1970s demonstrated the excessive and highly variable levels of protection from external competition afforded to industry by tariff barriers to trade in most developing countries. On the basis of these studies, it was shown that many existing industrial activities were in fact receiving negative protection while others received very high levels of implicit subsidies through the price system. The eagerness to encourage industrial investments in the earlier (and easier) stages of import substituion had led to disincentives affecting the development of intermediate and capital goods, and, most importantly, the development of exports. Domestic resource cost methodologies documented the significant cost penalties, relative to international prices (lack of international competitiveness), of the investments associated with these protection regimes.[8]

More recently studies of the dynamic costs of protection regimes in developing countries have indicated that the instruments by which protection from international competition is·afforded to domestic industries can affect productivity performance and, hence, international competitiveness, quite apart from the levels of protection granted.[9] The most consistent and significant of these results relate to the role of quantitative import restrictions in reducing levels of industrial efficiency. Quantitative restrictions on imports break the link between international and domestic relative prices and insulate domestic producers from movements in international prices. Because changes in international prices convey substantial information on productivity trends in the rest of the world, instruments that interfere with the transmission of these prices can make the productivity performance of competitors irrelevant and lead to deteriorations in international competitiveness over time.

Although there was almost general agreement on the desirability of shielding domestic industry from foreign competition, there was considerably greater variation in the approaches adopted by LDC governments toward regulating activity within the protected industrial sector. In many countries industrial licensing mechanisms, often called industrial development acts or investment codes, set out the terms and conditions for entry

---

[8] Three important contributions to the literature summarize these results: Little *et al.* (1970), Krueger (1978), and Balassa *et al.* (1982).

[9] For a formal discussion of the relationship between total factor productivity change and international competitiveness see Nishimizu and Page (1986). Studies of the relationship between the instruments of protection and rates of TFP change in industry include: Nishimizu and Page (1987), Samaniego (1988), and Mierau (1987).

into a wide range of industrial markets. The great majority of these acts were regulatory in spirit, vesting in the public sector substantial discretion over the ability of individual private producers to compete with established industrial firms.

Recent adaptations of the theory of contestable markets to industrial policy analysis in the LDCs has resulted in a new view of the linkage between international trade and domestic market structure and to renewed focus on the efficacy of competition in promoting cost discipline and productivity change.[10] The fundamental contribution of this literature is to focus attention on the degree to which markets are contestable by potential new entrants, rather than on the existing market structure. One basic prediction of contestable market models is that exposure to international competition dilutes the market power of domestic producers, affecting their production and pricing decisions accordingly (see e.g. Krugman, 1986). Another is that in sectors characterized by economies of scale protection can lead to excessive entry by inefficiently small producers, increasing unit costs despite an apparently competitive domestic market structure (Dixit and Norman (1980) summarize these and other results).

These arguments do not, however, diminish the relevance of domestic market structures for industrial performance, given the trade policy environment. It is often the case that contestable markets are absent from economies in which non-market allocation of resources dominates in the form of planning and/or market regulation. Since it is the contestability of a market, whether via domestic or international competitors, which provides the pressure on producers to carry out sustained efforts to improve productivity and product quality, domestic regulatory regimes have demonstrated many of the same negative impacts on industrial performance as highly distorted trade policies, and have therefore tended to reinforce their effects.[11]

Empirical work on the structure of LDC financial markets undertaken in the 1970s and early 1980s began to demonstrate the costs in terms of resource allocation of the directed credit and forced investment systems which many countries had established to channel investments into the industrial sector.[12] These mechanisms which operated primarily through mandating volume targets and interest rates for industrial lending by the banking system and/or through the rediscounting of commercial lending at subsidized interest rates, tended to supplant the development of term-

[10] For surveys of the literature on contestable markets as applied to LDCs see Kessides (1984), Caves (1985), or Krugman (1986).

[11] A recent series of World Bank 'Sector Studies' of industrial regulation and planning in such diverse economies as Hungary, Mexico, Argentina, and Turkey yield similar results with respect to the negative influence of policy-induced barriers to entry on industrial performance.

[12] The seminal work these issues is probably McKinnon (1973). A recent survey of financial market development in LDCs is contained in Virmani (1982).

financing mechanisms which would have been more responsive to market forces. Frequently the adverse effects of directed credit instruments on the development of term financing were reinforced by tax legislation which favoured debt over equity financing of investments.[13]

Theoretically, it is possible for the managers of a directed credit system to 'simulate the market' by channelling resources from low-productivity to high-productivity sectors in response to calculations of economic rates of return. In practice the directed credit systems—including the development banking systems—established in many financially repressed economies constituted an additional barrier to entry into industrial activities and inhibited efficient reallocation of resources in response to changing patterns of comparative advantage. In short in most LDCs the financial systems developed to support industrial development tended to reinforce the anti-competitive characteristics of the trade and domestic regulatory policy framework.

In the developing countries publicy owned enterprises account for a much greater percentage of industrial value added than in industrially advanced economies (see Dervis and Page, 1984). Recently institutional and empirical arguments have been advanced to support the view that levels of industrial efficiency could be improved by increasing the share of private ownership in the industrial sector.[14] There is not unanimity, however, on the relationship between ownership *per se* and industrial performance. Rather, it appears that the policy environment within which publicly owned firms are constrained to operate and the nature of their management structures and internal incentives may have more to do with their performance relative to private enterprises than ownership of their assets (see e.g. Levy, 1981, and Svejnar and Hariga, 1987 for econometric evidence).

Taken together, the three major policy instruments used by most developing countries in the pursuit of industrial growth during the period 1950 to 1980—limitations on competition (including trade policies), financial repression, and public investment—meant that industrial policy in the developing countries tended to foster a process of extensive growth. Rapid growth of industrial output was achieved in many countries at the expense of improvements in industrial efficiency with the consequence that the greater variability of industrial productivity growth rates observed in the LDCs arose largely from variations in their policy environments.

4. Industrial Policy in the 1980s: Changing Views

Recognition of the costs of extensive industrial growth and a reorientation of industrial policies in many developing countries during the 1980s arose primarily from the need for economy-wide adjustment to a series of major

---

[13] A recent survey of tax regimes in LDCs is contained in Lechor (1985).
[14] Aharoni (1986) provides a survey of this literature.

shocks that plagued the LDCs during the decade. The adverse impact on external balances of deteriorations in the terms of trade and in export demand during the 1970s were mitigated to some extent by expanded foreign borrowing by LDC governments late in the decade. But, rising real interest rates, coupled with continuing declines in the debt-service capacity of many economies due to deteriorating international competitiveness, culminated by the mid 1980s in what has come to be called the LDC 'debt crisis'.

Adjustment to the debt burden by most countries has involved attempts to combine programmes to reduce absoption with efforts to increase production through the realization of improvements in the efficiency of resource use; in short, attempts at 'stabilization with growth'. In terms of industrial policy, these efforts have primarily been focused in four areas—the promotion of industrial exports, measures to increase industrial competition, industrial restructuring, and privatization.

The size and diversity of the industrial sector in many middle-income countries, and the successful performance of a number of (primarily Asian) industrial exporters, resulted in a fundamental shift in perspective on the role of trade policy in industrial development in most developing countries: policies favouring world-market orientation and export promotion were no longer viewed as inimical to industrial development. Being 'pro-export' no longer means being 'anti-industry', and a consensus appears to be emerging that there is a need to correct the extreme anti-export bias in the industrial incentive structure. It is increasingly accepted that that semi-industrial economies should emphasize rapid development of manufactured exports in their basic development strategies.

In many countries initial efforts at industrial export promotion have attempted to compensate exporters for the impact of tariffs and other distortions which have resulted in the anti-export bias of the incentive structure. The most pervasive of these mechanisms is the creation of 'free trade status' for exporters by use of free trade zones, duty drawbacks, or temporary admissions schemes to permit duty-free import of intermediate goods for export production.

There is a danger, however, that pro-export policies can be taken too far, particularly in the absence of more fundamental changes in the structure of incentives. Financial market interventions which provide subsidized credit for term and working capital finance of exporters have achieved widespread popularity, and in some cases one suspects that these measures have reached the point at which the structure of incentives favours excessive expansion of exports. An important check on the ability of policy-makers to pursue these measures arises, however, from the threat of foreign retaliation.

There is less consensus among the developing countries on the need to pursue aggressive reforms to increase the level of competitive pressure faced by existing domestic industry. Powerful vested interests, including many foreign investors who entered heavily protected markets in the LDCs, can mobilize substantial political support to maintain their insulated positions. Nevertheless a number of middle-income countries, including Chile, Turkey, Mexico, and more recently Hungary, as well as such low-income countries as Ghana and Bolivia, have made efforts to foster greater competition through replacement of quantitative import restrictions with tariffs, reductions in domestic industrial regulation, and fewer restrictions on foreign investment.

In many low-income countries, however, considerable sympathy remains for generalized protection of the 'infant' industrial sector. And in some semi-industrialized countries, industrial policy continues to favour interventions to support the growth of basic or heavy industry through favourable treatment of producer goods sectors. This kind of attitude has traditionally had strong support in countries such as Hungary, India, Pakistan, Turkey, and Egypt. Finally, a number of countries have found it politically so difficult to reduce barriers to competition that little has changed in the domestic or international incentive regime, despite efforts at macroeconomic adjustment. Among the most prominant of these economies are Argentina, Brazil, Colombia, and Venezuela.

Reflecting these developments the debate on industrial policy in the developing countries is moving somewhat closer to that found in the industrialized economies. There are now 'sunset' industries in the more mature semi-industrialized economies. The steel industry, petrochemicals, and shipbuilding have been hard hit by the rise in energy costs and slow growth of international markets. Textiles, clothing, and footwear face growing competition from other LDC producers. And in countries pursuing changes in the incentive structure designed to increase international competitive pressure and reduce anti-export bias, there are calls from producer interests for 'adjustment assistance'. The need for restructuring and retrenchment which characterizes large segments of industry in the industrial nations is present in many of the more advanced semi-industrial economies.

Industrial restructuring can be thought of as the process of reallocating resources according to changing competitive conditions and improving cost competitiveness through productivity change. Put in this way, however, it appears that industrial restructuring seeks to accomplish two objectives that should be part of the natural process of industrialization. The need for specific government actions to accomplish these objectives arises in the LDCs from three phenomena.

First, the reorientation of industrial policy toward a more outward-orientated, competitive economic environment for firms implies a significant change in relative prices and market contestability. This presents a form of moral hazard for producers who had made their prior investment decisions on the basis of a different policy framework. Where producer interests are strongly represented in the political process their claims for assistance in meeting the new environment may derail policy reform if not met by concerted government action. Second, financial markets in the LDCs do not have great experience in evaluating many of the types of intangible investments required to improve productivity at the enterprise level, and in repressed financial systems the market will not readily provide credit for such innovations. Third, investments in knowledge, including product and process innovations, are notoriously difficult to appropriate fully at the enterprise level. Thus, externalities may lead to underinvestment in restructuring efforts even in well-functioning financial systems.

In general, industrial restructuring programmes, as initiated in such middle-income countries as Turkey and Mexico, have involved a combination of reforms in the policy environment, designed to promote competitive behaviour by firms and enhance cost discipline, with firm- and product-specific studies to provide information to both industry and the financial markets on viable programmes of market penetration, product upgrading, plant organization, and technological innovation or mastery. These efforts have generally been accompanied by credit and equity finance programmes to facilitate the development of merchant banking services and the financial restructuring of firms.

Reducing the direct role of the state in the process of industrial development is generally viewed in terms of limiting the extent of future public investment in the industrial sector and gradually privatizing existing assets. The financial performance of many public enterprises in most of the countries in which the public sector plays a major role has deteriorated to the point at which they are a constant source of dissaving for the consolidated public sector. The poor financial performance of these firms often has its origins in the widespread control of such basic economic decisions as pricing, employment practices, and production mix by the central government. Bureaucratic control with lack of corresponding management autonomy and incentives also plays a role. Moreover despite the rather sketchy and contradictory evidence available, there is widespread dissatisfaction with the economic performance of public industrial firms.

Efforts at privatization have only succeeded in raising levels of economic performance where price, quantity, and employment controls were eliminated concurrently. When this has failed to occur, private investors have not been forthcoming to take up the assets offered, or the agreements reached have included substantial elements of implicit subsidies which, while reducing the direct financial burden on the government, have not improved economic performance.

5. Directions for the Future

It is difficult to enumerate the elements of an appropriate industrial policy framework to apply to all developing countries. The interests and needs of the low-income countries are quite different from those of middle-income countries in the process of structural adjustment, and their needs in turn differ substantially from those of the highly successful developing industrial exporters. There are, however, a few common themes that cut across the spectrum of income levels and macroeconomic constraints.

First, there remains a critical need in most LDCs to take a comprehensive view of the industrial incentive regime in terms of its impact on market contestability and competition. The current policy environment in many countries contains a multitude of often contradictory interventions arising from the *ad hoc* manner in which incentives and controls were adopted and from the often contradictory objectives that were associated with industrial policy formulation. Notwithstanding the substantial body of literature on the topic, in most developing countries the net effect of the structure of incentives on domestic relative prices and competitive behaviour is still only imperfectly understood. The need to correct irrational and often contradictory incentives in order to promote both external and domestic competition and to moderate anti-export bias remains the first item on the industrial policy agenda.

Second, there is a critical need to focus attention on reform of the financial sector and on the development of viable capital markets. The recent history of adjustment efforts in Latin America uniformly shows the significant role played by the financial sector in facilitating or inhibiting structural adjustment in the industrial sector.[15] In repressed financial systems, resources do not move easily in response to changing market signals or economic performance, and high real interest rates in the uncontrolled segments of the capital market often have exceeded the social marginal product of capital. In many economies the precarious financial position of the banking system has led to disintermediation and a substantial increase in the spreads between lending and borrowing interest rates.[16]

Financial sector reforms should encompass both improvements in banking supervision and prudential regulation and progressive deregulation of the credit market. Removal of interest rate ceilings on deposits and loans as well as dismantling of the forced investment and directed credit systems are priority areas for policy action. Successful efforts and financial reforms have been undertaken in such disparate economies as Ghana, Bolivia, Argentina, and Ecuador, but much remains to be done.

[15] For a country case-study see Swanson and Tybout (1987).
[16] Extreme examples occur in Argentina and Bolivia where the *spreads* of banking institutions have in recent years exceeded the economic rate of return of most industrial investments.

Third, further efforts are required to achieve effective implementation of initiatives to restructure private industry and to privatize or reform the public industrial sector. If the policy interventions causing distortions are removed, economic agents will respond to the change in market price signals in two distinct and contradictory ways. Where rent-seeking behaviour is encouraged by the political process, efforts will be directed at reestablishing rent-generating policy regimes. These efforts will make no contribution to improvements in the efficiency of resource use nor in structural changes in the manufacturing sector, and if successful, will result in a resumption of the extensive pattern of industrial growth. Where rent-seeking is unlikely to be successful, producers will be forced to restructure their existing operations, seek new market opportunities afforded by the reformed policy regime, and/or exit the market.

Efforts are therefore required to provide policy-makers with a range of options which reduce the scope for rent-seeking and recidivism. Well-designed industrial restructuring programmes can provide both the incentives and the means to avoid a return to the protected, high-cost industrial development patterns of the past. There is a need therefore to proceed concurrently with broadly based trade and industrial policy reform and with industry-specific programmes to facilitate adjustment.

References

Aharoni, Y. (1986), *The Evolution and Management of State-Owned Enterprises* (Cambridge, Mass.: Ballinger).

Balassa, Bela *et al.* (1982), *Development Strategies in Semi-Industrialized Countries* (Baltimore: Johns Hopkins Univ. Press).

Bhagwati, Jagdish, Brecher, R. A., and Srinivasan, T. N. (1984), 'DUP Activities and Economic Theory' in D. C. Colander (ed.), *Neo Classical Political Economy* (Cambridge, Mass.: Ballinger).

Caves, Richard (1985), 'International Trade and Industrial Organization: Problems Solved and Unsolved', *European Economic Review*, 28.

Chenery, Hollis B. (1986), 'Growth and Transformation', in H. Chenery, S. Robinson and M. Syrquin (eds.), *Industrialization and Growth: A Comparative Study* (London: OUP).

Dervis, Kemal, and Page, Jr., John M. (1984), 'Industrial Policy in Developing Countries', *Journal of Comparative Economics*, 8.

Dixit, Avinash, and Norman, Victor, (1980), *Theory of International Trade: A Dual General Equilibrium Approach* (New York: CUP).

Kessides, Ionis (1984), 'Industrial Organization and International Trade: Some Recent Developments' (Washington, DC: World Bank), mimeo.

Krueger, Anne O. (1974), 'The Political Economy of the Rent Seeking Society', *American Economic Review*, 64.

——. (1978), *Foreign Trade Regimes and Economic Development: Liberalization Attempts and Consequences* (New York: NBER).

Krugman, Paul (1986), 'Industrial Organization and International Trade, *NBER Working Paper*, 1957 (New York: NBER).

Leamer, Edward E., and Stern, Robert M. (1970), *Quantitative International Economics* (Boston, Mass: Allyn & Bacon).

Lechor, Chad (1985), 'Tax Incentives for Industrial Development: An International Comparison' (Washington, DC: World Bank: Industry Department), mimeo.

Levy, Victor (1981), 'On Estimating Efficiency Differentials between Public and Private Sectors in a Developing Economy—Iraq', *Journal of Comparative Economics*, 5.

Little, I. M. D., Scitovsky, Tibor, and Scott, M. FG. (1970), *Industry and Trade in Some Developing Countries* (Oxford: OUP).

Martin, John P., and Page, Jr. John M. (1983), 'The Impact of Subsidies on X-efficiency in LDC Industry: Theory and an Empirical Test', *Review of Economics and Statistics*, 55.

Mierau, Barbara (1987), 'Trade Regimes and Productivity Performance: The Case of the Chilean Manufacturing Sector' (Washington, DC: World Bank), mimeo.

McKinnon, Ronald I. (1973), *Money and Capital in Economic Development* (Washington, DC: Brookings Institution).

Nishimizu, Mieko, and Page, Jr. John M. (1982), 'Total Factor Productivity Growth, Technological Progress, and Technical Efficiency Change: Dimensions of Productivity Change in Yugoslavia, 1965–1978', *Economic Journal*, 92.

——(1986), 'Productivity Change and Dynamic Comparative Advantage', *Review of Economics and Statistics*, 68.

——(1987), 'Economic Policies and Productivity Change in Industry: An International Comparison' (Washington, DC: World Bank), mimeo.

Nkrumah, Kwame (1963), *Africa Must Unite* (New York: International Publishers).

Samaniego, Ricardo (1988), 'Protection and Productivity Change in Mexican Industry' (Mexico, DF: Instituto Technologico Autonomo de Mexico), mimeo.

Svejnar, Jan, and Hariga, Moncer (1987), 'Public vs. Private Ownership, Export Orientation and Enterprise Productivity in a Developing Economy: Evidence from Tunisia', paper presented at the Northeast Universities Development Consortium Conference, Boston University.

Swanson, Eric, and Tybout, James (1987) 'Industrial Bankruptcy Determinants in Argentina' (Washington, DC: World Bank), mimeo.

Tollison, Robert D. (1987), 'Unresolved Issues in the Theory of Rent Seeking', (Fairfax: George Mason University), mimeo.

Virmani, Arvid (1982), *The Nature of Credit Markets in the Developing Countries*, *Staff Working Paper*, 524 (Washington, DC: World Bank).

Westphal, Larry (1982), 'Fostering Technological Mastery by means of Selective Infant Industry Promotion', in M. Syrquin and S. Teitel (eds.), *Trade, Stability, Technology and Equity in Latin America* (New York: Academic Press).

7

Vision and Reality of Public Sector Management: The Indian Experience

SUDHIR MULJI

1. Background: The Post-War Story

By the end of the Second World War, the belief that poor countries would have to depend upon state-owned enterprises for rapid development was more widely held than one would now care to admit. Although Bhagwati and Desai (1970, p. 127) argue that 'the phenomenal growth of the public sector in India during the three Plans is to be attributed largely to the 'socialist', ideological goals which the Indian National Congress embraced as early as the 1930s and to the leadership of Jawaharlal Nehru during the period of recent planning', it is unlikely that state enterprises would have received quite as much support if there had not been strong economic arguments for establishing them. General collectivist ideas apart, the notion of semi-autonomous corporations acting for the common weal had already met with academic approval. This after all was the age of Keynes, and as early as 1913 he had pleaded, in the teeth of considerable local opposition, for a state-owned central bank for India. In regard to England, at first, he was content to observe the evolutionary trends. He believed that the Bank of England had already been socialized. On the occasion of the centenary of Walter Bagehot's birth, Keynes wrote:

In point of law and history the Bank is a private institution worked for the profit of its shareholders like any other joint stock company. . . . It was Bagehot who first insisted that by force of circumstances, whether we like it or not, the Bank of England had become a national institution with national responsibilities, and could no longer function with primary regard to the profits of its shareholders. . . .

Bagehot's view has long prevailed, but even now we sometimes speak in the old way. Labour politicians demand the nationalisation of the Bank of England; Dr Leaf predicts that appalling disasters would ensue from such an act. They both waste their words. Bagehot nationalised the Bank of England fifty years ago. We may differ about what our monetary policy ought to be, but whatever it is, the Bank of England stands as an instrument of incomparable power to carry it out (Keynes, 1926a, p. 467).

This chapter would not have seen the light of day without Maurice Scott's persistent encouragement. I am grateful to him for ensuring that I used this opportunity for honouring Ian Little, a friend whom I greatly admire. The reader must thank, as I do, my wife's careful editing; without it the English would have been incomprehensible. I have greatly profited from Skidelsky's article on Keynes's political legacy.

Nor was the Bank unique as a private institution responsive to public needs; he found

more interesting than [the great Corporations] is the trend of joint stock institutions, when they have reached a certain age and size, to approximate to the status of public corporations rather than that of individualistic private enterprise. . . When this stage is reached, the general stability and reputation of the institution are more considered by the management than the maximum profit for the shareholders. The shareholders must be satisfied by conventionally adequate dividends; but once this is secured the direct interest of the management often consists in avoiding criticism from the public and from the customers of the concern (Keynes, 1926*b*, p. 289).

Keynes clearly approved of these developments. Earlier he had written in *The Times*

So far from wishing to diminish the authority of the Bank of England, I regard that great institution as a heaven-sent gift, ideally suited to the instrument of reform I advocate. We have here a semi-independent Corporation within the state, with immense prestige and historical traditions, not (in fact) working for private profit, with no interest whatever except the public good, yet detached from the wayward influences of politics. . . The Bank of England is a type of that socialism of the future which is in accord with the British instincts of Government and which—perhaps one may hope—our Commonwealth is evolving within its womb. The universities are another example of the semi-independent institutions divested of private interest I have in mind. The state is generally sterile and creates little. New forms and modes spring from the fruitful minds of individuals. But when a Corporation devised by private resources has reached a certain age and a certain size, it socialises itself or falls into decay (Keynes, 1925, p. 347).

Keynes's advocacy of large socialized corporations was in no way ideological. His own experience with the stock markets had made him aware of the fickle nature of the investing public. Over the years he was to be increasingly concerned with the divergence between a short-term outlook which made for success or failure in the markets and the longer-term vision required to ensure a steady flow of investment. His ideas gradually grew more revolutionary. By 1933 he was seriously concerned with the limitations of private enterprise.

In matters of economic detail, as distinct from central controls, I am in favour of retaining as much private judgement and initative and enterprise as possible. But I have become convinced that the retention of the structure of private enterprise is incompatible with that degree of material well-being to which our technical advancement entitles us, unless the rate of interest falls to a much lower figure than is likely to come about by natural forces operating on the old lines (Keynes, 1933, p. 240).

Later still, he concluded that the rate of interest could not be forced down sufficiently, and the the government would need to intervene directly. In the *General Theory*, therefore, he was anticipating a future when the state which he thought was

in a position to calculate the marginal efficiency of capital goods on long views and on the basis of the general social advantage [would take] a greater responsibility for directly organising investment; since it seems likely that the fluctuations in the market estimation of the marginal efficiency of different types of capital . . . will be too great to be offset by practicable changes in the rate of interest (Keynes, 1936, p. 164).

Now Keynes could not have seriously thought that the state was more capable of calculating the marginal efficiency of capital goods than were private investors. He was after all experienced in the ways of government and no doubt had a clear perception of the limited sagacity in these matters of those in authority. Keynes's main concern was that the risk associated with market fluctuations would, from time to time, frighten the private investor away with a consequent drop in output and employment. The fall in employment would be so damaging socially that the private sector could not survive. Besides, the loss in output was wasteful. Esoteric phrases, like 'the marginal efficiency of capital', were no doubt thrown in to soothe his economist colleagues; but his real message to the politicians—or at least what they understood it to be—was as Crossman said:

'Let us start by recalling Keynes's picture. The way he proposed to deal with mass unemployment was to dig a very deep shaft, bury millions of bank-notes at the bottom of it and then pay wages to workers for digging the bank-notes out again. There, he said, is the simple method of resolving the inherent contradictions of capitalism. Whether the work is socially useful or socially useless is of secondary importance: what matters is the provision of work' (Crossman, 1956, p. 60).

This message, powerful as it was in the developed world, was heady stuff in poorer countries. If the level of national income could be raised by the level of investment, and if the specifics of investment were not very important, the solution was self-evident. The state should undertake massive projects and all the rest would follow. Naturally it would be more sensible to undertake socially useful investment, but *any* ordering of priorities would yield fruitful results.

If Keynesian ideas had been revolutionary in the 1930s, they were surely conventional wisdom by the 1950s. It would have been an unusual leader of a developing country who could have withstood such a convergence of ideas for state initiative. The general trend of collectivist philosophy had made it socially desirable; it was now seen as economically correct, and in a poor country it was likely to prove politically popular.

Of course there is no necessary connection between using state initiative to raise the level of investment and investing through state-owned enterprises; it is equally possible to create conditions for stimulating investment in the private sector. But unlike developed nations, developing countries did not have large socialized joint-stock institutions that had grown to a size where the management could be relied upon to act for the public good. On the contrary, within the private sector in India, 'a large number of flagrant abuses in the promotion, management and financing of companies came to light in the late forties' (Hazari, 1964, p. 199).

In an investigation carried out by Justice Vivian Bose into the affairs of the Dalmia Jain group, the financial irregularities[1] discovered were such as to suggest to the public that, far from socializing their joint-stock companies as these grew, Indian businessmen were systematically milching them for private gains. Although this was a sweeping generalization it has to be admitted that the Indian private sector simply failed to command a sufficient degree of respect to justify control over large publicly financed investments.

In order to complete the picture it is necessary to understand Nehru's formative thinking on the role of planning. He had at an early stage been deeply influenced by the Soviet Five-Year Plans. In his letters he extolled the First Soviet Plan in the following words:

This Five-Year Plan has been drawn up after the most careful thought and investigation. The whole country has been surveyed by scientists and engineers; numerous experts had discussed the problem of fitting in one part of the programme into another. For the real difficulty comes in this fitting in. There was not much point in having a huge factory if the raw material for it was lacking; and even when raw material was available, it had to be brought to the factory. So the problem of transport had to be tackled and railways built, and railways required coal so coal mines had to be worked. The factory itself wanted power for its working. To supply it with this power, electricity was produced. . . . These are but a few instances of the amazing complexity of the problems raised by the Five-Year Plan. A single mistake would have far reaching results; a weak or backward link in the chain of activity would delay or stop a whole series. But Russia had one great advantage over the capitalist countries. Under capitalism all these activities are left to individual initiative and chance, and owing to competition there is a waste of effort. There is no coordination between different producers or different sets of workers, except the chance coordination which arises in the buyers and sellers coming to the same market (Silverman, 1972, p. 37).

I have quoted extensively from Nehru's letter because it seems to me that this was the primary vision that inspired his economic thinking. Three ideas are particularly significant: first, the importance of fitting things together where a single mistake would have far-reaching results. Second, that in capitalist countries co-ordination came about only by chance; and,

---

[1] 'Financial irregularities' increasingly excite the imagination of the public. It is therefore interesting to note that Keynes, at least publicly, praised Ivan Kreuger as a genius (*CW*, xxi, p. 39), but that may have been before his financial irregularities were discovered. For a romantic view of the need for financial irregularities see Neville Shute's beautiful novel *Ruined City*.

finally, that competition led to a waste of effort. To Nehru and many who thought similarly the whole business of development had to be planned; leaving it to chance was unscientific and irrational. Everything had to be thought out so that different parts fitted in one to another like pieces of some gigantic jigsaw puzzle which could be assembled by an ordered and scientific mind. An essential feature of this mode of thinking was that certain crucial areas—the commanding heights—had to be under direct control of the government; one could not afford to allow a weak link in the chain or any uncertainty that could delay or stop a whole series. Were these ideas part of a socialist ideology, or simply an engineer's way of looking at development? Certainly Professor Bauer—a severe critic of Indian planning—wrote disapprovingly of the engineering or military arguments for the priorities of the Second Plan (Bauer, 1961, p. 60), but that only begs the question of the relevance of non-economic arguments in development planning.

2. The Second Five-Year Plan

In the mid-1950s India was in the throes of preparing the Second Plan, generally regarded as reflecting 'a major watershed in India's economic thinking' (Chakravarty, 1987); and the basic notions were quite clear; as Professor Bauer pointed out at the time, 'the suggestion that the growth of income depends very largely on investment expenditure underlies much of the Second Indian Plan' (Bauer, 1961, p. 41).

The priorities of the Plan were explicitly stated in the 'Second Five-Year Plan' as follows:

The expansion of the iron and steel industry has obviously the highest priority since, more than any other industrial product, the levels of production in these materials determine the tempo of progress of the economy as a whole.

. . . Heavy engineering industries are a natural corollary of iron and steel works. The high priority accorded to them arises both on this account and from the fact that they will provide from within the country a wide range of industrial machinery and capital equipment such as locomotives for railways and power plants for the generation of electricity. . . . [they] have to be generally strengthened for undertaking such tasks as the construction of steel plants, fertilizer factories etc. In this context the creation of basic facilities such as the establishment of heavy foundries, forges and structural shops is absolutely necessary (Bauer, 1961, p. 45).

The similarity between this set of priorities and those of the First Russian Plan encouraged economists to describe this as a Soviet-type plan. For example Andrew Shonfield, economic correspondent of the *Observer* said: 'It is a Soviet-type plan. I do not use that label in any pejorative sense, but simply to indicate that it is a heavy-industry plan . . . the consumer gets a very small look-in. Within the total set aside for industrial investment dur-

ing the five-year period rather more than half goes to steel alone . . . '
(Bauer, 1961, p. 106).

Yet the author might equally have described it as a Japanese-type Plan.
India and the Soviet Union were not the only countries to found their
development on heavy industries. Trezise and Suzuki, while in general
denying the influence of the Japanese Government in industrial planning,
do admit 'In the early postwar period, the emphasis was naturally on the
basic industries: coal, fertiliser, steel and electric power—along with shipbuilding' (Trezise, 1976, p. 794).

It was not merely during the post-war reconstruction that Japan concentrated first on basic industries. Professor Minami attributes the acceleration in Japanese growth rates between 1877 and 1938 to the development
of heavy and chemical industries, and he goes further to argue that Britain
missed an opportunity by failing to switch to this group of industries when
her textiles faced competition. He draws the following conclusion:

Finally, we must say a little about the relationship between growth of heavy and
chemical industries and economic growth. On the one hand, the increase in these
industries' output accounted for a large part of the increase in GNP. Also they
stimulated growth in other industries; their 'forward and backward linkage effects'
were large relative to other industries. The growth of the iron and steel industry,
for example, increased the demand for iron ore, coal and electric power—
backward linkage, and facilitated the development of the automobile industry by
supplying products it needed—forward linkage (Minami, 1986, p. 137).

Now there is nothing in all this to suggest that what was right for Japan was
necessarily right for India. If, however, it was 'natural' for Japan without
any raw materials to place emphasis on basic industries, it surely could not
be so very unnatural for India or Russia with their large coal and ore reserves to do the same thing.

It is fashionable now to decry the particular mix of industries chosen by
Indian planners, but at the time most economists, and many were con-
sulted, did not think the choice wrong. Ian Little, for example, described
the 'broad strategy of Indian planned development' as 'eminently sound'.
(Little 1960). Even in retrospect it is difficult to disagree with this judgement; the Japanese would certainly argue that if they without any natural
resources could make a success of their steel industry, India with her raw
materials should have been able to produce steel at economic prices. The
fault lay not in the design but in the execution.[2]

---

[2] I do not wish to imply that India might not have done better with other priorities, only
that the ones chosen were not ideological but seemed quite sensible. Nowadays economists
have increasingly suggested that governments of developing countries should have devoted
their energies to agriculture rather than industry. It is salutary to remember therefore that
that is precisely what Russia has done recently without much success. In general, economists
pay too much attention to choice rather than execution and organization.

It is now 30 years since the inception of India's Second Plan; the document has been frequently analysed and criticized. With the clarity of hindsight, the flaws are self-evident; but at the time the story was entirely different. It is difficult to convey the sense of excitement and anticipation that the Second Plan brought. In a speech at Sholapur in 1953 Nehru had said 'Wait for another ten years and you will see that our plans will change the picture of the country so completely that the world will be amazed' (Gopal, 1979, p. 200).

Enthusiasm was not confined to politicians; Nehru's biographer Professor Gopal tells us 'A wise and experienced, if committed, observer wrote that the Second Plan papers and estimates constituted one of the most important documents in the world at that time.' He then quotes from Haldane's letter to Mahalanobis, the architect of the Second Plan:

Even if one is pessimistic, and allows a 15 per cent chance of failure through interference by the United States (via Pakistan or otherwise), a 10 per cent chance of interference by the Soviet Union and China, a 20 per cent chance of interference by civil service traditionalism and political obstruction, and a 5 per cent chance of interference by Hindu traditionalism, that leaves a 50 per cent chance for a success which will alter the whole history of the world (Gopal, 1979, p. 305).

Nor was it only great men who felt the excitement; in 1956 this writer was an undergraduate at Christ Church, a college less famed for its intellectual qualities than for its political maturity; for an Indian at university in England Nehru had already then become a hero for projecting India into world affairs. India had achieved a voice in the affairs of nations that no one could have anticipated at the time of independence. Now it seemed that the Second Plan was to be the other part of her process of catching up with the world.

But, if India's development depended upon the Plan, the Plan's success seemed to depend upon the public sector. When contrasting Soviet Plans with economic planning in capitalist countries Stalin had said 'Our Plans are not forecasts, nor guesses. They are instructions' (Kornai, 1959, p. 199). Nehru may not have used the language of Stalin but in conception the Second Five-Year Plan was nothing more than a set of instructions to the rest of the government and if these instructions failed to be implemented the Plan would fail. To carry them out there had to be some organization responsible for doing so. The private sector could not be depended upon; for though this could be prevented from doing things it could not be commanded to perform. If Plans were to be implemented there had to be a public sector subservient to the needs of the state. This was like a builder's preference for possessing essential tools; to the planners the public sector was a way of showing their craftsmanship in constructing an edifice of their design.

The late Shri L. K. Jha, a pupil in his university days at Cambridge of Keynes, Robertson, and Pigou, describes the mood of the time in the following words:

It was in the spirit of high adventure and profound confidence following independence that India embarked upon the programme of planned development to lift the economy out of centuries of backwardness. . . . The Planning Commission tried to provide plans larger than resources. . . . On the other hand, individual ministers, dissatisfied with the sectoral targets allocated to them by the Planning Commission, often tried to outstrip them.

The execution of public sector projects was undertaken in a lavish way, with much emphasis on increasing investment and enlarging capacity and little regard for the demands of their products and ultimate profitability (Jha, 1980, p. 7).

This early background to the modern Indian public sector was to have a profound effect upon its subsequent development. Firstly, it meant that notions of profits and prices were not strictly relevant; investment through the public sector was part of a grand design where the sole concentration was on production in quantitative terms. Secondly, autonomy of public corporations was necessarily restricted by the Plan. Of course certain operational decisions were left to individual enterprises, but in the wider context of what the public sector was expected to produce there was no freedom at all. Typically a heavy-engineering plant was not expected to plan its capacity on what the management of the corporation thought it could reasonably make and sell, but on what was expected of it by the Plan. These priorities were determined within the Planning Commission and were then passed on through the administrative ministries to individual organizations.

Finally, special mention must be made of the notion of competition. In an earlier passage we have seen that Nehru considered competition wasteful; he thought that individual planning without co-ordination must result in a squandering of resources; in the private sector, enterprises attempted to 'overreach or get the better of other individual concerns. Naturally this results in the very opposite of planning; it means excess and want side by side' (Silverman, 1972, p. 38).

Competition was apparently seen as the very antithesis of planning; and this way of thinking was implemented by a policy of restricting both private and foreign competition through industrial licensing and import control. The operational part of the plans consisted of setting targets for industrial capacity of each product, and the government ensured that these were not exceeded by sometimes penalizing the use of even existing capacity. Thus an economic situation was created 'where the possibility of competition from potential entry by domestic or foreign rivals was minimised' (Bhagwati, 1970, p. 272).

This state of affairs had particularly unfortunate consequences for the measurement of efficiency in the public sector. Ever since Adam Smith, classical economics had recognized the role of competition as a regulator of prices which in turn determined profits and thus provided a gauge for judging the efficiency of enterprises. These notions of classical economics had been so severely mauled that profits were no longer seen as a reliable guide for efficiency; but if this conventional mechanism was inoperable the government would have to rely upon other instruments to ensure accountability on the part of public sector managers.

3. Economic Efficiency and Project Selection

Ian Little was associated with many of these developments on the Indian scene, both as an observer and an adviser. He was one of the foreign economists to participate in the economic debates that took place within the Planning Commission at the time when the Second Plan had encountered difficulties and the Third Plan was being formulated. His interaction with Pitamber Pant, the head of the Perspective Planning Division, gave him a rare insight into the thinking and objectives of Indian planners. His associations with the Ford Foundation and later the World Bank gave him a unique opportunity to look at and understand the problems associated with assessing public sector performance; it was in studying these practical problems that he became aware of the real difficulties public sector managers faced when domestic prices and actual profits provided no guide to economic costs and benefits.

In 1965 he presented a paper suggesting the use of border prices for the valuation of inputs and outputs for public sector project selection in India. Subsequently with Tibor Scitovsky and Maurice Scott he explored problems faced by developing countries in the field of industrialization and trade particularly when prices were distorted; together they suggested macro-policies that could be adopted to reconcile social and actual prices. From an Indian point of view it is perhaps unfortunate that their conclusions led to the recognition that foreign trade had been neglected; this diverted attention to trade policies, although the methodology had equally important implications for the central problem of industrial efficiency. Later still, Ian Little returned to his original problem of finding methods for selecting investment projects; with Jim Mirrlees he constructed a set of rules for planners enabling them to reconcile social objectives in the selection of projects. But from the outset in 1965 he had emphatically warned 'that nothing which has been said. . . has anything to do with how projects should be run, and how their performance should be evaluated after they are chosen. . . in practice the management has to work with actual prices. . . the only practicable and economically sound general instruction to management is to maximize profits' (Little, 1965, p. 257). This simple maxim of Ian Little's was never accepted; instead the chimera of economic efficiency was endlessly pursued.

4. The Efficiency of the Public Sector

At first glance there seemed very little reason to suppose that, in socialist countries, where governments have substantial powers over the economy, public enterprises would have difficulties in achieving economic efficiency. Yet, as we look at the public sectors of different countries of the world, the one remarkable common feature is that nowhere have they been considered an outstanding success, neither in developing countries nor in developed, and if the present debate for *perestroika* and *glasnost* reflects a crisis of economic management in the Soviet Union, it suggests a degree of disenchantment even in socialist countries with the workings of state-owned enterprises.

The general criticism is that public sectors are not only financially unprofitable but also that they fail to meet the production criteria expected of them. The reasons for this apparent failure seem to vary from country to country; sympathetic critics have frequently complained that the type of industry that the public sector is asked to run is by its very nature likely to be a loss-maker; but such arguments cannot apply to countries where all the means of production are in the hands of the state. In a recent book on the *Economics of Perestroika*, the Chief Economic Adviser to Gorbachev, Abel Aganbegyan, writes that even when all the required resources have been made available many Soviet plants are unable to meet even the most ordinary requirements of its citizens. He gives an interesting example of the problem:

In 1987 the Soviet Union may exceed the 800 million mark in shoe production, i.e. 3.2 pairs per person per year. In Czechoslovakia 1.7 pairs per person suffices. In the USA where the population is little greater than USSR only 300 million pairs of shoes are produced and that has been sufficient. But in the USSR 800 million pairs were not enough, and we still purchased a large quantity of footwear. . . . All this footwear is being produced, but the quality is poor and having bought these shoes people are not satisfied and seek new ones. As soon as modern fashionable shoes come into the shops queues form, while poor quality shoes sit on the shelves swelling stocks. This applies to many other products (Aganbegyan, 1988, p. 37).

If, in overcentralized economies, the public sector is accused of a certain woodenness in management, in efficient market economies the problem apparently lies elsewhere. In Japan for example, Masu Uekusa tells us:

NTT (Nihon Telephone and Telegraph), JNR (Japan National Railways) and JM (Japan Monopoly Corporation) became Public Corporations to improve managerial efficiency. Initially the organisational change appeared to have been a success

but inefficiency has since become apparent. This results not only from their monopolistic positions (particularly NTT and JM) but also several other causes.

First strong intervention by the Diet has weakened these corporations' decision-
making autonomy and sapped their competence and volition to improve managerial efficiency. Second excessive or unreasonable Diet requests to corporations
(for instance to construct many local railroads in spite of predicted losses) have
eliminated cost-reduction incentives and led in JNR's case to huge financial losses.
Third, inappropriate prices established through pork barrel politics in the Diet and
lack of specialised understanding in the Diet of the fair return principle . . . has
generated managerial and allocative inefficiency. Finally, since many regulatory
authorities participate in public regulation, it is difficult to identify where the final
regulatory responsibility resides. These problems exist in every form of public
enterprise [and he might well have added 'all over the world'] (Uekusa, 1987, p.
508).

Clearly the problem of the public sector is not one of resources or demand but of the system within which they operate. It is not surprising
therefore that modern defenders of state-owned enterprises no longer
claim efficiency as the justification for their expansion. Mrs Gandhi wrote
in a preface to the Fourth Plan 'socialism involves a reordering of society
on rational and equitable basis, it can only be achieved by assigning an
expanding role to the public sector' (Chandy, 1986, p. 1.17). Now the
reordering of society through the public sector may be a desirable, indeed a
dominant, goal but it is a far cry from Tawney's vision of a professional
class motivated, not by money, but by *esprit de corps*, being able to bring
about a very much more efficient organization of scarce resources.

Efficiency is not everything; developing countries have many critics who
make this point very forcefully. In a recent article on 'Relevance of the
Public Sector in India', K. T. Chandy a distinguished ex-public sector chief
writes:

Protagonists of the capitalist approach to development argue that the industrial transformation of the country, the modernisation of her industry, and the
strengthening of her economic base . . . did not require the creation of a public
sector . . . and that such enterprises are intrinsically weak and would wilt in the
long run, because of the style of functioning of any Government.

They say that the examples of South Korea, Taiwan and Japan in the post-war
period prove this point. . . . The founding fathers of our democratic polity did not
subscribe to these views. Their evaluation of the historical experience of our epoch,
their assessment of the complexities of the domestic situation in the vast land mass
that is India, their determination to overcome mass poverty in the shortest possible
time, and their values derived from the freedom struggle, led them to adopt what
was termed by them as a socialistic approach. They were as much concerned with
the long term goals, in regard to the type of society to be built, as with the type of
instrumentalities to be fashioned. . . . in fact, their concept was that the spirit in-
spiring and determining the structure and performance of such instrumentalities as
the public sector should be derived from long term goals (Chandy, 1986, p. 1.16).

Mr Chandy's point is not entirely clear. Are we being told that eventually in the long run the Indian public sector will prove to have been economically more efficient? Or is the argument that, even though it is never likely to be a successful instrument for industrial development, it is nevertheless desirable? Perhaps the answer to these questions should not be sought, but certainly the earlier planners believed, not merely that the public sector would lead to socialist transformation, but also that modern industries would *per se* be more efficient than older ones, and thus their ownership would at the very least be profitable thereby increasing the flow of resources to the state.

In an article published in the *New Age* in 1957 Professor Mahalanobis summarized this point of view as follows: 'The rapid development of modern industries in the public sector gave the Chinese Government a dominant position in the national economy, ensured adequate and increasing flow of resources out of the profits of the State enterprises, and placed Government in a strong position to make rapid advance with Socialist transformation' (Bauer, 1961, p. 110) No one would wish to claim that the concept of profits was at all central to India's Plans, but equally it would be absurd to deny that an expectation of a surplus generated by the public sector was implicit in the process of planning. The industries chosen for public investment may have had a longer gestation period, but it was not anticipated that they were long-term loss-makers. In any event no sector, public or private, can retain support in the face of continuous losses. At some point in time the budgetary strains of financing these deficits and investments gather such momentum that governments are forced to look for alternatives; in developed countries a widely adopted solution has been to privatize nationalized industries. One reason for these policies being well received has been their dramatic effect on government funds; selling the family silver has at least helped balance the books; but for carrying out these policies an alternative ideology has to be acceptable.

In socialist or developing countries so radical a change has limited possibilities; in general the following comment by one of India's most powerful ex-bureaucrats, P. N. Haksar, still reflects the accepted wisdom. In an introduction to a collection of papers on the public sector published in 1986 he writes:

So there is much to debate about. However what is not debatable is the issue of Self-Reliance and the primacy of development strategies which palpably reinforce self-reliance and our Independence. Viewed in this light, whatever may be the abstract charms of efficiency of the market-place, Indian economic development cannot take place without a powerful intervention of the State. Public Sector, therefore, is an inescapable necessity and must be safe-guarded against the virus of the newly imported disease of 'privatisation' as advocated by the World Bank on the one hand and some eminent economists both indigenous and foreign on the other (Nigam, 1986, preface).

Yet the threat from this virus floating in the air has heightened the debate about the future of the public sector. As is the way of governments, various committees have been set up to examine the problem, the two most recent being the Jha Committee and the Arjun Sen Gupta Committee. Committee after committee and report after report have revolved round problems of management; the central issues have turned upon a discussion of two words: 'autonomy' and 'accountability'. Public sector managers claim that they cannot be made accountable unless they have sufficient autonomy, while their opponents argue that the sector has been molly-coddled and has not been subjected to the normal disciplines of industry. Although arguments on each side are unending, the essentials can be very briefly summarized.

5. The Control of the Public Sector

In any society where industry is owned by the state there will inevitably be a degree of interference from the bureaucracy and its political masters. We have already noted the consequences of parliamentary intervention in Uekusa's description of the problems of the Japanese public sector, but from their conception it has always been assumed that state-owned enterprises must be accountable to Parliament. Richard Crossman explains the general argument in the following passage:

The political and moral case for Socialism . . . was formulated in its classic form by Professor R. H. Tawney. He showed that Parliamentary democracy will only become a fully effective guarantor of individual freedom when it is combined with social control of economic power. Power, he argued, always degenerates into privilege when those who hold it are accountable to no one but themselves. In a democracy, therefore, those who own or manage the means of production must be made responsible to a popularly elected Government, and the most effective way to do this is to substitute public for private ownership of large-scale industries. Tawney's case for Socialism was not that it is easier to work than the Acquisitive Society but that it is morally superior—and politically essential to the realisation of freedom (Crossman, 1956, p. 63).

Now this case for socialist organization of industry is very different from, indeed diametrically opposed to, the Keynesian notion of self-regulating socialized public corporations and joint stock companies. As early as 1927, in a talk to the Liberal Summer School, Keynes made the point that two-thirds of the capital of large-scale undertakings had been invested in socialized or semi-socialized organizations like docks, railways, charity commissions, and building societies. His subsequent comments were reported in the *Manchester Guardian* as follows:

Mr Keynes considered next how the existing public concerns might be overhauled and set in order. He thought that Cabinet Ministers should have as little as possible to do with these concerns, whose gigantic operations should be kept separate from the state budget . . . Public Enterprises, so far as their organisation and management were concerned, might take a leaf out of the book of the private concern.

He advocated the running of these public services, national and local, by boards . . . . chosen solely for their business capacity. . . . and, in that way the advantages of public ownership and responsibility would be combined with the technical methods of management which private enterprise had evolved as the most efficient for large-scale affairs. The board should be as free from daily interference as the normal board of directors was (Keynes, 1927, p. 696).

Keynes thought the case for public ownership rested upon the divergence between private and social profits and not upon the control of companies. *That* problem was being adequately resolved by the separation of ownership and control. In large companies like Unilever and Shell, university graduates were already prominent. This new breed of intelligent men were no longer motivated solely by the interests of their shareholders, but by what was perceived by informed opinion to be good for society. At the heart of the Keynesian vision is the notion of like-minded persons, some in the civil service, others in joint stock companies, working things out in a professional manner for the benefit of society as a whole. Keynes believed that the socialists were tilting at the wrong windmill; the world had changed, and capitalists, those merchant princes and captains of industry, were no longer in power.

The self-made barons of Birmingham, Manchester, Liverpool and Glagow—where are they now? There are no such objects on the earth. Their office-boys (on salaries) rule in their mausoleums.

Thus for one reason or another, Time and the Joint Stock Company and Civil Service have silently brought the salaried class into power. Not yet a Proletariat. But a Salariat, assuredly. And it makes a great difference (Keynes, 1934, p. 34).

The difference it made was to vested interest; the old industrialists had acquired wealth and personal power while the salariat had no such possibilities. 'In England today no one has personal power', replied Keynes to Shaw. In the old system people in power had difficulty in accepting change because they had gained from the status quo, but the new élite would be more willing to take good advice; they would 'swallow it in gulps—the Salariat quicker than the Proleteriat' (Keynes, 1934, p. 34).

With much of this analysis Tawney would have been in agreement. He too had concluded that those who had profited from the old economic order would resist change; he too had recognized that a new breed of managers had come into power. But, unlike Keynes, the socialists found the power of the salariat almost as objectionable as the power of the old capitalists. Nothing it seems had changed; power had devolved to a small oligarchy that was not accountable to anyone.

Contrast Keynes's views with the following remarks of Crossman's to the Fabian Society:

Has Tawney's denunciation of the acquisitive society become less relevant in the last thirty years? On the contrary. One of the main post-war features of the Western world has been the steady concentration of economic power in the hands of the managerial class, whose responsibility to their shareholders is frequently titular. In Tawney's sense, the men who run our great industries today form an irresponsible oligarchy; and the degree of public control we have achieved is quite inadequate to ensure that they are in any sense accountable to the community.

The first task of Socialism therefore must be to expose this growth of irresponsible power; to challenge the new managerial oligarch; to show its monopolistic—or oligopolistic—privileges are a threat to democracy and to demand that it should become not the master but the servant of the nation (Crossman 1956, p. 63).

These passages show the essentials of the two opposing views in the modern debate about autonomy and accountability. It is important to observe that public ownership is not central to either protagonist's argument. Keynes thought nationalization was irrelevant but autonomy important; in characteristic prose he wrote

There is, for instance, no so-called important political question so really unimportant, so irrelevant to the reorganisation of the economic life of Great Britain, as the nationalisation of the railways . . . But we must keep our minds flexible regarding the forms of semi-socialism. We must take full advantage of the natural tendencies of the day, and we must probably prefer semi-autonomous corporations to organs of the central government for which ministers of the State are directly responsible (Keynes, 1926*b*, p. 390).

As a socialist, Tawney could not but approve of public ownership; but as far as he was concerned it was only a first step and not always a very important one. In the case of the railways for example he was quite prepared to accept that private ownership should remain 'private' as long as the public tolerated it (Tawney, 1918, p. 111). What really mattered was, first of all, that industry should be subordinated to the interests of the community and not just serve its owners; thus far Keynes and Tawney are at one. However, Tawney suggested further 'that its direction and government should be in the hands of persons who are responsible to those who are directed and governed, because it is the condition of economic freedom that men should not be ruled by an authority which they cannot control' (Tawney, 1921, p. 7).

It is on this second issue that Keynes and Tawney take separate paths. Indeed it is perhaps not too fanciful to argue that if either side had been pressed to compromise Keynes would have conceded public ownership provided the autonomous status of the organization could be retained, while Tawney might have agreed to private ownership so long as control was effectively in the hands of the people, or at least their parliamentary representatives. In a nutshell, Keynes wanted autonomy and Tawney accountability.

It is therefore a paradox to note that although the question of ownership was not essential to their argument it was in fact the structure of ownership that subsequently distinguished the type of control that industry faced. Very broadly, the Tawney vision has prevailed in the control of state-owned enterprises, while the Keynesian vision has dominated in the regulation of privately owned enterprises. Within its context, nowhere is this more evident than in India.

The industrial sector of the Indian economy is highly regulated. As early as 1956 the Indian Government took upon itself powers that enabled it to control almost the entire gamut of private industrial activity, powers as Mr Paul Bareau described them, 'of life and death over individual enterprises' (Bauer, 1961, p. 87). Subsequently these powers have, if anything, been enhanced; new laws relating to foreign exchange, monopolies and restrictive practices, and the strengthening of the Industrial Licensing Act, have reduced the independence that one associates with a private sector almost to vanishing point. But, in spite of this immense control, the absence of that accountability, which seems a consequence of state ownership, has left private sector autonomy more or less intact.

On the other hand, in the management of the public sector accountability has destroyed autonomy. Indeed accountability has grown like Topsy. It is not just to the relevant administrative ministry or Parliament that a manager is now accountable; for with the growing power of the press and the recently acquired skills of investigative reporting, public sector managers are now faced with continuous scrutiny and surveillance of a kind that is so exhausting and debilitating that very little time or energy remains for the conduct of ordinary business.

6. The Accountability of the Public Sector

Before discussing the need for and the nature of public sector accountability, it will be best to specify those aspects that will be specifically excluded from consideration. First there is a widespread belief that the corporate sector as a whole should be accountable to a wider group of persons than the shareholders of its companies. There may or may not be great merit in this notion; it was certainly what Tawney was arguing for; but it should not be confused with the specific problem of accountability in the public sector alone. If society requires a wider accountability from industry or trade, it should legislate for it taking into account the general background, and not restrict the issue to state-owned enterprises only.

It may be argued, however, that industries in the public sector are particularly of the type that need to be accountable to society on this wider plane. Frequently they enjoy monopoly power requiring some countervailing authority. In so far as this proposition is correct, society is better served by an examination of a particular industry. Simply using these arguments as a general basis for having a different system of accountability for state-owned enterprises does little either to resolve the problem or to distinguish precisely what it is one is attempting to resolve.

The other rather more powerful argument for accountability in the public sector has its origins in the fiduciary relationship between public funds and those who are required to dispense them. Administrators trained in the ways of modern governments stress this reason for imposing procedures and demanding accountability from managers of state-owned enterprises. Sound as this argument may be for government expenditure, it has little or no application to state-owned enterprises. First, a fiduciary relationship exists in the private as well as in the public sector. Directors of joint stock companies are equally aware that they are not spending their own money but that of the public. Second, in contrast with conventional government expenditure, the activities of state-owned enterprises are strictly measurable in terms of profit and loss. The distinction is that the value from output in government expenditure is in general not measurable, either because the service is provided free of charge as in the case of defence or social welfare, or because the charges are expected to cover only part of the cost. The difficulty of measuring output is really what distinguishes government expenditure from that of state-owned enterprises.

Unlike a civil servant's, the role of the public enterprise manager is not simply to *spend* money but to use it for producing saleable commodities. It follows therefore that if there is an adequate system for measuring the value of the costs incurred and output provided, then prima facie a system of accountability already exists and need not be duplicated on fiduciary or any other grounds. But this rather simple notion has never been accepted.

Although profits as a measure of gain is a familiar concept, the knowledge that social and private interests do not always coincide, as well as the fact that the virtue of profits was a tenet of the capitalist system, had brought the notion into considerable disrepute. Marx had given a pejorative interpretation of the concept as a measure of the surplus value of labour extracted by capitalists through ruthless competition. There was therefore a natural disinclination, particularly among socialists, to accept profits as the primary criterion for judging the efficiency of public sector enterprises. Some social measure was needed.

But unfortunately no easy solution could be found. We have seen earlier that Ian Little from the outset was very emphatic on this point. He recognized that his methods for project appraisal had nothing to do with rules for evaluating projects after they had been chosen. But his suggestion that the only sound instruction to managers was to maximize profits at actual prices seemed an unsatisfactory solution after he had so convincingly argued that market prices did not reflect the real costs of those commodities to the economy.

It is therefore sad to record that the outcome of drawing the valuable distinction between actual and social prices has been quite different from what had been hoped for by economists. While the notion has enabled those in authority to discard more effectively the criteria of conventional profits, it has failed to provide a satisfactory substitute for them as a measure of what it is that the manager is expected to optimize. Indeed the public sector manager is now faced with a new version of Morton's fork. If he makes profits that is no evidence of managerial efficiency, for it might simply reflect mispricing. On the other hand if losses are made, that is a clear case of squandering public money through inefficient management. The Indian Prime Minister, a sympathetic critic of the public sector, recently expressed the sharpness of the dilemma:

If the public sector loses hundred crores or a thousand crores of Rupees it means that a hundred crores or thousand crores of Rupees of anti-poverty programmes or development programmes are down the drain. And why? Because one unit cannot pull its weight; [On the other hand] . . . Profits; well we ask for profits, but these are highly dubious figures that we get, because invariably the prices are all fixed by us, we are not realistic; the profits are made on production costs plus something, which is a totally nonsensical way of doing things (Gandhi, 1986, p. 3.3).

It seems then that recognition of the distinction between actual and accounting prices has made the measurement of efficiency even more difficult; and the newly acquired wisdom has also opened a Pandora's box of social objectives which are now indiscriminately imposed on state-owned enterprises in the expectation that clever economists will be able to resolve the trade-offs.

In an article on public enterprise, Waris Kidwai, Secretary General of the Standing Committee of Public Enterprises (SCOPE), a sort of chief executives club, complained that public sector companies were given autonomy on paper but 'the soul of autonomy was taken away'. He shows by examination of government directives that there are at least 28 national objectives that state-owned enterprises are expected to pursue, ranging from building up surpluses and providing competition with the private sector to developing backward areas, developing indigenous technology, working as a model employer, and promoting a socially desirable pattern of consumption. In themselves, each one of these objectives is doubtless highly desirable, but together they provide a confused programme for the manager to implement.

Nor are government directives very helpful in achieving these objectives;

the Bureau of Public Enterprises has issued guide-lines to public sector
managers consisting of two volumes covering 1,100 pages describing in
detail what is expected of them. They cover diverse matters including such
trivia as the size of windows and the colour of staff cars. In themselves
there are very few sanctions for breaching most or all such advice; but
when a government decides to open investigations trivial accusations provide colour for painting a picture of general mismanagement and riotous
living. In the art of populist rhetoric a poor country has many skilled
artists.

The Arjun Sen Gupta Committee on Policy for Public Enterprises
claimed that 'Accountability to Parliament is a major reason for continuous surveillance and involvement by the Ministry or Departments of
the Government in the operations of public enterprises. The involvement
sometimes relates to matters which are wholly within the powers of the
Board of Directors of the enterprise' (Sen Gupta, 1984, p. 2.1278). But of
course once 'involvement' begins it does not restrict itself to the main
purpose. Various little rivulets of investigation for somewhat less laudable
reasons quickly develop, and if the enterprise objects to a particular
query on the grounds that Parliament has not raised it, the reply is always
'Parliament could raise the issue and the Ministry must be prepared with
an answer.' Once the right to ask and the right to probe has been accepted,
there is simply no end to the group of people who can ask for an explanation and not the least of these is the media. In this regard, Aubrey Silberston, a former non-executive director of the British Steel Corporation,
makes this shrewd observation:

the press is always interested in nationalised industries' conflicts. Some issues are
debated more in public than in private, e.g. the conflict between Tony Benn and
Monty Finniston over redundancy in steel, and the nationalised industry chairmen
have to grow accustomed to becoming public figures. The contrast in this respect
with the chairmen of even the largest private companies [and, he could have added,
with the senior echelons of the civil service or armed forces] is very marked (Silberston, 1978, p. 141).

Indeed, when the whole process of accountability is taken sufficiently far,
anyone who claims to speak for the public good must be satisfied. In a
democracy, Parliament is ultimately responsible to the people, so the
people must have the right to question.

It may be argued that these rights exist mainly on paper; that in reality
there is very little that the people can do to translate them into effective
action. It is here that the combination of the press, Parliament, and government becomes critical. The press can only raise an issue, but that is the
trigger for Parliament to start questioning. Ultimately however administrative ministries play a crucial role; the power to investigate depends not only

upon the desire to do so but upon resources in terms of trained manpower. Governments have this machinery readily available to them; in India there are accountants in the the office of the Comptroller and Auditor-General, there is a Vigilance Commission, and there is the Central Bureau of Investigation (CBI), a semi-police body that can be called in not only for special investigations but which also as a matter of routine keeps a close watch on the public sector. According to Dr Narrottam Shah of the Centre for Monitoring Indian Economy,

Fear is one dominant feeling among top executives of the Public Sector enterprises. There are several reasons for this. The CBI keeps, as a matter of routine, a close watch on all Public Sector transactions above a certain limit; such transactions run into thousands every year. The CBI may or may not start any enquiry in respect of a particular transaction; but the fear of any such enquiry haunts the executive while concluding even an honest transaction (Shah, 1986, p. 1.93).

It is not very surprising therefore that in an informal survey he found public sector managers 'hamstrung, humiliated and demoralised . . . one can marshall a mountain of evidence of the manner in which . . . the full time chairmen or managing directors are tortured by those above as well as those below them' (Shah, 1986, p. 1.92).

Once an investigation has begun it is a lengthy, slow, and elaborate process. Gathering evidence that might constitute proof in a criminal court is far from easy and many of these investigations lose momentum over time. Nevertheless the process can clearly be embarrassing and tortuous and is best avoided. Since sins of omission are very much more difficult to investigate than sins of commission, public sector managers become adept at procrastination.

In his great book *The Acquisitive Society* Tawney tells us 'In all cases where difficult and disagreeable work is to be done, the force which elicits it is normally not merely money, but the public opinion and tradition of the little society in which the individual moves, and in the esteem of which he finds that which men value in success' (Tawney, 1921, p. 186). There is no doubt that earning the respect of one's fellow men is important, and in poorer countries it counts for very much more than in richer nations. But this incentive to public service is lost if men fear condemnation for mistakes they may make. Tawney had hoped for an industrial corps developed along the principles that the Services have been built on, with their own professional conduct and their own ethical code. He hoped that the comradeship that goes with an honourable profession would compensate for material deficiencies; but in asking for maximum publicity and parliamentary control over leaders of industry he forgot that it is the essence of professionalism for individuals to be judged only by their fellow professionals; as a group they are accountable to society, but only a fellow officer or a fellow lawyer or a fellow doctor can cashier, condemn, or disbar another.

Nowhere is the ancient right to be judged by one's peers as necessary to a sense of justice as in the case of professionals. For, in the final analysis, the problem of accountability is that it requires as profound an understanding of the relevant issues on the part of those to whom one is accountable as is expected from those who are accountable. Ultimately one must have the right to turn around and say, 'You show me how it can be done.'

In their vision of the new world Tawney and later on Crossman were concerned with the preservation of social control against the growth of large and dominant industrial organizations. Their perception of power made them fearful of an unholy alliance between the state and the supposedly irresponsible oligarchs who controlled industry. Their chosen instrument was the citadel of all power—Parliament. But Parliament cannot have the time, expertise, and experience to be able to exercise its power judiciously. In its place authority is exercised by the Minister; as Nevil Johnson quoting Professor Hanson points out:

So long as the Minister is held by Parliament to be *generally* responsible for the performance of the nationalised industry under his supervision . . . he will continue . . . to ensure . . . predominantly by informal means that its activities are such that he feels he can reasonably defend before the House of Commons. [Johnson perceptively continues] Professor Hanson may, writing ten years ago, have underestimated the extent to which Ministers want to defend themselves before audiences other than the House of Commons. Nevertheless he put his finger on a key issue—the infinite temptations to which Ministers are exposed, the infinite flexibility which their relations with Parliament allow them to claim (Johnson, 1978, p. 143).

All this is familiar stuff; yet the problem of accountability is so intractable that even the wisest and most experienced administrators can find no solution to it. The Sen Gupta Committee consisted of men who had long served both in administrative services and in the public sector. They understood the process of government as well as the problems of public sector management. They were fully aware of the high state of demoralization throughout the Indian public sector and the causes for it. Yet when it came to the central issue of management they ducked the problem and indeed went so far as to say, 'The Committee recognised that in general Parliament's intervention to the overall performance of public enterprises had a very beneficial impact' (Sen Gupta, 1984, p. 2.128).

Now state-owned enterprises may *need* to function under a regime of public accountability; the apex of that regime may well be the surpreme organization of the land—Parliament; but to claim that such a system can have a beneficial impact on the performance of state enterprises is simply flying from truth. It is a well-known technique of committee reports to make a statement and then so modify the central proposition as to render a totally different interpretation, but you still cannot take matters so far as to say exactly the opposite of what you mean.

However, recognition of the difficulties that professional managers face in being held accountable by those whose knowledge is at best superficial is evident in the recommendations of the Arjun Sen Gupta Committee report. 'Beneficial' as they found Parliament's intervention in the public sector, they suggested the creation of holding companies as intermediaries between the enterprise and the government. The enterprise would then be accountable solely to its holding company which would presumably be directed by professional managers. In turn the holding company would be responsible to government and Parliament for the performance of its subsidiaries. Although the recommendation was couched in terms of resolving the problem of centralization and decentralization, the implicit purpose was clearly to insulate the operational levels of organizations from the pressures of political and bureaucratic demands. But, because they failed to grasp the nettle of accountability, the recommendation fell on stony ground. Managers of state-owned enterprises saw the holding comapny as an additional layer of bureaucratic control which did nothing to reduce their overall responsibility and merely deprived them of direct access to the government.

Before we turn to alternative solutions, let us review the theoretical arguments again. Keynes saw that the divorce of ownership and control would lead to precisely that type of professionalism that Tawney so avidly sought. But in the public sector the divorce did not take place because state ownership led on the contrary to a marriage of ownership and control, and as a result all the undesirable elements of later capitalism have come together again. For the essential problem of late capitalism was the inability of the owner to understand the needs of his grown empire. Like some absentee landlord dealing with his agents, all he could demand was performance and accountability. His notions of what could or could not be achieved were based neither on any real experience of prevailing conditions nor on any professional knowledge of what was required to put his estates in good heart, but on whatever suited his own requirements at the time. However the mere assertion of the rights of ownership by the principal and the evocation of fear in the agent cannot produce desirable results.

Keynes concluded that autonomy was essential and that state ownership was probably unnecessary for retaining social control; he recognized that *laissez-faire* as traditionally understood was doomed and that age and size tend to socialise companies. Tawney had the greater vision but Keynes knew how business actually worked. Yet Keynes was not blind to the Tawney vision; he recognised the attractions of Communism as 'a protest against the emptiness of economic welfare, an appeal to the ascetic in us all to other values' (Keynes, 1934, p. 35).[3] In India, with her philosophy of renunciation and sacrifice, that appeal is intellectually universal. There, public ownership weaves its own magic. In the Indian context at least, Tawney and Crossman were justified in claiming its moral superiority, but at the practical level Keynes's insight was greater. Indeed compared to his understanding of the workings of corporations both Tawney's and Crossman's seem naive.

Can these issues be resolved through indirect ownership by the state, though not perhaps in the form of holding companies envisaged by the Sen Gupta Committee? We have argued earlier that the demand for accountability is based on a false analogy between the running of state-owned enterprises and the conducting of government administration. Nevertheless, accountability to Parliament depends not only on Parliament's right of surveillance over the dispersal of public funds, but also on its inherent rights as the elected representatives of the people who are the ultimate owners of public enterprises.

We have recognized that state ownership for some larger enterprises may well be desirable particularly in recently developing nations which are not blessed with a sufficient number of semi-autonomous corporations that have over a passage of time socialised themselves. However, it has been suggested that the kind of accountability demanded as a consequence of state ownership is counter-productive. One answer may be to persuade Parliament to draw up a set of conventions of a self-limiting kind restricting its right to call for accountability; but it is unlikely that Parliament would wish to surrender its rights. '*Sed quis custodiet ipsos custodes?*' will surely seem a reasonable question to others but not to the guards themselves. Besides, Parliament rightly considers itself a watchdog over government, and it could not be asked to relinquish its authority without a corresponding dilution of the government's authority and control on the state-owned sector. We therefore need to find a solution that retains public ownership but at the same time removes state-owned enterprises from government control.

7. An Alternative Solution

The socialized autonomous joint stock company goes only half way to resolving our problem, for it still leaves the issue of ownership unsolved.

---

[3] There is a school of thought that Keynesian economics was not analytically conceived but a reaction against Puritanism (Deacon: *The Cambridge Apostles*). It is interesting to read therefore that Keynes was personally very frugal almost to the point of asceticism. According to Frances Spalding, his wife would have to send a telegram for his permission before she could serve wine to guests in his absence (Spalding: *Vanessa Bell*, Weidenfeld & Nicolson, London, p. 247).

Indeed, as we have seen, some socialist critics believe that the divorce of ownership and management has made matters worse for it gives the share-holders rentier profits for which they have not worked; but these objections would not hold, or at least would be considerably mitigated, if the rents were paid not to individuals but to national institutions.

In principle there is no difficulty in reorganizing ownership in this way; what we need is to find deserving owners like public institutions or at least other public sector companies. Indeed it is possible to devise an entirely circular system of ownership where A owns B, who in turn owns C who owns A. The construct of such ownership will seem very artificial but that is because the historical evolution of ownership and control in the West has been primarily with individuals as the base. In Japan, on the other hand, industrial ownership particularly of the core sector of industries is held through companies. In the early stages ultimate ownership belonged to a few powerful families, but when the *zaibatsu* were abolished a new system of circular group ownership took over with banks at the centre of the structure.[4] In other words, you have a system of companies owning shares in other companies, and once you allow for cross ownership it is entirely possible to interlock ownership in such a manner that a group becomes self-perpetuating.

To many this pattern of ownership represents the worst form of capital-ist machination, as it enables a small group to control large sections of industry; in India special legislation, the abolition of the Managing Agency System, was introduced to prevent precisely this form of interlocked con-trol; but what may seem an undesirable situation if ownership and control is in the hands of private organizations may seem less so if ownership is in the hands of state-owned companies. In other words, if a pattern of own-ership were to be created whereby different state-owned companies owned each other, or at least jointly owned each other, it might be possible to combine the benefits of state ownership with the kind of autonomy, accountability and management that allows for economic efficiency.

But how and to whom would such a group be accountable? First, it would not have to be one group only; the Japanese have sensibly grouped their companies round different banks and this scheme could be emulated in India as all the main banks are nationalized. Second, being grouped round a bank does not mean being a subsidiary of the bank. The interlock arrangements would operate in such a manner that if for example Bank A had an x per cent holding in Steel Company B, in turn B would have a holding in Bank A; mutual loyalty would be ensured by restricting A and B from purchasing shares in the initial stages in any other bank or steel com-

---

[4] The break-up of the *zaibatsu* was an American idea strongly resisted by the Japanese Government. The Japanese authorities were compelled to pass the anti-monopoly law, which however was soon circumvented with official connivance.

pany. Third, a typical group would have a steel plant, a fertilizer company, a bank, a trading company and an insurance company, so that each group would be financially sufficiently strong to compete with another on an equal basis. The essence of the scheme would be not so much state ownership as an absence of private ownership; nor would the groups have a right to sell shares to individuals; they could only be transferred to other state institutions. This would of course be a disadvantage, but it could be taken into account in determining the initial price at which the stock was transferred. But the great merit of the scheme would be that shares could be transferred from the state without accusations of privatization; and yet it would cut the essential cord that binds these companies to the state.

Each company within the group would be accountable internally to other members of the group and to society as a whole by virtue of competing with each other. These companies could still enjoy monopolistic privileges, to the extent that these were thought desirable, but the introduction of an element of competition between state industries could greatly enhance flexibility within the economy.

It is easy to be put off such a scheme because of its seeming artificiality; but great institutional developments are often created by apparent illusions. The growth of the Limited Liability Company had a seemingly unnatural birth, but has since been recognized as the single most powerful institutional development in the history of industrialization.

It is unfortunate, but true, that corporate capitalism, whether it is perpetuated by the state or by the private sector, usually rouses great suspicion among those who try to guard against the excessive power of men in authority. Yet the management of industry has its own compulsions which cannot simply be made subservient to the arbitrary demands of the state. Sovereignty apart, these claims have been based upon the rights of ownership; but in Japan, surely the most successful industrial nation in the world, a different system seems to prevail.

In Japanese law, as in American and European law, management is the servant of the stockholders. But this the Japanese treat as pure fiction. . . . Management is the servant of the going concern, which brings together in a common interest a number of constituencies: employees first, then customers, then creditors and finally suppliers. Stockowners are only a special group of creditors rather than the 'owners' for whose sake the enterprise exists (Drucker, 1986 p. 182).

It looks as though we have come full circle. Keynes's socialised joint stock company separating ownership from control does not seem very different from modern concepts of management in highly successful Japanese companies. Both represent a shift in the balance of power from owners to managers, from stockholders to directors. In contrast, Indian public sector companies have excessively weak managements and inherently powerful owners. It is ironic that the very remedy proposed by early Fabians to improve morale and professionalism in the public sector has caused its downfall. Tawney wanted 'industry to be conducted in the light of day' so that all would know its costs necessary or unnecessary; but this ruthless exposure, instead of making managers bolder, more competent and professionally prouder, has in fact led them to timidity, caution and a dangerous lack of will to make decisions. On the other hand the secretive, interlocked, self perpetuating systems of Japanese management, seem to have led to a greater concern for the employee and a wider perception of social obligations by professional managements than could ever have been anticipated. If there is a lesson in this for public sectors in general and the Indian public sector in particular, it is quite simply this: the structure of organizations matter; it is not just the substance but also the form which is important.

8. Conclusion

L. K. Jha in his book on *Economic Strategy for the 80s* told us that 'Perhaps no other single factor can make the same positive contribution to better performance of the economy in the 80s than improved functioning of public sector enterprises which occupy key positions in the most vital sector of the economy. They are poised for leadership, which they can only exercise if they enjoy the requisite measure of autonomy' (Jha, 1980, p. 38). No observer of the Indian scene could disagree with that, except to wonder how poised for leadership the public sector really is, 10 years later. In this paper it has been argued that the failure of the public sector has been due less to lack of resources, misguided investment and poor pricing policies than to bad management. Yet the men who serve the public sector are both intelligent and dedicated; the problem lies not in the people but in the system they are expected to operate within. It is a failure of governance that so important a sector of the economy should have come to be described by a distinguished commentator as one where chief executives are 'tortured' from above and below. Even the best salariat cannot perform in these circumstances.

The structure of management has been greatly weakened because in contrast to the evolution of joint-stock companies, the balance of power has swung dramatically in favour of the owners. A sovereign Parliament with the authority of the state can too easily impose its will on the nationalized sector; these decisions are normally justified in the name of social control and enforced through rights of ownership. The results however are not always what one might hope for. Paradoxically, strong managements and weak owners have been able to achieve much more in the way of socialized industrialization.

Perhaps we have underestimated the extent of autonomy required to make a success of business. Perhaps such autonomy is simply not possible with traditional modes of state ownership. One possible solution is a change in the form of ownership. In reconstructing the structure it may be worth bearing in mind that, during the First World War, it was said that there were two kinds of officers, those who led their troops from the front, the 'come on' type, and others who led from behind, the 'go on' type. The public sector has suffered too much from politicians, private businessmen, academics, and administrators of the 'go on' type. Accountability is more readily given to those who can lead from the front; if these changes do not come about we will need not managers but heroes. Some will welcome the acknowledgement of this fact and argue that great changes cannot be wrought without men of courage and high daring. Let them echo the words of Andrea in Brecht's play *Leben des Galilei*:

ANDREA. *Unglucklich das Land, das keine Helden hat!*
    (Unhappy the Land that has no heroes).

But for myself I prefer Galileo's reply:

GALILEO. *Nein, unglucklich das Land das Helden notig hat.*
    (No, unhappy the Land that needs heroes).

References

Aganbegyan, A. (1988), *The Challenge: Economics of Perestroika* (London: Hutchinson Education).

Bauer, P. T. (1961), *Indian Economic Policy and Development*. (London: Allen & Unwin).

Bhagwati, J. N., and Desai, P. (1970), *India Planning for Industrialisation* (Paris and London: OECD and OUP).

Bhuleshkar, A. V. (ed.) (1969), *Indian Economic Thought and Development* (Bombay: Bombay Popular Prakashan).

——(1972), *Towards a Socialist Transformation of India* (Bombay: Bombay Popular Prakashan).

Bose, Vivian (1963), *Report of Commission of Inquiry on Administration of Dalmia-Jain Companies* (New Delhi: Ministry of Commerce and Industry).

Butler, D., and Halsey, A. H. (eds.) (1978), *Policy and Politics: Essays in Honour of Norman Chester* (London and Basingstoke: Macmillan Press).

Chakravarty, S. (1987), *Development Planning: The Indian Experience* (Oxford: Clarendon Press).

Chandy, K. T. (1986), 'Relevance of Public Sector in India', in Nigam (1986).

Crossman, R. H. S. (1956), 'Planning for Freedom', reprinted in Crossman (1965).

——(1965), *Planning for Freedom* (London: Hamish Hamilton).

Drucker, P. (1986), *The Frontiers of Management* (London: Heinemann).

Gandhi, R. (1986), 'Policy Announcements for the Public Sector by Prime Minister, in Nigam (1986).

Gopal, S. (1969), *Jawaharlal Nehru—A Biography, Vol. ii* (London: Cape).

Hamouda, O. F., and Smithin, J. N. (eds.) (1988), *Keynes and Public Policy after Fifty Years* (Aldershot: Edward Elgar).

Hazari, R. K. (1964), 'The Implications of the Managing Agency System' First published in the *Economic Weekly*, annual number 1964, reprinted in Bhuleshkar (1969).

Jha, L. K. (1980), *Economic Strategy for the 80s* (Bombay: Allied Publishers).

——(1984), *Reports of the Economic Administration Reforms Commission on Government and Public Enterprises*, partly reprinted in Nigam (1986).

Johnson N. (1978), 'The Public Corporation: An Ambiguous Species', in Butler and Halsey (1978).

Keynes, J. M. (1925), Letter to the Editor of *The Times* 25 March 1925, quoted in *Collected Works (CW)*, Vol. xix.

——(1926*a*), 'Bagehot's Lombard Street', *CW*, Vol. xix.

——(1926*b*), 'The End of Laissez-faire', *CW*, Vol. ix.

——(1927), 'The Public and Private Concern', Lecture to the Liberal School; reported by the *Manchester Guardian*, *CW*, Vol. xix.

——(1933), 'National Self-Sufficiency', *New Statesman and Nation*, *CW*, Vol. xxi.

——(1934), 'Mr. Keynes replies to Shaw', *New Statesman and Nation*, *CW*, Vol. xxviii.

——(1936), *The General Theory of Employment, Interest and Money*, *CW*, Vol. vii.

Kidwai, W. R. (1986), '*The Threatening Storm over Public Sector in India*', in Nigam (1986).

Little, I. M. D. (1960), 'The Strategy of Indian Development', *National Institute Economic Review*, 9 (May).

——(1965), 'Public Sector Project Selection', in Bhuleshkar (1969).

——Scitovsky, T., and Scott, M. FG. (1970), *Industry and Trade in Some Developing Countries* (Oxford: OUP for the Development Centre, OECD).

——and Mirrlees, J. A. (1974), *Project Appraisal and Planning for Developing Countries* (London: Heinemann).

——Kornai, T. (1959), *Overcentralization in Economic Administration* (London: OUP).

Minami, R. (1986), *The Economic Development of Japan* (Basingstoke and London: Macmillan Press).

Nehru, J. N. (1934), *Glimpses of World History*, 2 vols. (Allahabad: Kitabistan).

Nigam, R. K. (ed.) (1986), *Towards a Viable and Vibrant Public Sector*. (Delhi: Documentation Centre).

Patrick, H., and Rosovsky, H. (eds.) (1976), *Asia's New Giant* (Washington, DC: Brookings Institution).

Royal Economic Society (1971–), *The Collected Writings of John Maynard Keynes* (London and Cambridge: Macmillan and CUP).

Sen Gupta Arjun (1984), 'Report of the Committee to Review Policy for Public Enterprises', in Nigam (1986).

Shah, N. (1986), 'Achievements and Failures of the Public Sector', in Nigam (1986).

Sudhir Mulji

Silberston, Z. A. (1978), 'Nationalised Industries: Government Intervention and Industrial Efficiency', in Butler and Halsey (1978).

Silverman J. (1972), 'The Ultimate Objective of Nehru's Socialism', in Bhuleshkar (1972).

Skidelsky, R. (1986), 'Keynes's Political Legacy', in Hamouda and Smithin (1988).

Tawney, R. H. (1918), 'The Conditions of Economic Liberty, in Tawney (1964).

——(1921), *The Acquisitive Society* (London: G. Bell & Sons).

——(1964), *The Radical Tradition* (London: Allen & Unwin).

Trezise, P., and Suzuki, Y. (1976), 'Politics Government and Economic Growth', in Patrick and Rosovsky (1976).

Uekusa, M. (1987), 'Industrial Organisation', in Yamamura and Yasuba (1987).

Yamamura, K., and Yasuba, Y. (eds). (1987), *The Political Economy of Japan* (Stanford: Stanford Univ. Press).

8

Trade Policy and Development

G. M. MEIER

THE 'neo-classical resurgence' in development economics, about which Ian Little has written so incisively (Little, 1982), has had its greatest influence as a guide to policies affecting international trade, agriculture, and project appraisal. This chapter concentrates on trade policy.[1] In considering the effects of trade policy on a country's development, we shall proceed from a summary of the 'old export pessimism' and experience with import-substitution policies (Section 1), to assessment of measures for export promotion (Section 2), and the superior performance of outward-orientated economies (Section 3), and finally to a critique of the 'new export pessimism' (Section 4). Our modest objective is to synthesize and sum up the essential features of mainstream thought on this subject.

1. The Old Export Pessimism

In neo-classical trade theory there is no conflict between realizing the gains from trade and the gains from growth. A movement along the production possibility frontier to specialization according to comparative advantage is tantamount to an expansion of the feasible set of consumption possibilities along an availability frontier that lies beyond the production possibility frontier. By conforming to comparative advantage an economy also follows its optimal growth path.

In the early post-war period of development economics, however, there was considerable dissent from this view and instead support for the contrary strategy of import-substituting industrialization (ISI). Pessimism with respect to the potential for development through the export of primary products was widespread, based on references to the dismal inter-war experience and the allegations of low price elasticity of demand, low income elasticity of demand, fluctuation in export receipts, and deterioration in the commodity and double factoral terms of trade.

Three versions of elasticity pessimism became prominent: Nurkse's inward-looking balanced growth, Rosenstein-Rodan's argument for co-ordinated investment in a balanced growth pattern, and Mahalanobis's case for heavy sector ISI (Bhagwati, 1984a, pp. 199–200). Nurkse believed

---

[1] The discussion draws on some parts of Meier, (1989).

that for the newly emergent countries international trade could no longer serve as an 'engine of growth'. If these countries could not rely on growth being induced from the outside through an expansion of world demand for their exports of primary commodities, they would then have to undertake

a balanced pattern of investment in a number of different industries . . . In the absence of vigorous upward shifts in world demand for exports of primary products, a low income country through a process of diversified growth can seek to bring about upward shifts in domestic demand schedules by means of increased productivity and therefore increased real purchasing power. In this way, a pattern of mutually supporting investments in different lines of production can enlarge the size of the market and help to fill the vacuum in the domestic economy of low incomes areas. This, in brief, is the notion of balanced growth (Nurkse, 1957).

In Rosenstein-Rodan's version of balanced growth, the balanced, co-ordinated growth requires a planning framework that will allow the realization of external economies from the simultaneous establishment of several complementary industries. Without such co-ordinated planning there will be no effective inducement to invest and no 'big push' to overcome rural underdevelopment. The dilemma that Rosenstein-Rodan poses would disappear if the country faced constant terms of trade at which it could sell what it wished. A necessary condition for Rosenstein-Rodan's prescription is, therefore, elasticity pessimism (Rosenstein-Rodan, 1943).

Mahalanobis in India also implicitly assumed an extreme form of elasticity pessimism by relying on a closed-economy model. In the two-sector version of his model, the state would have to plan for heavy sector ISI (Mahalanobis, 1953).

Development economists could also propound some logically valid arguments in support of the promotion of industry under an ISI strategy: dynamic external economies, the learning effects of an infant industry, and disequilibrium in the labour market (the wage in industry being greater than the social opportunity cost of labour).

In reality, however, ISI became the preferred trade strategy not because of the rational arguments of economists but rather because of expeditious 'third best or nth best' policies undertaken to cope with balance-of-payments crises and because of social and political forces acting on policy-makers. Interest groups were catered for in the political market. The promotion of a sheltered home market had a common appeal to the bureaucratic-authoritarian state, urban manufacturers, and multinationals that supplied technology and capital. Protection also met the state's objectives of pursuing revenue- and expenditure-maximizing activities through maximum revenue tariffs and export taxes.[2]

[2] For a political economy explanation of ISI see Hirschman (1968, pp. 3–32); Evans (1979); Magee (1984); Findlay and Wellisz (1982); Lal (1987, pp. 273–300).

The adverse effects of ISI have been reviewed in detail for numerous countries (Little *et al.*, 1970; Bhagwati, 1978; Krueger, 1978; Balassa, 1982). ISI was not targeted according to systematic economic criteria but instead was pursued in a chaotic, inefficient manner and for too long a time. At the micro level, too many plants produced too small an output; quality was inferior; capital was underutilized; and the industrial structure became increasingly monopolistic or oligopolistic. Few if any firms were able to realize the object of Krugman's 'protection as export promotion': the scale advantage of greater production that might be provided by protection did not succeed in moving oligopolistic firms down the learning curve to lower marginal costs, and hence to the eventual realization of higher profits by establishing a competitive position in export markets (Krugman, 1984).

Although the sheltered firm's profits in local currency could be high, the domestic resource cost was excessive, and the cost increased per unit of foreign exchange saved. Given high effective rates of protection, the domestic value added in some cases was actually negative at world prices. Moreover, economic resources were diverted to rent-seeking activities (Krueger, 1974) and directly unproductive profit-seeking activities (Bhagwati, *et al.*, 1984*b*).

In general equilibrium terms, the bias in resource allocation to the domestic production of importables caused agriculture to suffer as the rural–urban terms of trade deteriorated for agriculture. Moreover, as the ratio of the effective exchange rate for exports to the effective exchange rate for importables became less than unity (by a Bhagwati–Krueger type of calculation)[3] exports suffered.

Not only did the protecting countries fail to develop their exports of manufactures, but their exports of primary products also lagged. The handicap on exports, together with the import intensity of the ISI strategy itself, tightened the foreign exchange constraint. There was an increasingly stringent exchange control regime and a growing dependence on foreign capital.

Further, policy-induced price distortions—negative real rates of interest, excessively high wages for unskilled labour, and undervalued foreign exchange—were pervasive. As the import-substitution process continued from the easy first stage of replacing non-durable consumer goods, it entailed production that was increasingly high cost and less economic; the incremental capital/output ratio increased; the rate of growth in aggregate output slowed down; and employment lagged as further import

[3] The effective exchange rate for exports is the official exchange rate adjusted for export subsidies and taxes. The effective exchange rate for importables is the official exchange rate adjusted for taxes and other costs of imports in the entire foreign trade regime. Compare equation (8.1) below.

substitution became more difficult. In short, the ISI syndrome of policies imposed dynamic losses on the entire economy that were far greater than simply the loss of neo-classical static allocative efficiency.

2. Export-orientated Industrialization

At the end of the 1950s and during the early 1960s, a few countries departed from ISI after the first easy stage and adopted an export orientation programme—in particular, Hong Kong, Taiwan, Republic of Korea, and Singapore. In part, the policy change was influenced by the resurgence of neo-classical economics that highlighted the policy-induced distortions under ISI, the inefficient resource allocation, and the worsenening situation with respect to employment and income distribution. Policy-makers were also hard pressed to seek more effective measures that would accelerate growth and relax the foreign exchange constraint. There was a growing desire for domestic autonomy—a desire not to depend on foreign aid or external borrowing that had become necessary under ISI when the foreign exchange constraint tightened (Findlay, 1986, p. 21).

A variety of measures were therefore taken to promote exports. The essential effects of these measures were to remove the negative restrictions and disincentives on exports and to offer positive incentives so that it was no longer more profitable to sell domestically than overseas. Programmes of trade liberalization replaced quantitative restrictions with tariffs, followed by a gradual reduction in tariffs and the introduction of tariff exemptions for exporters and also for domestic suppliers to the exporters. Extremely important was an increase in the effective exchange rate for exporters so that the ratio of the effective exchange rate for importables to the effective exchange rate for exports became closer to unity. This was achieved by such measures as indirect tax exemptions, a fall in direct taxes on income earned in exports, accelerated depreciation allowances, reduced rates for public utilities, credit subsidies through lower interest, and automatic access to bank loans for working capital.

Consider equation (8.1) where EER is an index of the nominal effective exchange rate for exports, derived as the official exchange rate (R), adjusted for export subsidies (S); P_{wx} is the index of dollar export prices; P_x is the domestic price index for exports, inclusive of export subsidies; and P_d is the price index for non-export (domestic) goods. According to equation (8.1), the relative profitability of exports will improve if the official exchange rate, the rate of export subsidy, or the dollar prices of exports increase, or the prices of non-export goods decrease (Balassa *et al.*, 1986, p. 2).

$$\frac{R(1+S) \cdot P_{wx}}{P_d} = \frac{\text{EER} \cdot P_{wx}}{P_d} = \frac{P_x}{P_d} \qquad (8.1)$$

The government also made sure that the real exchange rate remained competitve through depreciation—if domestic prices rose more rapidly than foreign prices—and by an attempt to limit inflation and confine wage increases to increases in productivity. Confronting world prices for their inputs and for their exports, the established exporting firms became competitive in a virtual free trade regime. There was, however, some support for infant industries. But, as exemplified by Korea, the government was careful to have only selective, efficient intervention in industry. Protection was given only to those industries that gave good assurance of becoming privately, and socially, profitable in the medium- run, and continual monitoring of these industries was undertaken (Pack and Westphal, 1986).

Not only was a consistent set of policies undertaken in the Asian newly industrializing countries (NICs), but the governmental policies had credibility for businessmen. Business believed that the policies announced and undertaken by the government would be permanent or at least of sufficiently long duration so that they could be relied upon and investment could be undertaken. Policies for business were also established in consultation with the private sector and designed to be permissive in taking advantage of market opportunities. Moreover, private investment was not crowded out by a public deficit or by an inflationary tax on savings.

Although it is certainly possible to oversubsidize exports and go beyond export promotion to export protection, there are certain safeguards against so doing. Initially an export promotion programme begins within the legacy of a previous bias against exports. The promotion of exports can therefore go quite a way until the previous import bias is removed. Moreover, an export-orientation programme does not rely on quantitative controls, and it therefore avoids the adverse effects of such negative restrictions. An export-orientated set of policies also tends to be non-discriminatory among exportables. There is less variation in the protective or subsidy equivalents of export incentives than in incentives for import substitution. Further, export subsidization comes through the budget and is therefore much more transparent. The costs of export promotion are quickly self-evident and the policies must meet the test of competition in international markets (Krueger, 1984).

Together with the need to avoid oversubsidization of exports, the sequencing of a liberalization programme is also highly important. The timing and sequencing of a successful liberalization programme should be determined by an analysis of the determinants of an optimal path of liberalization. A liberalization programme will have a time stream of benefits and costs; the present value of the net social benefit should be maximized. While there are the ultimate benefits of greater efficiency in resource allocation and higher rates of economic growth, there are also transitional costs involving the balance of payments, employment, and income distribution. To reduce the costs, a gradual, multi-stage implementation of a liberalization policy is likely to be superior to a once-for-all immediate programme (Michaely, 1986).

Questions of trade liberalization involve the timing of a transfer of policies from quantitative restrictions to tariffs and then a reduction in the variance in effective rates of protection. The sequencing of trade liberalization must also be related to liberalization in the capital market and to balance-of-payments adjustment. A large-scale unilateral trade liberalization must be associated with real devaluation if the current account is not to deteriorate and if the employment losses in protected import-substituting industries are to be compensated by employment gains elsewhere, especially in export industries. Balance-of-payments adjustment requires exchange rate adjustment, and the longer-run equilibrium real exchange rate also depends on the degree of trade liberalization (Corden, 1987).[4] The process of capital market liberalization is likely to affect the real exchange rate. If the real exchange rate appreciates, this will make trade liberalization inconsistent with current account balance. If, however, capital tends to flow out after financial liberalization, the exchange rate will move in the right direction for the current account (by depreciating), but it will overshoot because the extent of depreciation required for the current account to be maintained with trade liberalization is less than that required for a temporary current account surplus to accommodate capital outflow. In general, the opening of the domestic capital market to the world market is likely to make it more difficult to manage the exchange rate. The rate will be put under capital-market-determined pressures, and this presents problems if it is desired to fine tune the exchange rate as part of a major trade liberalization programme.

Besides exchange rate policies and capital market policies, attention must also be given to economic policies that affect the rate of inflation. Although the superiority of an export-orientated industrialization programme has been empirically established, there is still need to analyse what might be the optimal path of a stabilization-cum-liberalization programme.

3. Superior Performance of Export Orientation

Both time-series studies of individual countries and comparative country studies are persuasive in demonstrating the economic superiority of export-orientation industrialization over import-substitution industrialization. Developing countries that have adopted an export-promoting strategy have had higher rates of increase in per capita income than those with an import-

---

[4] The issue of the process of trade liberalization and how it relates to macroeconomic and other policies is currently the subject of a comparative study by researchers at the World Bank. The World Bank project involves the study of 35 liberalization episodes in 19 countries. For a preliminary report, see Papageorgiou *et al.* (1986).

substituting strategy. They have also demonstrated superior performance in terms of increases in saving ratios, investment ratios, total factor productivity, employment, and real wages, a declining incremental capital/output ratio, a more equitable distribution of income, and better adjustment to external shocks.[5]

Why has export promotion had such a strong, favourable impact on development? As for the effect on the balance of payments one might think that there is little difference between earning a unit of foreign exchange through exports or saving a unit of foreign exchange through import substitution. But the domestic resource cost of earning foreign exchange has been shown to be less than the domestic resource cost of saving foreign exchange. Moreover, export-promoting countries have become more creditworthy and their foreign exchange constraint has been relaxed.

In terms of favourable effects on resource allocation an export-orientated industrialization strategy has resulted in not simply a once-for-all improvement in allocation according to the country's comparative advantage in international trade, but more importantly in the realization of dynamic benefits. While a reallocation of resources in conformity with comparative advantage can raise the level of income, the dynamic gains are significant in increasing the rate of growth in income.

There has been increased capacity utilization of plant, realization of economies of scale, the creation of employment through export of labour-intensive products, a multiplier effect that gives rise to increased demand for intermediate inputs and increased demand by consumers, and an increase in total factor productivity. Export expansion has been shown to be positively, and import substitution negatively, correlated with changes in total factor productivity (Nishimizu and Robinson, 1984, Table 5). Econometric analysis also indicates that marginal factor productivities in export-orientated industries are significantly higher than in the non-export-orientated industries (Feder, 1982). The difference seems to derive, in part, from inter-sectoral beneficial externalities generated by the export sector.

Most important has been a realization of dynamic efficiency in the sense of a fall in the incremental capital/output ratio, the realization of 'X efficiency', the extension of informational efficiency, enjoyment of external economies, and realization of Verdoon effects. Considering the latter, there is evidence that the faster export output grows, the faster is the growth in productivity. This is because of economies of scale, higher investment embodying capital of a more productive vintage, and a faster pace of innovation in products and processes (Amsden, 1985, pp. 271–84).

[5] See various empirical studies by Little *et al.* (1970); Balassa (1971); Donges (1976); Bhagwati (1978); Krueger (1978); Feder (1982); Lal and Rajapatirana (1987). A good summary of these statistical results is in Balassa (1987), Sect. III.

More generally, dynamic efficiency may be interpreted as a reduction in what Myint terms 'organizational dualism' (Myint, 1987). Myint interprets a developing country as being within its production possibility curve on a lower curve—its production feasibility curve. Even if one could remove all the policy-induced distortions, a substratum of 'natural' dualism would still exist in factor markets, goods markets, and in the administration and fiscal system because of institutional features and the costs of transactions, transportation, information, and administration. Given the incomplete state of development of its domestic organizational framework, the country is within its production possibility frontier. The gap between the production possibility curve and the production feasibility curve is not uniform, but is skewed against an increase in output of the traditional sector. This is because the frictions and the costs of overcoming them are not uniformly distributed. These frictional costs are higher within the unorganized traditional sector and in the transactions between the traditional and the modern sectors and are lower within the modern sector and in the transactions between the modern sector and the outside world.

The incompletely developed organizational framework of a developing country can be improved or repressed by appropriate or inappropriate trade policies. By overcoming indivisibilities and filling in the gaps in the organizational framework of the traditional sector, the expansion of exports may be able to shift the production feasibility curve upward. In moving from a position on the production feasibility curve to the production possibility curve, a developing country gains much more than simply a once-over change to comparative advantage. Organizational dualism is reduced in the sense of a reduction in the costs of transactions, transportation, information, and administration.

The improved effectiveness of the domestic economic organization allows the developing country to take advantage of available external economic opportunities in the form of international trade, foreign investment, technological adaptation, and ideas from abroad. There is institutional adaptation to realize the potential comparative advantage in trade. The mutual interaction between economic policies and economic institutions results in improvement of the organization of production, more effective incentives, and a strengthening of markets. Dynamic efficiency is realized as diseconomies of a small economy are overcome, the transformation capacity of the economy widens, and the learning rate of the economy accelerates.

Whereas proponents of the old export pessimism could criticize neo-classical trade theory and assert that the dynamic gains from ISI would outweigh the possible static costs of protection, it is now realized that the dynamic gains are far superior for export promotion. The case for development through trade can actually be expressed in stronger terms than in its neo-classical version.

With the experience of the NICs as evidence, it is now realized that the major explanation of the superior development performance of countries that follow export-orientated industrialization is to be found in the indirect dynamic benefits from trade that extend far beyond simply the direct static gains from a removal of distortions (Myint, 1987).

4. New Export Pessimism

There is now, however, scepticism regarding the potential for exports of manufactures from additional NICs. Cline (1982) has asked whether the East Asian model of development can be generalized. Lewis (1980) has expressed concern about the slowing down in the growth of world trade. Streeten (1982) has taken a cool look at outward-looking strategies for development.

Some of the scepticism rests on the contention that the success stories of the Asian NICs are special cases based on initial conditions that cannot be repeated elsewhere. A more balanced interpretation of initial conditions, however, might indicate that they were actually adverse. Korea and Taiwan suffered severely from the Second World War, and South Korea was left a devastated half-economy after the Korean War. Both countries were poor in natural resources and had extremely high labour/land ratios. The stength of their subsequent development performance is attributable to their undertaking of appropriate policy measures.

If the successes of the NICs were to be attributed to unusually favourable initial conditions, both domestically and externally, rather than to good policies, then one would have to be pessimistic about future development through trade. But the lessons of the NICs are that effective demand management and efficient supply-orientated policies have been the strategic policy variables accounting for their successful development performance. In considering the unique performances of the NICs, Little (1979) has given special importance to the non-distortionary trade policies of these countries. Neither commodity prices nor factor prices were seriously distorted, and a virtually free trade regime was created for exports.

Appropriate policy measures, such as those undertaken by the Asian NICs, need not be confined to any one country. As Ranis (1978, p. 398) notes, we must differentiate between those elements of 'non-transferability' that relate to obstacles 'in nature' versus those relating to obstacles 'in man'. The latter can be overcome by institutional choices and the political process. The lessons of the NICs can be transferred to other countries by the creation and extension of social, economic, and political institutions and mechanisms that promote the mobilization of resources, their efficient allocation, and increases in total factor productivity.

Another set of arguments underlying the new export pessimism focuses on the constraint of external demand. The fallacy of composition is invoked to maintain that it is impossible to generalize the experience of the Asian NICs. If many other developing countries reach the same high ratio of exports to GDP as have the NICs, would not the market be saturated? (Cline, 1982).

It is, however, unreasonable to expect that other countries will attain the same exceptionally high ratios of export to GDP as have the NICs. Moreover, one should not view the future problem of trade as simply a division of a fixed bill of exports; the range of exports is ever-changing.

It is characteristic of the export of manufactures that they become ever-more diversified. Empirical studies have shown that intra-industry trade through horizontal specialization has increased and that the extent of intra-industry trade in industrialized countries has grown much more rapidly with the developing countries than with other industrialized countries (Balassa, 1983). There appears to be wide scope for horizontal specialization or intra-industry specialization.

Most significantly, the outward-looking strategy has been successful because the NICs have been able to capitalize on dynamic forces that produce stages in comparative advantage and that allow a 'multiple catch up' process. The ever-changing structure of comparative costs allows a given country to proceed up the ladder of comparative advantage from specialization in resource-intensive exports to unskilled-labour-intensive exports, to skilled-labour-intensive exports, to capital-intensive exports, to knowledge-intensive exports. And as a given country moves up the ladder, another country in the queue is able to climb another rung on the ladder. Thus, as Japan has risen on the ladder, the East Asian NICs have become major suppliers of Japan's former exports.

As the NICs proceed through the various stages of comparative advantage, there is room for others to follow into the markets vacated by the earlier exporting countries. As factor endowments shift with capital accumulation in the more advanced countries, and as the advanced developing countries transform their industrial structure toward the production of more skill-intensive and capital-intensive activities, other countries will be able to enter more easily into labour-intensive industries.

As Hong Kong, Singapore, Taiwan, and South Korea advance to the higher stages of comparative advantage, their former positions are being taken by Thailand, Malaysia, Indonesia, and the Philippines. As the East Asian exporters increase their real wages and accumulate skills in capital, they should in turn become markets for other countries that acquire comparative advantage in the labour-intensive products that have been abandoned by countries that are rising up the ladder of comparative advantage.

It is, however, true that the period 1945–73 was indeed a unique period of growth in world real GNP and an even higher rate of growth in world exports. Against this exceptional period and the subsequent recession in the early 1980s, it is not surprising that much of the new export pessimism stems from the fear that the external demand for exports from the developing countries will be insufficient because of slower income growth in the more developed countries and the spread of protectionism against imports from developing countries. If external demand slackens, or if LDCs are denied market access, then it will of course be more difficult to maintain an export-led growth strategy.

But this fear can be overdrawn. Contradicting the commonly held belief that LDC export growth depends on income growth in the more developed countries, a study by Riedel emphasizes supply conditions in the developing countries rather than external demand factors as the principal determinants of a developing country's export performance in manufactures (Riedel, 1984). Unlike exports of primary products, the exports of manufactures are not so dependent on growth in the more developed countries. Exports from the developing countries can substitute for the production of competitive manufactured goods in the more developed countries. Several country studies also indicate that domestic policy is much more important than overseas market constraints in explaining export performance (see, for example, Wolf, 1982). Superior export performance has come not from passive acceptance of external demand but rather from what Kravis measured as the 'competitiveness factor' and the 'diversification factor', especially the former (Kravis, 1970, pp. 867–9).

The declining share of India's and Sub-Saharan Africa's exports during the 1970s while other developing countries increased their shares is attributable to their not being competitive on world markets rather than to the constraint of external demand.

Furthermore, during the decade of slow growth in the 1970s, the share of imports from developing countries in the consumption of manufactured goods in industrial countries increased considerably, but it was still only 4.3 per cent in 1980, varying from a low of 1.7 per cent in Canada to a high of 6.8 per cent in the Netherlands (Anjaria *et al.*, 1982, Table 4, p. 85). Given this low import penetration ratio, there is clearly considerable potential for growth in manufactured exports from developing countries. If they can be competitive on the side of export supply, their share of the import demand in the developed countries can increase even if consumption in industrial countries does not grow as rapidly as it did in the unique 1945–73 period.

Moreover, there is considerable potential for additional trade among the developing countries themselves—not as a substitution for, but as a complement to North–South trade in manufactures. For example, the East Asian NICs now export only about 3 per cent of their total exports to South Asia, while ASEAN countries export only some 4 per cent to other ASEAN countries. The application of the stages approach to comparative advantage would indicate that trade among countries at similar or at lower levels of development can be expanded. Lewis (1980) has emphasized this potential for South–South trade (see also Amsden, 1986, pp. 249–74). Taken as a group, the LDCs could quickly end their dependence on the more developed countries for fertilizers, cement, steel, and gradually throw off their dependence for machinery.

Finally, it should be recognized that protection does not exercise such a constraint on external demand as is popularly believed. Even though protectionism was increasing during the period, the share of developing countries in the world export of manufactures rose from 5 per cent in 1970 to 9 per cent in 1980 and to 12 per cent in 1983. Almost two-thirds of the developing countries' total manufactured exports went to developed market economy countries.

In a study of the period of the 1970s when protection increased, Hughes and Krueger (1984) presented the following empirical findings:

(i) The share of developing countries in the absorption of manufactured goods in the industrial countries continued to increase. About half of the developing countries' gain would have accrued had the developing countries merely maintained their share in the general expansion of imports in domestic markets, but the other half may be regarded as growth at the expense of imports from developed-country suppliers.

(ii) The gains from the exports of the developing countries were widely dispersed among the countries in general, although the Asian developing countries did the best.

(iii) The commodity composition of developing-country manufactured exports to industrial countries shifted toward more sophisticated products, with the largest increases in shares for fabricated metal products, machinery and equipment, manufactured chemicals, petroleum, coal, and rubber products.

Hughes and Krueger (1984, p. 413) concluded that 'the overwhelming impression is that despite all the public discussion of protection and the political pressures for it, the effects on imports of manufactures from developing countries of protectionist measures were relatively small. The rate of increase of LDC market shares was sufficiently great that it is difficult to imagine that rates would have been significantly higher in the absence of any protectionist measures.'

An OECD study also concluded that the most important effect of protectionist policies has been to accelerate the geographical diversification of LDC exports of manufactures. Protection directed against the LDCs has relatively little effect in the aggregate. During the late 1970s the five major export-earning NICs most subject to protectionist measures by industrial nations diverted a large share of their exports to non-OECD countries. Another change helping to maintain export growth has been the deliberate shifting of certain production activities out of the East Asian NICs into less-restricted, low labour cost countries. Further, in the 1970s middle-income countries with substantial manufacturing sectors that fostered outward-orientated growth have been able to capture market shares from the more inward-looking LDCs (OECD, 1985, pp. 177–98). As demonstrated since 1973, even during periods of slow growth in industrialized countries, manufactured exports from the developing countries can grow much more rapidly than real GDP in industrialized countries.

Note also the conclusion from an empirical study of manufactured exports by non-NIC developing countries in the 1970s:

when one observes that in the climate of slower economic activity since 1973, twelve countries of the new industrialized group have been able to continue export expansion at rates well in excess of the average for world trade and above that of other developing countries, and that despite the continuing dominance of the NICs, about a dozen developing countries have been able to increase their exports of manufactured goods even more rapidly than the NICs, it becomes difficult to resist rejection of export pessimism and adoption of a more optimistic view of export prospects for developing countries. The evidence of export performance by the most successful new exporters of the seventies does quite clearly say that many other countries besides the NICs can and have followed the same path to successful exporting as had the NICs earlier (Havrylshyn and Alikhani, 1982, pp. 660–1).

In the future, export growth will continue to depend more on internal-supply elasticities for price-elastic manufactures than on external-demand elasticities. Instead of lamenting conditions of external demand, developing countries should emphasize their own policies that make them competitive on world markets. Contrary to the new export pessimism there is considerable scope for differentiation of exports and export expansion.

References

Anjaria, S. *et al.* (1982), 'Developments in Trade Policy', IMF Occasional Paper, 16 (Washington, DC: IMF).

Amsden, Alice H. (1985), 'The Division of Labour is Limited by the Rate of Growth of the Market: The Taiwan Machine Tool Industry in the 1970s', *Cambridge Journal of Economics*, 9.

——(1986), 'The Direction of Trade—Past and Present—and the Learning Effects of Exports to Different Directions', *Journal of Development Economics*, 23.

Balassa, Bela (1971), *The Structure of Protection in Developing Countries* (Baltimore: Johns Hopkins Univ. Press).

——(1982), *Development Strategies in Semi-Industrial Economies* (Baltimore: Johns Hopkins Univ. Press).

——(1983), 'Comments', in William R. Cline (ed.), *Trade Policy in the 1980s* (Cambridge, Mass.: MIT Press), pp. 713–14.

——(1987), 'The Importance of Trade for Developing Countries', *World Bank DRD Discussion Paper*, Report no. DRD248.

——*et al.* (1986), 'Export Incentives and Export Growth in Developing Countries: An Econometric Investigation', *World Bank*, Report no. DRD159.

Bhagwati, Jagdish N. (1978), *Foreign Trade Regimes and Economic Development: The Anatomy and Consequences of Exchange Control Regimes* (Cambridge, Mass.: Ballinger).

——(ed.) (1982), *Import Competition and Response* (Chicago: Univ. of Chicago Press).

——(1984*a*), 'Comment on Raul Prebisch', in Gerald M. Meier and Dudley Seers (eds.), *Pioneers in Development* (New York: OUP).

——Brecher, R. A., and Srinivasan, T. N., (1984*b*), 'DUP Activities and Economic Theory', in Colander (1984).

Cline, William R. (1982), 'Can the East Asian Model of Development be Generalized?' *World Development* (Feb.), pp. 81–99.

Colander, David C. (ed.) (1984), *Neo-Classical Political Economy: The Analysis of Rent-Seeking and DUP Activities* (Cambridge, Mass.: Ballinger).

Corden, Max (1987), 'Protection and Liberalization: A Review of Analytical Issues', *IMF Occasional Paper*, 54 (Washington, DC: IMF).

Donges, J. (1976), 'A Comparative Study of Industrialization Policies in Fifteen Semi-Industrial Countries', *Weltwirtschaftliches Archiv*, 112/4, pp. 626–59.

Evans, P. (1979), *Dependent Development* (Princeton: Princeton Univ. Press).

Feder, Gershon (1982), 'On Exports and Economic Growth', *Journal of Development Economics*, 12, pp. 59–73.

Findlay, Ronald (1986), 'Trade, Development, and the State', Economic Growth Center, Yale University (mimeo).

——, and Wellisz, S. (1982), 'Endogenous Tariffs; The Political Economy of Trade Restrictions', in Bhagwati (1982).

Havrylyshyn, Oli, and Alikhani, Iradji (1982), 'Is There Cause for Export Optimism? An Inquiry into the Existence of a Second Generation of Successful Exporters', *Weltwirtschaftliches Archiv*, 118, pp. 651–63.

Hirschman, Albert O. (1968), 'The Political Economy of Import-Substituting Industrialization in Latin America', *Quarterly Journal of Economics*, 82/1.

Hughes, Helen, and Krueger, Anne O. (1984), 'Effects of Protection in Developed Countries on Developing Countries' Exports of Manufacturing', in R. E. Baldwin and Anne O. Krueger (eds.), *The Structure and Evolution of U.S. Trade Policy* (Chicago: Univ. of Chicago Press), ch. 11.

Kravis, I. B. (1970), 'Trade as a Handmaiden of Growth—Similarities between the 19th and 20th Centuries', *Economic Journal*, 80, pp. 850–72.

Krueger, Anne O. (1974), 'The Political Economy of the Rent-Seeking Society', *American Economic Review*, 64/3, pp. 291–303.

——(1978), *Foreign Trade Regimes and Economic Development: Liberalization Attempts and Consequences*, (Cambridge, Mass.: Ballinger).

——(1984), 'Trade Policies in Developing Countries', in R. W. Jones and P. B. Kenen (eds.) *Handbook of International Economics*, Vol. 1 (New York: North-Holland).

Krugman, Paul, (1984), 'Import Protection as Export Promotion', in H. Kierzowski (ed.), *Monopolistic Competition and International Trade* (Oxford: Clarendon Press), pp. 180–93.

Lal, Deepak (1987), 'The Political Economy of Economic Liberalization', *World Bank Economic Review*, 1/2.

——and Rajapartirana, Sarath (1987), 'Foreign Trade Regimes and Economic Growth in Developing Countries', *World Bank Research Observer*, 2/2, pp. 189–216.

Lewis, W. A. (1980), 'The Slowing Down of the Engine of Growth', *American Economic Review*, 70/4, pp. 555–64.

Little, Ian M. D. (1979), 'An Economic Reconnaissance', in W. Galenson (ed.), *Economic Growth and Structural Change in Taiwan* (Ithaca: Cornell Univ. Press), pp. 482–5.

——Scitovsky, T., and Scott, M. FG. (1970), *Industry and Trade in Some Developing Countries* (Oxford: OUP for OECD).

Magee, Stephen P. (1984), 'Endogenous Tariff Theory: A Survey', in Colander (1984), ch. 3.

Mahalanobis, Prasanta C. (1953), 'Some Observations on the Process of Growth of National Income', *Sankya*, 12, pp. 307–12.

Meier, G. M. (1989), 'The Old and New Export Pessimism: A Critical Survey', in *The Balance between Industry and Agriculture in Economic Development*, Proceedings of the 8th World Congress of the International Economic Association, Delhi, India, Vol. 5, Nurul Islam (ed.), *Factors Influencing Change* (London: Macmillan).

Michael, Michael (1986), 'The Timing and Sequencing of a Trade Liberalization Policy', in A. Choksi and D. Papageorgiou (eds.), *Economic Liberalization in Developing Countries* (Oxford: Blackwell).

Myint, Hla (1987), 'The Neoclassical Resurgence in Development Economics: Its Strength and Limitations', in Gerald M. Meier (ed.), *Pioneers in Development*, 2nd Series, (New York: OUP), pp. 107–36.

Nishimizu, Mieko, and Robinson, Sherman (1984), 'Trade Policies and Productivity Change in Semi-Industrialized Countries', *Journal of Development Economics*, 16.

Nurkse, Ragnar (1957), 'The Conflict Between "Balanced Growth" and International Specialization', *Lectures on Economic Development* (Faculty of Economics, Istanbul), pp. 170–6.

OECD (1985), *Costs and Benefits of Protection* (Paris: OECD).

Pack, Howard, and Westphal, Larry E. (1986), 'Industrial Strategy and Technological Change', *Journal of Development Economics*, 22, pp. 87–128.

Pagageorgiou, D., Michaely, M., and Choksi, A. (1986), 'The Phasing of a Trade Liberalization Policy: Preliminary Evidence', *World Bank CPD Discussion Paper*, 1986–42.

Ranis, Gustav (1978), 'Equity with Growth in Taiwan: How "Special" is the "Special Case"?' *World Development*, 6/3, pp. 397–409.

Riedel, James (1984), 'Trade as the Engine of Growth in Developing Countries, Revisited', *Economic Journal*, 94, pp. 56–73.

Rosenstein-Rodan, Paul (1943), 'Problems of Industrialization of Eastern and South-Eastern Europe', *Economic Journal*, 53, pp. 202–11.

Streeten, Paul P. (1982), 'A Cool Look at "Outward-Looking" Strategies for Development', *World Economy*, 5/2, pp. 159–69.

Wolf, Martin (1982), *India's Exports* (Oxford: OUP).

9

The Political Economy of Controls:
American Sugar

ANNE O. KRUEGER

IN economic theory, it is relatively straightforward to analyse the impact of government controls over economic activity. Whether the control is over feed-grain prices in Egypt, the quantities of imports of individual items in India, price controls on 'old' oil, or the 'voluntary' reduction in the number of automobiles exported from Japan to the United States, several conclusions follow straightforwardly. First and foremost, those controls (and most others) at best achieve their objectives in a more costly manner than would alternative mechanisms. Second, the presumed beneficiaries of controls are often quite different from those (if any) actually benefiting. Third, the costs of controls seem to be largely ignored or misunderstood in political decision-making, at least in the first instance.

Despite these well-established results, controls seem to persist. A major challenge confronting those concerned with their costs is to attempt to understand the reasons why the political process often generates and perpetuates high-cost solutions to stated objectives. To establish an understanding of the political economy of controls would appear to be a formidable, but important, challenge, if means are to be sought to lower the costs of attaining political objectives.

The purpose of this chapter is to attempt to further our understanding of the political economy of controls. Section 1 provides a survey of existing models of regulation. The remainder of the chapter is then devoted to an examination of how well those models perform in light of the history of one particular set of controls—the American sugar programme. In part, resort to an inductive effort to understand controls better seems logical in light of economists' puzzlement with their prevalence. In part, however, it seems likely that further advances in understanding of the political economy of controls can take place only with the accumulation of insights emanating

I am heavily indebted to Paul Pecorino for valuable research assistance in preparation of this chapter. Al Reifman was extremely generous with assistance in providing material from the Congressional Research Service. Richard Snape was exceptionally helpful and generous in commenting on several drafts of the entire manuscript and in sharing his extensive knowledge of the international sugar economy. Stanley Engerman and Maurice Scott provided useful comments on the penultimate draft. Helpful comments and suggestions were also made by members of the Political Economy Workshop at Duke University, and the International Economics Workshops at Virginia Polytechnic and State University, the University of North Carolina, Harvard University, and the University of Rochester.

from analysis of a number of particular cases. It is to be hoped that they will gradually yield 'stylized facts' upon which better theory can be built. Sugar was chosen for scrutiny for a number of reasons: the programme has had a long and chequered history since 1934; given the transparency of the American system, most of the contending interests have been documented to an unusual degree in Senate and House hearings; and good economic analyses of the programme have been undertaken at various times so that focus here can be on economic-political interactions.

Ian Little has been in the forefront of professional economists using their analytical tool-kit to demonstrate the costs of controls in a variety of settings. His work has been instrumental in convincing the vast majority of the economics profession that the economic costs of controls are far greater than were generally thought two or three decades ago. It is therefore appropriate that an essay in his honour should attempt to further understanding of the political economy of economic policy.

1. Models of Economic Policy Formulation

The absence among economists[1] of a widely accepted model of economic policy formulation is readily illustrated by the divergent implicit and explicit assumptions about the nature of intervention underlying policy analysis in the various sub-fields in economics. In international trade, the tradition was for long to assume that policy-makers were uninformed and that failure to adopt Pareto-optimal policies reflected ignorance on their part. International economists assumed that a benevolent government would, once informed of the benefits of free trade, immediately undertake policy reform. Considerable bewilderment then resulted from the many departures from Pareto-optimal policies in circumstances where infant industry and monopoly power in trade did not apply.

Several models of political-economic interaction in policy formulation have been set forth in an effort to understand the persistence of some policies. Brock and Magee (1978) modelled politicians as needing money to win elections but simultaneously losing votes if they support lobbyists' causes too ardently; an equilibrium occurs when the revenue from lobbying at the margin increases votes by the same amount as further support of special interests loses votes. Corden (1974), by contrast, attempted to explain international economic policy as a consequence of a 'conservative

---

[1] There is a large literature among political scientists focusing on the determinants of policy. I am heavily indebted to Robert Bates for long and useful discussions about this literature. In this section, I focus only on the economics literature on the subject, in part because of my own comparative advantage, but in part because the intent of the chapter is to focus on political-economic interactions, and the role of market forces in affecting the outcomes of policies adopted by politicians, topics largely neglected in both the economics and the political science literature.

social welfare function': in his view, politicians attempt to protect people's income streams, and thus provide assistance to those who are adversely affected by shifts in prices and competitive positions. Finally, Bhagwati and Srinivasan (1980) modelled 'directly unproductive activity', in which lobbyists spend resources in seeking legislation equal in value to the value of the protection to them.

In public economics, there has been a similar tradition: a presentation of economic efficiency conditions for optimality, with the accompanying assertion that non-fulfilment of these conditions—such as the presence of externalities—represented a case of market failure and therefore justified market intervention. Underlying these sets of policy prescriptions is the notion of government as a benevolent guardian, hampered only by ignorance of proper economic policy as it seeks disinterestedly to maximize a Benthamite social welfare function.

In the field of industrial organization, the tradition was similar until the 1960s. It was assumed that government bureaucrats were in fact pursuing the public interest in regulating whatever was regulated—transport, communications, public utilities, and the like. This view was challenged, and largely overthrown, in the 1970s by Stigler (1971), Peltzman (1976), and others, who instead posited full rationality of all actors. In their view, all political agents are rational and use the political process to effect wealth transfers. Thus, the view of the regulatory process changed fundamentally, from being a process fostering the 'common good' to being a rational outcome to private maximization through the political process. Participants were seen to be fully rational and acting in their own self-interest. In this model, policy analysis by economists would serve no useful purpose, as additional information would not change the behaviour of any participant in the regulatory process.

An interesting variant on the Stigler–Peltzman approach has been set forth by Becker (1983), who assumes that political interest groups form in their own self-interest, and that politicians rationally choose policies in response to the competing pressures these groups can exert. With competition among groups, and the assumption that anything which benefits one group must either be financed directly by a tax or indirectly by costing another group (including deadweight losses), Becker concludes that resources are allocated to the political process to maximize the benefits (which are for some groups negative) each group expects to receive.

Yet another approach is that of Olson (1965, 1982). Starting with the 'logic of collective action', in which the 'free-rider' problem prevents the effective collusion of large numbers of small losers, Olson formulated various hypotheses as to which effective pressure groups would emerge and the characteristics of industries and of other economic interest groups that would be likely to be able to organize and effectively represent their interests. These characteristics include both geographic and market concentration. Carrying his analysis further, Olson attempted to explain differentials in growth rates among nations after the Second World War. In Olson's world, interest groups organize to protect their interests as growth progresses. Over time, more and more groups and institutions are in place, and in the process economic efficiency diminishes and growth decelerates. War destroys these groups and interests, at least to some extent, so that war-devastated countries, such as Germany and Japan are enabled to grow rapidly, freed of many of the resistances to growth that arise over time in a war-free environment.[2]

Olson's model essentially posits that economically inefficient outcomes arise because of free-rider problems: it is rational for individuals not to join groups interested in consumer welfare, etc., because the benefits to them are independent of their own activities. This contrasts significantly with the Stigler–Peltzman–Becker view in two ways: institutional means are not available for large groups of small potential gainers or losers to represent their interests, and interest groups form gradually over time as they learn about their interests (and respond to the gains of other groups).

The final view of the political process is that of Buchanan and public choice theory. Here, the underlying assumption is that individuals behave in their interest in the political, as well as the economic, arena, but that the 'rules of the game' in the political arena may permit choices that, while individually rational, could clearly be improved upon by a different decision rule.

Each of these models doubtless contains elements of truth. None the less, one can ask whether they capture a sufficiently large fraction of it. One could question, for example, the implicit hypothesis underlying the views of Becker and Buchanan that all participants understand their own self-interest. An important issue is where the role of knowledge, and of the technocrats who implement controls, enters into such an analysis.

Moreover, almost all the models implicitly or explicitly address controls as if they were a once-and-for-all phenomenon. In many situations, one has more the impression that politicians impose a control with a certain naïveté as to its ramifications; that the market then reacts to minimize the cost of the control; that the politicians in turn find the market solution unacceptable and then alter the control, only to have the market once again react. If this view is correct, a control cannot be analysed as a static, unchanging set of regulations, and must be seen in light of the economic-political forces that it sets in motion to result in continuing evolution of the programme.

As will be seen, the evolution of the American sugar programme con-

---

[2] See Mueller (1983) for a series of papers examining the empirical validity of the Olson hypotheses regarding growth rates.

tains elements of almost all the models discussed above. Additionally, it is certainly a programme that evolved over time, where market interactions with controls affected not only outcomes, but even the position of various participants with respect to the desirability of controls. Moreover, it is also a programme whose evolution depended, in important ways, on the fact that it was highly complex; complexity in effect created a barrier to entry into the political arena, and thus facilitated the perpetuation of the programme; it also created a vested interest in the perpetuation of the programme on the part of knowledgeable parties. Finally, and perhaps most interestingly, the evolution of the sugar programme is full of 'mistakes', in the sense that various parties on not infrequent occasions took policy stances that turned out, at a later date, to be against their own self-interest.

Background information essential to understanding the sugar economy is presented in Section 2. Thereafter, the origins of the sugar programme are covered in Section 3; the programme during the post-war years from 1948 to 1960 is the subject of Section 4; Section 5 covers the period from 1960 to 1974; Section 6 the period from 1974 to 1981; and Section 7 traces the evolution of the programme on to the present time. Section 8 then assesses the implications of the sugar programme for a richer political economy of controls. The final section draws tentative conclusions.

2.   The Sugar Market

The economic effects of the American sugar programme have been extensively analysed, and are reasonably well know. In this section, the essential characteristics of the sugar industry, and the relation of the American market to the international sugar market, are described. Emphasis is on those aspects relevant for analysing the political economy of controls, at least as exemplified in the case of sugar.

2.1.   The Production Function[3]

Sugar is an unusual commodity. It can be made from either raw cane or sugar-beet, and yet the end-products of the two are perfect substitutes. Cane can grow only in tropical or semi-tropical climates while sugar-beet is grown in temperate climates. Both cane and beet require processing to make sugar. In both cases, initial processing must be undertaken within a very short time after harvest; it must therefore be done close to where the cane or beet is grown.

For beet-sugar, a single-stage refining process has produced refined sugar since the late 1800s. In the case of cane, however, second-stage re-

---

[3] This section draws heavily on Congressional Research Service (1985). The interested reader can consult that source for considerably greater detail. The facts, however, are in virtually all Congressional *Hearings* pertaining to the sugar programme.

fining is necessary to make sugar in the crystalline white form used in final consumption; raw sugar (i.e. that processed from cane near the site) can be refined anywhere.[4] While there are a few by-products of cane and of beet, they are not sufficiently valuable to warrant growing the crops in the absence of a demand for their sugar; at any event, the by-products made from cane and beet are similar.

Cane and beet mills and cane refineries are capital-intensive, and apparently have little or no alternative use. No farmer would consider growing cane or sugar-beet without a mill near by, and no mill would be established unless it was anticipated that there would be a proximate source of supply. For this reason, there is a considerable degree of vertical integration in the industry; in Hawaii, for example, most cane is grown in fields owned by the same parties who own the local sugar mill for first-stage refining.

Mills need a fairly steady flow of cane or beet in order to utilize their capacity reasonably steadily over a major part of the year. Arrangements for harvesting sugar-beet and cane therefore include fairly detailed provisions as to the date of delivery of the product to the mill.

One of the interesting political phenomena about the industry, given the evolution of controls, is its relatively small size. It is estimated that, in 1969 (which was the about the peak of sugar production and demand in the United States), there were only 28,000 American farms producing sugar, producing about $1.25 billion of gross output, and employing 150,000 (mostly seasonal and largely immigrant) workers.[5]

2.2.   The Demand for Sugar and Sweeteners

If it is conventional wisdom that producers are more likely to gain when they are highly concentrated relative to consumers, sugar is an exception. More than 70 per cent of US sugar consumption is by industrial users—bakeries, soft drinks, confectionary, cereals, etc. The remaining 25–30 per cent of consumption goes through distribution directly to consumers (defined as all sugar sold in bags of less than 50 lb.).

Consumption of refined sugar in the United States peaked at about 10.7 million tons in 1972, equivalent to about 102 lb. per capita. At that time,

---

[4] The United States had a tariff on raw imports, and a higher tariff on refined sugar imports, throughout most of the 19th century. At the time, beet-sugar required second-stage refining. The differential in tariffs between raw and refined sugar was high encough to make the effective rate of protection to refining greater than 100%. The best means of determining whether sugar had been refined was the 'Dutch colour test' which graded imports by the extent of brown colouration of the sugar being imported. Among the 19th-century problems with tariff administration was the importation of brown refined sugar. See Taussig (1924), pp. 101 ff. for a description.

[5] See Heston (1975) p. 26. Johnson's estimates (1974) as to the size of the industry are similar.

consumption of all caloric sweeteners, including sugar, corn sweeteners, honey, etc. was 13.3 million tons, or 126.7 lb. per capita.[6] By 1986, American consumption of sugar had fallen to 7.4 million tons, or 61.6 lb. per capita, while total caloric sweetener consumption had risen to 15.4 million tons or 131.6 lb. per capita.[7] This decline in sugar consumption resulted from the substitution of high fructose corn syrup (HFCS) for sugar in most of the commercial uses of liquid sugar (soft drinks being the largest) as a result of sugar's high price under the programme. As will be seen, this market response to the high support price for sugar (at approximately 4–5 times the world level) resulted in a major shift in the sugar producers' and sugar refiners' interests in the sugar programme, but simultaneously induced the corn-growers to support perpetuation of the programme in its existing form.

2.3. The International Sugar Economy

There are few countries in the world that do not intervene in their domestic sugar markets. Perhaps this is because both temperate and tropical countries can grow sugar. Regardless of the motives for intervention, the result is that about three-quarters of sugar grown in the world is consumed in the country of production.[8]

For this reason, the international market is somewhat thin, with about 27 million tons out of an estimated total world production of about 100 million tons (sugar equivalent, both cane and beet) entering into international trade (*Sugar and Sweeteners Situation*, June 1987, p. 35) in the 1985/6 crop

---

[6] This contrasts with an estimated consumption per capita of 9 lb. in the United States in 1822 (see Johnson, 1974, p. 5). Here and throughout, the reader should be alert to units; production is often measured in terms of tons (2,000 lb.) of cane or beet; these units (contrast Tables 9.2 and 9.3 below) are obviously different from those that measure the weight of refined sugar produced or consumed. Since the yield of cane and beet varies from year to year and place to place, conversion ratios are not constant. However, the conversion factor is close to 10:1—*for example* in 1986, 28.743 million tons of cane were produced, which was 3.4 million tons of sugar, raw value. For beet, 25.229 million tons were produced, with 2.989 million tons of sugar, raw value produced. See USDA, *Sugar and Sweetener Situation and Outlook Yearbook*, June 1981. For an amusing discussion of the problems of administering an import quota set in terms of raw value, see House *Hearings* (1974), pp. 95–101.

[7] Consumption of non-caloric sweeteners has also risen; in 1970 it is estimated that they accounted for 5.8 lb. per capita consumption, while by 1987 they were 18.5 lb. per capita. There are many grounds for believing that much of the increase in consumption of non-caloric sweeteners may have represented a shift in tastes, rather than a consequence of relative price changes. For that reason, the evolution of non-caloric sweetener production and consumption will not be further considered in this chapter. Taking it into account would not significantly alter the argument at any stage, as total consumption of non-caloric sweeteners still occupies less than 15% of the entire market for sweeteners.

[8] One of the many arguments for the sugar programme given by sugar interests has been that sugar is controlled almost everywhere. In most instances, however, it is subsidiary to other arguments put in support of the programme.

year. Even out of that total, the existence of a number of preferential arrangements (including the American quota and Cuban–Soviet trade) has meant that the 'free market' price has governed only a small fraction of transactions. American preferences are diminishing in importance, however, as American imports have fallen, for reasons that will become evident below, from 6.2 million tons in 1977 to an estimated 1.5 million tons in 1987.[9]

The price of sugar has always displayed volatility on international markets. Two factors contributed to this. First, there is an 18-month lag between planting of cane and first harvesting. Thereafter, cane is usually cut two more times at approximately six-month intervals before the field is cleared and a new crop planted. Thus, when sugar prices rise, there is a longer time-lag than for annual crops (although not as long as for some tree crops) before additional production reaches the market. When the sugar price falls, it can be an even longer time before the planting response is reflected in reduced sugar output, unless of course the price falls so low that harvesting proves unprofitable. Second, and at least as important, the fact that the international market is a residual has intensified these price swings.

Thus, after Cuba lost her US quota in 1960, world prices rose for several years.[10] Thereafter, new plantings (which took place predominantly in countries which received higher sugar prices because of their increased quotas in the American market) matured, and world sugar supplies rose sharply; the world price fell from a high of 8.50 cents per lb. in 1963 to 1.86 cents per lb. in 1966. That, in turn, apparently discouraged plantings, because by 1969 the sugar price was rising again. However, because of the world-wide commodity boom, the production response was apparently more sluggish and delayed than in earlier periods of high prices. Hence, the price of sugar rose continuously until November 1974, reaching over 40 cents per lb. in that month. There then followed another sharp decline in price as new supplies appeared by 1976, and the price fell for the next two years. By 1980, however, production had once again responded to

[9] In Dec. 1987, the United States Department of Agriculture announced that the permitted level of imports for 1988 would be 750 thousand tons. See *New York Times*, 16 Dec. 1987, p. 29. However, the political reactions to that announcement have not yet been completed. See below, Section 7.

[10] Cuba's exports and quota constituted the vast majority of sugar imports into the United States prior to 1960. In 1959, for example, Cuba exported 3,437,582 tons to the United States out of total imports of 4,273,000 tons. This contrasted with domestic production of 4,702,619 tons in that year. By 1961, Cuba's exports to the United States were zero. See Senate Finance Committee, *Hearings on Extension of the Sugar Act of 1948*, 1965, p. 11. Cuba's estimated share of the world sugar trade was 28.6% in 1961, and 24.7% in 1984. The Soviet Union replaced the United States as the major market for Cuban sugar in the 1960s. See Tan (1986) for particulars of the Cuban-Soviet sugar trade.

lower prices, and the price again rose sharply, reaching 29.02 cents per lb. by the end of 1980.

Starting early in 1981, the world price fell and remained depressed for a long period as American imports declined sharply and the European Community increased exports as its production surpluses mounted. It was estimated in 1985 that, if all countries were to adopt free trade in sugar, the world price would be about 12 cents per lb. contrasted with an actual world price of at that time 4 cents per lb. and a US domestic wholesale price of 20.3 cents per lb. (see Table 9.1).[11] By the end of 1987, the world price had risen substantially, to about 9.5 cents per lb., while the US price was virtually unchanged.

3. Origins of the Sugar Programme[12]

There have been few years in American history when sugar has not been the object of some degree of intervention. It has always been an importable. Starting in 1796, a tariff on imports was imposed. Until the late 1800s, revenue was the major motive for the tariff, as domestic production was less than 10 per cent of consumption and imports supplied more than 90 per cent of US consumption.[13]

Hawaii's relationship to the United States in the 1870s and 1880s was heavily centred around sugar: a free trade agreement with the United States had permitted Hawaiian sugar to be imported without duty, and had encouraged the expansion of Hawaiian cane-growing land. The American Congress then proceeded to rescind the duty on sugar, but to pay a bounty of 2 cents per lb. (about the same as the specific tariff earlier collected and equivalent to 100 per cent nominal protection) to American growers. The desire to have access to the American market at favourable prices seems to have been a major motive behind Hawaiian accession to US jurisdiction, after which the US reverted to tariff protection and Hawaii escaped the sugar tariff. From the 1890s until 1930, American tariff protection con-

---

[11] See Leu and Knutson (1987) for one attempt to estimate what the world price would be in the absence of the current US programme. See also Congressional Research Service (1985).

[12] This section draws heavily on Terpstra (1981). Only those aspects of the pre-1934 sugar tariff relevant for later development are discussed here. For a full account, see Taussig (1924), ch. II.

[13] House Agriculture Committee *Hearings* of 1951; Extension of the Sugar Act of 1948, HR 4521, pp. 34–5. Taussig attributed the expansion of sugar-cane production in Louisiana in the 19th century to the existence of the protective tariff, and documented USDA efforts in the middle and late 19th century that led to the development of sugar-beet production in the United States. See Taussig (1924), chs. IV and VII. According to Taussig, sugar would not have been produced at all in the continental United States had it not been for USDA encouragement. Thus, the sugar programme is an example of an industry whose origins lie in government protective policies, and not of government controls originating because of industry pressure.

TABLE 9.1. New York and world sugar prices, 1948–1987 (US cents/lb.)

	Caribbean price (f.o.b.) (1)	New York duty-paid price (2)	Ratio of Col (2) to Col (1) (3)
1948	4.17	5.6	1.34
1949	4.34	5.8	1.34
1950	4.98	5.9	1.18
1951	5.67	6.1	1.08
1952	4.17	6.3	1.51
1953	3.41	6.3	1.85
1954	3.26	6.1	1.87
1955	3.24	6.0	1.85
1956	3.48	6.1	1.75
1957	5.16	6.1	1.18
1958	3.50	6.3	1.80
1959	2.97	6.2	2.09
1960	3.14	6.3	2.01
1961	2.91	6.4	2.20
1962	2.98	6.3	2.11
1963	8.50	8.2	0.96
1964	5.87	6.9	1.18
1965	2.12	6.8	3.21
1966	1.86	7.0	3.76
1967	1.99	7.3	3.67
1968	1.98	7.5	3.79
1969	3.37	7.8	2.31
1970	3.75	8.1	2.16
1971	4.52	8.5	1.88
1972	7.43	9.1	1.22
1973	9.61	10.3	1.07
1974	29.99	29.5	0.98
1975	20.49	22.5	1.10
1976	11.58	13.3	1.15
1977	8.11	11.0	1.36
1978	7.82	13.9	1.78
1979	9.65	15.6	1.61
1980	29.02	30.1	1.04
1981	16.93	19.7	1.16
1982	8.42	19.9	2.36
1983	8.49	22.0	2.59
1984	5.18	21.7	4.19
1985	4.04	20.3	5.02
1986	6.05	21.0	3.47
1987	7.10	21.7	3.06

Source: USDA, *Sugar and Sweeteners Situation*, various issues.

tinued. Because the Hawaiians were exempt from the tariff (and Cuba also received a 25 per cent reduction in duty),[14] they benefited from protection in the sheltered American market. The Philippine sugar industry also started under the umbrella of American preferential protection.[15]

The Smoot–Hawley tariff in 1930, however, raised the rate of duty faced by Cuba to 2 cents per lb. (compared with a world sugar price of 0.73 cents per lb. in 1932), and the duty on imports from other countries to 2.5 cents per lb. In fact, however, imports from Cuba and the Philippines met US demands, and little sugar was imported from other countries. Indeed, during some periods of the year, the sugar price fell below the world price plus duty as Cuban sugar was more than sufficient to meet demand at that price.

During the Great Depression, sugar prices fell drastically. Among other consequences, the Cuban economy was extremely adversely affected, and, with it, the fortunes of American investors who owned sugar plantations there. Political instability in Cuba was another consequence: a general strike led to pressure from the Roosevelt Administration for a change in leadership, which in turn led to the resignation of President Machado; his successor also could not restore law and order, and an army revolt brought Sergeant Fulgencio Batista to power.[16] Simultaneously, the Roosevelt Administration was introducing parts of its New Deal programme. The Secretary of Commerce, Harold Ickes, reported that, with respect to sugar:

The President is chafing under the present system by which, under the heavy tariff on beet sugar, the whole population is taxed in order to pay a subsidy to the beet sugar growers . . . If it were not for the political questions involved, the President would put sugar on the free list and pay a subsidy. . . . He has discussed the possibility of wiping out the beet sugar industry over a series of twenty years (Ickes, 1953, p. 147).

Starting in 1933, the Administration attempted to bring about political stability in Cuba and address the 'sugar situation' by imposing production quotas on US producers, thereby raising prices. The sugar interests opposed this programme so vigorously that several early proposals were withdrawn.[17] In effect, opponents wanted more restriction of imports to increase prices, with no production controls. Finally, in 1934, the Jones–Costigan Act was passed. It provided for a system of production and

[14] Cuban sugar production rose rapidly in the first three decades of the century in response to this partial exemption. Much of the cane was planted, harvested, and processed (first-stage) on American-owned land and sugar-mills. By 1934, it was estimated that Americans owned 70% of Cuban sugar producing capacity (*Hearings* 1934, p. 106). See also House *Hearings* (1952), p. 35.

[15] Again, see Taussig (1924), ch. 6 and US Tariff Commission (1937).

[16] Heston (1975), p. 91. Heston says that an ultimatum was delivered that the marines would intervene if Machado did not relinquish power within 48 hours.

[17] See Heston (1975), pp. 102–13 for a description of the political forces opposing and supporting the 1934 sugar programme legislation.

marketing quotas for domestic producers and import quotas for foreigners (almost exclusively Cuba). The intent of the Jones–Costigan Act seems to have been primarily to shore up the Cuban economy and secondarily to increase American producers' incomes. There was, in addition to production and import restrictions, provision for direct payment to American producers. However, there was also a clear intention to contain the size of the industry. In his message to Congress, President Roosevelt's statement was that:

Steadily increasing sugar production . . . has created a price and marketing situation prejudicial to virtually everyone interested. Farmers in many areas are threatened with low prices for their beets and cane, and Cuban purchases of our goods have dwindled steadily as her shipments of sugar to this country have declined.

There is a school of thought which believes that sugar ought to be on the free list. . . .

I do not at this time recommend placing sugar on the free list. I feel that we ought first to try out a system of quotas with the threefold object of keeping down the price of sugar to consumers, of providing for the retention of beet and cane farming within our continental limits, and also to provide against further expansion of this necessarily expensive industry.[18]

Like much of the New Deal legislation, the Jones–Costigan Act was passed quickly within several days of its introduction and after hearings lasting only a few hours.[19] Although sugar producers were opposed to the Act, their representatives in Congress apparently gave in when threatened with the alternative of a reduced tariff and no programme. Beet-growers were particularly adamant in their opposition as the Act called for a 17 per cent reduction in sugar-beet production from the level of 1933.[20]

---

[18] *Sugar Beets and Sugarcane as Basic Agricultural Commodities under the Agricultural Adjustment Act*, HR 7907. 19 February 1934, House *Hearings*, p. 1. The Chief, Section of Sugar and Rice, Agricultural Adjustment Administration, testified that the domestic sugar industry was 'an expensive one from the point of view of the consumer and that lies behind the freezing of sugar beet acreage' (p. 13).

[19] See ibid.

[20] See Heston (1975) and *Hearings* (1934), pp. 84, 118, 121, 132, 145, 148, 152, 167. Because sugar was an import, its regulation should have come under the jurisdiction of the House Ways and Means Committee and the Senate Finance Committee. It did come under the latter. But one of the interesting 'accidents' with important consequences was that when the Jones–Costigan Act was first up for renewal in 1937, the Chairman of the House Agriculture Committee requested, as a favour from his colleague and friend, the Chairman of the Ways and Means Committee, that the House Agriculture Committee handle sugar matters. The Chairman of the House Ways and Means Committee acceded to the request, and the House Agriculture Committee has handled sugar matters ever since. See Price (1971) for an account. Because there is a tax on sugar imports, only the House may initiate legislation. This right of initiation, combined with the fact that sugar is the only agricultural commodity considered by the Senate Finance Committee, has resulted in unusually great power concentrated in the hands of the House Agriculture Committee for dealing with sugar. See the discussion of the 1962 bill below for one instance where the Senate opposed the House decisions but in the end was unable to prevail.

Even in the 1934 legislation, sugar refiners sought quotas to restrict imports of refined sugar. They claimed that the 1930 legislation (Smoot–Hawley) left them with a cost disadvantage *vis-à-vis* foreign producers (because Congress had assumed that it took one ton of raw sugar to make a ton of refined, whereas the actual conversion ratio was more like 1.07 to one).[21] So, quotas on imports of refined sugar were imposed to satisfy domestic (second-stage) refining interests; the quota was later replaced with a prohibition on importing fully refined cane sugar—a necessary condition for preserving the support of the sugar refiners who imported the raw (cane) sugar and refined it in their plants.[22]

As already indicated, the sugar growers opposed the introduction of these quotas in 1934, feeling it was against their interests. When the bill came up for renewal in 1937, however, they had switched sides, and actively supported the sugar programme and production and import quotas (see House *Hearings* (1937), pp. 16–45). Thus, just as the mainland sugar industry originated because of government efforts to encourage it, the 1934 sugar programme was put in place by the government with the opposition of the sugar interests.

Clearly, this sequence of events does not support the Bhagwati–Srinivasan model in which producers expend their resources to attain a programme aimed at supporting their interests. Rather, the USDA in the nineteenth century, and the Roosevelt Administration in 1934, seem to have viewed their roles as benevolent guardians of the social good. Once the programme was in place, however, sugar producers and refiners recognized their interests in its perpetuation, and generally supported it.[23] The major issue in 1937 was the size of the future quotas, and representatives of cane-sugar-producing states urged expansion of their quotas. Florida and Louisiana cane growers particularly pressured for larger quotas. Interestingly, it had been primarily beet producers that had opposed production ceilings in 1934; however, beet producers had not even filled their quotas under the original 1934 Act and did not seek large increases under the 1937 bill (House *Hearings* (1937), p. 145).

Unquestionably, then, the initial opposition of the beet growers had

---

[21] Johnson (1974), p. 30 believes that American refineries had lost their comparative advantage in the 1920s and used the 1.07 to one conversion ratio as an argument for protection which they needed on other grounds. Taussig's documentation, however, suggests that the protection accorded to American sugar refineries as early as the 1870s was more than sufficient to provide needed protection and monopoly profit. See his interesting discussion of the 'Sugar Trust' (Taussig, 1924, ch. VIII). Taussig (1924, p. 104) cites testimony before Congress in 1888 by the head of the American Sugar Refining Company (the Trust) to the effect that 'the mother of all trusts is the customs tariff bill'.

[22] The precise quotas set forth in the first bill may be found in House *Hearings* (1934), p. 2.

[23] Interestingly, a representative of the United States Sugar Corporation (based in Florida) opposed the 1937 bill on the grounds the Florida could expand prodution and indicated a preference for unrestricted sugar imports unless Florida's production quota was increased substantially (see House *Hearings* (1937), p. 168).

been irrational; they were unconstrained in how much they grew, since the quotas were not binding. Their own later support of the programme demonstrates this. As will be seen, this behaviour of the beet-growing interests is only one of the instances in the history of the sugar programme where it is unquestionable that actors took positions that were clearly against their own interest.[24]

When the sugar programme was up for renewal in 1939, production had expanded sufficiently to reach the assigned quotas in most producing regions, and pressures mounted to reduce imports and increase mainland quotas. The Act was renewed, however, with little change in production quotas and in the shares of domestic production and imports in anticipated total consumption. However, with the advent of the Second World War, the entire programme was suspended as the problem became one of increasing output, rather than controlling supply. During the war, Cuban sugar was exported to the United States, even when American prices were below those that could have been realized in other markets.[25]

4. The 'Support Cuba' Period, 1948–1960

At the end of the war, commodity prices were high and there was no sugar legislation in effect. It had been put in place as a New Deal programme to deal with low sugar prices and a Cuban political-economic crisis. Sugar producers, who had originally opposed it, had come to support it, but, with the high prices after the war, there was no particular pressure from them for a resumption of the programme.

However, the Sugar Act was reconsidered in 1948. At the time, of course, the world price was high (although the US price was about 30 per cent above it, see Table 9.1) and the real issue was the percentage of sugar that should be supplied from domestic rather than foreign sources. A major consideration in devising the legislation was the moral debt owed to Cuba, because of Cuban steadfastness in providing sugar to a wartime ally. As passed, the intent of the legislation was to 'protect foreigners' interests in the US market'. This was to be accomplished by continuing to restrict US production to 55 per cent of consumption and allocating the remaining rights to supply the high-price US market to foreign countries, which in practice meant primarily Cuba.[26]

---

[24] Puerto Rico and Hawaii had lost out in terms of their production quotas, but gained in terms of a higher sugar price. Both regions in 1937 focused on the prohibition in the 1934 bill which prevented exporting of second-stage refined sugar to the mainland. This provision was, however, not changed. See House *Hearings* (1937), pp. 55, 106.

[25] Sugar Act of 1948, House Agriculture Committee *Hearings* (1947), pp. 42–4. See also Gerber (1976) for a discussion.

[26] House Agriculture Committee *Hearings* (1951), HR 4521, Extension of the Sugar Act of 1948, pp. 34–5. The 55–45 formula had been set in the 1937 Extension of the Jones–Costigan Act.

By virtue of the production controls, the US price would be higher than the foreign price by more than the tariff; rights to sell in the US market would therefore be valuable. It was clearly the intent of the Administration that these rights be directed largely toward Cuba. The Cuban share was 98.64 per cent of total import rights and Cuba also received rights to unfilled quotas of other countries. In 1949, for example, the United States imported 3.103 million tons of sugar from Cuba, 525 thousand tons from the Philippines, and 56 thousand tons from all other foreign countries (Senate Finance Committee *Hearings* (1965), p. 19).[27]

It is perhaps significant that only one sugar consumer testified in 1948: the American Bakers' Association submitted a short letter indicating its support of a one-year extension of the Sugar Act, and urging a study of the effects of the sugar programme (House *Hearings* (1948), p. 54). This pattern was repeated whenever the programme was up for renewal in the 1950s and right up until 1973. A Sugar Users' Group had formed, and generally testified at hearings, supporting legislation and at most urging minor curtailments in the degree of restrictiveness of the bill.

The sugar programme was changed very little throughout the 1950s. Cuba's share of imports fell somewhat as other countries' production increased, but remained at 3.4 million tons in 1958, contrasted with 980 thousand tons from the Philippines and 291 thousand tons from all other foreign sources. The Sugar Act was renewed in 1951 to continue through 1956, and it was again extended in 1956 to last through 1960. The 1956 extension differed from the earlier ones in that production quotas for US producers were increased along with foreign quotas, and it was decided that quotas would thereafter be established so that American producers would maintain their share in the American market. Thereafter, market growth in excess of 8,350,000 tons was to be shared 55–45 between domestic and foreign producers.[28]

---

[27] The Philippine sugar industry was initially bolstered by the Payne Aldrich Tariff Act of 1909 which gave the Philippines the right to export 300,000 tons duty free to the United States. The duty-free allotment had then been expanded during the First World War. The Philippine production of sugar had expanded greatly in the 1930s. According to the US Tariff Commission, 'the most rapid expansion in both acreage and production occurred in the years 1932–4, when the question of Philippine independence was being debated by Congress. In as much as the several independence bills then under consideration provided for quotas on sugar to be allocated to individual mills and to planters on a production basis, there was an incentive to increase output and hence quota allotments. As a result, Philippine sugar production reached a peak of 1,509,000 short tons in 1934. Since that year it has declined because of the quota provisions of the Jones–Costigan Act and the Independence Act' (US Tariff Commission, 1937, p. 45). After the Second World War, the Philippines were again to be favoured with quotas; initially, however, it was recognized that war damages would prevent their filling their quotas and the unfilled portion was allocated to Cuba.

[28] Data are from US House of Representatives, Committee on Agriculture, *The United States Sugar Program*, 1971, p. 37. As an indication of how complex formulae can become, the 55% additional domestic production quotas were to be distributed as follows: of the first

During the 1950s, acreages allocated to cane and sugar-beet in the United States remained relatively constant, but production increased somewhat due to rising yields. In 1950, 406,000 acres of cane and 924,000 acres of sugar-beet had been harvested with yields of 34.9 tons and 14.7 tons per acre respectively. By 1960, 406,600 acres of land were devoted to sugar-cane and 897,000 acres were devoted to sugar-beet. Yields had risen respectively to 40.0 and 18.7 tons per acre (USDA, 1985).

5. Expanding Domestic Production and Acreage, 1960–1974

5.1. The Battle over the Cuban Quota

A major shift occurred after 1959, however, as American relations with Cuba soured. A first step was to amend the earlier legislation to permit the President of the United States to determine the Cuban quota for the period June 1960 to June 1962, and to permit imports from alternative sources not to exceed the amount by which the Cuban quota was reduced. Cuba's quota was thereupon reduced to zero from July 1960.

In so far as a major purpose of the sugar programme from 1948 to 1960 had been to support Cuba, one would have supposed that, at a minimum, country-specific import quotas would have been abandoned in favour of a global quota. Better yet, import quotas might have been replaced with an import duty. Even more preferable would have been a shift to deficiency payments, under which sugar producers would have received compensation to make up the 'deficiency' between a politically determined support price and the actual market price.

Certainly, the sugar producers should not have been interested in country-specific quotas: their interests lay more in increasing the share of domestic production in consumption. None the less, a major political battle over the future of government policy toward sugar then ensued. The original motives for the 1948 Act were no longer valid. Economists in the Administration and outside the government advocated the abandonment of quotas both on domestic production and on imports, and a return to free markets; if not that, at least a global quota (rather than country-specific allocations) would have made sense and was in fact finally supported by the Kennedy Administration. The domestic growers, and especially beet grow-

---

165,000 tons of increased quota, 51.5 was to go to sugar-beet and 48.5% to mainland cane; the next 20,000 and 2,000 tons were to go to Puerto Rico and the Virgin Islands respectively, and increases in excess of 188,000 tons were to be allocated in proportion to the initial quota allotments (ibid.). For foreign countries' 45% additional allocations, 43.2% was to go to Cuba, and 1.8% to other foreign countries in 1956, while in subsequent years Cuba was to receive 29.59% and 15.41% was to go to other foreign countries: the Philippines, however, were not to receive any change in quota. Meanwhile, if any domestic areas failed to fill their quotas, these should be reallocated to other domestic areas and Cuba only.

ers, however, seized the opportunity to urge that their production quotas be increased to make up part of the Cuban shortfall, and advocated a continuation of the programme including country-specific quotas.[29]

However, interests of the refiners of raw (i.e. cane) sugar did diverge from those of growers of cane and sugar-beet, and from those of beet and cane millers: reducing the quantity of raw sugar imported and increasing domestic production would necessarily reduce economic activity for raw sugar (cane) refiners. For most of the (second-stage) refiners of cane were located primarily in coastal areas, where imports of raw Cuban sugar (once-processed cane) had once been refined. In so far as domestic beet would substitute for imported cane, new sugar-beet processing capacity would be built near beet-growing areas, and second-stage cane refiners would not receive raw cane-sugar in quantities commensurate with their capacity.

After Cuba lost her quotas, the Chairman of the House Agriculture Committee apparently wanted to reassign a large share of the Cuban quota to the Dominican Republic, at the same time as the State Department was preparing sanctions against the Dominican Republic (under Trujillo). As described by Cater:

Quite a struggle ensued. For a period, it remained doubtful whose foreign policy would prevail—the U.S. government's or the sugar subgovernment's. Chairman Cooley forced a temporary increase of the Dominican quota, but the US Treasury slapped a special tax on it. With the change of Administrations in 1960, Executive resources were wheeled into the battle, Attorney General Robert Kennedy made it known that he was examining the spending habits of the affluent Dominican lobbyists for evidence of 'improper' efforts at persuasion . . . At long last, Mr Cooley retreated, and soon afterward General Trujillo fell. . . . Despite President Kennedy's desire to move toward a 'global quota' purchased at nonpremium prices, the old arrangement . . . has been preserved largely intact.[30]

Although opposition to the bill arose both from those opposing giving something of value to foreigners and from those who wanted to protect

[29] It should be recalled that the early 1960s were a time of 'surplus production' of agricultural commodities under agricultural price-support programmes. This enabled advocates of expanded sugar-growing areas to argue that enactment would reduce the extent of surpluses of other commodities. For an account of the political force that determined the outcome in 1962, see Berman and Heineman (1963).

[30] Cater (1964), pp. 19–20. The 1962 Congressional Almanac commented that 'Although sugar legislation is not a partisan issue, it has touched off some major Congressional battles in recent years. In general, the Senate has supported the Administration, while the House has followed the lead of its Agriculture Committee, where sugar legislation originates.

' . . . In 1962, the Administration and the House were in accord on increasing domestic quotas, but differed sharply over the foreign quota provisions, with the Administration resisting reassignment of a portion of the reserved Cuban quota to other countries on a permanent basis, and the House supporting such reassignment . . . A controversy arose over the role of lobbyists representing foreign interests, who stood to gain large fees if their clients' countries received quotas . . .' (*Congressional Quarterly Almanac*, 1962, p. 128). I am indebted to Rick Harper for calling this article to my attention.

domestic growers, the Sugar Act of 1962 none the less passed in a form which enlarged and/or extended quotas to other foreign producers but simultaneously allowed for increases in domestic production.[31] Thus, total acres of cane and beet harvested rose from 1,370,00 in 1960 to 2,065,000 in 1970.[32]

The 1962 amendments to the Sugar Act of 1948 included a provision under which there would be acreage allotments granted to yield 65,000 tons raw value of beet-sugar. Localities were to be selected without regard to earlier producing history, in accordance with the following criteria: 'firmness of capital commitment for construction of factory facilities, need for a cash crop, distance from other producing localities, suitability for sugarbeet production and accessibility to sugar markets. . .'.

157,000 acres were committed to localities in which six new beet mills would be constructed, and another 15,000 acres were allotted in areas where existing mills were thought to have additional capacity (USHR, 1971, p. 39). Over $20 million was invested in additional beet-refining capacity. The designated localities were Mendota, California (1963), Herefore, Texas (1964), Drayton, North Dakota (1965), Montezuma, New York (1965), Easton, Maine (1966), and Chandler, Arizona (1966).[33] This set of provisions appears to defy all of the models of control set forth in Section 1. First, it is not obvious why it was in the interests of existing sugar producers that other areas should enter into sugar-beet production. Second, of the six mills that were constructed, only two ever reached full operation: two never started because farmers in the area did not grow enough sugar-beet and two others never reached more than 50 per cent of capacity and went out of business. Thus, even if one were to assert that six additional districts were expected to support the sugar programme in the

[31] The version passed in the Senate was considerably more liberal than that passed in the House, but it was the House's version that survived the conference committee. See Berman and Heineman (1963) for an account.

[32] Almost all of this increase took place on the US mainland. Acreage planted in Hawaii rose about 200,000 acres between 1960 and 1970. However, acreage and production in Puerto Rico declined over this period, apparently due to the high costs of production relative to other US sources. It is difficult to determine the reason for Puerto Rico's apparent cost disadvantage. Sugar was grown on small farms in Puerto Rico, and it is probable that scale economies, combined with rising real wages in Puerto Rico, resulted in unprofitability of the crop. There is some discussion of Puerto Rico in the House Agriculture *Hearings* (1974) on the Sugar Act Extension of 1974, p. 293.

[33] Thirty-six Congressmen were on the House Agriculture Committee for the 87th Congress. The Chairman was from North Carolina and the Vice-Chairman from Texas. There was no Congressman from Arizona on the Committee and there were Congressmen from states with more apparent suitability for sugar-beet production than some of those mentioned above. (Committee membership included a representative from Idaho, two from Kansas, two from Iowa, and two from Oklahoma.) There were three Congressmen on the committee from cane-growing states (Hawaii, Louisiana, and Florida). See *Congressional Quarterly Almanac*, 1961, p. 48.

future, there was serious miscalculation as to the economic benefits to the six areas of beet production.

Cane production and milling capacity were also expanded: during the 1960s, eight new raw-sugar mills were constructed in Florida, so that there were nine large mills in 1970 compared to three in 1960.

Clearly, expanding mainland acreage in sugar did little for existing sugar interests; indeed, second-stage refiners located on the coast and dependent on imported raw sugar were positively hurt. Likewise, maintaining country-specific import quotas did not benefit sugar producers, and cannot be explained in terms of a producer-interest model. Even more interesting is the absence of the sugar users as a vocal and organized group to oppose continuation of the programme; at a minimum, one would have expected strong opposition to further expansion of domestic production capacity. It will be argued below that the chief beneficiaries were those who had learned the intricacies of the sugar programme and that the very existence of the programme, combined with the fact that it was necessarily complex because of market pressures, resulted in a large group of specialists whose human capital would have depreciated sharply had the programme been greatly simplified or eliminated.

5.2. *Administration of the Programme*

The Sugar Act of 1962 was renewed, with amendments, until 1974. There were difficulties in both administration and enforcement during these years. For example, sugar tended to be shipped to the United States early in the quota period, leaving US refiners with storage problems. The US Department of Agriculture therefore began restricting the amount of sugar that could be imported under quota in the first part of the year (USHR, 1971).

There was also a problem of how to keep domestic acreage within the desired limits. For some regions, including Hawaii for the entire post-war period and Puerto Rico after 1956, this was not an issue as prices were not sufficiently high to induce increased plantings. For other areas, however, the Secretary of Agriculture was to determine 'proportionate shares' to be allocated to individual farms. These shares were the fraction of a region's allotment that could be produced by the individual farm. These proportionate shares were enforced by a 'conditional payment' granted to farmers staying within their allotments, which constituted an important part of their income. Farmers could feed excess cane or beet to livestock without penalty but could not sell it to the mill; the mill, in turn, could buy it legally but had no incentive to do so because it would not have been able to market it.

This, in turn, caused difficulties in areas where it appeared there would be excess production, because each producer wanted to sell to the mill before the mill's allotment was exhausted. When this happened, 'panic selling' started. To stop this, the Secretary of Agriculture was entitled to impose marketing allotments for individual farms, indicating the proportion of each farmer's crop that could be sold to the mill.

Then, too, criteria had to be established for the allocation of foreign quotas.[34] These included:

(i) The governments must be 'friendly' and maintain diplomatic relations with the United States and any country was to be ineligible for a quota which discriminated against American citizens and/or failed to indemnify for any property expropriated.

(ii) The country must have demonstrated 'dependability as a source of sugar supply as reflected in the country's history in supplying the US market, its maintenance of sugar inventories and its potential for supplying additional sugar upon call during critical periods of short supply' (*US Sugar Progam*, p. 49).

(iii) A country that imported more from the United States, especially agricultural commodities, was to be more favoured.

(iv) 'Need of the country for a premium priced market . . . including (a) reference to the extent it shares in other premium priced markets,[35] (b) its relative dependence on sugar as a source of foreign exchange, and (c) present stage of and need for economic development' (ibid.).

(v) 'Extent to which benefits of participation of this market are shared by factories and larger land owners with farmers and workers together with other socio-economic policies in the quota countries' (ibid.).

(vi) Location of country, including considerations of how supplies might be affected in case of emergencies.

There were also provisions for the imposition of quotas upon the importation of sugar-containing products in the event it was determined that these would affect the US sugar market and the implementation of the programme.[36] Ironically, administration of the programme was not more

---

[34] There were even criteria for the allocation of quota deficits, but these were complicated and varied depending on which country was in deficit with respect to its quota, and are not covered here.

[35] This was primarily a reference to sugar exports to the United Kingdom under the Commonwealth Sugar Agreement.

[36] There was even quota-exempt sugar importation, for the following situations:

'(1) The first ten short tons, raw value, of sugar or liquid sugar imported from any foreign country, other than Cuba and the Republic of the Philippines';

(2) the first ten short tons, raw value, of sugar or liquid sugar imported from any foreign country, other than Cuba and the Republic of the Philippines, for religious, sacramental, educational, or experimental purposes;

(3) liquid sugar, imported from any foreign country, other than Cuba and the Republic of the Philippines, in individual sealed containers of such capacity as determined not in excess of one and one-tenth gallons each; and

complex because sugar prices did not elicit additional production: during most of the 1960s production quotas of mainland producers failed to be filled. This is one of the many pieces of evidence that suggests that the sugar programme resulted in large resource costs and few rents over the longer run, a topic to which attention turns below.

5.3. Interest Groups

Administrative complications and complexities notwithstanding, the Sugar Act continued to be approved, with amendments, until 1974.[37] Long before that, various groups interested in the sugar programme had organized themselves. As already mentioned, there was (and is) a Sugar Users' Group (consisting of bakers, soft drink bottlers, candy and confectionery manufacturers, etc.) and a Sugar Producers' Group (the growers, millers, and refiners), there were growers' associations in all the main regions, and associations of refiners (of imported raw sugar) and of beet-mill operators.

Foreign lobbyists were also important. Cater, in his Washington exposé of 1964, focused *inter alia* on the 'sugar subgovernment'. As he described it:

since the early 1930s, this agricultural commodity has been subject to a cartel arrangement sponsored by the government. By specific prescription, the sugar market is divided to the last spoonful among domestic cane and beet growers, and foreign suppliers. Ostensibly to insure 'stability' of supply, the US price is pegged at a level considerably above the competitive price in the world market . . .

Political power within the sugar subgovernment is largely vested in the Chairman of the House Agricultural Committee who works out the schedule of quotas. It is shared by a veteran civil servant . . . who provides the necessary 'expert' advice for such a complex marketing arrangement. Further advice is provided by Washington representatives of the domestic beet and cane sugar growers, the sugar refineries, and the foreign producers (Cater, 1964, p. 18).

Cater's reference to civil servants once again points to the importance of the technocratic element amongst the sugar interests. Heston (1975) cites the careers of many persons involved in sugar, who went from USDA to become officials of one of the producer groups. That people moved back and forth between administering the programme and lobbying for it should not be surprising: it required considerable knowledge of sugar to do either

---

(4) any sugar or liquid sugar imported, brought in, or produced or manufactured in the United States (*a*) for livestock feed or for the production of livestock feed, or (*b*) for the distillation of alochol (including all polyhydric alcohols), or (*c*) for the production (other than by distillation) of alcohol, including all polyhydric alcohols, but not including any alcohol or resulting by-products for human food consumption, or (*d*) for export as sugar or in sugar-containing products' (*US Sugar Program*, p. 64).

[37] The Chairman of the House Agriculture Bill introduced one set of amendments to the bill to the House with the introductory statement that the bill was so complex that no one could understand it, and it would be necessary for Congressmen to take his word for it!

job. Persons having learned the intricacies of the programme may have had the public welfare at heart, but they had a vasted interest in serving the public good through some sort of complex programme.

6. Cessation of the Sugar Act, 1974 and the Era of No Programme, 1974–1981

During 1973–4, the price of sugar sky-rocketed, rising from 9.61 cents per lb. on the world market in 1973 to 44.97 cents per lb. at the end of 1974, having reached a high of 57.17 cents in November of that year. The Sugar Act was up for renewal and came to a vote during the period of high prices. At that time, the US price was a little below the world price, so that the quotas to recipient countries were valueless and there was no protection to American producers. Indeed, there was discussion in the hearings as to whether it was 'reasonable' to expect Hawaiians to ship raw sugar to the mainland when they would receive a higher price in Japan. Simultaneously, consumer groups were protesting high retail sugar prices, which reached a dollar a pound at the retail level at about the time the hearings were held (see Council on Wage and Price Stability, 1975).

The National Consumer Congress testified in favour of failing to renew the Sugar Act, eliminating all quotas, and going instead to an income-support basis (deficiency payments) for sugar growers. The consumer group also advocated efforts to reach an international agreement to stabilize sugar prices (House *Hearings* (1974), p. 164).

The Department of Agriculture supported extension of the Sugar Act, but wanted to end domestic quotas and direct payments. It also requested a three-year extension (only) of the programme, with the stated intent of considering ways of bringing the sugar programme under general agricultural legislation. The Sugar Users' Group recommended a two-year extension of the programme, and advocated a wide corridor for the price targets of the Secretary of Agriculture. Simultaneously, it opposed bringing other sweeteners under the programme or controlling them in any way.[38] The National Confectioners' Association also supported extension of the bill, but advocated quotas on imports of confectionary products as an essential part of the legislation.

Thus, support still appeared strong for a sugar programme, but it was less cohesive than had earlier been the case. Cane- and beet-producers' support was somewhat less intense, in part because of the high price of

---

[38] As will be seen below, the emergence of high-fructose corn syrup ultimately curbed the sugar programme; the sugar users were clearly aware of its implications during the 1974 hearings, as is evident from their opposition to extension of the programme. One of the many apparent puzzles confronting the analyst trying to interpret producers' advocacy as rational behaviour is why they did not attempt to control the development of sugar substitutes.

sugar at that time.[39] In particular, raw-sugar refiners' support for the programme had weakened considerably, and the various producer and user
groups were more divided than had earlier been the case. In addition, a
consumer lobby—protesting against high prices in general but focusing to
some extent on sugar—for the first time provided a source of opposition to
the bill. The House Agricultural Committee passed a bill, and it was anticipated that the bill would pass both the House and the Senate. However, it
was defeated on the House Floor, and the Sugar Act was not renewed.

As a consequence, sugar was without a special programme for the first
time since 1948. It still fell under the general provisions applicable to agricultural commodities, however, and thus remained subject to agricultural
price supports. In addition there remained a duty on imported sugar.

By the early 1970s, a technology for producing a virtually perfect substitute for sugar in liquid uses from corn (high-fructose corn syrup—HFCS)
had been developed. Until the high sugar prices of 1973–4, however, it was
uneconomic relative to sugar. With the high prices of 1973–4, however,
HFCS came to be produced in increasing quantities and to be used instead
of sugar in some commercial uses. As can be seen from Table 9.2, HFCS
constituted less than 1 per cent of sweetener consumption in 1971, but its
share began rising sharply thereafter. Indeed, American sugar production
peaked in 1972; thereafer, the increment in demand was met by HFCS,
and later, HFCS began displacing sugar as a sweetener.

The price of sugar fell much less in real terms after its high of 1974 than it
had after earlier downturns. There were repeated pressures, none the less,
to reinstate the programme. By 1978, the sugar price had fallen to 7.82
cents and pressures were mounting. Another proposal for a new Sugar Act
surfaced. For the first time, however, the sugar refiners testified against it.
The representative of the US Cane Sugar Refiners' Association was asked
whether the refiners had not earlier supported legislation. The response
was: 'Yes and of course that was prior to the new HFCS technology which
completely changes it. It is an entirely different ball game . . .' (Senate
Hearings, p. 140). Simultaneously, the Sugar Users' Group advocated joining the International Sugar Association with deficiency payments to growers if the price fell out of the International Sugar Association range. This
would have permitted sugar prices to industrial users and consumers to
move with the international price and have supported farmers' incomes.
The Sugar Users' Group further opposed quotas, and advocated fees on
imports, if necessary, rather than quotas. Thus, by 1978, with the increas-

[39] In hearings on each renewal of the Sugar Act, supporter after supporter of the programme testified that one major reason to have the programme was because of price volatility in
the sugar market. The failure of the producers to recognize that the 1974 price was temporary
is almost incomprehensible, and it is certainly inconsistent with the proposition that they
understood their own economic self-interest in the longer term.

TABLE 9.2. Sugar and sweetener consumption; USA 1970–1987 (millions of tons)

	Refined sugar	HFCS	Total corn	Total sweeteners	Sugar % of total
1970	10.43	0.07	1.98	12.57	83.0
1971	10.60	0.09	2.16	12.91	82.1
1972	10.74	0.14	2.21	13.11	81.9
1973	10.68	0.22	2.48	13.31	80.2
1974	10.22	0.32	2.68	13.03	78.4
1975	9.63	0.54	2.97	12.75	75.5
1976	10.18	0.78	3.24	13.56	75.0
1977	10.37	1.05	3.44	13.96	74.4
1978	10.18	1.35	3.75	14.10	71.4
1979	10.05	1.67	4.09	14.30	70.2
1980	9.52	2.18	4.58	14.24	64.7
1981	9.13	2.67	5.12	14.39	63.4
1982	8.56	3.10	5.60	14.31	59.8
1983	8.33	3.60	6.12	14.61	57.0
1984	8.01	4.30	6.84	15.01	53.4
1985	7.58	5.39	7.96	15.70	48.2
1986	7.37	5.53	8.12	15.66	47.0
1987	7.44	5.65	8.29	15.89	46.8

Note: Non-caloric sweeteners consumption (in sugar equivalent weight) was 0.59 million tons in 1970 and rose to 2.23 million tons by 1986.

Source: USDA, *Sugar and Sweeteners Situation*, June 1987.

ing competition from HFCS (see Table 9.2), the unanimity of interests represented by growers, processors, refiners, and users broke down completely. In these circumstances, the Administration decided to have the United States join the International Sugar Organization as its proposed assistance to domestic sugar interests.[40]

Although action was proposed repeatedly in the mid 1970s as the world price of sugar fell, no bill passed in those years. In 1978 and 1979, price supports were put into effect under general agricultural legislation, but, in the following two years, the world price of sugar (see Table 9.1) once again soared, rising from 9.65 cents per lb. in 1979 to 41.09 cents per lb. in October 1980, and then falling almost as precipitously to 16.32 cents per lb. by July 1981 (Terpstra, 1981, p. 4).

---

[40] The United States did join the International Sugar Organization, which set 13 to 23 cents per lb. raw value as its target price range. As can be seen from Table 9.1, the ISA was unable to prevent the price from exceeding this range during 1980 and could not prevent its fall below the target range in 1982.

7. The Sugar Programme of the 1980s

It was while the price of sugar was high that a new sugar programme was passed. Unlike earlier measures, however, the sugar programme was treated as part of the overall Agriculture and Food Act of 1981, rather than as a separate piece of legislation. The new programme set domestic price support levels for the period 1982 to 1985, with an interim support level until March 1982 of 16.75 cents per lb.[41] No quotas were set on imports, as it was anticipated that the support price could be maintained by altering the tariff and fee applicable to sugar imports (which the President was authorized to do under existing legislation). It was anticipated that the purchase price would not be attractive relative to the world price, and that the domestic price could be adequately supported through import duties and fees (see Terpstra, 1981). One amendment to the bill, adopted, prohibited the financing of the sugar programme from government revenue. Thus, the Commodity Credit Corporation could not buy sugar that would not be repurchased by farmers, for it would have had to take a loss to do so.

Once the law was passed, a number of market reactions ensued. There were unusually large imports at the end of 1981 in anticipation of the higher tariffs that would be imposed (see Terpstra, 1981, p. 8). Also, by late May, the Department of Agriculture had to issue regulations that a sugar processor could not sell more to the government than the minimum he had had on hand over the preceding six-month interval. A *Washington Post* article suggested that sugar processors had deposited more sugar with the CCC than they in fact had with the intent of forcing the government to impose quotas (*Washington Post*, 6 June 1982).

As the sugar price fell on world markets, it became apparent that the Commodity Credit Corporation would end up holding some sugar that it had received from farmers in return for 'loans'. The tariff had already been

---

[41] The Administration had not advocated a support price for sugar, but apparently accepted it in return for support for other legislation. It seems likely that the Administration did not anticipate that the world sugar price would fall so drastically or so soon. Just as the producers in 1974 failed to recognize the cyclical nature of the prevailing high prices, the Administration drastically miscalculated the future course of the sugar market after 1981. As will be evident below, less than 6 months elapsed between the passage of the bill and the decline in the price to the point where the Administration was forced to take action under the law it had itself accepted. The Senate had passed a support bill, at an initial price of 16.50 cents a lb.; the House had rejected an amendment that would have made the price 18 cents a lb. for the 1982 crop, and had then voted down the programme. But sugar price supports were passed as part of the 1981 farm programme after the particulars had been worked out in conference committee. Loans until the end of March 1982 were to be made at the rate of 16.75 cents per lb. raw basis and 19.70 cents per lb. of refined beet-sugar. The Secretary of Agriculture was instructed to set the price for the 1982 crop at a level not less than 17 cents per lb., for the 1983 crop at 17.5 cents per lb., at 17.75 cents for 1984, and at 18.00 cents for 1985. Growers could get a loan at these prices from the CCC, and decide not to reclaim their produce, which in effect meant that they would repay only if the price rose above the support level. The CCC cannot sell commodities it is holding at less than 1.05 times the purchase price.

increased to the maximum extent permissible by law (50 per cent of the world price). As the world price fell (see Table 9.1), it became evident that maintenance of the support prices mandated by the 1981 law would not be possible without CCC purchases of crops that would not be repurchased by growers unless other action was taken. Since CCC retention was inconsistent with the amendment requiring no budgetary cost from the programme, something had to be done. In May, emergency quarterly import quotas were established on a country-by-country basis to avoid a 'loss to the Treasury'.[42]

This episode is perhaps the one most difficult to explain in terms of any of the political economy models discussed at the outset. First of all, the Administration should have anticipated that the sugar price would not remain at the very high levels of early to mid 1981. But, more importantly, having made that miscalculation, it was not forced to reintroduce country-specific quotas: a global quota would have sufficed! Yet, here was an Administration advocating market forces, which had wanted to end the sugar programme but apparently had not had political power to do so (and had 'traded' support of sugar for support of its budget), which then reintroduced the entire, costly, apparatus of country-specific import quotas.

At that time, it was estimated that the 'cost of production' of sugar was about 21–22 cents per lb. in the United States. Production was decreasing in Hawaii and in sugar-beet-growing areas, and mills were in fact closing down. There were no production ceilings on any US source (see Terpstra, 1981, p. 10).

Import quotas were established by the Administration on the basis of average deliveries over the preceding years when entry had been free. This was done to attempt to ensure conformity with the non-discriminatory clauses of GATT pertaining to the imposition of quotas.[43]

As can be seen from the price disparities in Table 9.1, the divergence between American sugar prices and world prices was now so great that

---

[42] One of the precipitating factors blamed by the Administration for its inability to maintain the domestic sugar price at the legally mandated level without CCC purchases was the fact that some sugar was being imported under the Generalized System of Preferences, under which some developing countries were permitted to export to the US at less than normal duty rates. Since most sugar imports came from developing countries, the GSP legislation undermined the effectiveness of the tariff. The Administration also pointed to the European Community sugar policy as a source of excess supply on the world market, and hence of the declining world price. Later on, a similar policy dilemma arose between the Caribbean Basin Initiative and sugar price supports.

[43] Until 1974, the US could impose quotas legally under GATT because its agricultural legislation had been in effect from GATT's initiation and had therefore been subject to 'grandfathering'. However, quotas had to be non-discriminatory to qualify when they were reimposed in 1981, as grandfathering no longer applied. When American policy toward Nicaragua shifted, the Administration eliminated the Nicaraguan sugar quota. Nicaragua sued the United States in the International Court of Law and won its case, although the United States failed to provide redress.

difficulties were bound to ensue. From the raw-sugar (cane) refiners' view-point, a major difficulty was that quarterly quotas prevented any futures contracts because of uncertainty as to how much would be importable, and from what source, more than three months hence. They therefore took the government before the US Court of International Trade. The Court, however, ruled in favour of the US Government, so quarterly import quotas persisted (Terpstra, 1981, p. 15).

At least six Presidential proclamations had to be issued between 1982 and 1983 to attempt to contain the side-effects. Among the more interesting were the effects on trade with Canada. Canada had no protection on sugar and imported it at world prices. Some Canadian firms at first added 6 per cent corn syrup to sugar, since anything less than 94 per cent sugar was not 'sugar' from the viewpoint of the regulations. This was then shipped to northern US points and sold to US producers of sugar-containing products. When these shipments reached 175,000 tons a year, they were banned. Then Canadian firms began producing high-sugar-content cake mixes and other products, which were exported to the United States where, once again, the sugar was extracted. Canadian firms also shipped sugar into the US as 'packets of cocoa and tins of maple syrup and in Aunt Hetty's Patent Pancake Mix' (*The Economist*, 1 June 1985, p. 31). These, too, were banned. However, other countries' exports of sweet products to the US also rose, so that by January 1985 emergency import quotas were placed on all imports of sweetened cocoa, cake mixes, and edible preparations. This latter category was filled by 5 March 1985, meaning that no Korean noodles (0.002 per cent sugar), kosher pizzas, or other products with any sugar could be imported for the remainder of the year (ibid.). Import prohibitions were put on all sugar-containing products after these, and other, responses to the price differential had been felt. Noteworthy were the protests of candy producers, after imports of confectionary products rose from 39,850 tons in 1980 to 95,553 metric tons in 1985: candy producers had been part of the Users' Group which earlier had supported the sugar programme.[44]

Data in Tables 9.1 to 9.3 tell the story thereafter. Support prices were set and import quotas established at levels designed to achieve them. However, the substitutability of HFCS was so great that sugar consumption began declining precipitously. All American soft-drink bottlers had shifted entirely to HFCS by 1985. Sugar accounted for less than half of all caloric sweetener consumption by 1985, when its price had risen to five times the world price.

---

[44] See USDA, Foreign Agricultural Circular, *Sugar, Molasses and Honey*, FS 2–86, Nov. 1986, pp. 18–24 for a listing of the 113 significant proclamations, Presidential signatures, notices filed, and USDA announcements pertaining to sugar over the 1982–6 period. See also Council of Economic Advisers, *Economic Report of the President*, 1987, p. 165.

TABLE 9.3. Sugar: Production by area, 1950–1986 crop years (1,000 short tons, raw value)

Crop year	Cane sugar				Total cane	Beet sugar
	Florida	Louisiana	Hawaii	Puerto Rico		
1950	108	456	961	1,299	2,824	2,015
1951	122	297	996	1,128	2,653	1,541
1952	154	451	1,020	1,372	2,997	1,519
1953	151	481	1,099	1,182	2,913	1,873
1954	132	478	1,077	1,204	2,891	1,999
1955	119	455	1,140	1,166	2,880	1,730
1956	129	432	1,100	1,152	2,813	1,971
1957	136	398	1,085	990	2,609	2,213
1958	136	443	1,158	934	2,278	2,214
1959	175	441	975	1,087	2,678	2,303
1960	160	470	936	1,019	2,585	2,475
1961	208	650	1,092	1,110	3,060	2,431
1962	380	472	1,120	1,009	2,981	2,595
1963	424	759	1,101	989	3,273	3,086
1964	574	573	1,179	989	3,315	3,332
1965	554	550	1,218	897	3,219	2,816
1966	652	562	1,234	883	3,331	2,853
1967	717	740	1,191	818	3,446	2,694
1968	546	669	1,232	645	3,092	3,510
1969	535	537	1,182	483	2,737	n.a.
1970	652	602	1,162	460	2,876	3,401
1971	635	571	1,230	324	2,760	3,552
1972	961	660	1,119	298	3,038	3,624
1973	824	558	1,129	255	2,804	3,200
1974	803	594	1,041	291	2,803	2,916
1975	1,061	640	1,107	303	3,237	4,019
1976	930	650	1,050	312	3,036	3,895
1977	894	668	1,034	267	2,951	3,108
1978	972	550	1,029	204	2,816	3,289
1979	1,047	500	1,060	193	2,893	2,879
1980	1,121	491	1,023	177	2,905	3,149
1981	963	712	1,048	153	2,986	3,388
1982	1,307	675	983	113	3,176	2,737
1983	1,223	603	1,044	100	2,799	2,699
1984	1,412	452	1,062	97	3,002	2,905
1985	1,413	532	2,021	109	3,109	3,000
1986	1,382	650	1,045	95	3,426	3,414

Sources: USDA, *Sugar and Sweetener Situation*, Oct. 1986 and June 1987. Figures for beet-sugar, 1950–68, from *Sugar Statistics and Related Data*, Vol. I (revised Dec. 1969), Statistical Bulletin no. 293, USDA, Feb. 1970.

By 1987, US imports had fallen to an estimated 1.48 million tons of raw sugar, down from 5 million tons as recently as 1979 and 1981. Estimates of the total cost of sugar support ranged from $800 million to $2.5 billion, depending on the estimated world price in the absence of the programme, with payments per sugar farm estimated to be $136,000. More than half of all caloric sweetener consumption was now high-fructose corn syrup, and the proportion continued to increase. Moreover, in 1987, it was announced that a technique for making crystalline dry corn sweetener had been discovered.

On existing trends, it is expected that the United States will stop importing sugar in either 1988 or 1989. As earlier mentioned, import quotas for 1988 have been set at 750,000 tons, half the 1987 level. When there are no longer any imports the policy choices available to the politicians will change and their costs will rise. If sugar prices are to be maintained at their present levels, production controls will have to be instituted, stocks will have to mount, or subsidized exports will have to start. If the political process is unwilling to accept any of these three options, price supports will have to be lowered.[45]

8. The Political Economy of the Sugar programme

No case can ever prove a rule, and the sugar programme is no exception. Like everything else, sugar is unique, and its uniqueness has undoubtedly influenced the evolution of intervention in the sugar market over the years. None the less, one can ask certain questions which pertain to the various models outlined in Section 1, and venture hypotheses as to some missing ingredients.

A first step is to assess the gainers and the losers at various stages of the

---

[45] This section was first written in Dec. 1987. On 7 Jan. 1988, the *New York Times*, under the headline 'Buried in Spending Law' reported that Senator Inouye (Hawaii), with the 'backing of domestic cane and beet sugar growers', had succeeded in getting a little-noticed provision into the $600-billion spending bill to permit an additional 400,000 tons of sugar—in addition to the 750,000 quota—imports into the United States in 1988 'to offset the impact on foreign producers of drastic cuts in American sugar imports in recent years'. The additional 400,000 tons, allocated to the Caribbean and the Philippines, is to be imported at American prices, refined, and may not be sold in the United States, i.e. it must be re-exported at world prices. The 1988 omnibus spending bill further allotted $100 million to cover the financial loss under this programme, equal to 12 cents per lb. Obviously, this additional sugar will increase the capacity utilization rate in domestic sugar refineries. The *New York Times* was silent on the issue of how the additional imported cane would be allocated between refineries. It would therefore appear that the final paragraph of this section was too optimistic: a new instrument has been created under which the US can import raw sugar and re-export it, which will make it relatively straightforward to export domestic surpluses when domestic production exceeds consumption. In March 1988, Secretary of Agriculture Lyng announced that USDA would not import the 400,000 tons because it could not technically do so in a manner consistent with other laws on the books!

programme's evolution. Next, some apparent puzzles in the evolution of the sugar programme are discussed. Thereafter, the evolution of the sugar programme is assessed relative to the models of political economy outlined in Section 1. Finally, the phenomena that seem important in analysing the sugar programme, which are absent from these models, are explored.

8.1. Who Gained and Who Lost?

To a first approximation, the cost to American consumers of the sugar programme is the difference between the domestic price and the world price that would prevail in the absence of the sugar programme: about 10 cents per pound, or a total cost of about $1.5 billion in 1987. Gross income to sugar farms was about $2.06 billion in 1987. Given the costs of purchased inputs, and alternative uses of land, it seems clear that there was great scope for improved resource allocation and compensation of such producers who might have lost from an abandonment of the sugar programme.

All the available evidence suggests that most American land devoted to sugar earns no more than it would in alternative uses. The only possible exception is Hawaii, which will be discussed further below. Even with the relatively high sugar prices of recent years, there has been little expansion of acreage devoted to cane and contraction of acreage devoted to beet.

Moreover, this does not appear to be a new situation. As already mentioned, Taussig believed that there was virtually no rent accruing to land growing sugar because of the high opportunity costs, especially for beet-sugar, in terms of crops in which the United States does have a comparative advantage.[46] When Johnson assessed the system in 1974, he concluded that the sugar programme was an 'evil system, costing between $500 and $730 million, depending on whether the premium per pound was 1.5 or 2.5 cents' (Johnson, 1974, p. 50). This contrasted with gross farm income from sugar at that time of about $870 million.[47]

Johnson estimated that the average income per sugar farm in 1972 was $619,856 in Florida, $312,611 in Hawaii, $75,089 in Louisiana, and above $30,000 in all sugar-producing states except Puerto Rico, Colorado, Montana, Nebraska, Utah, Michigan, and Ohio. There were altogether 175 thousand production workers in 1971, but their average hourly earnings (both in growing and processing) were significantly below the average for persons with comparable training and skills in each state.

Johnson concluded that:

---

[46] This is especially true of beet land in the Upper Midwest where soya beans, wheat, and corn constitute highly viable alternatives.

[47] Johnson, 1974, pp. 54–55. Johnson's estimates excluded Puerto Rican and Hawaiian-grown sugar. They were based on the assumption of a 2 cents per lb. quota premium in addition to the tariff. Taussig believed that no mainland acreage was profitable for sugar, given alternative uses, and attributed the development of sugar-cane acreage in Louisiana to American protection in the nineteenth century. See Taussig (1924), ch. IV.

the net benefits—the net increase in income going to farm-owned resources—are only a small fraction of the gross benefits. Most of the gross transfers are required because the US is a high-cost producer of sugar. Many resources are used in sugar production that would readily find employment elsewhere . . . Much of the gross transfer is required to induce these resources to be devoted to sugar production rather than their next best alternative (Johnson, 1974, p. 58).

Turning to analyse beet and cane separately, Johnson found no evidence that the price of sugar-beet land (near mills) was significantly different from the price of other land in beet-growing areas. He noted that: 'I must admit that these results surprised me. I had expected to find some positive effect . . . There has been considerable political pressure to establish new sugar beet producing areas, and it seemed reasonable to assume that farmers expected to gain from these efforts' (p. 61).

Of the six new beet-processing plants established after 1962, two (New York and Maine) were 'complete failures' (because they could not obtain enough sugar-beet to operate). The acreage allotted the sugar-beets in Arizona had been only half that anticipated when the plant was built (Johnson, 1974, p. 61). Moreover, the Secretary of Agriculture had not, at that time or since, had to impose 'proportionate allotments' on any producing area since 1966.

As for cane, Puerto Rican production and acreage had been declining for a decade at the time of Johnson's analysis. For Hawaii, most benefits went to the large producers, as noted above, as 25 out of the 705 sugar farms produced 93 per cent of the sugar.[48] In addition, field-worker wages in Hawaii were double the national average and Johnson concluded that 'it is quite possible that some of the economic rent from sugar production in Hawaii has been captured by approximately 5,000 farm workers' (Johnson, 1974, p. 67).[49]

During the 1970s, more beet- and cane-processing plants went bankrupt. USDA data show 58 beet-processing factories operating in 1970, 56 operating in 1975, 43 operating in 1980, and 36 operating in 1986. There were 75 sugar mills processing cane in 1970, and the number fell to 42 by 1986.[50]

Certainly, refiners of imported raw cane-sugar lost from the sugar programme, at least starting with 1970 and the increased inroads of HFCS. Some went bankrupt, and the total demand for their product fell sharply as beet and sugar substitutes replaced imported raw cane-sugar.

[48] Johnson noted the disappearance of data on size of sugar farms in Hawaii from the Census of Agriculture starting in 1969 (Johnson, 1974, p. 66).

[49] Taussig (1924, ch. 5, p. 65) pointed to immigrant workers as the chief gainers in Hawaii from sugar protection, asserting that native Hawaiians, like native Americans, would not work in cane fields.

[50] See *Sugar and Sweeteners Outlook and Situation*, June 1987, Tables 19 and 20. Total sugar capacity remained approximately constant as those mills still producing were handling larger average volumes.

There is little reason to question Johnson's conclusions today. Indeed, subsequent bankruptcies, the failure of the industry to expand despite greater protection and higher real producer sugar prices, all suggest that most of the cost of the sugar programme was absorbed by the excess cost of production. Indeed, even the argument first put forth in 1934—that the United States should have some domestic production capability in the event that foreign supplies were disrupted—no longer seems compelling in light of the HFCS substitution possibilities.[51]

If there were gainers in the United States, they would have been Hawaiian growers (who are low-cost relative to the mainland). But there, strong unions apparently appropriated most of the rents from higher sugar prices for the plantation workers, who therefore were the chief Hawaiian gainers. Since most workers are immigrants, they should not have a significant political voice.[52] The other identifiable gainers were, at least earlier on, the sugar exporters whose gains under quotas exceeded their losses from the lower world price. Even for them, it is questionable whether the present value of the sugar programme was positive, given that the longer-run effects were to build in a declining total demand for sugar in the United States and a gradual phase-out of American imports of sugar.

The conclusion, then, is that surely in the longer run there were few domestic economic interests that gained from the sugar programme; gains were at best short-term. Even then, it must be asked why the various lobbying groups fought hard for *expansion* of domestic American sugar acreage: increasing the number of mills in 1962 surely did not benefit existing sugar growers. Outside of Hawaii, more than half the acreage under production in 1985 was devoted to other crops as recently as 1960. It is interesting to speculate on the type of political-market model that would yield an outcome in which the chief gainers from controls had no voice in the decisions to adopt those controls.

8.2. Some Puzzles

One of the fundamental assumptions of economists is that individuals are rational in their own self-interest. Even with individual rationality, of course, a group does no necessarily maximize as models of the prisoners' dilemma readily demonstrate. A first question, therefore, is the extent to which individual actors acted in their own self-interest.

There are two issues here. First, how well did the representatives of the various interests (cane and beet growers, cane millers, beet refiners, and

[51] And if concern had genuinely been over the adequacy of foreign supplies, one wonders why distant, landlocked Sub-Saharan African countries should have a quota.

[52] Taussig noted this same apparent anomaly—that immigrant workers were the chief beneficiaries—in his analysis of the sugar programme. At that time, he concluded that the refiners had also gained, at least temporarily, through their formation of the trust.

raw-cane-sugar refiners) know their own interests? Second, was the under-standing of economics underlying behaviour approximately correct? Answers to these questions are prerequisites to assessing existing models of political economy and providing clues as to missing elements in those models.

It has already been argued that the long-term gains to sugar producers of the sugar programme have been small indeed: reduced sugar consump-tion, the availability of alternative uses of the land, and other reactions have resulted in the virtual elimination of any long-term rents that might otherwise have resulted from the sugar programme.

None the less, in the same way that more alternatives are always prefer-able to fewer, there must have been short-run gains to those already grow-ing sugar, or with the possibility of growing beet or cane, from the sugar programme at most points in time. Even that does not prove that the gains were maximized. Quite aside from the question as to whether pressure for other types of support might not have been more in the interests of sugar producers than the actual programme, the sugar programme could have been altered in ways which would have prevented the emergence of HFCS. For example, had the sugar programme in 1981 been established to provide deficiency payments to farmers (compensating for the difference between the price received by them and a target support price), HFCS could not have made the inroads it did on sweetener consumption.[53]

Moreover, even then, it seems apparent that many of the gains of the sugar programme prior to the 1970s did not go to American interests: many foreign countries were gainers.[54] Certainly there was considerable political opposition aroused by the activities of foreign lobbyists, especially in 1962 when they were widely blamed for having achieved the 1962 reimposition of country-specific quotas.[55] One might have thought the domestic sugar

[53] The only way to reconcile the growers' opposition to deficiency payments is to believe that obscurity was essential to the perpetuation of the programme. There is also a question as to why attempts were not made to prohibit HFCS—the European solution. This, along with other evidence, points to the role of knowledge, and of expertise, in controls. See Section 8.3 below.

[54] They did not gain by the full amount of the premium times their quota, of course, and some with small quotas into the American market probably lost. For most countries, sugar was sold both to the United States at premium prices and on the residual world market at much lower prices. To the (considerable) extent that the world price would have been higher in the absence of American quotas, only those sugar exporters gained whose quantity ex-ported to the United States times the excess of the premium over the world price in the absence of US quotas exceeded the quantity they exported to the rest of the world times the amount by which the world price was below its no-sugar-programme level. However, it was not until 1985 that any foreign representative in Washington publicly opposed the prog-ramme.

[55] See Berman and Heineman (1963). Since the focus here is on domestic economic-political interactions, many of the irrationalities involved in the allocation of foreign sugar quotas are ignored. Suffice it to note that the Dominican Republic under Trujillo was the big gainer from the 1962 legislation at a time when the Administration was attempting to impose sanctions on the regime. Berman and Heineman's comment was that 'It is not easy to find

interests would have dissociated themselves from the foreign interests, yet that does not appear to have happened.

Furthermore, there are several actions that were *not* taken that would have been in the interest of the producers, if one accepts the viewpoint that the overall programme was beneficial to sugar interests.[56] To cite just a few: (i) if large Hawaiian growers really profited from the programme, one would have expected them to support a price ceiling in 1974, rather than to permit the opposition that arose to the very high (and very temporary) price of sugar to defeat the entire programme; (ii) why did the sugar interests accede to American efforts to support the International Sugar Organization in the late 1970s rather than push for more effective action?; (iii) why in the early 1960s did the sugar interests so adamantly support country-specific quotas, when they could have bargained for a larger domestic fraction of the market with a global quota?

Then, too, there is a list of positive mistakes if one takes a narrow, short-run, self-interest model and accepts that the sugar programme did help American sugar over the short run. There seems little doubt that many of the large growers were among those most adamantly opposed to the programme in 1934, although they did change sides by 1937 (see e.g. Krauss and Alexander, 1965, p. 336). There is also the question of why soft-drink bottlers, cake-mix manufacturers, bakers, and confectioners were so willing to support the programme. Indeed, in terms of the interest-group models of controls sketched in Section 1, the failure of the sugar users to oppose the sugar programme is perhaps the major surprise. One can only conjecture that they regarded the demand for their outputs as reasonably price-inelastic, and were therefore not overly concerned about the increased costs of their input under the sugar programme. As experience with competing imports demonstrates,[57] however, that judgement repre-

---

rational justification for many of the quotas that were recommended by the House Agriculture Committee and included with little change in the final legislation' (p. 425). They proceeded to cite a quota of 15,000 tons for Panama (which had produced only 5,000 tons a year) and several other countries which could not meet their quota, as well as quotas for the Netherlands and Ireland (although a separate provision of the bill prohibited imports from countries that themselves imported sugar as these latter two countries do).

[56] There is abundant evidence world-wide that protection of domestic industries tends to weaken their competitive abilities and thus render them even higher-cost and more uncompetitive in the long run than they are when protection is first introduced. It is certainly conceivable that that has happened to American sugar. While it is unarguable that some sugar land has such good alternatives that it is inherently uncompetitive at any plausible world price of sugar, it is also possible that some lands, such as the Hawaiian, might have been considerably lower-cost producers had they been subject to foreign competition. Some Hawaiian growers opposed quotas initially on the ground that it would weaken their competitive ability. See Krauss and Alexander (1965).

[57] The explanation that belief in price inelasticity accounts for the failure of sugar users to oppose the programme is somewhat less plausible, however, in that testimony before the Council on Wage and Price Stability (1975) indicated that a number of bakers had gone bankrupt in 1973–4 due to the high price of sugar.

sented an underestimate of the degree of price elasticity. In addition, the support of the sugar refiners was clearly essential for the continuation of the programme and yet was obviously ruinous to them in the long run.

Finally, in the large, there have been several actions which could at best have been very short-term maximization. Given that the United States will shortly stop importing sugar altogether, and that high-fructose corn syrup and crystalline fructose corn can be expected to continue to take an increasing share of the market (along with non-caloric or low-caloric sweeteners which are better able to compete at higher sugar prices) it is interesting to ask whether the sugar programme has even been in the long-run interests of Hawaiian and other low-cost growers.

Moreover, there seems to have been no effort to bring HFCS under regulation to prevent its emergence as a substitute for sugar. Certainly if it was rational to seek a high domestic sugar price, the sugar producers should have sought a ban on high-fructose corn syrup, or if not that, at least a system of deficiency payments rather than price-raising measures. The declining consumption of sugar in the United States and the increasingly competitive position of corn substitutes were clearly not consistent with the longer-term interests of sugar producers, and even less so of refiners. Had sugar growers and refiners been willing to accept a deficiency payment programme in the late 1960s (so that payments to growers would compensate for any divergence between the world price-plus-margins and the domestic support price), much of the HCFS competition would have been avoided.[58]

At present, the corn producers strongly oppose any switch to deficiency payments on the grounds that they would provide 'unfair competition' to corn in the sweetener market. Indeed, Congressional representatives from corn-producing states now appear to be the strongest supporters of the sugar programme, including import quotas. Whether that support group would have developed had sugar producers correctly estimated the potential competition from corn is an open question. Certainly, to the extent that corn producers are the gainers from the sugar programme, there is no evidence of their apparent support for the programme prior to the 1970s.

The apparent reason for the sugar growers' opposition to deficiency payments seems to have been their concern that a ceiling would be placed on the size of the payment that might be made to any individual farm. This suggests that growers were sensitive to the degree to which benefits were to larger farmers, but it does not indicate why refiners and processors were willing to support import and production quotas. It is not clear whether

---

[58] The representatives of the corn refiners were at pains to assure Congress that their costs were high, and that 'sugar is still the standard of the sweetener industry' (testimony of Donald E. Nurdlund, Chairman of A. E. Staley Manufacturing Co., representing the corn producers, in House *Hearings* (1978), p. 138).

sensitivity resulted from the concern that, if the size of payments became known, the entire programme would be halted, or whether instead the desire was to protect payments to large growers.[59]

Even beyond that, however, there lies the question—alluded to by Johnson—as to why in the early 1960s it was anticipated that there would be great benefits to expanded beet-sugar production. These do not seem to have been forthcoming, and the evidence strongly suggests that such an expansion was not in the interests of existing producers and did not significantly benefit those in areas where new beet-sugar mills were established.

If one is to believe statements from representatives of the sugar interests, sugar producers have not been happy with the programme. According to *The Economist* after the 1985 bill was passed: 'It might be supposed that the sugar-growers, at least, would be happy with the absurd press for regulations. They are not. They get a government subsidy of 17 cents a pound, but say it costs them 20 cents to produce one. Acreage under sugar cane in Florida, Louisiana and Hawaii, or under sugar beet in the Midwest, continues to contract' (*The Economist*, 1 June 1985, p. 31 of American Survey).

There is then the curious episode with the International Sugar Association: the ISA could not contain the price of sugar even within a very wide band. In part this was because the EC did not join. However, it is difficult to imagine that, even with EC participation, the target range could have been maintained without resources considerably in excess of those available to the ISA. It is difficult to believe that the ISA was expected to be effective in stabilizing the sugar price: why, then, was support for ISA membership taken as an acceptable substitute by the sugar producers for a sugar programme?

Next, there is an interesting question as to why some arguments are convincing, or are thought convincing, in the political arena. Virtually all witnesses to Congressional hearings on the sugar programme listed as one of its major virtues the fact that 'it costs the taxpayer nothing'.[60]

A second oft-repeated argument pertained to the alleged instability of

---

[59] For an amusing sidelight to the story, see the testimony of Helen Rohrbach, Head, Quota Section, Special Operations Branch, Office of Operations, US Customs Service. This branch is (or at least was in 1974) in charge of administering all import quotas. Ms Rohrbach explained why her branch could not administer import quotas (which were set in raw value terms) as then currently laid down. Congressman Vigorito, who presided at the hearings, thanked her for her testimony with the statement: 'You have brought to my attention a small group in Customs that I did not know existed . . .' 1974 *Hearings*, p. 97).

[60] See e.g. the statement contained in the House Agriculture Committee pamphlet on the US Sugar Program (1971): 'The Sugar Act has given us this security of supplies at a reasonable cost to the consumer and at no cost to the taxpayer' (p. 45). Note, however, that the decision to permit the import and re-export of 400,000 tons of sugar in the omnibus spending bill passed by Congress in Dec. 1987 invalidates this argument because there will be a cost to taxpayers, and of course it sets a precedent for subsidies to support exports in future years.

the international sugar market and the 'need' for price stability for producers. This argument first appeared in Roosevelt's message to Congress in 1934, and was reiterated by almost all witnesses supporting the Sugar Program. Yet the programme was neither designed for 'stability' (since there was no price ceiling) nor were there efforts to set a 'band' within which the price might fluctuate. Whether it was thought that appeals for 'stability' were more convincing than appeals for support prices is open to conjecture, but the inconsistency of rhetoric pertaining to stability with the appeals for higher prices strikes one on even the most casual perusal of Congressional testimony.

Although a large number of other puzzles could be pointed to, it suffices to mention one more: surely in 1974 and again in 1981, it should have been understood that the prevailing price of sugar would not continue indefinitely. Even without any degree of sophisticated understanding of the sugar market domestically and internationally, all testimony before both Houses of Congress had for years emphasized the wide fluctuations in sugar prices as a reason for controls. Yet the Reagan Administration apparently believed that it had a sugar programme which would not require a return to the country-specific quotas that had earlier prevailed.

8.3. Conformity with Models of Political Economy

Without doubt, the saga of the American sugar programme over the 1934–87 period contains elements of a number of the models discussed in Section 1. In this section, the 'goodness of fit' of each model is considered in turn.

The 'benevolent guardian' of the public good theory of governmental behaviour seems to conform reasonably well to the motives of the Roosevelt Administration in 1934, and of the Reagan Administration in 1981 in its efforts to bring sugar into general agricultural programmes.

Other than that, however, there is very little of the 'benevolent guardian, social-welfare maximizing' government in the story, and that model fails to account for the evolution of the programme, and especially for the 1960–2 period, and the resumption of country-specific quotas in 1981.

Turning then to interest-group models, there is no doubt that lobbying groups emerged as a result of the sugar programme. However, the Brock–Magee model fails in that the politicians supporting the sugar programme were from sugar states and, by and large, appear to have gained votes as a consequence of their attainment of the sugar programme. Clearly lobbying was important, as the various components of the sugar industry sought to increase the benefits they perceived as emanating from the bill and foreign lobbyists did the same thing for their clients. Perhaps the Brock–Magee approach suggests that those politicians *not* from sugar-producing regions might have lost votes had the sugar programme become even more costly, but in light of what happened, it is difficult to believe that sugar prices could have been supported at very much higher levels than they in fact were.

An interesting point to note with respect to lobbying models, however, is that they do not fit Olson's prediction that interest groups would form when the group on the opposite side of the market consists of relatively small and fragmented entities. Sugar users were at least as large as sugar producers and none the less joined in the coalition. One would not have forecast the coalition of interests that did emerge because their interests were, at least from an economist's viewpoint, antagonistic. There was ultimately a significant conflict between the interests of domestic and foreign growers, between domestic growers and refiners, and between domestic producers and domestic industrial users. The latter were large, which is not normally anticipated in discussions of lobbying.[61] The puzzle here is thrown in even sharper relief when it is asked why sugar growers, millers, refiners, and users were all on the same side of the issue when there were clearly some divergent interests among them.

Lobbying, at least by domestic growers, was *not* significant in the inauguration of the sugar programme, however. Growers seem actively to have opposed it initially, and it is certain they did not lobby for it. In that respect, the Bhagwati–Srinivasan revenue-seeking model, in which resources are spent in an effort to obtain a programme of value, does not seem appropriate for the initiation of the sugar programme. Once the programme was in place, however, domestic sugar growers rallied to its support. Likewise, corn producers did not support the programme until after HFCS had become an important sugar substitute: had revenue-seeking taken place, corn producers would have supported the programme sooner.

The conservative social welfare function argument—that the political process attempts to protect incomes of those losing out for whatever reason—reasonably well fits the motive for introduction of the sugar programme in 1934; it does not explain its reintroduction in 1948, its continuation of country-specific quotas after 1960, nor the evolution of the programme thereafter. Certainly, the effort to increase mainland acreage after 1960 was not an effort to protect sugar growers.

The Stigler–Peltzman–Becker view of the political-economic process certainly has elements of truth in it once the sugar programme had been established. Sugar growers must have believed that the programme increased their incomes, and used the political process to attempt to effect a transfer.

---

[61] There is no doubt that Americans owned some sources of foreign supply. This was especially true in the 1930s. However, even then, only about a third of Cuban sugar was produced under American ownership. For the Philippines, the fraction did not reach that level until after Philippine preferences were in place, and the mechanism seems to have worked the other way round: the American preference induced American firms to start producing in the Philippines. See US Tariff Commission (1937).

However, the Stigler–Peltzman–Becker view does not help in explaining the inauguration of the programme in 1934, its reintroduction in 1981, nor why import quotas (and country-specific ones at that) were the instrument of choice, rather than tariffs. Were wealth redistribution among Americans the dominant political logic, foreign governments would not have been the beneficiaries of the sugar premiums.

8.4.   Ingredients for a Fuller Model of the Political Economy of Controls

There is no doubt that economic interests and lobbying go part way toward explaining the sugar programme. There are missing elements, however, to which attention now turns. First, it is apparent that institutional mechanisms were necessary in order to facilitate the continuation of the programme, and that alternative arrangements might have reduced the economic costs of the programme, even if they would not have eliminated it. Second, it is clear that markets reacted to the various shifts and turns in policy in ways which neither politicians nor sugar interests anticipated. In this sense, there never was 'the' sugar programme; rather, policies evolved over time as politicians reacted to market responses (and exogenous events) and markets reacted to the changes in policy. Finally, any reading of the evolution of sugar policies over time suggests that a number of key issues surrounding transparency, knowledge, and the role of technocrats must be addressed.

Institutional issues. Several institutional issues are noteworthy. First, there is the anomaly (for the American Congress) that sugar legislation was handled by the Senate Finance Committee (because it is an import) and the House Agriculture Committee (by historical accident). Moreover, because it was an import and thus had revenue implications, only the House had the power to initiate legislation. This gave the House Agriculture Committee considerably more power over sugar than it would have had had the counterpart body been the Senate Agriculture Committee, and the House Agriculture Committee had considerably more ability to focus its attention on sugar than would the House Ways and Means Committee.[62]

Second, the sugar programme could not have persisted in anything like the form that it did had sugar not been an import. At a minimum, there would have been a budgetary cost to any programme which raised price. As mentioned above, the 'lack of budgetary cost' was frequently mentioned as an important point by advocates of the programme. Had there

---

[62] Had the House Ways and Means Committee handled the legislation, its attention would have been spread over other issues with the result that it could not have devoted as much time to it as did the House Agriculture Committee. Moreover, membership on the House Ways and Means Committee would have been determined with respect to many more issues and thus could not have been as specialized as was the House Agriculture Committee. For a discussion of these issues, see Price (1971).

needed to be an explicit vote of funds to support the programme, it is evident that political opposition would have increased, as evidenced by the amendment in 1981 which prohibited budgetary expenditures in support of sugar prices. The fact that 'no cost to the government' was so frequently used in testimony before Congress suggests that the argument was appealing.

Likewise, because sugar was an import, the programme provided instruments of foreign policy (the sugar quotas) which would otherwise not have been present. Moreover, had sugar not been an import, it would have been dealt with together with other agricultural commodities: the ability of sugar interests to influence the outcome (for better or worse in their own self-interest) would have been less as other interests would have competed for scarce resources.[63]

Indeed, it is arguable that it was the ability of the sugar interests to distance themselves from other elements of a political situation that was crucial to the continuation of the programme: it was an import, and therefore came before the Senate Finance Committee and was not dealt with as part of other agricultural legislation. While an import, it was agricultural, and thus not dealt with in other trade legislation along with other importable commodities.

Third, it took the agreement of all producing interests—beet growers, cane growers, beet refiners, cane millers, and cane refiners—to ensure the continuation of the programme. Indeed, until the mid 1970s, what is remarkable is that the Sugar Users' Group did not oppose the programme. Why they failed to do so is one of the mysteries of the Sugar Program—one can only conjecture that either they believed that an increased input price did not affect them or that they believed they were unable to influence the outcome significantly. As already seen, the first possibility seems less than plausible in light of testimony about bankruptcies resulting from high sugar prices, while the latter was manifestly wrong, as all observers believed, and stated, that all parties had to agree to perpetuate the programme.

Fourth, the fact that the interrelationships were complex undoubtedly increased the political influence of those who did understand the economics and politics of the sugar programme: in a sense, the complexity of the issues stood as a barrier to entry of non-specialists.

Interaction of economic and political markets. Examination of the history of the sugar programme strongly suggests that, once created, a policy instrument will: (*a*) be seized upon by groups who perceive themselves to

---

[63] The above paragraph was written prior to the passage of the 1987 omnibus spending bill. That bill sets a precedent for expenditures on supporting sugar prices that may ease the way for subsidy payments when sugar is no longer imported. Even so, one might guess that pressures against sugar will mount when the programme has to be financed from the budget.

benefit (regardless of whether they had anything to do with initiating the programme or not); (*b*) induce economic market reactions which will minimize the costs of the programme; (*c*) lead to political responses to (*b*) by the groups formed under (*a*) to attempt to offset these economic market reactions, which in turn will lead to (*d*) increasingly complex policy instruments designed both to deal with the competing interest groups that form around the policy instrument and simultaneously to subvert the sorts of market responses perceived to be detrimental.

This sequence, which as articulated sounds very straightforward, is perhaps the most obvious, but also the most complex, of conclusions. For it suggests that, once an instrument is in place, a variety of political forces will emerge that will act upon it and try to seize it in ways that are largely unpredictable. In the case of the US Sugar Program, the instrument was initially opposed by the sugar producers, but they very quickly reversed their position and supported its continuation. Likewise, the sugar-exporting countries strongly supported the programme until the mid 1980s, and then reversed their position in response to the market forces set in motion by the price support programme.

Ironically in 1948 it was a perceived obligation to Cuba, rather than any motivation of domestic producers, that led to the reinstatement of the programme. During the years 1948 to 1960, Congressmen dealing with the sugar programme were regarded virtually as foreign agents—their interests appear to have been primarily in allocating import quotas rather than benefiting domestic interests.

There are two interesting mental experiments that can be performed: (i) what would have happened had the Cuban Government not changed?; and (ii) what would have happened if there had been no sugar programme prior to 1960 when the Cuban Government changed? In answer to the first, the most reasonable conjecture would appear to be that the US Sugar Program would have continued, much as before, and that there never would have been the expansion of beet acreage and high-cost (and possibly even ill-advised on the part of those who undertook them) expansions of beet-refining capacity that characterized the 1960s. It is hard to imagine the impetus that would have been necessary to increase substantially American acreage at the expense of imports.

With regard to the second question, had there been no sugar programme in 1960 the most likely outcome is that the United States would have continued buying sugar on world markets. It is difficult to imagine a sequence of events under which a changed Cuban Government could have been seized upon as a rationale for the inauguration of a Sugar Program.

In so far as these conjectures are plausible, they strongly suggest that it is much easier to adapt, or seize, an already-existing instrument, than it is to have a new one created. For that reason alone, an existing instrument is very likely to become used for objectives and by groups that may not have been the intended beneficiaries at all when the instrument was first formed.

There is then the question of market reaction. Clearly, the market will minimize the cost of any given policy-imposed distortion. In the case of sugar, this entailed two important reactions and several minor ones. The first important reaction was the shift in the location of production (with expansion of Florida land and reduction in beet land). The second was the development of substitutes and, with it, the potential disappearance of sugar as an importable good: that will make the Sugar Program, in its present form (with a legislated mandate to avoid any payments by the US government), infeasible. In the absence of a legal ban on development of all substitutes, it is difficult to see how the political process can further increase the real price of sugar, especially as and if crystalline corn sugar becomes economic. In the longer term, this market reaction to the sugar programme may result in the closure of the entire sugar industry in the United States—thereby doing the very thing that many supporters of the Sugar Program claimed they were trying to avoid.[64]

The minor reactions include: the importation of soft drinks, cake mixes, and other sugar-containing products from Canada and elsewhere; the need for detailed regulation of imports to avoid storage costs for American refiners; the seizure of the programme by sugar refiners as a basis on which to press for a ban on imported raw sugar or of refined beet-sugar; and the diplomatic and other complications arising out of establishing and implementing import quotas for a large number of countries. An interesting reaction, difficult to classify, has been the increased volatility of the international sugar price in response to the smaller and smaller volume of transactions going through the 'free market' (which would more appropriately be termed the 'residual' market).

These market reactions in turn have induced: political responses; bans on imports of cake mixes, and then of processed food products containing sugar; movement from annual to quarterly import quotas; reactions to the high sugar price of the early 1970s (which itself was arguably the outcome of the earlier decision to increase domestic production, which depressed the world price, leading to amplified fluctuations in plantings and in sugar

---

[64] HFCS was discovered in the 1960s, but was uneconomic to produce. Estimates are that it was economic at around 14 cents per lb. in the early 1980s, contrasted with a then-estimated world price of sugar of 12 cents per lb. if the US adopted free trade. Once established, of course, HFCS processors were likely to continue producing at a price somewhat below that which induced them to build capacity. Given that cost estimates for US sugar are well in excess of 20 cents per lb. from almost all sources, it seems likely that HFCS can compete for the entire liquid-sugar market. If crystalline corn becomes economic, as is said to be the case, it does not seem possible further to increase the producer price of sugar over the longer term except through direct subsidies (deficiency payments?) to producers. As already stated, the representatives of the corn growers vehemently oppose such a shift in the nature of the programme.

price cycles) which led to the (temporary) abandonment of the pro-gramme, and so on.

In a sense, this 'life of its own' hypothesis is the most disturbing for potential economist-policymakers. If the hypothesis is correct, it says that even if a programme is designed to meet socially desirable objectives in cost-minimizing ways, it will likely be seized upon by groups and in cir-cumstances only remotely related to the initial intent of the programme. Once put in place, a policy may evolve in ways unrelated to the initial purpose.[65]

Role of knowledge and technocrats. Partly because of the interaction of economic and political markets, any ongoing programme is likely to be-come very complex. While sugar may be especially so, it is at least arguable that price supports, production controls, or deficiency payments to other agricultural commodities, imports subject to quota, health regulations, and most other policy instruments inevitably become highly complex. One im-portant consequence is that a coterie of specialists is called for whose hu-man capital consists of their understanding of the programme, and one hopes, of the economic implications of alternative changes in policies.[66]

Complexity in and of itself provides a significant barrier to participation of non-specialist groups in the decision process. In the case of sugar legisla-tion, it seems evident that there were several efforts to resist changes that might have made the programme more transparent: sugar producers opposed deficiency payments (until it was too late) probably because the size of payment per farm would have been apparent and they feared a ceiling; import quotas were country-specific, rather than global, and there was opposition to any change; import quotas, rather than tariffs, were the chosen instrument for protection; raw-sugar refiners supported the pro-gramme and sought prohibition of imports rather than seeking protection from foreign refiners; and corn producers were adamant in wanting sugar prices supported rather than seeking higher support prices and deficiency payments for corn growers directly.

In addition, however, the specialists in a given policy instrument become

---

[65] One needs only to point to the complexity of American income tax laws (even after reform) and of the Multi Fibre Arrangement to convince oneself that the phenomenon is not limited to the sugar case.

[66] One indication of the ways in which these interests grow is to examine the length of hearings and the number of witnesses who appeared before the House Agriculture Commit-tee each time the Sugar Act was under consideration. The 1934 *Hearings* were 251 pages long, with 33 witnesses; in 1937 *Hearings* were 373 pages long, with 47 witnesses. In 1940, *Hearings* were 302 pages with 40 witnesses; the 1948 *Hearings* were short with 114 pages and 10 witnes-ses; 1951 *Hearings* were 323 pages with 46 witnesses and submissions; 1955 *Hearings* were 768 pages with 136 witnesses and submissions; 1962 *Hearings* were 552 pages with 81 witnesses and submissions; 1965 *Hearings* were 365 pages with 74 witnesses and submissions; 1971 *Hear-ings* were 789 pages with 132 witnesses and submissions. Even this understates the increase, as coalitions of supporters (such as the Sugar Users' Group and the Sugar Producers' Group) formed.

a vested interest in the maintenance of *some* policy.[67] Those with understanding of the US Sugar Program could seek employment as lobbyists for foreign governments, or as representatives of domestic groups, as Congressional staff assistants, or with the Department of Agriculture. For any non-specialist to enter the policy dialogue in a meaningful way would require a considerable investment.

All of these phenomena suggest that public discussion of policy options might be significantly improved if means could be found to keep policies transparent and simple. The opposition to deficiency payments and other transparent procedures was surely based at least in part on the belief that they would not have withstood careful scrutiny. Whether means can be found in complex markets of limiting the types of interventions that are permitted is a difficult subject, and one well beyond the scope of this chapter. None the less, it seems highly likely that, had the Sugar Program been transparent and readily comprehensible to an informed citizenry, it could not have persisted in anything like the form it did.

9. Some Tentative Conclusions

No case-study can provide the generalizations desirable to form a basis for a theory of political-economic interactions. The US Sugar Program is, none the less, interesting in that it raises some questions that are not readily handled with the use of traditional models. Its evolution demonstrates that a static analysis of the costs and benefits of the programme at a point in time would significantly misstate the programme's impact: clearly account must be taken of the ways in which economic and political responses will alter the programme over time. It is to be hoped that future research will enable the transformation of some of the questions raised here into testable hypotheses.

Several questions clearly call for further research. Among them: (i) to what extent are the economic outcomes of policies reasonably correctly anticipated and to what extent do side-effects render the outcomes unacceptable to the policies' advocates?; (ii) can one find meaningful characterizations of the logic of interaction between political and economic markets?; and (iii) can one classify policy instruments according to criteria (such as transparency) and then make meaningful predictions as to, for example, the likely excess cost of policies pursued with each of these instruments?

At this stage, the conclusions that emerge arise primarily with regard to

[67] It might be argued that they would prefer some changes because that generates more work, but that issue is secondary. The hypothesis here is that the loss of human capital that would be involved in the complete abandonment of a programme is probably so large as to induce specialists to advocate more rational programmes, rather than programme abandonment.

the sugar programme itself. First, when it was originally formulated in 1934, and then when it was reinstated in 1948, the intentions of its advocates bore little resemblance to the purposes to which it was put some 20 or 30 years later. Second, it seems highly unlikely that the electorate would support a programme that provides payments of over $136,000 per farm were that figure highly publicized. Third, at least some of the supporters of the sugar programme over the years—the importers and refiners of raw sugar and the beet-mill owners who went bankrupt at the very least— would not have been so enthusiastic had they known the outcome.

At a more general level, two tentative lessons emerge. First, at the very least, economists advocating government intervention in markets would be well advised to recognize that the measures they adovcate will, once enacted, have lives—including supporters—of their own. Second, in choosing between alternative policy instruments, there should be a strong presumption in favour of simple, transparent instruments: the likelihood that those instruments can be seized in ways unacceptable to a comprehending electorate would be reduced.

References

Becker, Gary S. (1983), 'A Theory of Competition among Pressure Groups for Political Influence', *Quarterly Journal of Economics*, 98 (Aug.), pp. 371–400.

Berman, Daniel M., and Heineman, Robert A. (1963), 'Lobbying by Foreign Governments on the Sugar Act Amendments of 1962', *Law and Contemporary Problems*, 28/2, pp. 416–27.

Bhagwati, Jagdish, and Srinivasan, T. N., (1980), 'Revenue Seeking: A Generalization of the Theory of Tariffs', *Journal of Political Economy*, 88/6, pp. 1069–87.

Borrell, Brent, Sturgiss, Robert, and Wong, Gordon (1987), 'U.S. Sugar Policy— Its Effects on the World Sugar Market', paper presented at International Sweetener Colloquium, California, Feb. 1987.

Brock, W. A., and Magee, S. P. (1978), 'The Economics of Special Interest Politics: The Case of Tariffs', *American Economic Review*, 68, pp. 246–50.

Buchanan, James M. (1987), 'The Constitution of Economic Policy', *American Economic Review*, 77 (June), pp. 243–50.

Cameron, Laurie A., and Berg, Gerald C. (undated), 'The U.S. Sugar Program, An Historical Overview', mimeo.

Campos, José Edgardo L. (1987), 'A Simple Political Economy Model of Price Supports', Ph.D. dissertation, California Institute of Technology.

Cater, Douglass (1964), *Power in Washington* (New York: Random House).

Congressional Quarterly Almanac (1962), 'Congress again Revises Sugar Quotas', *CQ Almanac*, pp. 127–30.

Congressional Research Service, (1985), 'World Sugar Trade and US Sugar Policy', Report no. 85–144, ENR, 12 July.

Corden, W. M. (1974), *Trade Policy and Economic Welfare* (Oxford: OUP).

Council on Wage and Price Stability (1975), *Staff Report on Sugar Prices* (May).

Ferguson, Allen R. (undated), 'The Sugar Price Support Program', mimeo.

General Accounting Office (1984), 'US Sweetener/Sugar Issues and Concerns', GAD/RCED 85–19, 15 Nov.

Gerber, David J. (1976), 'The United States Sugar Program: A Study in the Direct Congressional Control of Imports', *Journal of Law and Economics*, 19/1, pp. 103–47.

Harris, Simon (1985), 'Protectionism in the World Sugar Economy Revisited', (São Paulo), mimeo.

Heston, Thomas J. (1975), 'Sweet Subsidy: The Economic and Diplomatic Effects of the US Sugar Acts—1934 to 1974', Ph.D. dissertation, Case Western Reserve University, 1975.

Ickes, Harold I. (1953), *The Secret Diary of Harold I. Ickes*, Vol. 1: *The First Thousand Days* (New York: Simon & Schuster).

Johnson, D. Gale (1974), *The Sugar Program* (American Enterprise Institute).

Krauss, Bob, and Alexander, William P. (1965), *Grove Farm Plantation: The Biography of a Hawaiian Sugar Plantation* (Palo Alto: Pacific Books).

Leu, Gwo-Jiun Mike, and Knutson, Ronald D. (1987), 'U.S. Sugar Policy: Costs, Benefits, Consequences', Paper presented at Western Economic Association, July.

Maskus, Keith E. (1987), 'The International Political Economy of U.S. Sugar Policy in the 1980s', US Department of State, Bureau of Economic and Business Affairs, Planning and Economic Analysis Staff, WP/87/1.

Mueller, Dennis C. (1983), *The Political Economy of Growth* (New Haven: Yale Univ. Press).

Olson, Mancur (1965), *The Logic of Collective Action* (Cambridge, Mass.: Harvard Univ. Press).

——(1982), *The Rise and Decline of Nations: Economic Growth, Stagflation, and Social Rigidities* (New Haven: Yale Univ. Press).

Peltzman, Sam (1976), 'Toward a More General Theory of Regulation', *Journal of Law and Economics*, 19, pp. 211–40.

Price, David E. (1971), 'The Politics of Sugar', *Review of Politics*, 33 (April), pp. 212–231.

Snape, Richard H., (1963), 'Some Effects of Protection in the World Sugar Industry', *Economica*, 30 (Feb.), pp. 63–73.

Stigler, George J. (1971), 'The Theory of Economic Regulation', *Bell's Journal of Economics and Management Science* (Spring), pp. 3–21.

Tan, C. Suan (1986), *Cuba-USSR Sugar Trade*, Commodity Studies and Projections Division, World Bank, Division Working Paper no. 1986–2 (Washington, DC: World Bank).

Tarr, David G., and Morkre, Morris E. (1984), *Aggregate Costs to the United States of Tariffs and Quotas on Imports*, Federal Trade Commission (Dec.).

Taussig, Frank William (1924), *Some Aspects of the Tariff Question* (Cambridge, Mass.: Harvard Univ. Press).

——(1931), *A Tariff History of the United States* (New York and London: Putnam & Sons).

Terpstra, A. Ellen (1981), 'U.S. Sugar Policy and Proposals Since 1974', Congressional Research Service, HD 9100 (July).

USDA (1985), 'Background to 1985 Sugar Legislation', Economic Research Service (US Dept. of Agriculture).

USHR (1974), Subcommittee on Domestic Marketing and Consumer Relations of the Committee on Agriculture, *Examination of Sugar Marketing Conditions Since Defeat of Sugar Bill*, 9, 10, 11, 12, and 19 Dec. 1974. Serial 93–XXX. Referenced as Sugar Marketing Hearings, 1974 (US House of Representatives).

USHR (various dates), Committee on Agriculture, Hearings on Sugar Program, cited as House *Hearings*, with date indicated (US House of Representatives).

US Tariff Commission (1937), *United States-Philippine Trade*, Report no. 118, 2nd Series (US Government Printing Office).

10

The Theory of Political Economy, Economic Policy, and Foreign Investment

JAGDISH N. BHAGWATI

1. Introduction

In this chapter I consider recent developments in the analysis of foreign investment that reflect the new thinking in economic theory along the lines of political economy. Section 1 provides an overview of the developments in the theory of political economy generally, focusing equally on its profound implications for the theory of economic policy. Section 2 turns then to the analysis of foreign investment in light of this overview, discussing how analysis of foreign investment changes in light of political economy-theoretic considerations, drawing particularly on the new theory of quid pro quo foreign investment.

2. The Theory of Political Economy: An Overview

The new theory of political economy is distinguished chiefly by its explicit consideration of political action by economic agents in the simultaneous determination of economic policy and economic phenomena.

2.1 Puppet Government: Echoing the Economist

Conventional economic theory typically postulates a government whose role is to echo the policy that the economist, presented with the technocratic information on the economy and choosing an appropriate objective function, proposes as the optimal one from a set of policy instruments. The government is therefore in essence a fictitious device. It simply represents a surrogate for the economist, impervious to any identity of its own as a participating agent in the economic process and equally to any activities by other economic agents to influence policy outcome in their preferred direction. I therefore call this manner of modelling government in conventional

---

In discussing recent developments in both the theory of economic policy and the theory of foreign investment, I hope that this chapter provides an appropriate tribute to Ian Little in view of his seminal theoretical contributions to the former and his insightful policy writings on the latter. An early draft of the paper on which this chapter is based was presented to the American Economic Association meeting in Chicago, December 1987, and has profited from the comments of David Colander and Mancur Olson.

(and indeed dominant) economic theory the *puppet government* view of how government functions. The economist is the puppeteer: the government is only, and exclusively, his voice.

The new theoretical developments in political economy essentially depart from this approach by endowing the government with autonomy from the economist. But they vary in the way in which the government then interacts with the conventionally defined economic system (e.g. the Walrasian value-theory model of general equilibrium) to define both economic policy and outcome. Two approaches to endowing an explicit role to the government can be distinguished.

2.2. Self-willed Government: Full Autonomy

One approach has been to endow the government with its own objective function and the power to determine policy, with the rest of the economic system providing simply the playground for the government to maximize its own welfare. The government is fully autonomous: it neither echoes the economist nor is it responsive to the forces of pluralist politics. This is essentially the approach underlying modelling in the spirit of Niskanen (1968) whose government bureaucrats maximize revenues for their own benefit, the Leviathan writings of Brennen and Buchanan (1977), and the purely predatory views of government espoused by others. There is no active feedback from the economic system to the government in such models: it is just that the government, now autonomous of the economist, has its own preference function and corresponding agenda.

The welfare-theoretic analysis of policy-making in such analysis cannot consist in devising optimal policy and ranking alternative policy instruments in a hierarchy of welfare outcomes. Instead, it must turn to asking what the welfare effect of a government setting its own agenda will be on the rest of us.

To see this contrast sharply, consider the conventional argument for trade policy for a large, open economy. Under the orthodox *puppet government* approach, we choose the *optimal* tariff (Johnson, 1950–1; Graaff, 1949) as the first-best among available policy instruments whereas domestic interventions appear as second-best improvements (Bhagwati and Ramaswami, 1963) over *laissez-faire*. On the other hand, a Niskanen government will choose the *maximum-revenue* tariff (Johnson, 1950–1). The welfare consequence of the maximum-revenue tariff for society can then be calculated as the loss relative to what the optimal tariff would yield.

2.3 Clearing-house Government: Primacy of Pluralist Politics

An altogether contrasting approach, on the other hand, has been to make the government again lose its autonomy, not to the economist, but now to the economic system whose agents within a pluralistic political regime play the policy-influencing game that determines the policy outcome.[1] The lobbies compete for policy outcomes; the government is *de facto* a playground where this competition or conflict results in policy outcome. The government has no ego, no identity, in this approach. It is best described as the *clearing-house government* approach to political economy modelling.

Thus, in recent models of tariff-seeking which endogenize tariff formation, the traditional general-equilibrium models of the open economy are augmented by a set of political equations which reflect the lobbying activities aimed at influencing the policy choice. Essentially, political markets are introduced as methods of affecting policy and hence one's income: these augment the conventional economic ways of earning income.

To take a specific example, in the Findlay–Wellisz (1982) model of tariff-seeking, the specific-factors 3×2 model of general equilibrium is augmented by lobbying functions for the specific factors in each of the two sectors. The specific factor in the import-competing sector gains from a tariff; that in the other sector loses from it. The model is solved for the endogenous tariff that equates the return from lobbying to its cost, both at the margin.

As I observed, the government here is captive to the economic system whose agents essentially operate in political markets to equate returns from them with the returns to activity in the conventional economic markets.[2] (The Niskanen–Brennan–Buchanan type of approach, on the other hand, has the economic system captive to the government which plays (or perhaps preys) on it to pursue its own ends.)

I should add that, in an implicit fashion, the role of the government as an autonomous agent can be imagined none the less in this approach. For, the effectiveness of lobbying for a tariff in these models for instance can be

---

[1] Mancur Olson's (1965) classic work on the free-rider problem and the logic of collective action is a pioneering contribution to this approach.

[2] The recent literature on activities by economic agents to secure profits or income (i) by influencing policy—e.g. tariff-seeking (Tullock, 1969), or (ii) by earning rent from existing policy, e.g. rent-seeking (Krueger, 1974) by chasing import quotas already in place, or revenue-seeking (Bhagwati and Srinivasan, 1980) to secure tariff revenues resulting from tariffs imposed endogenously or exogenously, or (iii) by evading policy, e.g. smuggling (Bhagwati and Hansen, 1973); (Johnson, 1974); (Kemp, 1975); (Pitt, 1980); (Panagariya and Martin, 1981)—now describes them as DUP (directly unproductive profit-seeking) activities (Bhagwati, 1982). They are undertaken by using resources to produce profit or income but not (socially valued) goods or output. On immediate impact, or *directly*, therefore, they are unproductive. But *indirectly*, in terms of final impact on welfare, they may be beneficial (owing to second-best considerations). Krueger's (1974) quota-rents-generated rent-seeking lobbying activities are an important *subset* of such DUP activities and should not be confused as being identical with them. Cf. Bhagwati (1982, 1983).

DUP activities of type (i) above, which endogenize policy-making, lead to important analytical consequences such as the Determinacy Paradox noted in the text below. Not so, DUP activities of types (ii) and (iii) if the policy that triggers them is still left exogenous. Cf. Bhagwati *et al.* (1984).

considered to be a function, not merely of the expenses incurred by oneself and by the opposing lobby, but also of 'ideology' or the objective function of the government. But just as weather shapes the production function in agriculture but plays no role in microeconomic analysis, this view of the government's ideology plays no analytical role in the pluralistic, lobbying models of *clearing-house government*.

Once again, however, the analysis of economic policy undergoes a shift. With policy endogenously determined, it becomes impossible to seek to rank policies by their welfare impact as in conventional, *puppet government* analysis. The degree of freedom to do this is not available, in general, any longer. This is what is now known as the *determinacy paradox* (Bhagwati, *et al.*, 1984; Bhagwati, 1986). The role of policy analysis and welfare economics is not lost, however. It just shifts to *variational* questions around the observed, political economy equilibrium. Thus, if any parametric shift occurs, either in the economic or in the political part of the model, we can ask: how will policy change, and how will the associated welfare change?

While the preceding two classes of modelled departures from the *puppet government* approach are polar cases, a realistic analysis of political economy must often draw on *both*. The government typically has objectives; and different branches of governments often have different objectives as well, so that it is often necessary to disaggregate.[3] By setting policy defined over the economy, the government can and does pursue these objectives. At the same time, economic agents within the economy typically seek to influence policy to their advantage in light of their own preference functions.[4] The interaction of these two sets of agents, the government and others, whether strategic or not, leads to the policy and associated economic outcome.

3. Foreign Investment: Quid Pro Quo DFI *et al.*

The underlying core of the theory of political economy, as just outlined, provides a necessary introduction to the recent political economy-theoretic analysis of foreign investment.

The conventional analysis of international capital and labour flows and of direct foreign investment (DFI) typically analysed *either* the consequences of exogenously imposed policies (e.g. tariffs) on variables such as

---

[3] A two branch model of government is developed in Feenstra and Bhagwati's (1982) analysis of the Efficient Tariff.

[4] Sometimes, the theory of political economy is supposed to embrace the extension of economic analysis to preference functions that go beyond goods-orientated utilitarianism. But this is simply confusing. Such extension, which international economists have considered and analysed under the theory of non-economic objectives since the later 1950s long before it became fashionable for others to consider non-utilitarian objectives, is fully compatible with the conventional *puppet government* approach.

the international flows of productive factors[5] or the optimal policy intervention when countries trading with one another also had international factor mobility between them.[6] But political economy-theoretic considerations have recently emerged in the theoretical analysis of international factor flows, and new ideas have been modelled in consequence in the theory of foreign investment.

These ideas have surfaced mainly in the context of response to import competition. Thus, the conventional economic analysis simply argues that, if import competition intensifies (i.e. the terms of trade improve), then a country will be better off (under the potential welfare-improvement Pareto criterion).[7] A benign 'puppet' government will continue its free trade policy; or, if there is monopoly power in trade, it will suitably adjust its optimal monopoly-power-in-trade tariff to the new situation.[8]

But suppose now that the response to import competition is to trigger lobbying by the adversely affected economic agents to change economic policy so as to cushion this impact. Then, government policy becomes a function of this lobbying among factors.

The conventional modelling in trade theory of such endogenized policy-making focused on *one* policy instrument, i.e. tariffs (or, their quantity counterpart, import quotas). However, starting in the early 1980s, the question of the *choice of instruments* was raised, in the context of response to import competition, in Bhagwati (1982). There, I considered in different models the differential incentive of different economic agents to seek one of several possible policy interventions.[9] In particular, I distinguished between 'capital' and 'labour'. I also explicitly considered policy instruments that went beyond trade policy to international factor mobility. Thus, I con-

---

[5] This is exemplified by the celebrated Mundell (1957) analysis of how factor-price equalization can lead to commodity-price equalization when an exogenously specified tariff is combined with international factor mobility in a Heckscher–Ohlin world.

[6] This is exemplified by the analysis of Kemp (1966) and Jones (1967) which considered the optimal structure of taxes and subsidies on trade and capital flows from the viewpoint of one country's advantage, in a world economy characterized by two countries and international capital mobility. In principle this analysis carries over to labour mobility as well. However, there is an overwhelmingly critical difference. For, when labour moves across borders, the important question arises: should such labour be excluded then from the set over which one defines the welfare function to be maximized for national advantage? Cf. Bhagwati (1972) and Bhagwati and Wilson (1989).

[7] This intuitive proposition needs some careful and extended argumentation: cf. Krueger and Sonnenschein (1967).

[8] If a suboptimal trade policy is in place when import competition intensifies, the theory of immiserizing growth (Bhagwati, 1968) tells one immediately that the result may be paradoxically to worsen, rather than improve, one's welfare. Cf. Batra and Pattanaik (1970).

[9] The analysis of differential incentives for different agents in Bhagwati (1982) was followed up by Dinopoulos (1983) and Sapir (1983). Subsequently, Rodik (1986) and Mayer and Riezman (1987a, b) have also considered the choice between tariffs and production subsidies as possible instruments of protection in more complete models.

sidered the following possibilities in response to import competition in
Schumpeterian industries:

(i) seek protection (tariffs or quotas) or promotion (subsidies);
(ii) seek relaxed immigration quotas (as in the *gastarbeiter* system of
Western Europe) to import more cheap labour to compete better;
(iii) go abroad (the Atari option) where labour is cheaper, thus undertaking DFI abroad; and
(iv) use the threat of protection to get successful foreign rivals to invest
here, thus getting their DFI into the home country.

This last option, a novelty in recent years, implies foreign firms investing
in the home country to defuse the threat of protection in a variety of ways.
Thus, for instance, Toyota undertakes a joint venture in the US with
General Motors, essentially giving General Motors an apparently gra-
tuitous share in profits from Toyota's superior know-how on small cars. In
exchange, however, General Motors breaks ranks on VER (Voluntary Export Restraint) renewal. The quid pro quo for Toyota from an otherwise
uneconomical DFI in the US is then the reduced threat of protection that
follows. Hence, I have christened this political economy-theoretic phenomenon as 'quid pro quo' foreign investment (Bhagwati, 1984, 1985).

Such quid pro quo investment by foreign firms can also appeal to domestic labour threatened by foreign competition. For it can help maintain jobs.
Thus, UAW's interest in auto-protection would be inversely related to
Japanese willingness to invest in the US, though the threat of protection .
must be created and sustained to induce this investment.

Therefore, domestic agents, both firms and unions, can be expected to
create a protectionist threat to induce investment in one's country by successful foreign rivals in joint ventures *à la* GM–Toyota in the former case
and more generally to placate labour in the latter case. This argument
therefore is explicitly political economy-theoretic. It says that Japanese
DFI is undertaken to affect US trade policy: by 'rewarding' US firms and/
or labour, it co-opts them into reducing the protectionist effort that they
would otherwise undertake. Hence I also call this the *tariff-threat-reducing*
DFI, to distinguish it from the traditional *tariff-jumping* DFI where the
tariff is both realized and exogenously specified in the manner of conventional analysis.

(i) The arguments above suggest that the foreign (e.g. Japanese) *firms*
would seek DFI in order to defuse the threat of protection in their external
market (e.g. in the US). This requires, of course, that the firm be large
enough, and the counterpart (US) firm and/or union be significant enough,
for this political quid pro quo to be a significant factor in the firm's
decision-making. If these conditions are met, then a natural way to formu-

late the resulting DFI is to consider a foreign, say Japanese, firm in a two-period setting, with two alternatives: producing in Japan and selling in the US and producing (at higher cost) in the US and selling in the US. In period 1, given the quid pro quo phenomenon, the firm would gravitate towards the latter option to the extent that it equates the marginal cost in period 1 from higher-cost production in the US with the discounted expected marginal benefit in period 2 from reduced probability of the US market being closed by protection. In essence, this is the underlying structure of the early formulation in Dinopoulos and Bhagwati (1986) and the later, more complete analysis in Dinopoulos (1987), my former Columbia student.

(ii) But suppose that the Japanese firms are not in a position to seek such quid pro quos. Even then, there may be a *generic* case for Japan, seeking national advantage, to increase the size of Japan's DFI in the US to reduce anti-Japanese, protectionist sentiment in the US Congress. In this case, the quid pro quo angle arises, not necessarily through co-opting of the economic agents who lobby Congress, but by reducing the willingness of Congressmen to respond to domestic protectionist pressures by these economic agents. Japan Inc. can reap the quid pro quo of reduced protectionism by encouraging Japanese DFI abroad. The simplest, economical way to model this generic argument for quid pro quo investment then would be to introduce, in a competitive model, a protectionist threat function which has first-period investment as one argument, with the partial derivative less than zero. This is, in essence, the type of analysis that we have recently undertaken (Bhagwati *et al.*, 1986).

(iii) But these analyses, whether oligopolistic and at firm level in Dinopoulos et al. or perfectly competitive and at national level in Bhagwati et al., consider the threat to protect in period 2 as *exogenously* specified. The firm, or the government, then chooses an optimal DFI level in period 1 so as to maximize an intertemporal profit or welfare function. Let me elaborate.

Thus, consider the following agents:

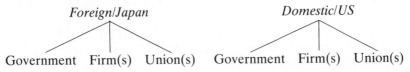

Foreign/Japan			*Domestic/US*		
Government	Firm(s)	Union(s)	Government	Firm(s)	Union(s)

The Dinopoulos analysis assumes that the Japanese firm undertakes DFI in period 1, to influence the probability of the US Government imposing a tariff in period 2.[10] The threat is exogenously specified but a function of

---

[10] Two models are used: one where there is a Japanese firm and a US firm, another where there are two Japanese firms.

Japanese DFI; no intermediation of protectionist lobbying by co-opted domestic agents is explicitly modelled. The analysis, like that in recent work on the small-group analysis of strategic trade policy, is partial equilibrium and basically shows how, even in the absence of Japanese Government action, firms in imperfectly competitive small-group situations will change the level of trade and investment when their investment can serve to defuse protectionist threats.

In the Bhagwati–Brecher–Dinopoulos–Srinivasan analysis, the protection-defusing action belongs to the Japanese Government instead. In a perfectly competitive world, the non-governmental agents in both countries are not modelled as influencing US policy. Rather, the Japanese Government intervenes to influence US trade policy by influencing Japanese investment in period 1 since that influences the exogenously specified protectionist threat in period 2. The analysis is then an extension of the analysis of optimal policy intervention (Bhagwati and Srinivasan, 1976) when a country finds that its exports in period 1 can (adversely) affect the prospects of a market-disruption-related quota being invoked by the importing country in period 2.[11] The analysis is in general equilibrium and focuses on optimal intervention by the Japanese Government and associated impact on foreign investment.

(iv) A recent analysis by Kar-yiu Wong (1987), another of my Columbia students, has however addressed the modelling of quid pro quo investment in a manner that is, in some respects, more satisfactory. He endogenizes the threat by explicitly modelling a US union whose lobbying activities reflect the unemployment resulting (in a fixed-wage context) from imports sent by a monopolist Japanese firm. The quid pro quo investment then reflects the fact that, by reducing unemployment in the US, the Japanese firm is able to reduce the lobbying by the US union and hence act towards defusing the protectionist threat in the US. The analysis is in partial equilibrium but extended to the welfare impact of quid pro quo investment on either country.

The three ways of modelling quid pro quo investment, sketched above, are not exhaustive. By looking at the possible set of agents that I set out earlier, we can see that a variety of other models is possible.

Thus, in an imperfectly competitive setting, the explicit modelling could reflect the Toyota–GM variety of quid pro quo investment where a Japanese firm undertakes joint production with a US firm, at a first-period loss to itself and gain to the US firm, and the lobbying effort of the US firm to get protection is then influenced favourably. This analysis would endogenize the protectionist threat, as in Wong's US-union-centred analysis,

---

[11] Whereas therefore Bhagwati and Srinivasan (1976) define the threat as a function only of first-period exports, Bhagwati *et al.* (1980) define it also as a function of first-period capital outflow.

and generate quid pro quo investment equally. Doubtless, other models, with different mixes of the foreign and domestic agents, can and will be built to analyse quid pro quo investment.

Evidence. While the analysis of such political economy-theoretic quid pro quo investment is proceeding rapidly since I started writing about it in the early 1980s, the question arises: is there systematic evidence for such investment?

That quid pro quo investment was a phenomenon from Japan to the US in the early 1980s is not to be doubted. I developed the hypothesis, and the subsequent theoretical analysis, on the basis of casual empiricism, the classic route to new theorizing. In particular, I had been impressed by a luncheon conversation with Mr Toyoda at Columbia University early in 1980, when he was expressing great hesitation about investing in the US but suggesting that the political pressure on him, to avert the US protectionist threat through investment and hence expression of goodwill by Japan to the US, was considerable. He really wanted to know, not whether his and other Japanese investments would create goodwill in the US and hence moderate the protectionist threat, but whether that threat was really serious. I assured him that it was.

That Mr Toyoda was under pressure from the Japanese Government to invest in the US, because the Japanese Government was conscious of the protectionist threat in the early 1980s, and encouraged Japanese investment in the US on quid pro quo grounds, was evident. In fact, in a recent article, Professor Toshio Shishido (1986) of the International University of Japan recalls a conversation with Mr Toyoda as follows:

In 1978, I had a talk with Mr Eigi Toyoda, the President of Toyota Motors. . . At that time, Mr Toyoda stated that Toyota had no intention to practice local production in America. I then said to him, 'Judging from the tense relationship between Japan and the US, why don't you think about an expansion of car production in America, in the form of cooperation [with] the government policy [in] national interest?' He said, 'Toyota is not making an automobile for the nation.' He clearly defined the standpoints of private enterprise. He clearly . . . was not able to do the direct investment [in] America, thinking [only] about the profit of Toyota (p. 15).

The interesting question of course is whether, independently of Japanese governmental pressure, the big Japanese firms thought of foreign investment *themselves* on quid pro quo grounds. For example, did Mr Toyoda finally invest in a joint venture with General Motors simply because it would be doing a good turn to Japan generally by helping to moderate Japan-bashing outbreaks of US protectionism or because he saw the quid pro quo more directly in terms of gains to Toyota in consequent increase in the probability of auto VER termination? The fact that he teamed up finally with General Motors, the most important US firm with the biggest polit-

TABLE 10.1. Motivations for direct investments abroad (to advanced countries after 1980) (%)

	Avoiding trade friction	Market expansion	Following clients	Superiority on cost	Others
Business machines	96.7	3.3	—	—	—
Machine tools	77.1	14.3	—	—	8.6
Consumer electric machines	53.6	13.6	10.7	14.3	7.8
Electronics	30.0	32.1	11.3	10.8	15.6
Automobiles	66.0	24.0	—	—	10.0

Source: MITI, 'Research on Foreign Local Production of Japanese Enterprises' (cited in Shishido, 1986, p. 25).

ical clout, and that General Motors broke ranks and successfully opposed VER renewal subsequently, suggests that Mr Toyoda may finally have seen some substantial quid pro quo for himself and not just for Japan.

In any event, I should mention that Shishido reports on a MITI survey on motivations for Japanese investments in developed countries abroad after 1980, reproduced in Table 10.1 here. While there is not sufficient information on the category 'Avoiding Trade Friction', which is the major reason advanced by the interviewees, it is certainly consistent with the hypothesis that quid pro quo considerations were important in motivating Japan's direct investments abroad.

The correspondents were not saying that, because they expected trade friction to result in trade protection, they were investing abroad in markets that they expected to close. Rather, they were saying that they expected to avoid trade friction and hence presumably trade protection by investing in the US. What is not clear from Shishido's all-too-brief summary report is whether this expectation, if it reflected industry-level quid pro quo considerations, was because the foreign investment would (*a*) produce goodwill in the US Congress and hence resistance to any given demand for 'high-track' (VER-style) administered protection in the industry, and/or (*b*) co-opt the economic agents and hence reduce the demand for protection itself by these agents, and/or (*c*) simply make 'low-track' administered protection related to market disruption and safeguards action under Section 201 more difficult to sustain beacuse it must relate to import levels. The *exact* modelling of quid pro quo investment, from among the possibilities I discussed, and others, should reflect the choice among these alternative routes through which the Japanese investors expect the quid pro quo to operate.

Motivational studies, however, are not sufficient, for obvious reasons. It should be possible to test for the quid pro quo investment by examining Japanese investment in the US for 1980–5 before the dollar–yen exchange rate began to adjust and made quid pro quo reasoning obsolete by making Japanese DFI in the US profitable on straightforward, conventional economic grounds.

A key problem, of course, is in distinguishing between tariff-threat-defusing and tariff-jumping investment. If one takes the firm-level decision-making as leading to quid pro quo foreign investment, how is one to decide, from cold data, whether a Japanese direct investor came into the US because he expected his export market to close or because he expected that his investment would help to moderate that threat for any of several quid pro quo-type arguments considered here? One approach, suggested by Robert Lawrence of Brookings, is to see if the large Japanese firms (which could reasonably expect to have such quid pro quo influence) came first into the US in the sequence of Japanese firms entering an industry. Another approach, since the model applies to the Japanese against whom protectionism is typically threatened, would be to see if Japanese preceded European investment in the US in specific protection-threatening industries. Dinopoulos and others are engaged in this empirical investigation currently.[12]

4. Concluding Remarks

The political economy-theoretic analysis of foreign investment, and indeed of other economic phenomena, thus offers a rich agenda for novel and important theoretical and empirical analysis.

By endogenizing the government and policy in an essential fashion, this type of analysis opens up a significantly different way of analysing both economic policy and economic phenomena, raising in turn (as noted in Section 2) some fundamental questions as well.

Hence, of the two recent developments since the early 1970s in international trade theory—the development of imperfectly competitive analysis (Brander, Dixit, Eaton, Grossman, Helpman, Krugman, Lancaster, Spencer, etc.) and of political-economy DUP-theoretic analysis (Anam, Baldwin, Bhagwati, Brecher, Findlay, Hillman, Krueger, Mayer, Srinivasan, Wellisz, Wilson etc.)—the latter would appear to be the more interesting and significant. The former consists in fitting the old bicycle (competitive trade theory) with a new motor (imperfectly competitive markets) whereas

---

[12] Kar-yiu Wong has drawn my attention to the remarkable fact that, during each year of the period 1982–6, Japanese direct investments in manufacturing in the US made losses although there were good profits for foreign investments as a whole in this sector. This would seem to provide prima facie evidence in support of the quid pro quo hypothesis for Japanese investment in the US.

the latter consists in taking the old bicycle (puppet-government trade theory) down a new road (explicit government trade theory). Surely one does not need to say which is more fundamental.

References

Bhagwati, J. (1982), 'Shifting Comparative Advantage, Protectionist Demands and Policy Response', in J. Bhagwati (ed.), *Import Competition and Response* (Chicago: Chicago Univ. Press).

——(1985), 'Protectionism: Old Wine in New Bottles', *Journal of Policy Modelling*, 7, pp. 23–34.

——(1986), 'Investing Abroad', Esmée Fairbairn Lecture, Univ. of Lancaster, UK (Nov.), mimeo.

——(1982), 'Directly-unproductive Profit-seeking (DUP) Activities', *Journal of Political Economy*, 90 (Oct.), pp. 988–1002.

——(1983), 'DUP Activities and Rent Seeking', *Kyklos*, 36, pp. 634–7.

——and Hansen, B. (1973), 'A Theoretical Analysis of Smuggling', *Quarterly Journal of Economics*, 87 (May).

——and Ramaswami, V. K. (1963), 'Domestic Distortions, Tariffs and the Theory of Optimum Subsidy,' *Journal of Political Economy*, 71 (Feb.).

——and Srinivasan, T. N. (1976), 'Optimal Trade Policy and Compensation under Endogenous Uncertainty: The Phenomenon of Market Disruption', *Journal of International Economics*, 88, pp. 1069–87.

——and Wilson, J. (eds.) (1989), *Income Taxation and International Mobility* (Cambridge, Mass.: MIT Press).

——Brecher, R., and Srinivasan, T. N. (1984), 'DUP Activities and Economic Theory', in D. Colander (ed.), *Neoclassical Political Economy* (Cambridge, Mass.: Ballinger Publishing Company), pp. 17–32.

——Dinopoulos, E., and Srinivasan, T. N. (1987), 'Quid Pro Quo Foreign Investment and Welfare: A Political-Economy-Theoretic Model', *Journal of Development Economics*, (1988).

Brecher, R., and Diaz-Alejandro, C. (1977), 'Tariffs, Foreign Capital and Immiserizing Growth', *Journal of International economics*, 7, pp. 317–22.

Brander, J. A., and Spencer, B. J. (1986), 'Foreign Direct Investment with Unemployment and Endogenous Taxes and Tariffs', mimeo.

Brennan, G., and Buchanan, J. (1977), 'Towards a Tax Constitution for Leviathan', *Journal of Public Economics*, 8 (Dec.), pp. 255–73.

Brock, W., and Magee, S. (1978), 'The Economics of Special Interest Politics: The Case of the Tariff', *American Economic Review*, 68 (May), pp. 246–50.

Buck, J. (1986), 'Direct Foreign Investment as a Game between Home and Host Country Firms and the Host Country Government', (Madison.: Univ. of Wisconsin), mimeo.

Dinopoulos, E. (1983), 'Import Competition, International Factor Mobility and Lobbying Responses: The Schumpeterian Industry Case', *Journal of International Economics*, 14, pp. 395–410.

——(1987), 'Quid Pro Quo Foreign Investment', Paper presented to the World

Bank Conference on Political Economy (June) forthcoming in *Economics and Politics*, 1(2), Summer 1989.

——and Bhagwati, J. (1986), 'Quid Pro Quo Foreign Investment and Market Structure', presented at the 61st Annual Western Economic Association International Conference in San Francisco (July).

Feenstra, R., and Bhagwati, J. (1982), 'Tariff Seeking and the Efficient Tariff', in Bhagwati (1982), pp. 245–58.

Findlay, R., and Wellisz, S. (1982), 'Endogenous Tariffs, the Political Economy of Trade Restrictions, and Welfare', in Bhagwati (1982), pp. 223–34.

Graaff, Jan (1949–50), 'On Optimum Tariff Structures', *Review of Economic Studies*, 17/42.

Johnson, Harry G. (1950–51), 'Optimum Welfare and Maximum Revenue Tariffs', *Review of Economic Studies*, 19.

——(1974), 'Notes on the Economic Theory of Smuggling', *Malayan Economic Review* (May 1972), reprinted in J. Bhagwati (ed.), *Illegal Transactions in International Trade*, Series in International Economics (Amsterdam: North-Holland).

Jones, R. (1967), 'International Capital Movements and the Theory of Tariffs and Trade', *Quarterly Journal of Economics*, 81, pp. 1–38.

Kemp, M. (1966), 'The Gain from International Trade and Investment: A Neo-Heckscher-Ohlin Approach', *American Economic Review*, 56, pp. 788–809.

——(1967), 'Notes on the Theory of Optimal Tariffs', *Economic Record*, 43/103.

Krueger, Anne (1974), 'The Political Economy of the Rent-Seeking Society', *American Economic Review*, 66 (May), pp. 1–19.

——and Sonnenschein, H. (1967), 'The Terms of Trade, the Gains from Trade and Price Divergence', *International Economic Review*, 8, pp. 121–7.

Mayer, W. (1984), 'Endogenous Tariff Formation', *American Economic Review*, 74 (Dec.), pp. 970–85.

——and Riezman, R. (1987*a*), 'Endogenous Choice of Tariff Instruments', *Journal of International Economics*, 23 (Nov.).

——(1987*b*), 'Endogenous Choice of Trade Policy Instruments', paper presented to World Bank Conference on Political Economy: Theory and Policy (June).

Mundell, R. A. (1957), 'International Trade and Factor Mobility', *American Economic Review*, 47, pp. 321–35.

Niskanen, W (1968), 'The Peculiar Economics of Bureaucracy', *American Economic Review*, 58, pp. 293–305.

Olson, M. (1965), *The Logic of Collective Action*, (Cambridge, Mass.: Harvard Univ. Press).

Pitt, M. (1981), 'Smuggling and Price Disparity', *Journal of International Economics*, 11 (Nov.).

Rodrik, D. (1987), 'Tariffs, Subsidies and the Theory of Optimum Subsidy', *Journal of International Economics*, 72 (May).

Sapir, A. (1983), 'Foreign Competition, Immigration and Structural Adjustment', *Journal of International Economics*, 14, pp. 381–94.

Shishido, T. (1986), 'Capital transfer from Japan to U.S. for Avoiding Trade Friction', in *Beyond Trade Friction*, Japan–U.S. Symposium (1–2 Sept. 1986), Tokyo, Center for Japan–US Business and Economic Studies, New York University.

Tullock, G. (1967), 'The Welfare Cost of Tariffs, Monopolies and Theft', *Western Economic Journal*, 5.

Wong, K. Y. (1986), 'Are International Trade and Factor Mobility Substitutes?' *Journal of International Economics*, 21, pp. 25–43.

——(1987), 'Optimal Threat of Trade Restriction and Quid Pro Quo Foreign Investment', (Seattle, Univ. of Washington), mimeo forthcoming in *Economics and Politics*, 1(3), Winter 1989.

11

International Capital Flows and Economic Development

DEEPAK LAL

Introduction

The role of international capital in economic development has been one of
Ian Little's major interests. His 1965 book, *International Aid*, with Juliet
Clifford still provides one of the few balanced discussions of 'the flow of
public resources from rich to poor countries' (as stated in its subtitle).
Since then he has developed the well-known Little–Mirrlees method of
project analysis (Little and Mirrlees, 1969, 1974) which is now widely used
in the appraisal of aid-financed projects in developing countries. He has
also provided clear-headed accounts of the costs and benefits of direct investment in developing countries in Little (1972), and his 1972 study with
David Tipping of the Kulai palm-oil estate was one of the first empirical
social cost benefit analyses of a major foreign investment in a developing
country.

All these discussions and analyses were timely, as official capital flows
and direct investment have been the major forms of international capital
available to the Third World since the Second World War. But since the
mid 1970's (see Fig. 11.1 and Table 11.1) these have been overshadowed
by private portfolio lending in the form of syndicated bank loans (which in
the late 1970s were almost of the same magnitude as official flows) and
private export credits (which were almost of the same magnitude as direct
investments in the same period).

These new forms of foreign capital have, however, turned out to be a
mixed blessing for their recipients, many of whom are now in a 'debt crisis'
which has dominated discussions of the international economy in the 1980s.
Not surprisingly, much of the analytical and empirical work by economists
in the last decade has therefore been concerned with various aspects of this
'debt crisis'. But given the continuing importance of official capital flows in
the overall flow of capital to developing countries, and the growing 'aid
fatigue' of the major donors in the 1980s, there has been revived interest in
justifying and evaluating the contribution that official capital flows can
make to development. There has also been a revival of interest in promot-

I am grateful to Maurice Scott for comments on an earlier draft which greatly helped to
improve this chapter.

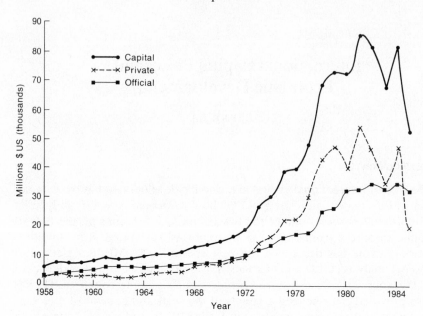

Fig. 11.1   (*a*) Capital, official and private flows, 1956–1985

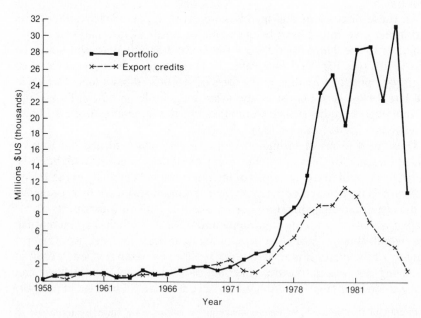

Fig. 11.1   (*b*) Portifolio and export credits, 1956–1985

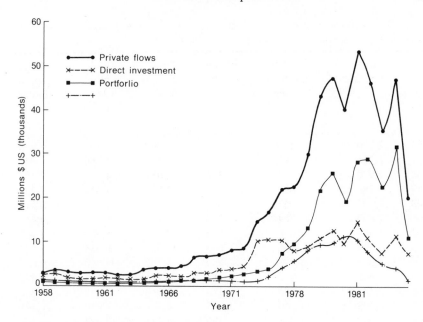

Fig. 11.1   (*c*) Private flows, 1956–1985

ing private foreign investment in developing countries, with the realization that the transfer burden associated with foreign borrowing in the form of direct investment may be less onerous than that based on bank borrowing at floating interest rates. Thus the older discussions of foreign aid and direct investment, to which Ian Little made such notable contributions, are again becoming relevant as the attention of economists and policy-makers shifts from the narrower issues concerning the management of the debt crisis.

This recent intertwining of interest in the role of the 'older' and 'newer' forms of foreign capital in economic development is, moreover, taking place during a momentous change in the nature of the global economic environment. I refer to the emergence of a globally integrated capital market which has resulted from the ending of capital and exchange controls in developed countries and the instantaneous linking of their national capital markets through the new information technology which reduces transactions costs, and is hence like a large reduction in transport costs for traded goods.

This capital-market integration parallels that in goods markets which was achieved in the first two decades after the Second World War as a result of various GATT rounds of multilateral tariff reductions. We know,

TABLE 11.1. Private capital flows and official grants and loans from DAC countries to developing countries, 1956–1985 (million $US)

Year	Direct investment	Portfolio and bank lending	Private export credits	Total private flows	Total official flows (inc. grants)	Total capital flows (inc. grants)
1956	2,350	190	458	2,998	3,260	6,258
1957	2,724	601	454	3,779	3,856	7,635
1958	1,970	733	214	2,917	4,387	7,304
1959	1,782	691	347	2,820	4,311	7,131
1960	1,767	837	546	3,150	4,965	8,115
1961	1,829	704	573	3,106	6,143	9,249
1962	1,495	386	572	2,453	5,984	8,437
1963	1,603	296	660	2,557	6,015	8,572
1964	1,572	1,298	859	3,729	5,916	9,645
1965	2,468	902	751	4,121	6,199	10,320
1966	2,179	625	1,124	3,959	6,431	10,390
1967	2,105	1,269	1,007	4,381	7,060	11,441
1968	3,043	1,738	1,596	6,377	7,047	13,424
1969	2,910	1,630	2,047	6,587	7,192	13,779
1970	3,557	1,251	2,211	7,019	7,984	15,003
1971	3,874	1,617	2,724	8,215	9,030	17,245
1972	4,306	2,695	1,429	8,430	10,195	18,625
1973	10,254	3,543	1,196	14,993	11,841	26,834
1974	10,350	3,795	2,482	16,627	13,499	30,126
1975	10,494	7,792	4,142	22,428	16,611	39,039
1976	7,824	9,169	5,424	22,417	16,971	39,388
1977	8,792	13,096	8,100	29,988	18,015	48,003
1978	10,906	23,265	9,400	43,571	25,381	68,952
1979	12,745	25,537	9,408	47,690	25,714	73,404
1980	9,769	19,171	11,490	40,430	32,536	72,966
1981	14,639	28,548	10,593	53,780	32,243	86,023
1982	10,385	28,843	7,328	46,556	35,191	81,747
1983	7,792	22,370	5,249	35,411	32,471	67,882
1984	11,269	31,815	4,239	47,322	34,934	82,256
1985	7,690	10,927	1,506	20,123	32,783	52,906

Note: Private flows = Direct investment + Portfolio and bank lending + Private export credits

Capital flows = Total official flows + Total private flows.

Sources: OECD *Development Co-operation Review* (1986) and earlier editions of the same.

largely as a result of Ian Little's pioneering research (Little *et al.*, 1970) that the relative economic performance of many developing countries in the 1960s and 1970s was in part determined by their reaction to the vastly expanded and growing opportunities for foreign trade. Hence, we may hypothesize that the future prospects of particular Third World countries will depend upon how they react to the new opportunities presented by the integration of world capital markets.

It may, therefore, be useful to provide an eclectic, but by no means comprehensive, survey of the insights to be gleaned from the large litera-ture on foreign capital and economic development to see how public policy in developing countries can best be adapted to these new emerging trends in the global economy. This is the purpose of this chapter, which is in three sections. The first, examines analyses which attempt to explain the deter-minants and effects of capital flows at an aggregate level. Our purpose in this section is also to provide a translation of various recent theoretical models whose mathematical virtuosity is rarely matched by expository clar-ity. We attempt to show that they can be integrated fairly simply into the standard geometric tool-kit employed by more old-fashioned economists! It might therefore serve a heuristic purpose. It also attempts to judge these models in terms of the historical evidence on capital flows.

Section 2 of the chapter examines the arguments surrounding the deter-minants, and costs and benefits, of particular forms in which capital has been transferred to developing countries.

Section 3 looks at the role capital flows could play in development in an increasingly integrated global economy, from the more novel viewpoint of 'neo-classical' political economy.

1. Theoretical Determinants and Effects of Aggregate Capital Flows

At its simplest, foreign capital flows transfer savings from one group of countries to another. Writing in 1961, Sir Alec Cairncross noted:

When we turn to the theory of international capital flows we are struck at once by its astonishing formalism. . . . I doubt whether even today we have formulated a theory of investment that does justice to the historical experience. . . . Existing theory does not even pose, much less answer the questions. . . . What governs the division of a country's savings between home and foreign investment? What deter-mines which countries will lend and which will borrow? What causes the total volume of international investment to expand or contract? . . . Why do countries that are not inherently incapable of mastering the techniques of modern industry fail to obtain from abroad the resources that might transform them? (Cairncross, 1961, p. 50).

In this section we outline the answers which have or could be provided to Cairncross's questions, as well as our judgements on their validity in the light of the historical record. As Cairncross noted, it is useful to categorize the answers in terms of two different approaches. The first is the main-stream neo-classical general equilibrium framework in which 'we make comparisons between the marginal productivity of capital in different coun-tries and relative rates of interest and profit in order to bring out the mar-ket forces governing the international flow of capital' (Cairncross, 1961, p. 51). The second is what nowadays would be called the 'structuralist' approach, which views 'capital requirements as a more or less fixed propor-tion of output, without much regard to interest rates or variations in capital/output ratios' (Cairncross, 1961).[1]

As much of conventional development economics has been formulated within the second framework we briefly outline the rationale for capital inflows it has provided before examining recent explanations within the former neo-classical framework.

1.1. 'Structuralist' Theories

The structuralist rationales are in a direct line of descent from neo-Marxist theories of the determinants of capital flows between developed and de-veloping countries, due to Hobson and Lenin. They expound what Cairn-cross calls the 'sink' theory of capital flows. It is assumed that there are fixed capital/output ratios in each country, and that at some stage rich capi-talist countries save more than they can invest at home. They then 'need a convenient "sink" for [these surplus savings] such as foreign investment could provide' (Cairncross, 1961, p. 51). There is a large neo-Marxist liter-ature on the resulting economic imperialism towards which developed countries are impelled. It has a modern garb in 'dependency theory' of which Ian Little provided a masterly critique in his book on *Economic Development*. We cannot appraise these neo-Marxist theories in this chap-ter, (but see Lal, 1983). However, it is important to note that the dominant 'structuralist' theory which even today views developing countries as being endemically short of capital, harks back to this neo-Marxist origin. Keynes, too, flirted with this view because of his fears about secular stagnation in developed countries resulting from over savings (see Cairncross, 1961). Such views seem particularly strange today, when the largest capitalist economy, the USA, is currently suffering from an acute shortage of savings (see Lal and Wolf, 1986).

In developing countries this neo-Marxist and neo-Keynesian 'structural-ist' view is used 'to demonstrate that, underdeveloped countries have a

---

[1] The latter approach looks at the world as being relatively inflexible in production and consumption. I like to call it, 'kinky', as it is based on assuming kinky production and con-sumption sets, such that there is little substitutability in production or consumption. See Little (1982) and Lal (1983, 1985) for critiques.

chronic shortage of capital and would develop more rapidly if they could borrow more abroad or find an assortment of fairy godmothers, preferably of international extraction, to bless them with grants and low interest loans' (Cairncross, ibid.).

The most famous of the structuralist explanations for a chronic need in developing countries for capital inflows is the so-called 'two gap' or 'foreign exchange bottleneck view' propounded by Chenery-Strout (1966) and McKinnon (1964).[2] This was enshrined in various formulae for determining 'aid requirements' by international and bilateral aid agencies. Its logic and limitations can be readily explained (see Lal, 1972).

In these two-gap theories, Nurkse's (1961) pessimism about the post-war export prospects of developing countries was carried to its logical extreme by assuming that the export proceeds of developing countries could not be increased. Furthermore it was assumed that domestic production required imported inputs, in the form of capital and intermediate goods, in set proportions. Production could not, therefore, be increased above a level determined by the quantity of imports which the fixed export earnings could finance. Even if a country was willing to save and invest a larger proportion of its income to finance growth, it would not be able to transform the savings into higher income and output because of the inexorable limit set by the 'fixed' export earnings. The incremental savings could not be transformed into the foreign exchange to finance the import requirements of additional investment.[3] The country was now stuck in a foreign exchange bottle-neck independent of any savings constraint.

This chronic balance-of-payments constraint on a country's development could not be cured by the orthodox means of raising the price of foreign exchange (through a devaluation) to induce an increase in the supply of and a reduction in the demand for this 'good' which was inhibiting growth. For both these effects had been ruled out by assumption. Either the volume of exports was limited by world demand; or an increased volume of exports could be sold only at declining prices on world markets without any rise in foreign exchange earnings. Thus, raising the price of foreign exchange would not increase its supply, whilst the technologically fixed import requirements of domestic output meant that, for any quantity of output, raising the price of foreign exchange would have no effect on demand for it.

---

[2] Ian Little, indeed, can be looked upon as an early proponent of this view, see Little (1960). But he has since eschewed it. See Little (1982).

[3] There are four assumptions which must hold simultaneously for a country to be in a foreign exchange bottle-neck: (i) the import content of current production must be unalterable; (ii) there must be no further possibilities of import substitution; (iii) export earnings must be completely inelastic, and (iv) the marginal social utility of current consumption must be zero. If *any* of these assumptions is relaxed the country cannot be in a foreign exchange bottle-neck. See Lal (1972).

The only available options were for government to husband its foreign exchange fund for use in 'essential' industries and to seek to augment it through concessional foreign loans and grants.

The assumptions required to generate a foreign exchange gap independently of a savings gap are highly unrealistic. First, even if export earnings from traditional primary commodities are inelastic it is possible to diversify exports into lines where foreign demand is more elastic, as many countries have done (see Riedel, 1984). Second, it is only in the very short run that the import intensity of domestic production will be fixed. Over the medium term import substitutes can be readily developed. Third, it is difficult to believe that the social utility of current consumption in countries which are poor could ever fall to zero—another necessary assumption for the foreign exchange bottle-neck to exist. Thus, the 'foreign exchange' gap aspect of the 'two gap' theories is extremely implausible. In fact, as the development of the Gang of Four—whose significance was first noted in Little *et al.* (1970)—and many other countries has shown, those which have maintained relatively open trade regimes and developed broadly in line with their comparative advantage have faced no chronic foreign exchange shortage. Instead, it is those 'inward-looking' countries of which India remains a prime example whose protectionist trade and exchange rate policies have created an artificial scarcity of foreign exchange. For these countries the theory of the foreign exchange bottle-neck became a self-fulfilling prophecy by *leading* to the very retardation of export earnings and irreducibility of minimum import requirements which were its premises (see Lal, 1983, 1985).

In historical perspective, even the 'savings gap' version of the 'two gap' view as an explanation of the determinants of capital flows is puzzling. First, as Lewis (1978) has emphasized, in the nineteenth century when some of the current developed countries were developing, the flow of international capital was not always from rich to poor countries. Thus nineteenth-century per capita income was higher in the major borrowing countries (the United States, Australia, and Argentina) than in the lending countries (the UK, France, and Germany). Second, it is likely that saving rates were higher in the borrowing countries of new settlements than in Europe in the nineteenth century. It is not evident that capital has necessarily flowed from high-to low-savings countries (see Kuznets, 1966, Table 5.3). Third, the savings performance of developing countries in the post Second World War period (see Lluch, 1986) shows that nearly all the developing countries (including those in Africa until the early 1970s) have steadily raised domestic savings rates since the 1950s. Whilst an economic explanation of this unexpected and remarkable savings behaviour is still awaited, it would seem to undermine the view that foreign capital is necessarily required to supplement fixed and inadequate domestic savings. Finally, differences in economic performance (in terms of growth rates) seem to be related more to the differences in the productivity of investment than its level.

1.2. Neo-Classical Theories

We therefore turn to the neo-classical, general equilibrium explanations for the determinants of international capital flows. The basic framework used has been an extension of the autarkic Solow–Swan neo-classical growth model (with one or two sectors) to two large countries (or regions) with perfect capital mobility between them, or to one small country which shifts from portfolio autarky and is faced by an exogenously determined world interest rate. To set ideas, it is useful to consider the simple static version of these two-country models due to MacDougall (1960), Kemp (1966), and Jones (1967). Differences in the autarkic interest rates (which are assumed equal to the respective marginal products of capital) in the two countries lead to capital flows between them until a common interest rate (and hence marginal productivity of capital) is established. There are the normal 'gains from trade' depicted in Fig. 11.2 (whose note provides an explanation), and this establishes the superiority of foreign trade in capital services to portfolio autarky within the standard neo-classical framework. Also, in parallel with the results from trade theory, if a country can influence the terms on which it can borrow or lend, then there is an 'optimum tariff'-type case for an optimum tax on the relevant capital flows (see Jones, 1967). This is the basis of Harberger's (1986) argument that as most developing countries face an upward-sloping supply of syndicated bank credit, they should levy an optimal tax on such borrowing to equate its tax-inclusive average cost to the higher marginal cost.

1.3. Steady-State Growth Theories

A dynamic version of the Kemp–MacDougall model can also be readily provided (Ruffin, 1979). There are a number of other dynamic models which have been propounded, but most of these are, in Ian Little's words, 'useless theoretical toys'. We provide an outline of the simplest of these steady-state models, which establishes whatever insights there are to be gleaned from this literature.[4]

Consider two standard Solovian economies with *differing* technologies but *identical* growth rates of the effective labour force, producing a single traded commodity which can be consumed or invested either at home or abroad. The accumulated investments of the commodity represent the capital stocks (K and K^*) *owned* by the two countries (but not necessarily located in them). The savings rates are constant and a fixed proportion s and s^* of the per capita income y and y^* in the home and foreign countries

---

[4] See the surveys in Jones and Kennen (1984) by Ruffin (1986), Findlay (1984).

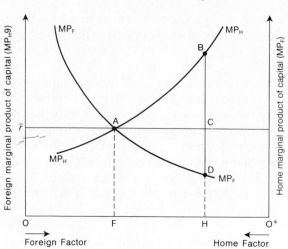

Fig. 11.2

Note: MP$_H$ is the home country and MP$_F$ the foreign country's marginal product of capital curve. Before capital mobility the foreign country's capital stock is OH, the home country's O*H. With capital mobility a common interest rate of r is established and HF of the foreign country's capital stock is placed in the home country. The foreign country gains ACD and the home country ACB. For the foreign country loses output ADHF (the area under the MP$_F$ curve) and it gains capital income of ACHF (the capital flow HF times the interest rate r) whilst the home country gains output ABHF (area under MP$_H$ curve) but has to pay area ACHF for the capital inflow.

respectively. Labour in efficiency units, L and L^*, in the home and foreign country is assumed to be growing at the same rate n. Assume that the home country locates D units of its capital abroad. The per capita capital stocks producing output in the two countries are then:

$$k_h = k - d \quad \text{(where } k = K/L \text{ and } d = D/L)$$
$$k_f = k^* + bd \quad \text{(where } b = L/L^*).$$

(11.1)

Output in both countries is a function of the capital stocks *located* in the two countries ($f(k_h)$; $g(k_f)$). With perfect capital mobility, as in the Kemp–MacDougall theory, the rate of interest (r) is equated to the marginal products of the capital stocks *located* in the two countries that is

$$r = f^1(k_h) = g^1(k_f).$$

(11.2)

Per capita incomes in the home (y_h) and the foreign (y_f) country are then the domestic output plus (minus) the interest payments on the capital stock located abroad (at home). That is

$$y_h = f(k_h) + rd$$
$$y_f = g(k_f) - rbd. \tag{11.3}$$

Per capita savings is sy_h and s^*y_f in the two countries, whilst the investment required to maintain the current capital/labour ratios are nk and nk^* in the home and foreign countries respectively. Therefore, the capital accumulation or decumulation per worker owned by each of the two countries is given by

$$\dot{k} = sy_h - nk$$
$$\dot{k}^* = s^*y_f - nk^* \tag{11.4}$$
$$(\text{note } \dot{k} = dk/dt).$$

In Fig. 11.3 (the standard Solow diagram), OZ and OZ* are the production functions for the two countries, and the nk line shows the capital requirements to maintain capital per man intact for each capital/labour ratio, given the *common* rate of growth of the effective labour force of n. Initially assume that, under autarky, the two economies are in steady-state equilibrium with capital/labour ratios (both owned and those nationally located) of k_1^*, in the foreign and k_1 in the home country. Output and income per head is $Z_1^* = y_{f1}$ and $Z_1 = y_{h1}$ respectively, and savings per head are s_1^* and s_1 which are just sufficient to maintain the respective autarkic capital/output and capital/labour ratios constant with effective labour growing at the rate n. The marginal product of capital at Z_1^* is greater than that at Z_1.

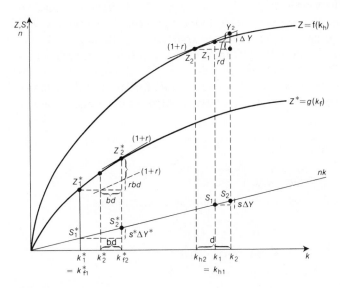

Fig. 11.3

Once free trade in capital is allowed the two economies will converge to the new output equilibrium given by Z_2^* and Z_2; with *owned* capital/labour ratios of k_2^* and k_2, and domestically located capital/labour ratios of k_{f2}^* and k_{h2} for the foreign and home country respectively. This new steady state will have come about as a result of steady-state capital flows per head of d (the difference between k_{h2} and k_2) for the home country, which are equivalent to inflows of bd (the difference between k_2^* and k_{f2}^*—also note that as drawn we are assuming that $b = L/L^* < 1$, namely that the capital-importing country is more populous than the exporting one).[5] The marginal product of capital on the *nationally located* capital stocks is the same and equal to the common world interest rate r. Per capita income is given by $Z_2 + rd = Y_{h2}$ for the home country, and by $Z_2^* - rbd$ for the foreign country. In the new open-economy steady state the extra savings generated by the increases in per capita income Δy^* and Δy, namely $s^*\Delta y^*$ and $s\Delta y$ are just sufficient to maintain the new steady-state capital/labour ratios constant in the two economies.

Clearly, as a result of capital mobility, income per head, as well as *owned* capital per head will be higher in both economies. However, as in the capital-exporting economy, the marginal product of nationally located capital rises (from the slope at Z_1 to Z_2), the wage rate will fall. The converse change in factor prices will occur in the capital-importing country.

1.4.   Stages in the Balance of Payments

This is as much as can be learnt from this steady-state analysis. As with much of growth theory its relevance to the real world is likely to be tenuous. For instance, these models seem to suggest that there would be a tendency for some countries to be perpetual capital exporters and others to be capital importers. However, from the historical evidence this has not been true—most dramatically in the case of the US, which was a large borrower for much of the nineteenth century, became a lender for much of this century, and has recently become the world's largest borrower of foreign capital.

---

[5] Stated in terms of the capital stocks *located* in the two countries the flows of investment between the two countries are:

$$\text{for the home country } I_h = [sy_h - nk_h]L$$
$$\text{for the foreign country } I_f = [s^*y_f - nk_f]L^*.$$

Using (11.1) we have the investment flows in terms of *owned* capital stocks.

$$I_h = [sy_h - n(k - d)]L$$
$$I_f = [s^*y_f - n(k^* + bd)]L^*.$$

In the steady state as $\dot{k} = \dot{k}^* = 0$, we have from (11.4) that

$$sy_h = nk \text{ and } s^*y_f = nk^*,$$

$$\text{so } I_f = I_h = dL = bdL^*.$$

These fluctuations in the status of particular countries as importers or exporters of capital have to be matched by equivalent fluctuations in their balance of payments on current account to effect the necessary transfers on the capital account. Cairnes (1874) was the first to suggest a theory of stages in the balance of payments corresponding to various stages in the development of an economy. This idea has been developed by Kindleberger (1968) and a number of models have been devised to explain this supposedly historical phenomenon (see Fischer and Frenkel, 1972). This 'stages' approach also underlies the various arithmetic models of debt cycles (see Domar 1950, and Avramovic *et al.* 1964) which have been popular in the literature on developing countries, and have recently been revived to outline adjustment paths for the major debtor countries (see Selowsky and van der Tak, 1986).

In a sense the 'stages' approach to the determinants of capital flows and the evolution of debt and the balance of payments follows from a purely mechanical arithmetic model, which is in effect the basis of most current 'debt cycle' models. Recent theoretical models (see Fischer and Frenkel, 1972) by contrast have attempted to provide some general equilibrium analyses which would generate the 'debt cycles' as part of the endogenous evolution of a growing economy as it approaches the steady state. It is argued that a developing country will pass through various stages, from being a debtor to a mature creditor. During this transition, initially the debtor will run deficits on both its trade and current accounts. Then as it becomes an adult debtor it will have a surplus on trade but a deficit on current account because of debt-service obligations. In the following stage as the country repays its debt it will still be a net debtor but will run a current account surplus till it becomes a net creditor when both its trade and current accounts are in surplus, and then the final stage is reached when the country is a mature creditor with a trade deficit, but current account surplus based on its interest earnings from its foreign assets.[6] Ruffin (1979) and Engel and Kletzer (1987) show how the interaction of savings and investment decisions in each country can lead to the balance-of-payments stages in the approach to the steady state. In terms of the model depicted by Fig. 11.3, this would involve a cyclical adjustment of the *owned* capital stocks (k, k^*) in the approach to the steady state (see Ruffin, 1979). We cannot go into the details but the economics of these models are rather contrived. Moreover, it does seem that these models are probably

---

[6] Bazdarich (1978) in an optimal savings model shows that these stages cannot exist! This is because he assumes a constant rate of time-preference. Engel and Kletzer (1987) show how the 'stages' in the balance of payments can be generated if the dubious Uzawa (1968) assumption that the rate of time-preference increases with the level of steady-state consumption is incorporated into a two-sector model consisting of traded and non-traded goods.

trying to explain a non-existent historical phenomenon. Even in his 1968 resurrection of the 'stages' notion Kindleberger noted that the historical experience of the UK and US does not fit the model too well—a conclusion which is strengthened with the 'mature' US currently a big borrower running a massive current account deficit.

1.5. Urbanization and the Need for Foreign Capital

More interesting for our purposes are two empirical features of the historical record of foreign borrowing emphasized by Lewis. The first as we have noted is that, unlike most of the models discussed above, capital flows have not necessarily been from 'rich' high-saving and, therefore, presumably low time-preference to 'poor' low-saving and hence high time-preference countries. In fact, as Lewis puts it: 'If Britain and France were saving enough to be lending in the middle of the 19th century, when they were not much richer than Ceylon or Brazil is today, why cannot the developing countries now save for themselves all the capital they need?' (Lewis, 1978, p. 39). His answer to this rhetorical question is that it is differences in rates of urbanization which explain which countries in the past were lenders or borrowers—the second feature of past foreign capital flows. In the ninetheeth century, European countries whose urban populations were growing by less that 3 per cent p.a. loaned to the countries—mainly of 'new settlement'—where urban populations were growing well above that rate. Urbanization Lewis claims is intensive in the provision of infrastructure which uses both more physical and human capital per unit of output than equivalent rural infrastructure. Thus, in Lewis's view, the urbanization induced by population growth in the Third World since the Second World War is the prime determinant of their excess demand for capital and hence for foreign borrowing.

Prima facie, this view has some plausibility. Consider a standard neoclassical two-good two-factor model of an open economy, where the two goods are a composite tradable good (assuming a small country which faces given world prices for its exports and imports) and a non-traded good, produced by capital and labour. Assume that there is perfect capital mobility so that the domestic rental on capital is equated to the world interest rate. With the world price of tradables and the interest rate given by world markets, the price of non-traded goods and the real wage will also be fully determined.

Assume that, initially, at this relative price of the two commodities the economy is in internal and external balance with no net capital inflows and outflows, and hence the desired and actual domestic capital stocks are the same. Now assume with Lewis that there is an increase in urbanization and hence in the demand for the non-traded good, *which is more capital-intensive* than the tradable good. The emerging excess demand for the non-traded good cannot, *ex hypothesi*, be met through foreign trade. It requires an expansion of non-traded good output. If, however, non-traded good output were to expand, induced by an increase in the short run in the relative price of the non-traded good, the real wage would have to fall and the rental on capital to rise. For the labour-intensive tradable good sector will be releasing less capital relative to labour than is required by the expanding non-traded good sector. The rise in the domestic rental rate on capital would induce an inflow of capital to restore the original wage/rental ratio and permit the old relative price equilibrium to be restored, but (following Rybczynski, 1955) with an absolute increase in the output of non-traded and fall in the output of traded goods. Fig. 11.4 illustrates the argument. It shows how in a general equilibrium framework there can be an excess demand for capital generated by a pattern of domestic demand which is biased towards non-traded capital-intensive goods.

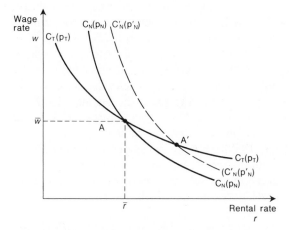

Fig. 11.4

Note: C_T and C_N are the iso cost curves for the two composite commodities, 'tradables' and the 'non-tradables' repectively. It is assumed that, the non-traded good is more capital-intensive than the traded good, and hence C_N has a steeper slope at every wage–rental combination than C_T. The price of the traded good P_T and the rental rate $\bar{r}$ are given by the world market. This then determines P_N and $\overline{W}$. Initially, equilibrium is at A. With a rise in the demand for non-traded goods, the D_N curve shifts outwards. The short-run equilibrium is at A' with a lower wage and higher rental rate. The latter induces a capital inflow which expands non-traded good output, reducing its price, and thus restoring the initial equilibrium (in factor prices space) at A, but with (following Rybczynski) a reduction in the output of the traded and expansion in that of the non-traded good.

1.6. Foreign Finance of Public Sector Deficits

Moreover, if as is common in most developing countries, a significant portion of non-traded goods in the form of infrastructure services are publicly provided there will be an excess demand for capital in the *public sector*. As I have argued elsewhere (Lal and van Wijnbergen, 1985) endemic public sector deficits may then emerge which cannot be financed through domestic taxation or borrowing. Governments may then seek to close the deficits either through levying the inflation tax (as has been common in many developing countries) or through foreign borrowing. We would therefore expect that there would be a positive association between urbanization and public expenditure and between government deficits and the growth of the debt/GDP ratio across developing countries. The evidence on the former is discussed in Lluch (1986), which broadly confirms that the level of urbanization and the share of government expenditure are correlated in a sample of 50 countries (Mitra, 1978). The evidence on deficits and debt was recently examined in the World Bank's *World Development Report 1985* and is reproduced in Fig. 11.5. This confirms a statistically significant positive association between the growth of debt and of government budget deficits in many developing countries between 1972 and 1982.[7]

Just as there are demographically determined pressures for capital-intensive urbanization which create an excess demand for capital in the provision of publicly provided infrastructure in developing countries, in recent years demographic pressures arising from the ageing of OECD populations, related to old-age-related public expenditures on health and pensions, have also put pressure on public finance in developed countries. In Lal and van Wijnbergen (1985) we have developed and calibrated a global model in which the interaction of the public sectors in developed and developing countries is the major determinant of world interest rates (as well as the terms of trade between the North and the South) in an integrated world economy.[8]

Consider a world consisting of three regions, the OECD, OPEC, and LDC's. Each is completely specialized in producing its 'own' good. OPEC produces oil, which is used as an intermediate input in the production of

---

[7] The mechanism envisaged in the *World Development Report* is that the growth in government expenditure leads to *growing* fiscal deficits which lead to balance-of-payments crises which in turn lead to the *growth* of debt.

[8] The discussion of global interactions in Part I of the *World Development Report 1984* was based on this model, whilst an updated econometrically estimated version by van Wijnbergen (1985) formed the basis for the global projections in the *World Development Report 1985*. The econometrics, not surprisingly, can be questioned as is usual of this genre. See the discussion of van Wijnbergen (1985) in particular by Wickens (1985). But I would still stand by the argument justifying the structure and the qualitative conclusion concerning the global outcomes resulting from the interactions of public sectors analysed by the model, as discussed at length in Lal and van Wijnbergen (1985, 1986).

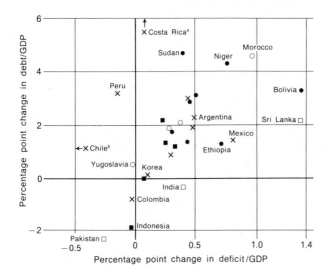

x Latin America and Caribbean

□ South Asia

○ Europe and North Africa

● Sub-Saharan Africa

■ East Asia and Pacific

Fig. 11.5 Growth of debt and government budget deficits in selected developing countries, 1972–1982

[a] Percentage point change in debt/GDP for Costa Rica equals 7.0.
[b] Percentage point change in deficit/GDP for Chile equals −1.3.
Note: Percentage point changes in debt/GDP and deficit/GDP are annual averages based on trend line calculations. Deficit data are not available for all countries for each year in the period shown. The positive relationship between growth of deficits and debt is significant at the 99 % confidence level, with $R^2 = 0.51$ for a sample of 25 countries.

Source: IMF *Government Finance Statistics* 1984; World Bank data.

From *World Development Report 1985*, OUP, 1985, p. 62.

the single, final consumer-good produced by each of the other regions. It is assumed that savings rates are highest in the OPEC region, followed by those in the OECD region, with LDC's being the lowest net savers. There is free trade in commodities and capital. There are two endogenous variables which are determined as part of the world equilibrium—the world rate of interest (r), and the terms of trade of the LDC's *vis-à-vis* the OECD (t). Two basic equations can be derived for the world equilibrium, one of which requires the *world* current account W to be equal to zero. The other requires excess demand for OECD (D) goods to be zero.

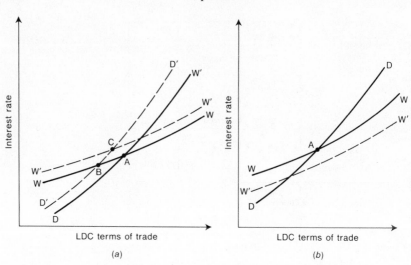

Fig. 11.6

$$W(r, t) = 0,$$
$$(+)(-)$$

$$D(r, t) = 0.$$
$$(-)(+)$$

(The signs below the variables indicate the expected signs of the partial derivatives.)

As regards the current account equation, higher world interest rates (r) lead to an incipient current account surplus, whilst an improvement in the LDC's terms of trade leads to a deficit as they imply a transfer of income from high to low savers. The WW curve in Fig. 11.6 therefore slopes upwards, as the incipient deficit due to a rise in interest rates requires an improvment in LDC terms of trade to eliminate the deficit.

The second equation sets the excess demand for the OECD good to be zero. Higher world interest rates reduce expenditure and hence lead to excess supply for OECD goods, whilst higher relative prices of LDC goods switch expenditure towards OECD goods and cure the excess supply. The DD curve in Fig. 11.6 will therefore also be upward sloping, but for the equilibrium to be stable (as it is assumed to be) the curve must be steeper than the WW curve, so that an incipient world current account surplus pushes down interest rates and an excess demand for the OECD goods pushes up their relative price.

Now consider an increase in the budget deficit in the OECD region resulting from either increased public expenditure unmatched by tax increases, or unchanged public expenditure but with a tax cut. The increased public consumption leads to excess demand for OECD goods shifting DD to the left. If the increased public dissaving is matched by an equivalent increase in private savings, as predicted by the so-called Ricardian equivalence theorem (see Barro, 1974), then private savings will offset the increased budget deficit and the world current account schedule WW will not shift. The equilibrium will be at B with lower world interest rates and a deterioration in the LDC terms of trade. If, however, increased private savings do not accommodate the budget deficit, so that there is 'crowding out' of private investment, then there will be an incipient world current account deficit, which shifts the WW curve upwards. If the incipient deficit *is large enough* it could shift the WW curve to lead to an equilibrium at C where world interest rates *rise* and the developing countries' terms of trade deteriorate. This appears very much like the outcomes in the world economy in the early 1980s.

A second shock to the world economy—a rise in oil prices—which was of importance in the 1970s can also be examined with the model. Higher oil prices transferred income from low- to high-savings countries leading to an incipient world current account surplus so the WW curve shifts down in Fig. 11.6(*b*). Depending upon whether as a result of the rise in the price of oil (a 'co-operative' factor of production in OECD output) OECD supply falls more than demand, there could be excess demand or supply for OECD goods. Hence the DD curve could shift to either the left or the right. In either case, however, world interest rates *fall* (unless there is a large shift to the right in the DD curve), but the LDC terms of trade could go either way. This scenario seems to be close to the outcomes in the world economy after the oil shock of 1973–4.

2. Determinants and Effects of Alternative Forms of Foreign Capital Flows

Whilst the above models provide some rationale for the flow of capital to developing countries, and effects in raising their per capita output and consumption, much of the policy debate has concerned the quality of the particular *forms* of capital flows and their presumed side-effects that are not captured by these highly aggregative models.

As Table 11.1 shows, the three major forms of capital flows to LDCs are official foreign aid, direct foreign investment, and—more recently—syndicated bank loans. In this section we briefly outline the reasons adduced for the determinants of these particular forms of capital flows and their presumed costs and benefits.

2.1. Official flows

Foreign aid has aroused the fiercest passions. This form of capital flow both in its magnitude and global coverage is novel. Though there are numerous historical examples of countries paying 'bribes' or 'reparations' to others, the continuing large-scale transfer of capital from official sources to developing countries is a post-Second World War phenomenon. Humanitarian, political, and purely economic justifications have been provided for the transfer of capital on concessionary terms through bilateral or multilateral agencies. The efficiency of concessional flows in subserving these multiple ends has been questioned (see, in particular, Bauer, 1972).

The most balanced discussion still remains that in Little and Clifford (1965). They recognized (p. 93) early on that the humanitarian motives for giving aid justified transferring Western taxpayers' money to poor *people* not poor *countries* and that giving money to the latter may have no effect on the former. Nor can the poor of the world claim a moral *right* for welfare transfers from the rich, on the line of argument used to justify *domestic* welfare payments. For the latter depends upon the existence of *national* societies with some commonly accepted moral standard. No similar *international society* exists within which a *right* to aid can be established (see Lal, 1978, 1983).

On the political reasons for giving aid, little can be said except to recognize the partial truth of Bauer's contention that, by and large Western Political interests have not been well served by foreign aid, which has instead fostered the formation of anti-Western coalitions of Third World states seeking 'bribes' not to go communist. As a recent study by Mosley (1987) concluded 'as an instrument of *political leverage*, economic aid has been unsuccessful' (p. 232). So it is by its broad economic effects that foreign aid needs to be judged.

The early justifications for aid were based on the two-gap type theory we discussed in the previous section. As these models are no longer credible this form of justification of aid has worn thin.

Recent attempts have therefore been made to assess the general impact of foreign aid on the growth prospects of recipient countries including the redressal of poverty (see Cassen, 1986; Mosley, 1987; Krueger *et al.*, 1988). The results of the statistical study by Mosley concluded unsurprisingly that 'at the world level' the efficiency of aid in *promoting growth* in the recipient country 'appears to be neutral: neither significant and automatically positive, as many defenders of aid assume, nor negative, as argued both by Bauer and by many writers on the extreme left' (Mosley, 1987, p. 233).[9]

[9] By 'neutral' Mosley seems to mean the effects differ with the circumstances, and no broad generalization of positive, negative, or zero effects of aid can be deduced.

The growth impact seems to depend on 'public sector behaviour [which] is not subject to general laws of behaviour which predetermine the effectiveness of aid; rather it varies from country to country and from period to period' (p. 23–4). On the poverty redressal effects of aid Mosley concludes from his empirical analysis that 'it appears to redistribute from the reasonably well-off in the West to most income groups in the Third World *except* the very poorest' (p. 233). Another finding of some importance is that 'over the last fifteen years aid has had a significant effect on development in Asia and very little in Africa' (p. 234).

The last point is important in forming judgements on the future role that aid can and should play in economic development. Apart from the dubious structuralist reasons given for aid programmes in the 1950s and 1960s, a straightforward welfare case for capital mobility exists in the context of differential rates of return in the neo-classical models discussed in the previous section. However, immediately after the Second World War, Western private capital markets—of which the US was the most important—were in effect shut to LDC borrowers. This was the consequence of the widespread defaults in the 1930s on Third World bonds (the major form of international capital flows before the Second World War), and the imposition of the so-called 'blue sky law' by the US which forbade US financial intermediaries from holding foreign government bonds. Meanwhile European markets were closed through exchange controls. In this environment official flows to LDCs at *commercial interest rates* (for instance through the non-IDA lending of the World Bank) would have been justifiable, purely on grounds of global efficiency.

This argument for official financial intermediation may seem to have become weaker with the explosion in bank lending in the 1970s. However, with the onset of the debt crisis and the cessation of voluntary commercial lending to at least the high-debt countries,it is argued that in effect the 'debt overhang' will prevent the commercial capital market functioning efficiently. The 'debt overhang' implies that current debts are so high relative to current income that future income increases will have to be used to finance current obligations. Hence as Krueger (1986 p. 65) has argued:

because foreigners correctly perceive this claim on future income, they will not lend even for new projects that would yield acceptable returns. This inability to insulate new claims from existing debt leaves countries in a vicious circle: they cannot restore creditworthiness without growth, and they cannot grow till creditworthiness is restored. The private capital market may thus fail despite the rational behaviour of all participants, and there is a strong analytical case for official assistance on commercial terms.

This argument would seem to provide a justification for the continuing financial intermediation of multilateral agencies like the World Bank.

The case for continuing official *concessional* assistance is less secure. If, as the evidence suggests, its growth and poverty-redressing impact is at best neutral, and given the declining political support for such programmes in developed countries, particularly as they are seen not to serve selfish political or economic interests, we can expect the share of concessional aid flows in the capital flows to LDCs to decline.

It is arguable that, at least in the early stages of development, much of the infrastructural investment which is required for growth has to be publicly provided—partly because of significant externalities (education, health) and partly because of the difficulty of levying user charges (because of low and slowly growing utilization of lumpy investment projects). If the domestic tax and financial systems are also underdeveloped, governments may not be able to finance public infrastructure through taxation. Borrowing on commercial terms is infeasible because, for the same reasons which preclude domestic financing, the government would not be able to meet the debt-service charges on the foreign loans. Concessional offical assistance is then advocated. Against this, we have to set Bauer's (1972) argument that 'the view that a substantial infrastructure is a precondition of development is unhistorical, as it ignores the fact that the infrastructure develops in the course of economic progress, not ahead of it' (Bauer, 1972, p. 111). Moreover, he emphasizes that the difficulty in financing infrastructure has been due in part to the poor treatment many developing countries have offered to foreign capital, and for their 'tendency to divert resources into subsidised manufacture, which reduces the funds available for the construction and maintenance of the social overhead capital' (Bauer, 1972, p. 111).

There are various other issues concerning the impact of aid on domestic savings, whether it should be given to programmes or projects, and what, if any, form of 'conditionality' should be attached to it. These have been discussed *ad nauseam* in the aid literature. I have reviewed some of these debates elsewhere (see Lal, 1978, 1983). They are not particularly relevant for the argument which I am trying to develop in this subsection, namely that whilst there is likely to be a continuing role for official (chiefly multilateral) capital flows at *commercial* interest rates (at least till the 'debt crisis' unwinds), the economic and political case for official *concessional* capital flows has become weaker.

2.2. Direct Investment

Private capital flows comprise (*a*) portfolio lending in the form of bonds (the predominant nineteenth-century and early twentieth-century form) and syndicted bank lending (the major form of lending in the 1970s), and (*b*) direct foreign investment.

Direct foreign investment (DFI) arouses even stronger passions than foreign aid. The malign as well as the benign effects attributed to DFI are completely disproportionate both to its past and likely future role in Third World development. Historically, DFI has been important in the development of natural (mainly mineral) resources and public utilities in the Third World. These traditional avenues for foreign investment have been steadily blocked by the rise of economic nationalism and the desire of host countries to acquire all the rents from the exploitation of their natural resources. The current conventional wisdom is that utilities should be in the government sector. DFI is today increasingly found in manufacturing industry where its virtues and vices are seen to stem from the associated attributes it brings of managerial expertise, new technology, and modern marketing methods, including advertising and foreign marketing connections.

Whereas the determinants of portfolio lending need to be sought in the interest rate differentials emphasized by the aggregative open-economy models discussed in Section 1, those for DFI are to be found in the strategic game-theoretic factors underlying the decisions of firms to invest in oligopolistic industries in different national markets (see Hymer, 1977; Kindleberger, 1969; Caves, 1971, 1982; Vernon, 1977).[10]

Vernon (1977) has shown that imperfections in the 'markets' for knowledge (due to increasing returns and/or externalities in its production and dissemination) and in those for organization (due to imperfections in information) are probably the most important reasons for DFI flows between developed countries. In developing countries, on the other hand, it is the imperfections in product markets created by their tariff structures which are the primary reason for the type of defensive DFI which predominates in their manufacturing sectors (see Reuber, 1973; Lal, 1975; Lall and Streeten, 1977).[11] The major determinants of DFI flows into natural resource based industries, as well as in the development of the international 'putting out' system in some industries, such as electronics, are the increasing returns to scale that can be attained by global vertical integration in some oligopolistic industries based in developed countries. In the latter industries, traditonal relative factor price differentials within

---

[10] As Caves (1971, p. 1) notes: 'In the parlance of industrial organisation, oligopoly with product differentiation normally prevails where corporations make "horizontal" investments to produce abroad the same lines of goods as they produce in the home market. Oligopoly, not necessarily differentiated, in the home market is typical in industries which undertake "vertical" direct investments to produce abroad a raw material or other input to their production process at home. Direct investment tends to invoke market conduct that extends the recognition of mutual market dependence—the essence of oligopoly—beyond national boundaries'.

[11] The recent examples of Japanese 'quid pro quo' investment in the US studied by Bhagwati (1986) and Dinopolous (1987) would also be examples of defensive investment to forestall the introduction of tariff barriers on Japanese goods.

the Hufbauer–Posner–Vernon 'product cycle' model of international trade are the major determinants of the DFI flows.

More recently there has been DFI by developing countries mainly in other developing ones (see Wells, 1983). Much of this investment, like a considerable part of so-called South–South trade, is from countries which have created heavily subsidized heavy industries (such as India), in which there is chronic excess capacity. The direct foreign investment is then based on acquiring equity on the basis of exporting the excess capacity of these heavy industries (Lal, 1978*d*). It is the counterpart of what can be termed bureaucratically created, artificial 'vent for surplus' trade (see Havrylshyn, 1987).

The passions surrounding DFI and other forms of capital flows concerns their welfare effects on the host country. In the 1960s, statistical demonstrations were provided of the inimical effects of capital inflows (both official aid and DFI) on domestic savings and thence on the growth rate of developing countries (e.g. Griffin and Enos, 1970; Weisskopf, 1972). These exercises were soon shown to be spurious since the definition of 'domestic savings' they used tautologically required 'domestic savings' to fall whenever there was a capital inflow (Papanek, 1972; Miksell and Zinser, 1973; Lal, 1978). But since it is the rate of investment that influences the growth rate, and no evidence was provided that foreign capital inflows reduce domestic investment, no harmful effects can be deduced from this fall in 'domestic savings'.

The next attack was based on estimates of the so-called 'balance-of-payments' effects of DFI flows. These also were shown to be illogical on the ground that the balance-of-payments effects of DFI which, *ex hypothesi*, raises national income and hence is socially desirable, can be whatever a government chooses (Little, 1972; Lal, 1975, 1978*d*). For, in a fundamental sense, the balance of payments reflects the difference between domestic output and domestic expenditure. Even if domestic output rises as a result of DFI—which is a good thing—a government can, through fiscal and monetary means, raise domestic expenditure by even more and thus engineer a balance-of-payments deficit—a bad thing! But the 'problem', if there is one, is with the government's fiscal and monetary policies, and not with DFI.

The cost-benefit framework, ideally of the Little–Mirrlees variety, does however provide an adequate measure and evaluation criteria to determine when foreign borrowing is desirable. Such criteria which take account of current and future constraints on saving, taxation, and terms-of-trade effects induced by making the requisite transfers have been derived (see Lal, 1971, 1975). Empirical studies of the effects of DFI on host country welfare based on these social cost-benefit welfare criteria can be found in Lal (1975) and Lall and Streeten (1977). These show that the welfare effects of DFI are by and large negatively correlated with the degree of effective protection provided to the industry in which the DFI takes place.[12]

If the deleterious effects of DFI are exaggerated by its opponents, so are its beneficial effects by its proponents, As noted above, compared with other forms of foreign capital inflows, DFI brings 'extras' in the shape of technology and managerial expertise. Since, however, most developing countries in the early stages of manufacturing are likely to have a comparative advantage in either light consumer goods or the simpler capital goods (like lathes, hammers, and other products of light engineering), their need to scale any great technological and managerial heights requiring DFI is doubtful. The technology of textile mills, and even steel mills, is fairly well known and can be readily purchased without having to rely on DFI. Korea, for instance, though it made use of foreign technology, which it bought, and foreign capital, which it borrowed, has made little use of DFI in its spectacular development. Thus, whilst there may be a valid case for more reliance on private enterprise in developing countries, it is by no means co-terminous with that for DFI.

2.3. Portfolio and Bank Lending

Commercial bank loans are the third major form of foreign capital inflows into developing countries. From modest beginnings in the mid to late 1960s, they became the principal source of external capital for LDCs in the 1970s.

The major nineteenth-century and early twentieth-century source of foreign capital for development—portfolio lending from the richer to poorer countries—was blocked to developing countries until fairly recently because of their widespread defaults in the 1930s. Bilateral and multilateral aid flows in the 1950s and 1960s can thus be justified as providing alternatives to the traditional channels of capital to developing countries. However, these forms of capital transfer (aid and DFI) share the disadvantage, in contrast with portfolio lending, of requiring a fairly intimate relationship between the borrower and lender with all the accompanying misunderstandings and politicization of economies. The old form of portfolio lending was anonymous and apolitical; lenders were only concerned that their interest payments were made on time.

The same American banking regulations which had led to the demise of the old portfolio lending were responsible for the development of the offshore banking facilities known as the Euro-currency markets. These were based on deposits in banks outside the USA, initially in dollars but later in other currencies also. In the early years, the main depositors were East

---

[12] Various deleterious 'social' effects due to the inappropriateness of the products produced or technology used have also been adduced against DFI (see Stewart, 1977; Lall and Streeten, 1977). However, there is little logic or empirical evidence to substantiate these—see Lal (1975, 1983).

European countries, but more recently they have been OPEC countries worried about opening deposits in US banks. The lending based on these deposits has become one of the major sources of external capital, at least for the semi-industrialized developing countries and those poorer ones with some readily exploitable mineral resources.

By the 1970s many middle-income developing countries particularly those in Latin America which for the reasons cited earlier had endemic public finance problems made ample use of this market. As real interest rates were low and for some years negative this borrowing could have been justified even to finance public consumption if the decision had taken in account risk and the future ability to repay the loans. Despite the undoubted waste associated with some of this foreign borrowing, Sachs (1981) concluded that by and large much of the borrowing went into public investment with social rates of return above the cost of borrowing.

In the late 1970s as a result of the common attempts to control inflation in OECD countries, there was a world-wide deflationary shock, which raised world interest rates to historically unprecedented levels and also led to depression in the prices of primary commodities of importance for many debtor countries in Latin America. The Mexican Government's inability to continue debt service in 1982 precipitated the debt crisis.

The problem arose because most of the borrowing was made by countries with weak fiscal systems through commercial bank loans of short maturity and with a floating rate of interest. The changes in the world capital market in the late 1970s exposed the fiscal weakness in the major borrowing countries. The debt crisis was and remains in large part a crisis of confidence in the ability of the *public sector* in many borrowing countries to generate the requisite net resources (either by cutting back public expenditure or by raising taxation) to meet the rising cost of real public debt service.

That the cause was these differences in domestic circumstances rather than the global recession or because debt-service ratios were intolerably high is borne out by the differential incidence of the 'debt crisis'. Thus many countries in South-East Asia (for instance Korea) suffered the same global shock as the 'debt crisis' countries of Latin America, Africa, or Eastern Europe, and yet did not become crisis debtors (see Balassa, 1985, Mitra, 1986). This was because their ability to generate the required domestic surpluses and to convert them into foreign exchange (by relatively smooth switching of output and employment from non-traded to traded goods production) was not in doubt. By contrast the crisis debtors, due to their endemic fiscal deficits and policy-induced inflexibilities in the working of their price mechanisms, found that the *costs* of meeting their higher debt-service obilgations had become intolerable.

Many observers argued that the 'debt crisis' reflected the inability to pay of the affected countries. But, as has been increasingly emphasized, it is not the *inability* of *sovereign* debtors to repay (either because they are illiquid or insolvent) but their *unwillingness* to repay (which will occur before they are unable to do so) which leads them to default—or reschedule their debts.

The distinction between unwillingness and inability to pay is crucial for all forms of sovereign lending, and explains why the current series of defaults is only one in a long historical series of 'boom–bust' cycles in private lending to sovereigns. The Bardi and Peruzzi banks were ruined by Edward III's default in the fourteenth century, whilst the British Council of Foreign Bondholders, formed in 1868, continued till 1988,[13] to seek compensation for the losses suffered in the repudiation by a number of American state governments in the 1840s of their bonds held by British investors (see Makin, 1982). Yet lending to princes has continued. Thus despite their heavy losses in the fifteenth century to King Edward IV, 'rather than refuse deposits, the Medicis succumbed to the temptation of seeking an outlet for surplus cash in making dangerous loans to princes' (de Roover, cited in Makin, 1984, p. 28). As Lewis (1978) notes, since the defaults on sovereign loans or 'rescheduling' as they are now called were common in each of the major recessions since the 1820s, 'The European capital market took such defaults in its stride. It knew that borrowers would have to come back for more money, and could then be made to recognize outstanding obligations before becoming eligible for new borrowing' (Lewis, 1978, p. 49).

Do these 'boom–bust' cycles in private international lending suggest that there is some market failure which requires corrective public action? There is one view due to Minsky (1972, 1982) recently popularized by Kindleberger (1978) which views these 'boom–bust' cycles as being endemic in capitalist economies due to the supposedly 'irrational' behaviour of private speculators, so that speculative bubbles in which there is overlending are followed by collapse and crisis. A lender of last resort is then advocated to mitigate the deflationary impact of the financial crisis.[14]

Whatever the merits of the view in the domestic context (and that too is

---

[13] It was finely disbanded in April 1988, even though there was still one US state which was in default on its 19th-century bonds. Most other defaulters have come to terms with their bondholders!

[14] The following is the mechanism envisaged: 'Suppose an economy is subject to random shocks generated in a stationary way. A chance period of stability will be misinterpreted as implying that fewer precautions need to be taken, thus increasing the economy's vulnerability to the next "normal" shock. As applied to financial structures, enterprises adopt excessively exposed geared, levered positions in a period of stability that does not in fact reflect a favourable shift in the economy's stochastic environment' (Flemming, 1982, p. 40). As Flemming goes on to note: 'the argument depends on agents failing to distinguish a run of good luck from a favourable structural shift in their environment. Such errors are not only identifiable but also optimal if agents attach the correct non-zero probability to structural changes. If Minsky believes that people are too willing to believe that such changes have occurred, he should consider suggesting to the authorities that they intervene randomly in financial markets—by increasing their variance, such intervention would hinder the recognition of genuine shifts and should also inhibit false inferences.'

doubtful for the reasons given in the previous footnote) is it valid in international lending? To sort out ideas it is useful to see the essential differences between domestic credit markets and those for sovereign loans. As Eaton *et al.* (1986) have emphasized, both sets of markets have to deal with problems of enforcement, moral hazard, and adverse selection. The major difference lies in the lack of any legal means of enforcement in international lending as opposed to the legal framework which is available within most national frontiers. Nor is there an equivalent of bankruptcy at the international level. Nevertheless, there are various penalties—withdrawal of trade credit, moratorium on future lending, sequestration of foreign assets—which would influence the sovereign's decision to default.

The sovereign borrower will continue to service the debt incurred as long as the expected utility from his income stream if he repays is greater than if he defaults. This implies (sec Eaton and Gersovitz, 1981; Kletzer, 1984; Eaton *et al.*, 1986) that because of sovereign risk there will be credit rationing in the international capital market, and that lenders are unlikely to extend credit to levels that would exist if contracts were enforceable. Instead, with sovereign risk, 'long before a country's ability to pay would become relevant, its willingness to pay constrains its access to credit' (Eaton *et al.*, p. 499). In that sense it is unlikely that there will be an over-extension of credit in the presence of sovereign risk.

What of panics? Following Diamond and Dybvig (1983), Eaton *et al.* (1986) argue that sovereign borrowers are rather like domestic banks with illiquid assets and liquid liabilities, and their commercial bank creditors are like the depositors in the domestic banking system. Bank runs arise when the 'bank' has short-run liabilities and many creditors. Then there may be an externality in that, when some creditors run, they may increase the likelihood that other creditors will be unable to recoup their loans. Moreover, these runs can be avoided if the loan contracts have a well-defined seniority structure, or as in the case of mutual funds the value of the debt is continuously revalued. If panics can thus be easliy forestalled, it is likely that the appropraiate adjustments to this form of lending would have been taken by rational actors given repeated runs. If they have not, perhaps the 'boom–bust' cycles are not best represented by the 'mania–panic' model.

In fact an alternative interpretation can be given of defaults or reschedulings. Rescheduling or defaults will only arise if it is impossible to contract completely against all possible contigencies. Eaton *et al.* (1986) report an unpublished model due to Ozler (1984) in which in a two-period model there are two uncertainties about the second period—the borrower's income and the default penalty. Once the loan is made under competitive conditions in the first period, the sovereign borrower and syndicated bank lender face each other as bilateral monopolists in the second period. Apart from the case where the debtor's second-period income and default penalty exceed the repayments due when debt service is met (when repayment will be made in full), there are two other situations. The first favours the lender—the borrower faces a pure liquidity problem and the default penalty is still higher than the repayment obligations. In this case the loan will be rescheduled at more favourable terms to the lender than the original loan. This seems to have been the case according to Ozler for the reschedulings in the 1970s, and was reflected in higher interest rate spreads on the rescheduled loans than on voluntary lending. The second situation arises where the default penalty falls below the repayment obligation. This favours the borrower who can use the threat of default to secure better terms than the original loan. This seems to have been the character of the recent 'debt crisis' reschedulings with interest rate spreads on rescheduled loans being lower than on voluntary loans.

Ozler's model therefore suggests that the 'bust' phase of the 'debt cycle' can be expected to be a natural (but not inevitable) part of sovereign lending. Given the impossibility of complete contingent contracting and the problem of sovereign risk, rescheduling can be expected to be part of the only feasible loan contracts that can be devised. In that sense contracts which lead to periodic 'panics' may be second-best Pareto-efficient.

Some support for this view is provided by the empirical estimates that Eichengreen and Portes (1986) have derived on the realized rates of return to maturity (including periods in which they were in default) on various US and UK bonds with government guarantees (issued between 1924 and 1930 for the US and between 1923 and 1930 for the UK bonds). They find that for the UK, the internal rate of return of 5.41 per cent exceeded the average yield on consols of 4.48 per cent, whilst for the US the returns were 3.25 per cent compared with a 5.3 per cent on Aa corporate bonds. Moreover they found 'that [as] the return on continuously serviced sterling loans was lower than that on comparable dollar loans whilst the cost of the average default on dollar loans was higher it reinforces the hypothesis that this differential default risk was recognized in the 1920s and incorporated into the required rate of return on the two categories of assets' (p. 628)

Secondly Edwards's (1984, 1986) econometric excercises on the pricing of bonds and bank loans to LDCs in the 1970s tends to confirm the hypothesis that this lending did take account of the changing default risk. In particular he found that the continuing risk premiums were positively related to the debt/output ratio and negatively to the ratio of investment to GDP. He also found that, on the basis of yields on Mexican and Brazilian bonds in the secondary market, the Mexican crisis of 1982 was anticipated though only by a few weeks by the financial market, which after the onset of the crisis heavily discounted Brazilian and Mexican debt.

If the above argument and evidence is accepted, then the reschedulings associated with the 'debt crisis' are part of the 'normal' cycle of sovereign lending. There is still no case for public concern or intervention. However it has been argued (see Cline, 1984) by analogy with domestic banking panics that the debt crisis raises the spectre of bank failures (amongst the most heavily exposed commercial banks). This in turn through the interaction of the global interbank market could lead to a collapse of the international system of finance and credit. Hence, analogously to the role of domestic central banks as lenders of last resort, it is argued that there should be an application of Bagehot's rule at the international level. Bagehot's rule to guide a central bank during a generalized financial panic was to discount the bills of those firms which were illiquid because of the general panic, but to liquidate those firms which were insolvent as the value of their assets was below their liabilities.

In the recent international debt crisis, however, there has been no general panic and the issue of illiquidity or insolvency should (following Bagehot) relate to the paper assets of the banks, not to the liabilities of the sovereign debtors. There is no reason to believe that financial markets would not correctly value the assets of banks. If the total market value is sufficiently below the total face value of their assets (by the amount of bank capital), the relevant banks are insolvent. As in any other case of insolvency, the stockholders should bear the resulting losses and if necessary the bank should be taken over or allowed to fail. Cline (1984, p. 132) disagrees with this 'solution'; he asserts these 'proposals apper naïve in that they do not address their dire implications for bank capital'. But this is a *non sequitur*. Consenting adults make all sorts of contracts, some of which lead to a loss of all their capital. Does this mean that Cline would support the public underwriting of any loss from all such private gambles? None of the dire consequences of allowing insolvent banks to be liquidated is stated. I take it, of course, that central banks know how to prevent any reduction in the overall national money supply from bank bankruptcies, and that in most countries small depositors are protected against bank failures by suitable provision, including deposit insurance.

By confusing the potential insolvency of some banks, with the liquidity problem of some debtor countries, Cline is able to argue that there should, in effect, be a global application of Bagehot's rule through an implicit international 'bail-out' of the banks, albeit through individual 'deals' with particular debtor countries. But it is arguable that it is precisely the moral hazard associated with such expected bail-outs which has led to the protracted debt crisis. Given the temper of the times, both the debtors and commercial banks had hoped after 1982 that, playing on the historical memories of the bank failures during the 1930s, they could force a bail-out by Western governments, ideally through the concealed means of intermediation by an international agency such as the World Bank. The 'willingness to pay' model suggests that, because of the 'moral hazard' associated with such perceptions, the perceived penalties of default and hence the willingness to pay of the borrowers would decrease. At the same time the banks by holding back on calling a default could avoid the inevitable downward revaluation of their assets.

In May 1987 the major New York banks with high exposure to Third World debt decided to set aside larger reserves against their Third World loans. Since then, various methods, like the recent Mexican swap arrangement to, in effect, buy back part of its existing debt at close to its value in the secondary market, reflect the growing realization of both the debtors and lenders that they will not be bailed out by the world's taxpayers. They are now negotiating the terms of the rescheduling which will determine how the losses embodied in the changed present value of past promises (contracts) will be shared.

The most important lesson for public policy of the 'debt crisis' for developed-country action therefore would seem to be—forbear. The 'debt crisis' in our judgement would have been resolved much earlier if today's Western governments had explicitly stood by the position expressed by Britain in the nineteenth century in the face of spectacular defaults on foreign bonds. In a famous circular of 1848 Palmerston, whilst eschewing any public action, noted: 'The British government has considered that the losses of imprudent men who have placed mistaken confidence in the *good faith* of foreign governments would provide a salutary warning to others' (cited in Lipson, 1985).

3. The Political Economy of Global Financial Integration

Despite the current debt crisis the future flow of capital to the Third World is most likely to be private (see Section 2.1). Its dimensions will inexorably be tied to expectations about the willingness to pay of sovereign nations. This is just another way of defining the political risks associated with foreign investment. The great nineteenth-century booms in foreign lending were promoted by the extension of norms of conduct based on European capitalist individualism—in particular the sanctity of private property rights—to much of the Third World, through the expansion of *Pax Britannica*, and its influence on the local legal institutions even of many independent states, as in Latin America. A strict set of legal rules was established through a number of commercial treaties between European states (see Lipson, 1985). The legitimacy of these nineteenth-century rules was not challenged until the Soviet and Mexican revolutions, and the explicit introduction of *étatist* policies by Turkey (under Atatürk) as a means of national economic development. Since then, there has been a gradual erosion of public acceptance of the sanctity of private property rights when faced with social policies designed to promote the general—usually nationalist—weal.

There was a partial restoration of these international property rights which underpinned the nineteenth-century economic order with the establishment of *Pax Americana* after 1945. But it has not successfully withstood the explosion of economic nationalism, following decolonization and the formation of numerous Third World nation-states determined to assert their rights of national sovereignty against any purported international property rights.

As direct foreign investors provide more local hostages to fortune, they have borne the brunt of the deleterious effects of this disintegration of the legal order. Moreover, most governments of developing countries, being both nationalist and *dirigiste*, have sought to regulate, tax, or nationalize particular foreign investments on grounds of national social utility rather than out of any general antagonism towards private property as such. This has meant that the US has been unable to identify expropriation of foreign capital with ideology (communism or socialism), as the nationalization of companies in the late 1960s and early 1970s by right-wing regimes in the Middle East proved.

This inexorble erosion of the old standards of international property rights might however be ending. The recent emergence of Third World multinationals, the importance of many OPEC countries as portfolio lenders, and with the US becoming the world's largest debtor, the old distinction between the divergent interests of developed capital-exporting countries interested in protecting international property rights, and of Third World capital-importing countries keen to circumscribe them, is becoming less valid. In the future the interests of developed and developing countries may converge and lead to an increasing acceptance of rules protecting international property.

This is all the more likely because of the rapid and remarkable integration of world capital markets that is currently taking place. This has resulted from: the ending of capital and exchange controls and the accompanying deregulation of domestic capital markets in most developed countries; the instantaneous linking of national capital markets through the new information technology which reduces transaction costs and is alalogous to a large reduction in transport costs for traded goods; the introduction of new financial instruments—the 'securitization' of all forms of debt—so that, even those forms of debt, such as house mortgages, which were previously considered to be intrinsically non-traded outside national boundaries, can now be traded internationally. At the same time many institutional investors—particularly pension funds, whose beneficiaries increasingly include a large portion of the developed countries' labour force—are holding an internationally diversified portfolio. These trends have a number of interesting implications for the conduct of public policy in developed countries, and point to the required changes in developing countries' policies which would help them to make the best use of these emerging global opportunities.

As far as developed countries are concerned, recent political economy models have sought to endogenize the pressures for protection in these countries. One such model due to Mayer (1984) is particularly useful for our purpose. He considers an economy described by the standard two-good, two-factor Hecksher–Ohlin model. The political system is based on majority voting, and it is assumed that voters vote their economic interests. The latter are determined by the income they receive from their individual endowments of the two factors of production—capital and labour. The *mean* of the distribution of factor ownerships is just the average capital/labour ratio of the economy (k). Under majority voting, with no voting costs and if voters have 'singled-peaked' preferences, then as Black (1948) demonstrated, public policy will be determined by the *median* voter's preferences. If, *ex hypothesi*, voters seek to serve their narrow economic interests, namely to raise the returns to the factor which is more abundant in their individual factor endowment, then the policy pursued will depend upon the *median* voter's factor endowment (k_m). Assuming that the distribution of factor ownership is unimodal, a tariff (subsidy) on capital-intensive imports will be voted in if the median (k_m) is greater (less) than the mean (k) of the distribution of factor ownership. If this distribution is symmetric then the median and mean are the same $(k_m = k)$, and the voters will support free trade (as that from standard trade theory maximizes the real income of a 'country'). However 'for most non-socialist countries there is strong evidence that capital–labour ownership distributions are not symmetric, but skewed to the right. Accordingly, one would expect a built-in tendency towards protection of labour's interests, through subsidies on capital-intensive imports or tarriffs on labour-intensive imports' (Mayer, p. 338).[15]

But now suppose there is complete global capital market integration.

---

[15] Strictly speaking the model would establish labour's interest in various non-tariff domestic subsidies to expand the domestic output of the labour-intensive industry, as these will dominate the tariff as second-best methods of achieving the non-economic objective of raising labour's share in national income. Also as Mayer emphasizes this is a long-run model and would explain 'long run tariff trends, especially in relationship to changes in voter eligibility rules, voting costs, or overall factor ownership distributions. It is much less suitable, however, in explaining more short-term attempts by individual industries to gain tariff protection. In particular, it sheds no light on the frequently observed phenomenon that a single industry succeeds in raising tariffs on its product, even though the vast majority of eligible voters do not benefit from such a policy.' He then goes on to develop 'a many industries model with specific factors to show how majority voting can result in tariff protection of a small industry'. It would take us too far afield to outline this short-run model which shows how 'a small minority of gaining factor owners can become a majority of actual voters for a tariff increase on a given commodity' (Mayer, p. 338). For our relatively long-term purposes, the above long-term version of Mayer's model will suffice to make the major point we wish to make in this section.

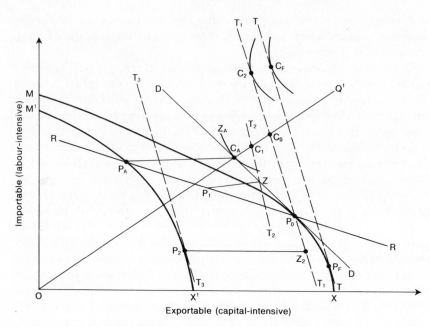

Fig. 11.7

One of the consequences will be that the interest rate on domestic capital will be exogenously determined for each 'small' country by the world economy. With given world prices for the two traded goods in the model, the wage rate will also then be fully determined. Suppose under majority voting in a capital-abundant country, the median voter has a factor endowment *less* capital-intensive than the economy. An imposition of a tariff on the labour-intensive import good would cause an incipient rise in the wage and fall in the rental rate. The latter would immediately lead to an outflow of capital, and the unviability of the capital-intensive export industry at the given world rental rate, as the economy's output shrinks along its Rybczynski line with the outflow of domestic capital.[16] As Mundell (1957) showed in his model of international trade and factor mobility in the new equilibrium, the free trade commodity and factor/price ratio would be restored, but with the elimination of commodity trade.

Fig. 11.7 sets out the argument. It depicts the standard Hecksher–Ohlin model, in which the home country faces given terms of trade TT, and produces both an exportable good (X) which is more capital-intensive than the

[16] The Rybczynski line would show the absolute decrease in the outputs or the capital-intensive good (at the new tariff inclusive commodity price) as capital fled, with the production possibility frontier for the two goods shifting inwards.

importable. MX is the production possibility frontier, free trade equilibrium is at P_F, with consumption at C_F. The domestic rental on capital is equated to the world interest rate through perfect mobility of capital.

With the imposition of a tariff the production point moves to P_0 and the consumption point to C_0, on the income consumption curve OQ^1 (drawn as a straight line for convenience) for the tariff-distorted relative commodity price ratio given by DD. The labour-intensive M industry expands and hence from the Stolper–Samuelson theorem, the rental rate falls and the wage rate rises. With perfect capital mobility the lowering of the domestic rental rate relative to the given world interest rate leads to an outflow of capital and the economy's production point moves leftwards on the Rybczynski line RR (for the constant domestic price ratio DD). Say, initially, it moves to P_1. The outflow of capital yields an income of P_1Z_1 at the tariff-distorted domestic price ratio DD. (We are assuming that there is no foreign taxation of the home country's earnings on capital placed abroad.) This is the difference in the value of output at the initial production point P_0— before the capital outflow—and that at the new production point P_1. The income given by point Z_1, can be converted into any combination of the two traded goods along the unchanged terms of trade, given by T_2T_2. Consumption will therefore be at C_1, on the income consumption curve OQ^1.

However, as at P_1, where the domestic tariff-distorted price ratio DD still rules, the rental on capital is still below the world interest rate, capital will continue to flow out until the point P_A on the Rybczynski line RR on the shrunken production possibility frontier X^1M^1 is reached. At P_A income from the capital placed abroad is P_AZ_A, and the income corresponding to Z_A will also be the consumption point C_A, as Z_A lies on the income consumption curve OQ^1. *There will be no trade at C_A*, and thus the domestic price of the importables, will no longer be determined by the world price plus the tariff. If there is an infinitesimal outflow of capital at P_A, and rise in the output of the importables its relative price will fall, which in turn will *raise* the domestic rental rate, thereby reducing its gap from the world interest rate and hence the inducement for capital outflows. The relative fall in the price of importables will continue until *domestic relative prices have returned to their initial free-trade ratio given by DD*. Production will then be at P_2, income from capital abroad will be P_2Z_2 and consumption at the domestic price ratio (now equal to the free trade one) will be at C_2. There will of course still be no trade in commodities, but as far as the factor-price configuration is concerned it will have returned to its original free-trade one. (Also see Minabe, 1974, and Brecher and Diaz-Alejandro, 1977.) For our purpose the lesson of the model is that, with perfect capital mobility, within the (admittedly unrealistic) Hecksher–Ohlin framework, labour's attempt to raise its wage above the free trade level by voting in protection of the labour-intensive good would have been foiled!

Clearly, in practice well before the economy reaches the trade-extinguishing point, P_A, in Fig. 11. 7 the collapse of the exportable industry and any attendant balance-of-payment crisis that may ensue in the absence of the smooth adjustment assumed in the Mundell model, would lead in this world of perfect capital mobility to attempts by the polity to return to the status quo ante by rescinding the tariff. Thus by making it difficult for the median voter to achieve the desired distributional changes associated with a tariff 'equilibrium' (which can be achieved when capital is *immobile*), essentially because of the capital flight that would be induced by squeezing domestic returns to capital, global capital-market intergration could provide that essential bulwark against the inevitable long-run political pressures for tariffs in developed countries as modelled by Mayer. It could thus provide most democratic developed economies a means of 'tying themselves to the mast' to save themselves from the siren calls of their politics.

What of developing countries? Given the differential incidence of the debt crisis, it is clear that differences in domestic policy were largely responsible for the divergent performance of highly indebted countries when faced by the global rise in interest rates and primary commodity price falls in the early 1980s. The two major policy failures of the past have been the tendency to run unsustainable fiscal deficits and the maintenance of inward-looking trade regimes. It is essential that, if developing countries are to utilize foreign borrowing efficiently in the future, they will first have to set their domestic house in order. Paradoxically, global capital-market integration can help in stiffening the spine of Third World governments to undertake this economic liberalization and to stick by more liberal economic policies in the future.

Elsewhere, we have argued (see Lal, 1987) that Third World governments have usually undertaken sustained economic liberalization only when the costs of maintaining repressed regimes to *them*, in terms of their control over the economy, had become too high. The past *dirigisme* of most Third World states has led to the gradual expansion of politically determined entitlements to current and future income streams to favoured groups. The accompanying (implicit or explicit) tax burden to finance them leads at some stage to generalized tax resistance, avoidance, and evasion. With taxes being evaded, with domestic and foreign credit virtually at an end, and with private agents adjusting to inflation to evade the inflation tax, the government finds its fiscal control of the economy vanishing. It is to restore this control that, most often, liberalization is undertaken.

In the 1980s, the integration of the global capital markets accelerated this dynamic process whereby the expansion of what can be called the 'transfer state' leads to the unexpected and very un-Marxian withering away of the state. For one important feature of the debt crisis was that the macroeconomic imbalances which in part were its cause, also led in many countries to capital flight (see Cuddington, 1986). For despite exchange controls, economic agents sought to protect their capital against the domestic depredations of asset values arising from the endemic inflation that accommmpanied macro mismanagement. With improved domestic prospects, and particularly with macroeconomic stability and more realistic exchange rates, flight capital has returned in many countries. But the important lesson is *not* that tighter capital controls should be maintained by developing countries. For with the expansion of trade and the growing familiarity of at least the richer residents of developing countries with international capital markets, capital controls are at best a short-term palliative. As Cuddington (1986) rightly concludes:

over expansive monetary and fiscal policies, an incompatible exchange-rate policy, and a repressive set of financial policies designed to divert resources toward the public sector will cause widespread distortions and imbalances even in the short run. Capital flight is an important symptom of these policy-induced distortions. While attacking this symptom directly by imposing capital controls may be essential in a crisis, it hardly represents a long-term antidote for destabilizing exchange-rate, fiscal and financial policies. Without capital controls, the threat of capital flight might impose much needed discipline on policy makers.

Thus, again as in the case of developed countries, integrated capital markets may be able to tie the hands of developing-country governments so that they no longer act to subserve base interests but the common weal. The major benefits for the economic development of Third World countries from free world-wide capital movements are therefore likely to come not primarily from the conventional sources of a better allocation of the world's savings, as is emphasized in most of our traditional economic models (surveyed in earlier sections), but from this political economy of global capital-market integration.

It is increasingly being realized that the role of open foreign trade regimes is probably more important in terms of their effects in inducing the establishment of a domestic economic system which is conductive to growth (see Lal and Rajapatirana, 1987). As Keynes (1926) emphasized, the classical case against mercantilism was essentially based on limiting state action to areas where such action was indispensable. What I have been arguing in this section is that free capital movements are likely to provide an even more effective shackle on the irrational *dirigiste* impulses of governments in both developed and developing countries.[17] The direct

---

[17] The political importance of capital-market integration in overcoming the territorial instincts of states is also of importance and is argued in a brilliant book by Rosecrance (1986). His arguments and those of the Luddites who wish to prevent capital-market integration in order to foster national autonomy in public policy are reviewed in Lal (1988).

effects of capital flows on growth (as of trade) are not likely to be substantial, as Cairncross (1962) perceptively noted. Thus we can extend Kravis's (1970) view of 'trade as the handmaiden of growth', to trade not merely in commodities but more importantly to the services of capital.

The handmaiden's primary role is to create incentives for our rulers to maintain a domestic economic framework where the state provides the indispensable public goods—law and order, stable money, and social overhead capital—for development, without over-extending itself and generating those policy-induced distortions which have done more damage to Third World prospects than the so-called endogenous distortions in these economies that the policies were meant to cure. Many economists have become hoarse preaching these economic virtues to states—but with little effect. But as most states seem to agree with the Bard that, 'there is no virtue like necessity' (*Richard II*), the 'political economy' consequences of the global integration of capital markets may yet force them to make a necessity of these virtues!

References

Avramovic, D. *et al.* (1964), *Economic Growth and External Debt* (Baltimore: Johns Hopkins Univ. Press).

Balassa, B. (1985), *Change and Challenge in the World Economy* (London: Macmillan).

Barro, R. (1974), 'Are Government Bonds Net Wealth?' *Journal of Political Economy*, Nov.–Dec.

Bauer, P (1972), *Dissent on Development* (London: Wiedenfeld & Nicolson).

——(1981), *Equality, the Third World and Economic Delusion* (London: Methuen).

——(1984), *Reality and Rhetoric: Studies in the Economics of Development* (London: Weidenfeld & Nicolson).

Bhagwati, J. N. (1986), 'Investing Abroad', Esmée Fairbairn Lecture, Univ. of Lancaster.

Brecher, R. A., and Diaz-Alejandro, C. F. (1977), 'Tariffs, Foreign Capital and Immiserizing Growth', *Journal of International Economics*, 7 (Nov.).

Buiter, W. H. (1981), 'Time Preference and International Lending and Borrowing in an Overlapping-Generations Model', *Journal of Political Economy*, 89 (Aug.).

Cairncross, A. K. (1962), *Factors in Economic Development* (London: Allen & Unwin).

Cairnes, J. E. (1874), *Some Leading Principles of Political Economy* (London: Macmillan).

Cassen, R. *et al.* (1986), *Does Aid Work?* (Oxford: Clarendon Press).

Caves, R. E. (1971), 'International Corporations: The Industrial Economics of Foreign Investments', *Economica* 38 (Feb.).

——(1982), *Multinational Enterprises and Economic Analysis* (Cambridge: CUP).

Chenery, H. B., and Strout, A. M. (1966), 'Foreign Assistance and Economic Development', *American Economic Review*, 56 (Sept.).

Cline, W. R. (1984), *International Debt: Systemic Risk and Policy Response* (Washington, DC: Institute for International Economics).

Crawford, V. P. (1987), 'International Lending, Long-Term Credit Relationships and Dynamic Contract Theory' *Princeton Studies in International Finance*, no. 59, (Princeton).

Cuddington, J. T., (1986), 'Capital Flight: Estimates, Issues and Explanations', *Princeton Studies in International Finance*, no. 58 (Princeton).

Diamond, P. A. (1965), 'National Debt in a Neo-classical Growth Model', *American Economic Review*, 55 (Dec.).

Diamond, D., and Dybvig, P. E. (1983), 'Bank Runs, Deposit Insurance and Liquidity', *Journal of Political Economy*, 91 (June).

Dinapolous (1987), 'Quid Pro Quo Foreign Investment', paper for World Bank conference on Political Economy, June 1987.

Domar, E. (1950), 'The Effect of Foreign Investment on the Balance of Payments', *American Economic Review*, 40 (Dec.).

Eaton, J., Gersovitz, M., and Stiglitz, J. E. (1986), 'The Pure Theory of Country Risk', *European Economic Review*, 30 (June).

Eaton, J., and Gersovitz, M. (1981), 'Poor Country Borrowing and the Repudiation Issue', *Princeton Studies in International Finance*, no. 47 (Princeton).

Edwards, S. (1984), 'LDC Foreign Borrowing and Default Risk: An Empirical Investigation', *American Economic Review*, 74 (Sept.).

——(1986), 'The Pricing of Bonds and Bank Loans in International Markets', *European Economic Review*, 30 (June).

Eichengreen, B., and Portes, R. (1986), 'Debt and Default in the 1930s', *European Economic Review*, 30 (June).

Engel, C., and Kletzer, K. (1987), 'Saving and Investment in an Open Economy with Non-traded Goods', *NBER Working Paper No. 2141*, (Cambridge, Mass.: NBER).

Findlay, R. (1978), 'An "Austrian" Model of International Trade and Interest Rate Equalization', *Journal of Political Economy*, 86 (Dec.).

——(1984) 'Growth and Development in Trade Models', in Jones and Kenen (1984), Vol. i.

Fischer, S., and Frenkel, J. (1972), 'Investment, the Two-Sector Model, and Trade in Debt and Capital Goods', *Journal of International Economics*, 2 (Aug.).

Fisher, I. (1930), *The Theory of Interest*, reprint, 1965 (New York: Augustus M. Kelley).

Flemming, J. S. (1982), 'Comment on Minsky', in Kindleberger and Laffargue (1982).

Griffin, K., and Enos, J. (1970), 'Foreign Assistance: Objectives and Consequences', *Economic Development and Cultural Change*, 18 (Apr.).

Harberger, A. C. (1986), 'Welfare Consequences of Capital Inflows', in A. Choksi and D. Papageorgiou (eds.), *Economic Liberalization in Developing Countries*, (Oxford: Blackwell).

Havrylyshyn, O. (ed.) (1987), *Exports of Developing Countries—How Direction Affects Performance*, (Washington, DC: World Bank).

Houthakker, H. S. (1965), 'On Some Determinants of Saving in Developed and Underdeveloped Countries', in E. A. G. Robinson (ed.), *Problems in Economic Development*, (London: Macmillan).

Hymer, S. (1977), *The International Operations of National Firms: A Study of Direct Foreign Investment* (Cambridge, Mass.: MIT Press).

Ihori, T. (1978), 'The Golden Rule and the Role of Government in a Life Cycle Growth Model', *American Economic Review*, 68 (June).

Jones, R. W. (1967), 'International Capital Movements and the Theory of Tariffs and Trade', *Quarterly Journal of Economics*, 81.

——(1979), *International Trade: Essays in Theory* (Amsterdam: North-Holland).

——and Kenen, P. B. (eds.) (1984), *Handbook of International Economics*, 2 vols. (Amsterdam: North-Holland).

Kemp, M. C. (1966), 'The Gain from International Trade and Investment: A Neo-Hecksher–Ohlin Approach', *American Economic Review*, 56.

Keynes, J. M. (1926), *The End of Laissez-Faire* (London: Hogarth Press).

Kindleberger, C. P. (1958), *International Economics* (Homewood: R. D. Irwin).

——(1969), *American Business Abroad* (New Haven: Yale Univ. Press).

——(1978), *Manias, Panics and Crashes* (New York: Basic Books).

——and Laffargue, J. P. (eds.) (1982), *Financial Crises—Theory, History & Policy* (Cambridge: CUP).

King, M. A. (1985), 'The Economics of Saving: A Survey of Recent Contributions' in K. Arrow and S. Honkapohja (eds.), *Frontiers in Economics* (Oxford: Blackwell).

Kletzer, K. M. (1984), 'Asymmetries of Information and LDC Borrowing with Sovereign Risk', *Economic Journal*, 94 (June).

Kravis, I. B. (1970), 'Trade as a Handmaiden of Growth-Similarities between the 19th and 20th centuries', *Economic Journal*, 80 (Dec.).

Krueger, A. O. (1986), 'Aid in the Development Process', *World Bank Research Observer* 1 (Jan.).

——(1987), Michalopoulos, C., and Ruttan, V. (1987), *The Impact of Development Assistance to LDCs* (Baltimore: Johns Hopkins Univ. Press).

Kuznets, S. (1966), *Modern Economic Growth* (New Haven: Yale Univ. Press).

Lal, D. (1971), When is Foreign Borrowing Desirable? '*Bulletin of the Oxford University Institute of Statistics*, 71 (Aug.).

——(1972), 'The Foreign Exchange Bottleneck Revisited: A Geometric Note', *Economic Development and Cultural Change*, 20 (July).

——(1975), *Appraising Foreign Investment in Developing Countries* (London: Heinemann Educational).

——(1978a), 'On the Multinationals', *ODI Review*, no. 2.

——(1978b), *Poverty, Power and Prejudice—The North-South Confrontation*, Fabian Research Series no. 340 (London: Fabian Society).

——(1978c), 'Industrial Co-operation Agreements', in *Industrial Co-operation*, Commonwealth Economic Papers No. 11, (London: Commonwealth Secretariat).

——(1978d), 'The Evaluation of Capital Inflows', *Industry and Development*, no. 1 (reprinted in *World Bank Reprint* Series, 84).

——(1983, 1985), *The Poverty of 'Development Economics'*, Hobart Paperback 16 (London: Institute of Economic Affairs). American edn. with new preface and additional Appendix (Cambridge, Mass: Harvard Univ. Press 1985).

——(1987), 'The Political Economy of Economic Liberalisation', *World Bank Economic Review*, (Jan.).

——(1988), 'By Land or by Sea, the Merchant Shall Inherit the Earth', *World Economy*, 11 (Mar.).

——and Rajapatirana, S. (1987), 'Foreign Trade Regimes and Economic Growth', *World Bank Research Observer*, 2 (July).

——and van Wijnbergen, S. (1985), 'Government Deficits, the Real Interest Rate and Developing Country Debt: On Global Crowding Out', *European Economic Review*, 29 (Dec.); reprinted with extensions in Lal and Wolf (1986).

——and Wolf, M. (eds.) (1986), *Stagflation, Savings and the State* (New York: OUP).

Lall, S., and Streeten, P. (1977), *Foreign Investment, Transnationals and Developing Countries* (London: Macmillan).

Lewis, W. A. (1978), *The Evolution of the International Economic Order* (New York: Princeton Univ. Press).

Lipson, D. (1985), *Standing Guard—Protecting Foreign Capital in the 19th and 20th Centries* (Berkeley: Univ. of California).

Little, I. M. D. (1960), 'The Strategy of Indian Development', *National Institute Economic Review*, 9 (May).

——(1972), 'On measuring the value of private direct overseas investments', in G. Ranis (ed.), *The Gap Between Rich and Poor Nations* (London: Macmillan).

——(1982), *Economic Development* (New York: Basic Books).

——and Clifford, J. M. (1965), *International Aid* (London: Allen & Unwin).

——and Mirrlees, J. A. (1969), *Manual of Industrial Project Analysis*, vol. 2, (Paris: OECD Development Centre).

——(1974), *Project Appraisal and Planning for Developing Countries*, (London: Heinemann Educational).

——Scott, M. FG., and Scitovsky, T. (1970), *Industry and Trade in Some Developing Countries* (London: OUP).

——and Tipping, D. G. (1972), *A Social Cost-Benefit Analysis of the Kulai Oil Palm Estate* (Paris: OECD Development Centre).

Lluch, C. (1986), 'ICORs, Savings Rates and the Determinants of Public Expenditure in Developing Countries', in Lal and Wolf (1986).

Makin, J. H. (1984), *The Global Debt Crisis* (New York: Basic Books).

Mayer, W. (1984), 'Endogenous Tariff Formation', *American Economic Review*, 74 (Dec.).

MacDougall, G. D. A. (1960), 'The Benefits and Costs of Private Investment from Abroad: A Theoretical Approach', *Economic Record*, 36, special issue; also published in *Bulletin of the Oxford Institute of Statistics*, 22/3 (1960).

McKinnon, R. I. (1964), 'Foreign Exchange Constraints in Economic Development', *Economic Journal*, 74 (June).

Minabe, N. (1974), 'Capital and Technology Movements and Economic Welfare', *American Economic Review*, 64 (Dec.).

Mikesell, R. F. and Zinser, J. E. (1973) 'The Nature of the Savings Function in Developing Countries—A Survey of the Theoretical and Empirical Literature', *Journal of Economic Liternature*, 11 (Mar.).

Minsky, H. P. (1977), 'A Theory of Systematic Fragility', in E. I. Altman and A. W. Sametz (eds), *Financial Crisis: Institutions and Markets in a Fragile Environment* (New York: Wiley).

Mitra, A. K. (1978), 'An Intertemporal Cross-country Analysis of the Impact of Economic and Demographic Factors on Growth Expenditure Share', PhD dissertation, Duke University, North Carolina.

Mitra, P. (1986), 'A Description of Adjustment to External Shocks: Country Groups', in Lal and Wolf (1986).

Modigliani, F. (1970), 'The Life Cycle Hypothesis of Saving and Inter Country Differences in the Saving Ratio', in W. A. Eltis, M. FG. Scott & J. N. Wolfe (eds.), *Induction, Growth and Trade* (Oxford: Clarendon Press).

——(1975), 'The Life Cycle Hypothesis of Saving Twenty Years Later', in M. Parkin and A. R. Nobay (eds.), *Contemporary Issues in Economics* (Manchester: Manchester Univ. Press).

Mosley, P. (1987), *Overseas Aid* (Brighton: Wheatsheaf Books).

Mundell, R. A. (1957) 'International Trade and Factor Mobility', *American Economic Review*, 47 (June).

Ozler, S., (1984), 'Rescheduling of Sovereign Government Bank Debt, (Stanford: Stanford University), mimeo.

Papanek, G. (1972), 'The Effects of Aid and Other Resource Transfers on Savings and Growth in Less Developed Countries', *Economic Journal*, 82 (Sept.).

Reuber, G., Crookell, H., Emerson, M., and Gallais-Hamonno, G. (1973), *Private Foreign Investment in Development* (Oxford: Clarendon Press).

Riedel, J. (1984), 'Trade as the Engine of Growth in Developing Countries, Revisited'. *Economic Journal*, 94 (Mar.).

Roover de R. (1948), *The Medici Bank* (New York: New York Univ. Press).

Rosecrance, R. (1986), *The Rise of the Trading State* (New York: Basic Books).

Ruffin, R. J. (1979), 'Growth and the Long-Run Theory of International Capital Movements', *American Economic Review*, 69 (Dec.)

——(1984), 'International Factor Movements', in Jones and Kenen (1984), Vol. i.

Rybczynski, T. (1955), 'Factor Endowments and Relative Commodity Prices', *Economica*, 22 (Nov.).

Sachs, J. (1981), 'The Current Account and Macroeconomics Adjustment in the 1970s', *Brookings Papers on Economics Activity*, no. 1.

——(1984) 'Theoretical Issues in International Borrowing', *Princeton Studies in International Finance*, no. 54 (Princeton).

Samuelson, P. A. (1958), 'An Exact Consumption Loan Model of Interest with or without the Social Contrivance of Money', *Journal of Political Economy*, 66 (Dec.).

Selowsky, M., and van der Tak, H. G. (1986), 'The Debt Problem and Growth', *World Development*, Sept.

Stewart, F. (1977), *Technology and Underdevelopment* (London: Macmillan).

Uzawa, H. (1968), 'Time Preference, the Consumption Function and Optimum

Asset Holdings' in J. N. Wolfe (ed.): *Value, Capital and Growth* (Edinburgh: (Edinburgh Univ. Press).

Van Wijnbergen, S. (1985), 'Interdependence Revisited: A Developing Countries Perspective on Macroeconomic Management and Trade Policy in the Industrial World', *Economic Policy*, Nov.; also comments by R. Dornbusch and Michael Wickens.

Vernon, R. (1977), *Storm over the Multinationals* (London: Macmillan).

Weisskopf, T. E. (1972), 'The Impact of Foreign Capital Inflow on Domestic Savings in Underdeveloped Economies', *Journal of International Economics*, 2 (Feb.).

Wells, Jr., L. T. (1983), *Third World Multinationals* (London: MIT Prerss).

World Bank (1984), *World Development Report 1984* (New York: OUP).

——(1985), *World Development Report 1985* (New York: OUP).

12

Principles of Taxation for Developing Countries

EHTISHAM AHMAD AND NICHOLAS STERN

1. Introduction

Tax systems should be judged and proposals for reform analysed in relation to systematic criteria and principles. Central amongst these will be the effects on the behaviour and welfare of participants in the economic system. The purpose of this chapter is to set out the simple theory of taxation in a form which leads to principles which can guide proposals for reform and practical, but sound, methods for their analysis. In this we trust that we follow the spirit of Ian Little's work—whilst he has always been interested in practical proposals he has been constant in his insistence on a firm basis in serious economic analysis.

If one asks how the tax system could be improved, or how extra revenue should be raised, then one must consider, in relation to objectives, the effects of possible tax changes on revenue, on incentives, on the distribution of welfare, and on the pattern of production. These effects will be closely linked through the behaviour and objectives of participants in the economy. One should also ask how the changes are to be enforced and at what cost. Any proposal under study should be examined systematically in relation to criteria which embody these considerations. The links between the four issues described are illustrated, for example, if one considers the effects of a tax change on the incentive to save. One is then concerned with the distribution of consumption across individuals at different points of time, and must ask what happens to revenue in each period (which will depend on behaviour). One must also examine how the pattern of production will change to meet the changed demands. Similarly a discussion on the progressivity of the income tax will involve possible effects on incentives to work, and thus revenue and production, together with concern for the distribution of disposable income. The theory in this chapter will be directed towards developing principles and methods for the simultaneous treatment of these issues.

The arguments in this chapter are set out more fully in a paper by the authors, 'Taxation for Developing Countries', in H. B. Chenery and T. N. Srinivasan (eds.), *Handbook of development economics* (North-Holland, forthcoming), and are also contained in D. M. G. Newbery and N. H. Stern (eds.), *The Theory of Taxation for Developing Countries*, (Oxford University Press for the World Bank, 1987). We are grateful to Maurice Scott for very helpful comments on an earlier draft.

Administration is not our main focus here but it plays an important role in the theory in terms of the taxes to be examined, their relative prominence, and their coverage. In most of the theory it enters through the constraints on possible taxes rather than in terms of explicit cost calculations, although as we shall see such costs can be made explicit in the theory of reform. Our main concern is with the medium or long term and the concentration is on indirect taxes, excises, tariffs, sales taxes, VAT, and the like, although personal and corporate income taxes will also be considered.

The theory plays two related roles. First we can use it without numbers to develop principles, train our intuition, sort out coherent from incoherent arguments, and to help identify the important assumptions or parameters. In this attempt to aid our understanding it is important to keep the models as simple as possible consistent with capturing the essentials of the problem. Section 2 contains this type of theoretical discussion. The second role of theory is in the organization and direction of empirical analysis and it is important to develop theory in such a way that it can be integrated explicitly into methods for applied work. Thus it should tell us what data are required and provide an analytic basis for the empirical calculations. The development of the theory in this way involves not only analytical skills but an appreciation of the demands and difficulties of empirical work; it provides part of the subject-matter of Section 3 in which we discuss applied policy models. An important element in that analysis will be the calculation of the effect of tax changes on price, or tax-shifting.

There are difficulties and dangers associated with each role for theory. In the first, clear results are an advantage in showing where different assumptions lead but we should not let their definiteness cloud our judgement of the relevance of those assumptions. This danger is particularly severe where there are strong preconceived views on what policy should be (e.g. the uniformity of indirect taxation, see below). And we should not be deluded into thinking that the presence of numbers indicates a serious applied study. For example in models which are too complicated to yield clear results the numbers may be used simply to illustrate possible theoretical outcomes.

In Section 4 we shall set the methods in context by showing how they form part of the general theory of tax reform, using shadow prices. This not only provides a considerable extension of their applicability but also a link with other chapters on policy, particularly cost-benefit analysis, in that we see how policy problems of different kinds have a similar underlying structure. Extensions of the models to deal explicitly with dynamic issues are described in Section 5. Taxes and production are discussed in Section 6.

The final four parts of this chapter move closer to practical policy. We look at agriculture in Section 7—its importance in the economies of developing countries and its particular features imply that it should not be treated as just another production sector. In Section 8 we look at the taxation of income and profits and in Section 9 some problems of indirect taxation. In the final subsection we summarize by formulating some simple practical guide-lines from the theory.

2. Theory

The development of basic principles requires an analytical foundation so that we can understand the circumstances in which they apply and the critical assumptions in their justification. In this subsection we shall, therefore, present an outline of the standard models of normative tax theory and then ask what lessons they offer for taxation in developing countries.

As a bench-mark and a simple starting point we take two of the standard frameworks in the theory of taxation, first where revenue can be raised in a lump-sum manner directly from households, and second where revenue has to be raised by the taxation of transactions between consumers and producers. In the former case if there are no externalities, and indifference curves and isoquants have the usual convex shape, then any Pareto-efficient outcome can be achieved as a competitive equilibrium in which the government raises revenue and redistributes purchasing power using the appropriate set of lump-sum taxes. The policy is clear: there are no taxes of any kind (neither on commodities nor income) except those which are lump-sum. Whilst the model is presented mainly as a bench-mark it does immediately generate a general principle which is of value in guiding policy: revenue should be raised and redistributed in ways which, as far as possible, are lump-sum. There are examples such as land or poll-taxes which are relevant but generally governments will also have to consider taxes which are not lump-sum.

In the second case we retain the competitive framework and the assumption of no externalities but now revenue has to be raised by the taxation of commodities bought and services supplied. The standard theory in the tradition of Pigou, Ramsey, Samuelson, Boiteau and Diamond-Mirrlees is to formulate the problem as one of the choice of the indirect taxes to maximize a Bergson–Samuelson social welfare function whilst raising a given revenue. The use of a Bergson–Samuelson welfare function is not *per se* restrictive since it simply says that our judgements of welfare are conducted basically in terms of the living standards of the households in the community (current and future). Neither does it presuppose a benevolent all-knowing government. We ask simply how a commentator interested in raising living standards and in the distribution of welfare would evaluate policy in this simple framework. An absence of understanding of the logic of policy in this simple example would preclude us from generalizing to more complicated worlds.

The problem is to raise a given level of revenue using commodity taxes whilst lowering the welfare of households as little as possible. Formally we choose a tax vector **t** to

$$\text{maximize } V(\mathbf{q}) \tag{12.1}$$

$$\text{subject to } R(\mathbf{t}) = \mathbf{t} \cdot \mathbf{X}(\mathbf{q}) \geqq \bar{R}, \tag{12.2}$$

where **p** are the prices faced by producers; **q**, equal to $(\mathbf{p} + \mathbf{t})$, are the consumer prices; the level of welfare in household h corresponding to **q** is $v^h(\mathbf{q})$ and the household levels of quantities demanded are $\mathbf{x}^h(\mathbf{q})$; $\mathbf{X}(\mathbf{q})$ is the aggregate demand vector, and $V(\mathbf{q})$ is social welfare, arising from those prices; $R(\mathbf{t})$ is indirect revenue, and $\bar{R}$ the required revenue. Notice that we are assuming that there are no incomes accruing to households other than from what they sell so that the demands and welfare of households (and thus social welfare) depend only on the prices which they face for the goods and services which they buy and sell. The assumptions on production are essentially that all production is either by the government or by competitive private firms, with constant returns to scale, all trading at the same prices. We are assuming that there is no taxation on transactions between producers but that all final sales to the consumer can be taxed. One can show that these assumptions allow us to conduct the analysis as if producer prices are fixed. Goods will be denoted by subscript i and households by the superscript h.

The formulation of the problem should make it clear that the same model applies to public sector pricing of good i where we interpret p_i as the marginal cost (assumed constant for simplicity although this is not essential) and t_i as the excess over marginal cost. Thus it is immediately obvious that the final price of a good sold directly to the final consumer by the public sector should *not* be marginal cost since optimal t_i would only exceptionally be zero. Public sector prices should include an element of taxation for goods sold to the final consumer, i.e. there should be a contribution to resource mobilization or revenue raising.

The solution to problem (12.1)–(12.2) gives us the many-person Ramsey rule for optimal commodity taxation. It is useful to have this in front of us since it is the simplest embodiment of the basic trade-off between equity and efficiency in taxation. The rule is derived straightforwardly from the first-order conditions for the Lagrangean, $V + \lambda(R - \bar{R})$, for the above maximization problem; λ is the Lagrange multiplier on the revenue constraint, i.e. the social marginal utility of government income. We have

$$\frac{\partial V}{\partial t_i} + \lambda \frac{\partial R}{\partial t_i} = 0. \tag{12.3a}$$

A little manipulation yields

$$\frac{\Sigma_k t_k \Sigma_h s_{ik}^h}{X_i} = -\sigma_i, \qquad (12.3b)^1$$

where we define σ_i in the many household case, by

$$\sigma_i = 1 - \bar{b} \, \Sigma_h \frac{x_i^h}{X_i} \frac{b^h}{\bar{b}}, \qquad (12.3c)$$

where s_{ik}^h is the compensated (Slutsky) effect of a marginal increase in the price of the kth good on the demand for the ith good by household h (the relevant utility level is at the post-tax equilibrium) and σ_i is negatively related to the covariance between the (net) social marginal utility of income, b^h, of household h. 'Net' means here that there is an adjustment to the social marginal utility, β^h, for the marginal propensity to spend on taxes out of extra income. The average of b^h is $\bar{b}$—with an optimal lump-sum grant $\bar{b} = 1$. The consumption of good i by household h is x_i^h. Thus σ_i is higher the more the good is consumed by those who have a low social marginal utility of income (e.g. the rich). The left-hand side of (12.3b) may be interpreted as a proportional change in quantity (see below) of the ith good. So (12.3b) tells us how much the ith good is 'hit' by taxation in terms of its proportional reduction.

We may interpret (12.3) in terms of a trade-off between efficiency and equity. If there is a single household then we may think of the problem as one of efficiency—raising a given revenue from the household at minimum cost. Of course in that case a poll-tax might well be an option and, if it is, it provides the best way of raising revenue. If, however, we are confined to commodity taxes then we can characterize their optimal structure by noting that, with one household, σ_i is independent of i (from (12.3c)'). Then 12.3(b) gives us the Ramsey rule that the left-hand side is independent of i: this is often interpreted as saying that (for small taxes) the proportional reduction in compensated demand arising from taxes should be the same for all goods (t_k measures the price change and the Slutsky terms the compensated responses in demand to the price change). The same result holds if we are not concerned with distribution in the sense that b^h is independent of h. Crudely speaking the efficiency result is to tax goods which are in inelastic demand, although as we have seen the correct expression is in

---

[1] We substitute

$$\partial V/\partial t_i = -\Sigma_h \beta^h x_i^h, \text{ and } \partial R/\partial t_i = X_i + \mathbf{t} \cdot \partial X/\partial t_i$$

and we use the Slutsky decomposition of demand derivatives ($\partial x_k/\partial t_i = s_{ik} - x_i \partial x_k/\partial M$) where M is lump-sum income. In the one-person case $\partial V/\partial t_i = -\alpha x_i$, where α is the marginal utility of income, and σ_i is given by

$$\sigma_i = -\alpha + \lambda(1 - \Sigma_k t_k \partial x_k/\partial M). \qquad (12.3c)'$$

terms of quantity reductions and compensated demands. The partial equilibrium version of this analysis is to tax goods in inverse relation to the price elasticity of demand (where we ignore income distribution). Some intuitive support survives the transplantation to general equilibrium but the partial version can be highly misleading, for example, when we discuss uniformity of proportional commodity taxes (see below). This may seem inegalitarian in that it would lead to taxation of necessities but then we have explicitly ignored distribution.

If, in the many-consumer case, with the possibility of combination of a poll-tax and indirect taxes, the government is indifferent to distribution (b^h is equal for all h), then the right-hand side of (12.3b) is zero. All revenue is then raised through the lump-sum tax and indirect taxes are zero. In this case indirect taxes may be justified on distributional grounds, as they finance reductions in the poll-tax, which bears more heavily on the poor.

Where we *are* concerned with distribution then (12.3) tells us that the reduction in compensated demand should be more for goods consumed relatively more by those with low net social marginal utility of income (b^h). We might think of those with low b^h as the rich and it is in this sense that we orientate taxes towards the consumption of the better-off. Thus (12.3) captures the essential elements of the trade-off between equity and efficiency in the standard analysis of optimal commodity taxation. Some further insight into the structure of these equations is provided when we discuss marginal tax reform (see equations (12.5) – (12.7) below).

The expression (12.3b) is known as the many-person Ramsey rule and also allows us to investigate the relationship between indirect taxation and other tax or subsidy instruments and the appropriate balance between them. Suppose, for example, we can make lump-sum transfers which depend on the demographic characteristics of the household. An example would be a subsidized rice ration where the amount depends on household composition. The model of (12.1) and (12.2) is then augmented to include the influence of the grants on household welfare and demands and we take off their costs from $t \cdot X$ in (12.2). The optimality condition for the transfers can then be combined with (12.3) to analyse the appropriate construction of policies. One can then show (see Deaton and Stern, 1986) that if the Engel curves are linear and parallel but where the intercepts can vary with household composition, factors supplied are separable in the utility function from consumption goods, and if the grants are set optimally then commodity taxes should be at the same proportional rate. Intuitively, all the redistribution that is desirable is carried out through the lump-sum grants which are financed by uniform commodity taxation, and there is no justification for further redistribution through differentiation of commodity taxes since everyone has the same marginal propensity to spend on each good. To put it another way efficiency points us to taxing necessities and distribution towards luxuries; under special assumptions about the shape of preferences *and* the setting of direct taxes, the two effects cancel and the role of indirect taxes is simply to raise revenue for the grants which act as a basic income guarantee related to household composition.

The formal results of the last few years have allowed a better understanding of both indirect taxation and of the balance between direct and indirect taxation than was possible from previous discussions which simply listed some of the things to be borne in mind. Having seen the assumptions which are used in establishing the results we are in a position to see how far they help in analysing the problems of developing countries. In our judgement they are valuable in three ways. First, they train the intuition to understand what is important in an argument about the structure of taxes and thus help in organizing practical enquiry and in using empirical results. Second, they help in further research because in modifying the models to be more appropriate for developing countries one has a baseline for building new models and judging results. Third, they lead rather naturally to the theory of reform which allows one to devise practical checks on optimality conditions and on desirable directions of movement. Formula (12.3) does not provide a practical basis for calculating what taxes should be. The optimum-tax model is a bench-mark, not a device for calculating optimal taxes in practice. The amount of information on the demand structure which would be required could not be available (see Deaton, 1987).

An example of the first concerns the level of the lump-sum grant which emerged in the special model considered by Deaton and Stern as the central redistributive tool. This leads us to ask whether a system of lump-sum grants related to household structure is possible. In many developing countries one does find some transfers through rationing systems (particularly for food) which are rather like lump-sum grants, the rations being often related to family structure (subsidized education or health services provide further examples). Where rations are resaleable then from the formal point of view they are just like lump-sum transfers (and even if they are not resaleable they are like lump-sum transfers if the level is lower than total purchases of the commodity). Thus a prominent feature of an argument concerning whether indirect taxes should be uniform is a judgement concerning the optimality or otherwise of the rations. This judgement can itself be structured since we have an explicit condition for the optimality in terms of the net social marginal utilities of income, the b^h; the average value of these net social marginal utilities in terms of public income should be one (if the average value were greater, for example, the transfer should be increased). With explicit value-judgements (the welfare weights, β^h), a knowledge of taxes, t, and an estimate of the demand system this can be checked (see, for example, the Ahmad and Stern analysis of reform in India, Section 3). More generally the results tell us that the interrelations between different parts of a tax system will be crucial in that the design of one part depends sensitively on the existence of options and the choice of policy elsewhere. Thus it is of special importance in developing countries to scrutinize carefully the availability of a wide range of instruments and to ask whether those that are used have been appropriately adjusted.

The second class of lessons involves the relaxation of some of the assumptions of the simple model to better describe developing countries. There should be no delusion that one can specify a single model for all developing countries—see Newbery and Stern (1987*a*) for a collection of models. There are, however, at least two common features of poor countries which should be accommodated. Production often takes place in units which cannot be described adequately by (competitive) firms facing prices distinct from those of consumers and producing under constant returns to scale. Peasant agriculture is an obvious and central example. Further, one cannot reasonably assume that all goods can be taxed. Whilst models which deal with these features in a direct way can be, and have been constructed, it is important to recognize that they do not require us to jettison immediately all of the standard model and its lessons. Thus, for example, if production goes on in the peasant household which faces consumer prices for its purchases and sales then the model is formally unaffected and one simply interprets demands and demand responses as being net of household production. And the optimal tax rules (12.3) are first-order conditions for those taxes which can be chosen and thus apply for the subset of taxes which are set optimally.

The shadow value, λ, of government revenue is endogenous in the model of (12.1) and (12.2) and does not need separate specification. It will depend, however, *inter alia* on the revenue requirement $\bar{R}$. In terms of the first-order conditions (12.3) for the problem $\bar{R}$ plays no explicit role (it comes into the solution, of course, since the constraint must be satisfied) but we can think of a desire for more revenue being reflected in a higher λ. Thus one can write government objectives to include a term for government revenue, suppress the constraint containing $\bar{R}$, specify λ, and then think of the eventual revenue as being endogenous. Then the weight on revenue can be discussed in terms of λ, and, for example, a government that attached a high value to public investment would have a high λ. In the dynamic context the value of investment is itself endogenous and this is discussed in Section 5. Generally, as should be obvious, the higher is λ the higher are taxes and the lower subsidies.

The third class of lessons from the standard optimization models concern their extension to reform. Suppose we start from a given status quo which is not an optimum and try to identify improving directions of reform. We show how such an investigation may be usefully structured. We retain the notation and model of (12.1) and (12.2) but no longer assume optimization. We define

$$\lambda_i = -\frac{\partial V}{\partial t_i} \bigg/ \frac{\partial R}{\partial t_i}. \tag{12.4}$$

We can interpret λ_i as the marginal cost in terms of social welfare of raising an extra unit of revenue from increasing the taxation of good i; $-\partial V/\partial t_i$ represents the welfare cost of a unit change and the inverse of $\partial R/\partial t_i$ tells us the magnitude of the change in t_i required to raise one rupee. What matteres for policy then is the relative size of the λ_i, i.e. if $\lambda_i > \lambda_j$ then we increase welfare at constant revenue by increasing the tax on good i and decreasing it on good j (optimality would require λ_i to be independent of i). The analysis places the status quo in a central position and asks 'Given where we are, in what direction should we move?' It seems quite likely (and it is confirmed by our experience) that the type of language involved is more easily understood by the policy-maker than the notion of a large move towards some optimum which may emerge from a model of which he is suspicious. This may be an advantage for the applied worker who is collecting data, although much of his underlying model is the same (but he can assume rather less, see next subsection). We assume here that producer prices are fixed. The assumptions are examined further in Section 4.

As we shall see in Section 3 an advantage of this approach is that it uses less information than is required for optimality—essentially we need only 'local' information (demand responses around the status quo), rather than the 'global' information (a full description of demand functions for all price vectors) required for the analysis of optimality. Further it allows considerations which are not captured in the model to be set alongside the calculated welfare increase in an appraisal of the costs and benefits of change. This type of discussion is less straightforward when the full optimum is computed since it is not easily integrated into a calculation whose output is a specific set of optimal rates. A disadvantage is that directions only and not step size are identified. And there will usually be a choice between many welfare-improving directions which, like that for step size, must be taken using criteria outside the model. Examples of relevant considerations might be (*a*) adminstrative convenience (e.g. which directions are easily achievable using existing tools), or (*b*) political acceptability which may limit how far one can go, or (*c*) confidence in estimates of the critical parameters working in favour of a particular direction, or (*d*) the existence of 'paternalistic' social preferences (e.g. the taxation of 'bads' such as alcohol or tobacco). Such questions are typically ignored in the optimality calculation. The use of expression (12.4) requires the simple assumptions about production used in the model of (12.1) and (12.2) and is discussed further in Sections 4 and 6.

The basic theories of public economics can then take us quite a long way in thinking about the problems of developing countries. In the remainder of this chapter we shall discuss some of the complications and difficulties of extending and applying the theory, before putting together some simple principles and lessons.

3. Applied Policy Models

Applied policy models can have many sectors or just a few and they can be used to study both marginal and non-marginal reform. Each of the four possible cases which arise has its uses and examples are available in the literature. We discuss them briefly in turn.

Policy models with many sectors and for the study of non-marginal changes are often grouped under the heading of computable general equilibrium models (CGEs). It is unnecessary to review these in detail because there are excellent surveys (see e.g. Shoven (1983), Shoven and Whalley (1984), and Robinson (1989), for applications see e.g. Dervis *et al.* (1982), or for a country case-study (Mexico) see Kehoe and Serra-Puche (1983). Typically production functions are constant elasticity of substitution (CES), factor markets are perfect, and preferences are of a fairly standard type (often also CES). The free parameters in the model are chosen so that the national accounts structure fits for a particular base-year. Policy variables are then changed and the new equilibrium is recomputed. Household utilities can be compared before and after the change to come to a judgement as to whether the change is beneficial.

This is not the place to discuss these models at length and we shall confine ourselves to some brief comments concerning their use in policy discussion. First, they require a very large number of parameters many or most of which are essentially imposed exogenously. Second, the scope for sensitivity analysis is rather narrow. Thus one can vary an elasticity of substitution fairly easily but it would generally require a great deal of work to change the structure of a market. Third, and related to the first two points, it is not easy to make an intuitive assessment of the role of crucial assumptions in determining the answers. Thus they often have a tendency to be used as black boxes with few questions asked as to where answers are coming from. Fourth, the detail they provide on the consumption side is generally rather less than would be required in coming to a judgement about the different types of gainers and losers—typically there may be 20 or so household groups compared with a household survey of five or ten thousand households. Frequently it is the fate of different types of households which is crucial in determining the attractiveness or otherwise of a reform and one cannot characterize in advance just which those households will be. Increasingly the appraisal of taxes is being influenced by analyses utilizing the detail at the household level (see Atkinson and Sutherland, 1987).

On the more positive side the models are explicit and they do allow some flexibility. The greater detail in production may pick up important points which might be missed in a more aggregated framework. And the models allow estimation of changes in factor prices. However, some of the detail in the results is spurious in the sense that it is the consequence of fairly arbitrary assumptions and the calculations for a particular industry would be unlikely to substitute for an industry study if some special sectors were at issue.

There are two main advantages of using more aggregated computable applied models. First, it is often possible to gain a good intuititive understanding of how the model works. Second, they can allow optimization. There are a number of recent examples of the study of non-marginal changes in such policy models (e.g. Braverman *et al.*, 1987). Heady and Mitra (1987) provide in addition some optimization. They also show how the model's simple structure can be used to discuss the analytical framework before embarking on computations.

The marginal approach, as described briefly at the end of Section 2 can be followed in both multi-sectoral and more aggregated models. Its first detailed application was by Ahmad and Stern (e.g. 1984, 1987, and forthcoming) in the study of Indian indirect taxes and (1986) for Pakistan. In order to see what is involved we write out (12.4), the expression for the marginal social cost of revenue arising from an adjustment of the ith tax (12.4), more fully.

$$\lambda_i = \frac{\Sigma_h \beta^h x_i^h}{X_i + \mathbf{t} \cdot \dfrac{\partial \mathbf{X}}{\partial q_i}}. \tag{12.5}$$

Intuitively the numerator represents the money cost (x_i^h) to households of a unit price change weighted by the welfare weight, β^h, and aggregated across households. The denominator measures the response of revenue to the tax change and involves the vector of demand responses, $\partial \mathbf{X}/\partial q_i$. Note that only the *aggregate* demands and demand responses appear in the denominator. An alternative way of writing (12.5) is as the distributional characteristic D_i divided by a tax elasticity.

$$\lambda_i = \frac{\rho_i D_i}{\eta_i}, \tag{12.6}$$

where

$$D_i = \frac{\Sigma_i \beta^h x_i^h}{X_i}, \ \rho_i = \frac{t_i X_i}{R}, \text{ and } \eta_i = \frac{t_i}{R} \frac{\partial R}{\partial t_i}. \tag{12.7}$$

The distributional characteristic is the average of the x_i^h weighted by the β^h divided by the unweighted average, ρ_i is the share of the ith good in tax revenue, and η_i is the elasticity of tax revenue with respect to the ith specific tax. One may see λ_i therrefore as the product of a distributional term and an 'efficiency' term since distributional judgements do not enter ρ_i and η_i.

The data requirements are an estimated demand system, the tax element in the price of final goods, and an expenditure survey. These are available in practice in a number of countries. One also needs to specify the welfare weights and we would want to display a number of examples to show how different views on distribution would affect favoured directions for reform. As for the optimality analysis, results will depend on the shape of demand functions but in this case the marginal analysis is less sensitive since we need to assume only knowledge of demand derivatives around the status quo and use actual values for current consumption levels (from a household expenditure survey) and not those which have been fitted to a demand equation. The calculation of the tax element in the price of final goods requires knowledge of the role of intermediate-goods taxation and the input–output structure, together with assumptions concerning shifting (see Ahmad and Stern (1987) for a discussion of an Indian example). It must be acknowledged, however, that one cannot be confident about the data inputs, particularly demand responses. This is not a worry specific to this method, however, since any reform has to be concerned with revenue response and this will depend on how demands will change.

The discussion, so far, has been based on the notion of 'effective taxes', as if the government were able to raise its required revenue from the taxation of consumption goods. However, most developing countries rely on the taxation of intermediate goods to a greater or lesser extent, given the availability of convenient tax handles. As Little *et al.* (1970, p. 137) also argue, this is generally inadvisable, since it creates distortions affecting input choices. The arguments in favour of taxing intermediates are largely administrative: that collection costs are lower for taxes on intermediate goods, which are also less easy to avoid; or that the intermediate good enters mainly into the production of a consumption good that is not so easy to tax. Examples include the taxation of petroleum as a means of taxing the transport sector and road-users, or the taxation of yarn as a means of taxing textiles. As Ahmad and Stern (1987) show, the taxation of intermediates can have unintended consequences. For example, in India while the government in the mid 1970s had a policy of encouraging the handloom and khadi industry, and there was a direct subsidy for this sector, there was in fact a positive 'effective tax' given the heavy taxation of intermediate goods.

The costs of administration may be formally incorporated into the reform analysis as follows. Suppose that an extra rupee collected via the ith

good costs γ_i in administration so that, net $1 - \gamma_i$ is raised. Then to raise one rupee net we have to collect $1/(1 - \gamma_i)$ gross so that the marginal social loss from one rupee net is $\lambda_i/(1 - \gamma_i)$. We would switch a net rupee on the margin from tax i to tax j if

$$\frac{1}{(1 - \gamma_i)}\lambda_i > \frac{1}{(1 - \gamma_j)}\lambda_j \tag{12.8}$$

or

$$\frac{\lambda_i}{\lambda_j} > \frac{1 - \gamma_i}{1 - \gamma_j}. \tag{12.9}$$

Although estimates of γ_i and γ_j may not be easy (for example allocation of tax authority expenditures is not straightforward), it may be possible once estimates of λ_i and λ_j have been obtained to come to a judgement as to which side of (12.9) is the larger. For example if λ_i/λ_j is 1.5, then if we guess that γ_i is around 0.25 rupees per rupee of gross revenue, then provided γ_j is less than 0.50 we would want to switch on the margin from i to j.

The marginal method is now being applied to some of the more aggregated models (see e.g. Newbery, 1987a). This allows one to avoid some of the more unsatisfactory assumptions about production and factor markets made in the more detailed framework (although at the cost of less information on the consumption side). These assumptions can also be relaxed by using shadow prices, the subject of Section 4.

4. The General Theory of Reform and Shadow Prices

The reform analysis discussed in Section 3 forms part of the more general theory of shadow prices. This has been examined at length in Drèze and Stern (1987) and a detailed discussion will not be provided. Our aim here is to bring out the general principles and show how they provide a unifying framework for much of policy analysis. The treatment is based on Drèze and Stern (1987). Technical details are provided in the Appendix.

The shadow price of a good is defined as the increase in social welfare made available by an extra unit of public supply of the good (equivalently it is the opportunity cost in terms of social welfare if we think of a reduction in supply). In the models we have been discussing (using the Diamond–Mirrlees framework) shadow and producer prices will be equal. Generally this will not be true because, for example, there is rationing, monopoly, limits on government tax tools, a desire to influence income distribution via the relative profitability of different activities, and so on. When shadow prices and producer prices are unequal it is remarkable that much of the previous analysis generalizes simply by replacing producer prices by shadow prices.

One can show that, under fairly general conditions, a reform in some policy tool can be evaluated by looking at its direct effect on household welfare and then subtracting the cost at shadow prices of the extra demands generated. For example, an increase in the old-age pension can be appraised by comparing the social value of the direct benefit of an extra pound to pensioners (their social marginal utility of income appropriately measured) with the cost at shadow prices of the extra demands for goods from the pensioners arising from their extra income.

It can also be demonstrated that the reform analysis of equations (12.5)– (12.8) can be generalized by introducing the notion of shadow taxes and shadow government revenue. Shadow consumer taxes are the difference between consumer and shadow prices, and shadow producer taxes, the difference between shadow prices and producer prices. Shadow government revenue is defined correspondingly (see Appendix). A proposed reform is then appraised by comparing the direct effect on households with its impact on shadow revenue. Thus we should cost government schemes *not* in terms of their effects on government revenue but on shadow government revenue.

There are many economies where shadow prices have been calculated. We have seen here that their use is not confined to project appraisal but applies also to the analysis of policy reform in general. Care should be taken, however, to ensure consistency of the models used in the reform discussion and those used to calculate shadow prices.

The shadow prices capture a great deal of information, essentially the full general equilibrium effects on welfare of a policy change. In principle they should be derived from a fully articulated general equilibrium model and one could argue that if such a model is available then welfare effects of policy changes can be calculated directly. However, in many cases the set of shadow prices will be a tool which is more flexible, reliable, less demanding, and more easily understood than the full model. They provide sufficient statistics for policy from the full model and can be discussed directly. And one supposes that corresponding to any plausible set of shadow prices one could construct a general equilibrium model and welfare judgements which would be consistent with the shadow prices. Hence, for example, if one argued that population growth, and better labour-market policies were likely to bring about a substantial reduction in the shadow wage, one could then examine fairly rapidly the consequences for tax policy. On the other hand it may involve a great deal of effort to redesign a large model (if such already exists) to take account of the changed assumptions. At the same time one hopes that (or should try to check that) variations of assumptions in one area do not produce huge changes in the whole shadow price vector, otherwise the credibility of the approach would be undermined (although such a situation would be likely to make any approach perilous).

5. Dynamic Assumptions

The theories described so far have had n goods and time has not appeared explicitly. We now ask how they can be reinterpreted in a dynamic context and what extensions or modifications would be desirable (for a more detailed discussion of the issues raised see Newbery and Stern, 1987b). The familiar Arrow–Debreu model of general equilibrium which underlies the standard models presented in Section 2 can be interpreted in the usual way as a full intertemporal model provided all goods are distinguished by their date of availability. Thus, if there are N physically different goods and T periods, there will be NT markets (a similar interpretation in terms of uncertainty and different states of nature is also possible). The standard results in welfare economics relating competitive equilibrium to Pareto efficiency then apply (and one can extend this to infinite horizons provided one adds an assumption about asymptotic behaviour to rule out oversaving). Similarly the Diamond and Mirrlees taxation model can be applied to this framework too. Thus consumers maximize utility, defined over the indefinite future, with knowledge of future consumer prices and incomes and make commitments for supplies of services and purchase of goods. Producers maximize the present value of profits at the producer prices which they face. The Ramsey taxes which are the difference between consumer and producer prices then define a tax system over the indefinite future. All producers face the same interest rates, profits taxation applies to present values and is not based on period-by-period returns, and savings would in general be taxed (producer and consumer prices will differ) to raise revenue and improve the intertemporal and interpersonal distribution of income.

The model is a useful point of reference but raises a number of basic difficulties for applied policy analysis for developing countries, many of which apply to analyses for developed countries also, and examples of which follow. First, many of the postulated markets do not exist. Second, it is difficult to separate savings and investment decisions (and thus consumer and producer intertemporal prices) for a large fraction of the private sector. For example, many or most business start-ups are financed out of individual savings (see Little *et al.* 1987). This problem arises in part from lack of markets but also has to do with the poor development of financial intermediaries, asymmetric perceptions or information (the bank may not share my view of my chances of success), and costs of enforcing arrangements in an informal sector. Third, the kind of dynamic optimization by individuals and firms which is assumed is implausible for individuals who may have a hazy vision of the future and ill-formed and complex preferences over future outcomes. This is not to say that they are irrational but that the detailed dynamic optimization model with unrestricted trading possibilities may not have an overwhelming claim as the appropriate representation of their behaviour. There is no doubt that all these problems arise in some shape or form in the static model but they are particularly pervasive and severe in the dynamic context. There has not in our judgement been great success in the literature in intergrating these features into a dynamic tax analysis, but we shall discuss below some models which are specifically designed for a dynamic context.

Further, there are particular features and difficulties which arise when we move to dynamic problems. For example, there may be incentives to renege on previous commitments or announced policies (sometimes called 'dynamic inconsistency'). Second, the open-endedness of the economy can lead to problems of dynamic inefficiency of the kind which do not arise in a static economy (e.g. it is easy to write down growth problems where no optimum exists, essentially because there appear to be grounds in the model for postponing consumption indefinitely). Third, there are problems associated with how individuals are forced to observe budget constraints (there have to be mechanisms to prevent build-up of debt in circumstances where individuals can promise to pay later). Fourth, in models of overlapping generations, transfers between generations can produce types of inefficiency which do not arise in static problems (e.g. if each generation is endowed with a chocolate than the first generation can be made better off by each generation passing a chocolate to the preceding generation whilst none of the others is worse off).

The discussion of practical policy towards taxation in developing countries has avoided the more esoteric modelling problems and has expressed the dynamic issues in terms of broader or more aggregated concepts such as savings, investment, and growth. Much of the early post-war literature on development (see e.g. Lewis, 1954) placed the rate of growth at the centre of the stage and many authors have singled out government concern, and perceived responsibility, for raising the rate of saving and so, it is hoped, growth as a major distinguishing feature of public finance in developing countries (e.g. Eshag, 1983; Goode, 1984; Prest, 1972). Developed countries may worry about the growth rate too but often greater emphasis is placed on the rate of technical progress than on savings and investment *per se*. And the experience of developing countries in the 30 years since Lewis was writing tells us that raising the savings rate is not necessarily a sufficient condition for rapid growth. For example, India and many other developing countries have savings and investment rates between 18 and 25 per cent in common with most of the industrial market economies (see World Bank, 1988).

If the growth objective is firmly adopted then governments should take careful account of the effects of its policies on saving and the level and productivity of investment. Policies for the encouragement of savings and

investment include favourable tax treatment of saving, promotion of financial institutions, and interest rate policy. One would like to examine these
policies in the consequentialist manner by first predicting their outcomes
and then evaluating the changes. A major problem is that the elasticities of
response are very hard to judge. This applies to both savings and investment.

There has been a considerable recent literature on modelling and estimating savings responses in developed countries. A useful survey is provided by King (1985) who argues that one often finds that life-cycle models
are consistent with behaviour for 70–75 per cent of the population but not
for the remaining 20–25 per cent, and one may suggest that for this minority credit constraints may be important. Whilst the data underlying these
studies are very rich compared to those available for developing countries,
the researchers have not found it easy to pick up the response of savings to
post-tax returns, an aspect which is crucial for the design of tax policy. The
lessons for developing countries of these studies may be as follows. First,
the 20–25 per cent for whom life-cycle models are inappropriate may
be much larger in developing countries where financial markets are less
well-developed. Second, it is unlikely to be possible given current data to
establish an interest elasticity of saving for developing countries. In the
meantime policy has to be formulated and it seems sensible to avoid
losing substantial amounts of tax revenue in schemes for the promotion
of savings whose net effect may be very obscure. Further one should try
to avoid creating tax anomalies which may arise from special treatment of
different kinds of savings since they can lose tax revenue and redistribute
income in favour of the more rich and knowledgeable, and may have little
further effect other than the rearrangement of some portfolios.

There have been a number of applied policy models focused on taxation
and savings for developed countries but they will not be reviewed in detail
here (for recent discussion see Chamley, 1983; Kotlikoff, 1984; and Newbery and Stern, 1987a). In most of the models, however detailed, the interest elasticity is a crucial variable yet it is one on which we have little
reliable in the way of estimates, see e.g., Giovannini (1985). The policy
simulations have often been concerned with switches from income to
consumption-based taxes and a central issue has been the effect on capital
accumulation via saving.

Our conclusion from this brief discussion of dynamic issues is that similar
priciples to the static analysis can be applied but that our present state of
knowledge of response is not firmly based. Nevertheless a concern to
promote saving and growth can be embodied in the techniques which we
used to guide public policy. Thus, for example, a premium on savings can
be incorporated in shadow prices (see e.g. Little and Mirrlees, 1984; Drèze
and Stern, 1987). One should try to discover the consequences of proposed

reforms for savings but be circumspect about confident claims for the likely effects of special tax concessions. There is no convincing theoretical argument in favour of expenditure rather than income taxes although one should be aware of revenue losses associated with separate treatment of capital and income. On the investment side promising areas for study of the dynamic effects of public policy are the potential of financial markets in supplying credit more easily, constraints on investment associated with infrastructure such as water and electricity supplies, and the pricing of public sector enterprises. Thus there may well be substantial scope for promoting the profitability of investments in ways which do not involve big tax concessions. Arguments for tax concessions should be examined rather carefully to check that any claimed response is likely to be present. Otherwise the concessions may simply act as a transfer payment. It should be emphasized that there is no assertion here that we should assume from our lack of knowledge that savings and investment actually are inelastic. Our ignorance should make us cautious and we should not therefore tax investment heavily on the dubious grounds that we 'may as well assume' it is interest-inelastic. At the same time the static analysis of taxes implicitly assumes that there are no strong intertemporal linkages particular to certain goods which are sufficiently large to change the whole picture.

6. Taxes and Production

One of the most striking contrasts between discussions of public economics for developed and for developing countries lies in the treatment of taxes and production. The concentration in the theory for developed countries has been on government revenue, on the allocation of consumption, and on factor supply—issues which are within the spirit of the standard model of Section 2. The assumption of fixed producer prices is common. On the other hand in the study of developing countries great attention has been focused on the incentives facing producers in terms of the effects of government policies on the prices they face—these considerations lie at the heart of discussions of effective protection, shadow prices, and so on. Thus many have argued that the consequences of government policy, particularly concerning taxes, in developing countries have been the wrong pattern of outputs, whereas in developed countries criticism is often focused on the alleged curtailment of incentives for factor supply and on the distributive effects on different types of household.

The basic principles of the normative analysis of policy reform when shadow prices are not equal to producer prices are provided in Section 4. One calculates the direct effect on households of a policy change and then adjusts this for the value at shadow prices of the net changes in excess demand associated with the direct effects in order to pick up the general equilibrium repercussions of the change. It is interesting to contrast this approach with discussions based on effective protection, a very popular applied tool used in discussions of tariffs and the pattern of production (see the *Journal of International Economics* symposium (1983), where a number of aspects of effective protection are examined). The first point to note is that the rate of effective protection, defined as the value added at domestic prices less that at world prices (as a proportion of value added at world prices) is not a normative concept but an attempt to describe what happens to value added in different industries as a result of tariffs. It is often rapidly transformed into a normative statement with the suggestion that resources should be transferred to sectors with a lower effective rate of protection from those with a higher.

As a normative suggestion concerning resource movements the argument is unsatisfactory. First, it takes no account of possible divergences between market prices and social opportunity costs (or shadow prices) for non-traded and factor inputs. Once proper account is taken of the former we have domestic resource cost (or DRC) calculations and the further step of treating the social opportunity cost of factors carefully takes us to a system of shadow prices. Second, the adjustment prescription based on effective protection takes no account of the scale of movement. If coefficients for non-factor inputs are fixed it would appear to tell us to transfer an indefinite amount into the activity with the lowest effective protective rate. Third, one cannot in general argue that when there is substitution amongst inputs and factors that resource flows follow the direction indicated by rates of effective protection; thus the effect of a tariff structure may be to direct resources to an industry with a lower rate of effective protection (see Dixit and Norman, 1980, ch. 5). Fourth, the question as to why one might want to protect is not put. Whilst the arguments for protection are often spurious one should not assume that they always are.

Effective protection calculations are also often used in discussions of tariff reform in that it is suggested that tariffs should be adjusted to make lower the effective protection rates for industries with higher rates of protection. Again this is unsatisfactory. There is nothing to suggest that uniform effective protection rates have any general optimality properties. As we argued in the previous section, in the absence of lump-sum taxes a government concerned with incentives and distribution should in an open-economy competitive world have taxes on final sales only, irrespective of origin. Thus there would be no tariffs or any other taxes affecting relative producer prices. And the taxes on final sales would not usually be uniform. One would require an articulated model with a careful statement concerning constraints on policies to justify any assertion that uniform effective rates of protection are optimal and it is very unclear how such an argument could be constructed (except for the first-best economy where net effective rates of protection would be uniform at zero).

The main advantage of calculations of effective rates of protection lies in reminding policy-makers that their actions affect not only output prices but also input costs and in making some of these effects explicit. As we have argued, however, they are unreliable guides to policy reform. The central notion in the area is that of shadow prices and greater use of this concept outside the area of project appraisal could be valuable.

The analysis of tax reform which incorporates an account of production and general equilibrium when producer prices and shadow prices are unequal would essentially add an extra term to an analysis of costs and benefits of tax reform. Thus, in addition to revenue and direct effects on household welfare one takes account of the losses associated with any shift in demand towards industries with shadow prices higher than producer prices, i.e. one subtracts $(v - p) \, \Delta X$ corresponding to a demand shift ΔX arising from the tax reform (see equation (12.16) in the Appendix to this chapter). This is a suggestion which should apply to policy reform for both developed and less developed countries. We find the general assumption that producer prices are equal to shadow prices for developed countries a little surprising. Is it true, for example, that the labour market clears under conditions of perfect competition? Are there tariffs? Does the pricing policy for major inputs to production such as electricity, oil, transports, and so on, avoid either implicit taxes or subsidies and reflect social marginal costs? Are all final goods taxed and are the rates optimally set? If the answer to such questions is negative then one must take seriously the possibility that producer and shadow prices do not coincide.

7. The Taxation of Agriculture

The analysis has, to this point, been mainly theoretical. We have been trying to assemble what theory has to offer in the provision of methods of applied policy analysis and in the formulation of principles for the setting of policy and by which it may be judged. In the remainder of the chapter we shall draw this analysis together in a discussion of particular taxes and in a set of guide-lines or principles which summarize some of the lessons of the theory. In so doing we must bring to the centre of the stage some of the practical difficulties which governments and tax authorities face. We begin with the taxation of agriculture.

There are many reasons why the taxation of agriculture deserves special study in developing countries and cannot be treated as just another example of a production activity in the standard competitive model. First, it is of central importance in both employment and output, the contributions often being in the region of $\frac{1}{2}-\frac{3}{4}$ and $\frac{1}{4}-\frac{1}{2}$ respectively. Second, there are strong limitations on the tax tools available to the government, in particular it is often impossible to tax transactions between producers and consumers, the difficulty arising both when the 'transaction' is within the household and when sales are between households or in informal markets. Third, the rural labour market and working arrangements dominated by agriculture, interact directly and indirectly with labour markets throughout the economy with important repercussions for all households and production activities. Fourth, land is a crucial input so that the problems with taxing rents must play a role. Fifth, the government is often the main or only supplier of vital inputs such as water and electricity so that its pricing policy must be integrated into the taxation of production. Sixth, food, its availability, distribution, and price is of such importance to welfare that all governments have to take some responsibility for its price, quality, and security.

The subject is clearly a major one and we do not have the space to go into details of data, arguments, and models. In this section we shall simply try to bring out some of the major issues; we draw on the introductory chapter (Newbery) to Part V of Newbery and Stern (1987*a*). We examine briefly some of the main influences on the incidence of agricultural taxes; the question of the extent of taxation of agriculture as a whole, and the allocation of resources between agriculture and industry; and availability and use of different kinds of tax instruments towards agriculture.

7.1. Tax Incidence

With agriculture playing such an important role in output and labour markets it is clear that one has to take a general equilibrium view and, therefore, there will be many influences on the incidence of taxes. We consider, briefly, four: the difficulty of taxing food transactions within the country, the elasticities of supplies and demands, effects operating through the labour market, and the variety in technological choice by farmers.

First, if transactions between producers and consumers of a food commodity cannot be taxed then the price for producers and consumers (apart from selling and transport costs) will be the same. Let us suppose for example that the good (rice, say) is imported (without quantity restrictions and from a competitive world market) and subsidized. This will act as a tax on producers, as well as subsidy to the domestic price (the domestic price is the world price less the subsidy). This means that the (marginal) incidence of the subsidy is as an imposition on producers related to their production and as a benefit to consumers related to their consumption.

Second, where the good is non-traded, the incidence of a tax will depend on supply and demand elasticities. Consider for example a tax on an input such as water. The effect on food prices will depend on the elasticity of net supply of foods with respect to input and output prices and the elasticity of demand. Third, taxes on agriculture will in general affect the wages and real incomes of both urban and rural workers. They will affect different kinds of workers in different ways. A number of models can be constructed and we shall not go into details, but it should be clear that the consequences flowing through the labour market may be of importance for the incomes of the poor, for profits, and for government revenue. Fourth, on judging incidence one must remember the very broad range of production techniques one finds within agriculture, indeed within a single village. One cannot assume that techniques are homogeneous and thus the pricing and taxing of inputs and the relation of input patterns to outputs should take account of these differences in practices amongst peasant householders and other producers.

7.2. *The Balance between Agriculture and Other Sectors*

The terms of trade between agriculture and industry and the allocation of resources between agricultural and non-agricultural sectors has long been a central topic in discussions of development, see e.g. the early Indian Five-Year Plans (Dixit, 1973; Lipton, 1977). We examine briefly here the influences of some of the issues raised for the analysis of tax policy. There are a number of arguments which have been advanced for turning the terms of trade against agriculture. Given that the discussion is often in terms of a single price and we are looking at the agricultural sector as a whole the discussion is at a fairly aggregated level. First, it may be suggested that aggregate agricultural supply is relatively inelastic. Second, one might argue that investible surplus should be extracted from agriculture to finance growth elsewhere. Third, it might be argued that food producers are relatively well off whereas consumers, rural or urban, are not. We examine these suggestions briefly.

A recent survey by Binswanger *et al.* (1985) has suggested that aggregate own-price elasticities of supply for food are indeed quite low (between 0.1 and 0.3). Individual crop elasticities will, of course, be higher (see e.g. Askari and Cummings, 1976 and Timmer *et al.*, 1983). The second argument which concentrates on dynamic aspects would require detailed justification. The allocation of investment is related to but distinct from its source of finance. One has to look at the revenue costs from different sources and the returns to investment in different sectors. The third suggestion relates to the incidence of taxes. It is not obviously correct that food producers are relatively well off, and incidence may not only be on landowners or producers.

Overall we would suggest that there are no strong and general arguments one way or another. The appropriate terms of trade and their control by government policy would depend on the structure of the economy, investment possibilities, and the availability of tax tools in a particular context. And it should be remembered that agriculture versus industry may not be a very useful way of putting any question. Welfare does not reside in industries or sectors but in households. We should be asking about the distribution and incentive effects of combinations of taxes and of investment policies in different parts of agriculture and industry.

The land tax. As we have emphasized the appropriate policy for any particular tax instrument will depend on the availability and levels of other taxes and policies. We shall therefore examine briefly some of the instruments that exist for the taxation of agriculture and how they might interact. An obvious and important example is the *land tax*. It can be argued that land is in inelastic supply and its distribution is unequal. From the viewpoint of both efficiency and equity it would seem the natural base for taxation and has been seen as such by economists from David Ricardo and Henry George. And historically (see e.g. Bird, 1974) the land tax seems to have been of substantial or dominant importance in many countries (e.g. in India under Mogul and British rule). Now, however, land taxes seem to be a negligible source of revenue. One of the main reasons for this would seem to be that the rich and powerful have been particularly successful in resisting the tax (see Bird, 1974, and Wald, 1959). Land taxation would require careful land records but this is not in principle so difficult (compared to measuring the base for other taxes) when landowners have a strong incentive to establish the legal title to their lands. It can be made progressive by taxing only holdings above a certain level. An important problem arises, however, with land quality. One would want to measure this by looking at its potential income. A number of countries (e.g. Pakistan) do have records which are linked to quality. This raises, however, the further question of whether improved land is in inelastic supply and the answer would often be negative. To this extent the attraction of the efficiency argument for taxing land is diminished.

The reason land taxation becomes difficult is that resistance to proper valuation and collection can be fierce and effective. Apart from possible disincentives to the improvement of land this resistance to effective implementation seems the crucial argument against land taxation. There are two possible reactions. One can either advise governments to attempt to force measures through or take the absence of land taxation as a constraint and devise other taxes. The former course can be perilous for the government, possibly also for the economist, and may damage his credibility as an adviser. We shall discuss some of the alternatives, but, the possible political difficulties notwithstanding, one should not remove land taxation from the agenda without careful discussion and thought concerning the circumstances in the particular country under examination.

Taxation of inputs and outputs. It is interesting to ask how far taxes on inputs and outputs substitute for a land tax. Clearly if the prices of all outputs and inputs are reduced in the same proportion then this is equivalent to a proportional tax on land. This would involve an output tax and an input subsidy. Such a combination is clearly impossible, however, since labour could not be subsidized in this way. An attempt at such a system would therefore distort incentives towards purchased inputs. The example does show, however, that one must examine carefully the effects of combinations of taxes. A tax on marketed surplus, for example, is equivalent to a tax on the purchases by the agricultural sector of non-agricultural goods. This is equivalent to changing the terms of trade against agriculture and is perhaps the most common form of taxation of the agricultural sector in developing countries.

Other possibilities for taxing agriculture include an agricultural income tax and export duties. The first of these raises severe administrative difficulties in measuring income. The second has been quite popular (e.g. for cocoa in Ghana and cotton in Pakistan) but can create considerable distortions given that elasticities of supply of particular crops may be quite high. Note that if supply is inelastic, an export tax is like a land tax, and if the exportable is produced by richer farmers, this need not have an adverse distributional impact.

The different possible methods we have indicated suggest that a careful study of the potential for reforming different combinations of the taxation of outputs, the pricing for publicly supplied inputs, and the taxation of purchased inputs may well yield substantial improvements for revenue, efficiency, and distribution. It is an area where it can be very misleading to look at one agricultural tax in isolation and for which a general equilibrium framework will be important. For examples of empirical work of this kind, see Braverman *et al.* (1987), Heady and Mitra (1987), and Newbery (1987*a*).

8. The Taxation of Income and Profits

From the point of view of a theory which sees change in welfare in terms of effects on households the corporation has a limited role. In the class of models considered in Section 2 the pure profits tax should in general be used where possible (assuming owners of firms do not have very high net social marginal utilities of income) but a corporation tax does not otherwise appear in the models unless one considers it as in part a tax on entrepreneurial or capital services provided by households. In answering the question, however, why there should be a corporation tax within the type of theory we have been examining one can point to four possible responses. First, it acts in part as a tax on monopoly rents or pure profits. Second, it provides a way of taxing foreign owners. Third, it may help in policies designed to promote savings or investment if it is designed so as to encourage the retention rather than distribution of profits. Fourth, because it is already there, in the sense that its removal would provide a windfall gain to groups which are far from impoverished. All of these arguments apply to both developed and developing countries but they may well be stronger in the latter case. Hence the more prominent role of the corporation tax, relative to the personal income tax, in developing countries is not without foundation in the principles we have been discussing. Perhaps the most important reasons, however, for taxing corporations is as a means of collection of taxes on personal incomes. As we have already noted, this applies to foreign owners but it applies to domestic owners too where the system of domestic personal income taxation is weak and easily evaded, particularly by owners of corporations who, we suppose, are not usually amongst the poorest of the population.

The form of the corporation tax can vary greatly depending on its treatment of distributed and undistributed profits, depreciation allowances, inflation, interest payments, and so on. Profits can also be manipulated by multinationals through transfer-pricing, e.g. inflating the costs of certain inputs, or deflating output prices to depress measured profits in countries where corporate taxation is high. These complications require careful scrutiny in the examination of policy for a particular country.

Theoretical and empirical research on the corporation tax is even less easy to present in a coherent and integrated form than it is for other taxes, partly because it sits somewhat unhappily in the economic theory of tax policy. Discussion has focused on a number of issues concerning the possible effects of the tax rather than on attempting to construct a theory of policy design. Further, the effects of the tax are rather difficult to quantify both theoretically and empirically. Thus concentration has often been on the incentives and disincentives associated with different systems rather than the explicit modelling of the full effects of these incentives. Most of the work has been for developed countries although, as ever, the issues apply to developing countries too. However, in the latter case one suspects that the immediate problems are more in devising ways to actually collect revenue rather than fine tuning. This should not, however, lead us to ignore the possible effects on the level and allocation of investment and saving. The revenue from the corporation tax is likely to grow over time as more advanced sectors develop and it is important to have a sensible system in advance. It is surely possible to learn from the experience of developed countries where, for example in the UK, the corporate tax system has grown as a series of rather *ad hoc* responses to short-term pressures (see Kay and King, 1986).

A particular focus of attention has been the extent to which the corporate tax, together with the personal income tax, discriminates between different sources of finance. The *classical system*, where the corporate tax applies to all profits, distributed or undistributed, and in addition the personal income tax is levied on dividends, has been particularly criticized on the grounds that it favours loan as opposed to equity finance. The other major form of corporate taxation is the *imputation system* where tax withheld on dividends is credited against the corporate tax at a rate known as the imputation rate. The bias in favour of loan, as against equity, finance is reduced but remains whilst the imputation rate is lower than the corporate rate.

In such an intricate, and rather messy, problem one cannot expect to be able to provide a synthesis of the basic determinants of optimal policy in the manner attempted for indirect taxes. King's response (1977, p. 249), is to seek criteria of neutrality or ask that the system be non-distortionary. Thus, for example, it is suggested that, unless there is special reason it should not distinguish amongst different forms of finance or amongst different forms of assets. Possibilities are (*a*) a classical system without deductibility of interest payments, together with capital gains taxed at full personal rates; (*b*) full integration of corporate and personal income taxation (with deductibility of interest); or (*c*) a cash flow corporation tax (where the cash flow excludes financial transactions). Space limitations prevent further detail here but it should be clear that the merits of any particular system will depend on what is practically possible in the country under study.

Special incentives for investment are very common in developing countries. Amongst these tax holidays are particularly popular (see e.g. Shah and Toye, 1979). However, as Gersovitz (1987) points out, there are a number of problems and abuses which may lead simply to a loss of tax revenue without any corresponding increase in investment. And any tax bonus for investment should be very carefully justified. Are there externalities to investment which are not reflected in market prices? If so, perhaps taxation or subsidy policy should be focused directly on those prices which are supposed to be wrong. Is the tax incentive which is proposed compensating for some alleged disincentive elsewhere in the tax system of the kind we have been discussing? If so, then perhaps it is the disincentive which should be tackled directly. Or is it being argued that for reasons of intertemporal allocation (e.g. future generations being underrepresented) the tax wedge should be negative rather than positive? Again, the position is unclear. Too often, it is taken as obvious that special tax incentives for investment are needed. The evidence that they have much incentive effect is scanty and it is likely that revenue losses are substantial.

Our conclusions from the somewhat unsatisfactory state of the subject are that the guiding principles should probably be simplicity, practicality, and neutrality. Complex provisions without clear rationale should be discarded, particularly where they lose revenue. Special treatment for particular industries should be viewed with suspicion. Allowable deductions should be scrutinized very carefully. Finally we would suggest that the withholding of tax on dividends is likely to be a practical way of actually collecting the revenue.

As we have seen, the theory of the optimal personal income tax is rather better developed than that of the optimal corporate tax. However, it probably has limited applicability to developing countries where the coverage of the income tax is usually limited. Nevertheless, like the corporate income tax, it has potential for the future and one should think ahead. Again it is sensible to focus on simplicity and practicality in designing policy.

One area where theory and practicality come together concerns transfers where distributive objectives can be effectively pursued by direct transfers to the poorest. The personal income tax is not a useful tool for protecting the poorest. How far it is a useful tool for redistribution by taxing the rich is largely a question of coverage and enforcement. Here, as broad a base as possible, together with moderate marginal rates, probably provides the best marriage between theoretical and administrative considerations. There is no general theoretical argument for anything other than a broad base. Permissible allowances should be confined to aspects of horizontal equity, principally concerned with family structure. Non-cash fringe benefits such as housing, cars, and education should, as far as possible, be included. A broad base provides scope for lower rates and we find that calculations of optimal taxes in which redistribution and incentives are traded off do not provide arguments for very high rates (see e.g. Mirrlees, 1971 and Stern, 1976). It is often argued that very high rates encourage evasion so that theory and administration, in this case, point the same way. As with the taxation of dividends, the withholding of tax at source for all types of incomes is an important tool for collection.

We have seen in Section 2 that theory has quite a lot to say about the optimal balance between income and indirect taxes. The crucial elements are (*a*) the sources of differences between households, (*b*) the structure of preferences, and (*c*) the form of the available income tax. It is probably reasonable to suggest that the relatively small role for the income tax in developing countries can be attributed to costs of administration rather than judgements about items (*a*)–(*c*). Nevertheless as the economies grow, the population becomes better educated, and accounting more widespread, one may suppose that the income tax will play an increasing role and one should think carefully how to structure the tax system to take advantage of the potential for growth. An advantage of the theory is that it points to tax tools and to comparisons which might otherwise be missed (e.g. the central role of lump-sum transfers or taxes linked to household characteristics).

9. Indirect Taxation

Indirect taxation can take a number of different forms. We briefly discuss four here: tariffs (and quotas), domestic excises, sales taxes and VAT. In general, trade quotas are inferior to tariffs. One could improve on a quota system by auctioning the licences and the auction price is then the equivalent of a tariff—the value of the quota licence goes to the government rather than the firm getting the licence. Further one can argue that tariffs are inferior to taxes (sales taxes or VAT) on final consumption goods, whether domestically produced or imported, since tariffs distort the allocation of resources in favour of the domestic production of the good under tariff (see Dixit, 1985). More formally one can show that if lump-sum taxes are impossible then the optimal indirect tax system (with respect to a welfare function embodying both incentives and distribution) in an open economy is to have taxes on final sales. This is essentially an application of the Diamond–Mirrlees (1971) efficiency theorem—see Dixit and Norman (1980, ch. 6) for an explicit formal argument. A tariff plus an equal excise on domestic production would have the same effect as a sales tax, for goods which are for final consumption only.

Arguments in favour of tariffs as against final-point sales taxes would then be associated with administration or with the desire to protect a particular domestic industry. No doubt the administrative considerations are of substance but it is important for revenue growth over time to build up an efficient internal tax administration and to encourage formal accounting, so that one would not want to hold fast to an administrative argument in favour of tariffs over the indefinite future. The protection argument would have to be examined directly in terms of the particular industry, whether it was likely to grow or whether it should grow, whether or not there were better ways of encouragement than the tariff, and so on. It seems that some of the more recent theories of international trade without the competitive assumption have added arguments for protection although not all the theorists would want to emphasize this point (see e.g. Dixit, 1984, and Helpman and Krugman, 1985). For example, as Dixit (1984, p. 14) puts it, there is the 'possibility that a partly countervailing duty may be desirable when a foreign country subsidises exports'. On the other hand, if oligopoly is associated with increasing returns to scale, then there are potential gains from specialization which are not included in the standard model of gains from trade.

Our last comparisons will be amongst domestic excises, sales taxes, and the VAT. Excises on domestically produced goods distort production in an analogous manner to tariffs—this time in the opposite direction. If coupled with a tariff they have the effect of a sales tax if the good is for final consumption. Distortions arise, however, if the good concerned is also an input into production. Domestic excises, as with tariffs, may lead to unintended consequences. For example, in our calculation of effective taxes in India we found (see Ahmad and Stern, 1987) that some goods for which the government offered subsidies (e.g. khadi and handloom cloth) were in fact taxed if one took into account taxes on inputs, and the particular culprit was domestic excises. As with tariffs the main argument for domestic excises would appear to be administration. It is interesting to note that in India the revenue from domestic excises has overtaken that from tariffs as the productive base of the economy has expanded (see Section 2) as in the story told by Hinrichs (1966). In the Indian case an important element is also the federal structure. Excises on production are the preserve of the centre whereas sales taxes are generally in the hands of the states.

The most attractive taxes from the point of view of theory are the final point sales tax and the VAT. The former has the advantage that it need involve only the final sale. Thus firms throughout the economy are not involved as they are with VAT. A disadvantage with this sales tax is that the final stage has to be identified and this can lead to much evasion. However, many countries, e.g. India, have some success in levying a sales tax at the wholesale stage. The VAT has been introduced in a number of countries in recent years; Tanzi (1987) noted 22 developing countries, stimulated in part perhaps by its extensive use in the European Economic Community. It has the advantage of the inbuilt checking system whereby buyers have an incentive to reveal the purchase (in order to get credit for tax paid on inputs) thus discouraging concealment by a seller. Further it can be applied to services as well as goods since it does not require the specification of a unit of output (although a sales tax could be extended in this way too). It is also straightforward to rebate VAT on exports. A major disadvantage is that it involves everyone in the production chain thus imposing a substantial administrative cost both on the authorities and the enterprises.

One advantage that should *not* be claimed for the VAT is uniformity. There is nothing in the logic of a VAT to require uniformity and neither, as we have seen, is uniformity generally a desirable property of an indirect tax system.

This discussion therefore suggests a fairly clear strategy for indirect taxes. This consists of a replacement of trade taxes by taxes on final goods. These taxes should be differentiated to take account of the distributional pattern of consumption with such differentiation being less important the more successful is the direct income support system. Whilst this advice is useful as a description of a long-term goal, the strategy is not something that most developing countries could introduce very quickly. Administration is a central problem and many developing countries would have difficulty in levying taxes at the retail stage. This would appear to be true, for example, for much of Africa and Bangladesh. On the other hand, many other countries do levy taxes at the retail stage with some success. For example, in 1985, Turkey introduced a full-scale VAT including the retail stage which with a 12 per cent rate now raises around 3 per cent of GDP. Thus the coverage is one-quarter of GDP (with a notional legal coverage estimated around 50 per cent of GDP). The Mexican VAT is also collected fairly successfully, as is sales tax in a number of Indian states. The appropriate sequencing of an introduction of a consumption tax through to the final stage will depend on the circumstances of the country concerned. Most countries should be capable of handling the import and manufacturers stage and many could include wholesale. Probably the majority could not go directly to the retail stage although one should not assume it is impossible without careful scrutiny. It is an advantage of the VAT that it can be introduced incrementally through the system, gradually increasing coverage and revenue. Thus if a stage is lost it does not imply that a good escapes tax altogether, whereas with a final stage tax (such as the old UK purchase tax) all revenue is lost if evasion takes place at the final stage. There is then a great advantage of the VAT over other types of indirect taxation where introduction has to be gradual. Even with VAT, however, partial coverage will shift sales to untaxed goods or outlets.

Where an indirect tax is not at the final stage then retail and/or wholesale margins will influence the proportion of tax in the price. In these circumstances an 'effective tax' calculation of the type described in Ahmad and Stern (1986) would be necessary and input–output information including retail and wholesale margins would be necessary.

We shall not discuss in detail here the precise form of a VAT. One has to define the base for taxation and how the taxes are to be calculated and administered. The 'consumption base' allows the deduction of capital inputs in computing value added but the 'income base' does not. The most common method of administration is the 'subtraction' method whereby the taxpayer levies taxes on all output and subtracts from this tax collection the taxes paid on his inputs to compute the tax he must transmit to the authorities. For further discussion of experience with the VAT, see Tait (1988).

The basic theories of public finance do then provide help in judging the balance of taxes of different types. Further, if developed, and with enough data and assumptions they can be constructively applied to guide decisions on possible reforms. Examples of explicit calculations comparing the impacts of different types of tax increases, domestic excises, tariffs, sales taxes, and so on are contained in Ahmad and Stern (1987).

10. Some Simple Guiding Principles

As a partial summary we shall draw out some simple guiding principles from the analysis. We shall attempt to keep the statements short and direct and as such the many qualifications which would be necessary are omitted.

We have discussed the relevant assumptions and the underlying logic in the preceding Sections.

(i) Where possible lump-sum taxes and transfers, or close approxima-tions should be used to raise revenue and transfer resources. Examples are land taxes (although incentives to improve land must be considered) and subsidized rations. It is not easy to find other examples where the lump-sum taxation can be appropriately linked to a relevant criterion (particular-ly wealth or poverty) without the tax or transfer ceasing to be lump-sum. Head or poll taxes are further examples but are unattractive on distribu-tional grounds. See Section 2 for further discussion.

(ii) It can be very misleading to look at one set of tax tools in isolation from what is happening elsewhere in the tax system. For example, we should not allocate redistribution to the income tax and revenue raising to indirect taxes. Both taxes affect distribution, affect resource allocation, *and* raise revenue; further the presence and role of the one set of taxes strongly influences the appraisal of the other. In particular the desirability of the differentiation in commodity taxes on distributional grounds is closely re-lated to other policies towards distribution. The stronger are the other tools the smaller is the redistributive role for commodity taxes. See Section 2.

(iii) The focus of indirect taxation should be final consumption. This means that intermediate goods should not be taxed unless there is difficulty in the way of taxing final goods or there are special distributional reasons for taxing these intermediates. This applies also to tariffs, which should be rebated on intermediate goods and linked to other taxes on final goods. They should be used for protection only when the case for supporting a particular domestic industry (and penalizing its users) is very strong and where other means of stimulating the industry are less satisfactory. It must be recognized that the elimination of tariffs except for protection is a long-term goal which for revenue reasons could not be achieved in the short or medium term in countries with very few tax handles. But it should be pur-sued in the sense that tariffs should be reduced as and when the revenue from final goods taxation can be built up. Again in the short term, it is generally preferable to replace quotas by tariffs so that the rent from the quota flows directly to the government rather than to those agents who allocate or receive the quota. See Sections 6 and 9.

(iv) Public sector prices should be set according to the same principles as indirect taxes: price equal to marginal social cost for intermediate goods (except for the cases noted in (iii) above) and marginal social cost plus an element for taxation for final goods. See Section 2.

(v) The appropriate microeconomic criterion for the expansion of in-dustries is profitability at shadow prices of the incremental output. Other indicators (such as effective protection rates or domestic resource costs) are reliable only where they coincide with shadow prices. Similarly a reform rule based on the other indicators, such as adjusting tariffs to move towards uniform effective protection, is incorrect. See Sections 4, 6, and 9.

(vi) Indirect taxes should be guided by a trade-off between efficiency and equity and in the absence of well-functioning schemes for income support there is no prescription for uniformity of indirect taxation. See Section 2.

(vii) A central argument for a corporate income tax is as a means for taxing personal incomes and thus an analysis of the tax should be closely linked to the personal income tax. See Section 7.

These principles have all been derived from theoretical models. They do, however, focus attention in a practical way for the appraisal of the basic elements and direction of tax reforms and for the design of such reforms. Further the theory can be used in a direct way to structure detailed empirical analysis. The use of economic theory in these different ways, to establish principles, to guide policy proposals, and to structure empirical analysis was a hallmark of much of Ian Little's work. For example, his early work on direct and indirect taxation (1951) showed clearly that analytically income and commodity taxes should be treated in much the same way and that one could not claim the former to be undistortionary and the latter not. This is an example of good theory exposing bad arguments and changing the way we perceive problems. And he showed in his work on Indian taxes (1964) how simple theory could help in the structuring of real decisions, and as ever showed appreciation of the difficulties and constraints which surround practical problems. Further in his work on cost-benefit analysis he showed how a theoretical framework could structure detailed policy appraisal in a constructive way. The spirit of Little's work pervades the analysis of taxation for developing countries much as it does many other problems of policy.

References

Ahmad, S. E., and Stern, N. H. (1984), 'The theory of reform and Indian indirect taxes', *Journal of Public Economics*, 25/3, pp. 259–95.

——(1986), 'Tax reform for Pakistan: Overview and effective taxes for 1975/76', *Pakistan Development Review* (Spring), pp. 43–72.

——(1987), 'Alternative sources of government revenue: illustrations from India for 1979/80', in Newbery and Stern (1987a).

——(forthcoming), *Tax Reform and Development* (Cambridge: CUP).

Askari, H., and Cummings, J. T. (1976), *Agricultural Supply Response: A Survey of the Econometric Evidence* (New York: Praeger).

Atkinson, A. B., and Sutherland, H. (eds.) (1987), 'Tax-Benefiit Models', Suntory-Toyota International Centre for Economics and Related Disciplines, London School of Economics, mimeo.

Binswanger, H., Mundlak, Y., Yang, Maw-cheng, and Bowers, A. (1985),

'Estimation of aggregate agricultural supply response from time-series of cross-country data', *Working Paper*, 1985-3 (Washington, DC: Commodity Studies and Project Division, World Bank), mimeo.

Bird, R. M. (1974), *Taxing Agricultural Land in Developing Countries* (Cambridge, Mass.: Harvard University Press).

Braverman, A., Hammer, J., and Ahn, C. Y. (1987), 'Multi-market analysis of agricultural pricing policies in Korea', in Newbery and Stern, (1987a).

Chamley, C. (1983), 'Taxation in dynamic economies: some problems and methods' (Washington, DC: World Bank), mimeo.

Deaton, A. S., (1987), 'Econometric issues for tax design in developing countries', in Newbery and Stern (1987a).

——and Stern, N.H. (1986), 'Optimally uniform commodity taxes, taste differences, and lump-sum grants', *Economics Letters*, 20, pp. 263–6.

Dervis, K., de Melo, J., and Robinson, S. (1982), *General Equilibrium Models for Development Policy* (Cambridge: CUP for the World Bank).

Diamond, P. A., and Mirrlees, J. A. (1971), 'Optimal taxation and public production I: production efficiency; II: tax rules', *American Economic Review*, 61, pp. 8–27 and 261–78.

Dixit, A. K. (1973), 'Models of dual economies', in Mirrlees and Stern (eds.), *Models of Economic Growth*, (London: Macmillan).

——(1984), 'International trade policy for oligopolistic industries', *Economic Journal*, 94 (Supplement), pp. 1–16.

——(1985), 'Tax policy in open economies', in A. Auerbach and M. Feldstein (eds.), *Handbook of Public Economics*, *I* (Amsterdam: North-Holland).

——and Norman, V. (1980), *Theory of International Trade* (Cambridge: CUP).

Drèze, J. P., and Stern, N. H. (1987), 'The theory of cost-benefit analysis', in A. Auerbach and M. Feldstein (eds.), *Handbook of Public Economics* (Amsterdam: North-Holland).

Eshag, E. (1983), *Fiscal and Monetary Problems in Developing Countries* (Cambridge: CUP).

Gersovitz, M. (1987), 'The effects of domestic taxes on foreign private investment', in Newbery and Stern (1987a), ch. 23.

Giovannini, A. (1985), 'Saving and the real interest rate in LDCS', *Journal of Development Economics*, 18/2–3, pp. 197–218.

Goode, R. (1984), *Government Finance in Developing Countries* (Washington, DC: Brookings Institution).

Heady, D., and Mitra, P. (1987), 'Optimal taxation and shadow pricing in a developing economy', in Newbery and Stern, (1987a).

Helpman, E., and Krugman, P. R. (1985), *Market Structure and Foreign Trade* (Brighton: Wheatsheaf Books).

Hinrichs, H. H. (1966), *A General Theory of Tax Structure Change during Economic Development*, Harvard Law School International Tax Programme, Cambridge, Mass: Harvard University Press).

Kay J. A., and King, M. A. (1986), *The British Tax System*, 4th edn. (OUP).

Kehoe, T. J., and Serra-Puche, J. (1983), 'A computational general equilibrium model with endogenous unemployment: An analysis of the 1980 fiscal reform in Mexico', *Journal of Public Economics*, 22/1, pp. 1–26.

King, M. A. (1977), *Public Policy and the Corporation* (London: Chapman & Hall).

——(1985), 'The economics of saving: a survey of recent contributions', in K. J. Arrow and S. Honkapohja (eds.), *Frontiers of Economics* (Oxford: Blackwell).

Kotlikoff, L. J. (1984), 'Taxation and savings—a neoclassical perspective', *Working Paper*, 1302 (Cambridge, Mass.: NBER).

Lewis, W. A. (1954), 'Economic development with unlimited supplies of labour', *Manchester School*, 22/2, pp. 139–91.

Lipton, M. (1977) *Why Poor People Stay Poor: Urban Bias in World Development* (London: Temple Smith).

Little, I. M. D. (1951), 'Direct vs indirect taxes', *Economic Journal*, 61 (Sept.), pp. 577–84.

——(1964), 'Tax Policy and the Third Plan', in P. N. Rosenstein-Rodan (ed.), *Pricing and Fiscal Policies A Study in Method* (London: Allen & Unwin).

——Mazumdar, D., and Page, J. (1987), *Small Manufacturing Enterprises: A Comparative Study of India and Other Economies* (Oxford: OUP: World Bank).

——and Mirrlees, J. A. (1974), *Project Appraisal and Planning for Developing Countries* (London: Heinemann).

——Scitovsky, T., and Scott, M. (1970) *Industry and Trade in Some Developing Countries: A Comparative Study* (Oxford: OUP for the OECD).

Mirrlees, J. A. (1971), 'An exploration in the theory of optimum income taxation', *Review of Economic Studies*, 38/114, pp. 175–208.

Newbery, D. M. G. (1987a), 'Agricultural taxation—the main issues', in Newbery and Stern (1987a).

——(1987b), 'Identifying desirable direction of agricultural price reform in Korea', in Newbery and Stern (1987a)

——and Stern, N. H. (eds.) (1987a), *The Theory of Taxation for Developing Countries* (New York: World Bank and OUP).

——(1987b) 'Dynamic tax issues', in Newbery and Stern (1987a).

Prest, A. R. (1972), *Public Finance in Under-Developed Countries* (London: Weidenfeld & Nicolson).

Robinson, S. (1989), 'Multisectoral models of developing countries: a survey', in H. B. Chenery and T. N. Srinivasan (eds.), *Handbook of Development Economics, II* (Amsterdam: North-Holland).

Shah, S. M. S., and Toye, J. F. J. (1979), 'Fiscal incentives for firms in some developing countries: surveys and critique', in J. F. J. Toye (ed.), *Taxation and Economic Development* (London: Frank Cass).

Shoven, J. B., (1983), 'Applied general equilibrium tax modelling', *IMF Staff Papers*, 30 (June), pp. 350–93.

——and Whalley, J. (1984), 'Applied general equilibrium models of taxation and international trade', *Journal of Economic Literature*, 22, pp. 1007–51.

Stern, N. H. (1976), 'On the specification of models of optimum income taxation', *Journal of Public Economics*, 6/1–2, pp. 123–62.

——(1987), 'Aspects of the general theory of tax reform', in Newbery and Stern, (1987a).

Tait, A. A. (1988), *Value Added Tax: International Practice and Problems* (Washington, DC: International Monetary Fund).

Tanzi, V. (1987), 'Quantitative characteristics of the tax systems of developing countries', in Newbery and Stern (1987a).

Timmer, C. P., Falcon, W. P., and Pearson, S. R. (1983), *Food Policy Analysis* (Baltimore: Johns Hopkins Univ. Press for World Bank).

Wald, H. P. (1959), *Taxation of Agricultural Land in Underdeveloped Countries* (Cambridge, Mass.: Harvard Univ. Press).

World Bank (1988), *World Development Report 1988* (New York: OUP for the World Bank).

Appendix

On the General Theory of Reform and Shadow Prices

We provide a brief formal account of the principles mentioned in Section 4. The government is concerned with the selection of certain policy variables, for example, taxes, quotas, or rations. At the initial position some are chosen optimally and the remainder are fixed at predetermined positions—the vector describing the former group is s and the latter group ω. The choice of s for given ω may then be described by the solution of the problem (12.10).

$$\text{maximize}_{s} \quad V(s, \omega)$$

$$\text{subject to} \quad E(s, \omega) = z, \tag{12.10}$$

where V is the social welfare function E net excess demands, and z public supply (many components of which may be zero). We suppose the problem is feasible so that the dimension of s is at least as great as that of z. When the two dimensions are exactly equal then, if $E(\ )$ is invertible (given ω), s is defined as a function of z and there will essentially be no choice. Thus the situation where the policy variables are fully determined and there is no scope for optimization is a special case of the model. The equality in the constraint in (12.10) and the assumption that the dimension of s is at least as great as z are not strong assumptions but involve merely the assertion that there is a process by which equilibrium is established and goods are allocated in the economy (it may well be of the non-competitive variety with fixed prices, rationing, and so on).

The Lagrangean for (12.10) is

$$L(s, \omega) = V(s, \omega) - v\,[E(s, \omega) - z], \tag{12.11}$$

where v is the vector of shadow prices. The shadow price of a good is *defined* as the increase in the value of the social welfare function when an extra unit of public supplies becomes available, and it is a standard result that it will equal v in (12.11) (whether or not the model is fully determined). Thus the increment in social welfare from a given project dz (at constant ω but with s endogenous), from the definition of v, is $v\,dz$.

The first-order conditions for a maximum in (12.10) are

$$\frac{\partial V}{\partial s} - v\frac{\partial E}{\partial s} = 0. \tag{12.12}$$

A reform is a change $d\omega$ in the variables ω which had previously been seen as predetermined. In order to satisfy the constraints we must have

$$\frac{\partial E}{\partial \omega} d\omega - \frac{\partial E}{\partial s} ds = 0. \tag{12.13}$$

Using (12.12) and (12.13) we have

$$dV = \left(\frac{\partial V}{\partial \omega} - v\frac{\partial E}{\partial \omega}\right) d\omega. \tag{12.14}$$

This is the general result on policy reform. It tells us that the welfare impact of a reform is given by the direct effect on social welfare less the cost of the extra net demands at shadow prices $v\,\partial E/\partial \omega$. This is a unifying principle which underlies very many discussions of policy change. It is at one level simple and obvious but it often seems to be imperfectly understood.

The model (12.10) and the derivation of (12.14) we have used makes it very clear that the shadow prices will depend critically on how equilibrium is re-established after a change in z or ω, i.e. they will be different for different specifications of the endogenous variables s. For example we can think of a change in net demands of an imported good (whose world price is fixed) from a parameter change being satisfied by extra imports with no price change or by rationed imports with an increase in the domestic price. In the former case it is the net imports that form part of s and in the latter case the price. The general equilibrium effect on social welfare will be different and thus so too will be the shadow prices.

The marginal analysis of the preceding section can readily be seen as a special case of (12.14). The details are not provided here (see Stern, 1987) but one way of expressing the generalization provided by (12.14) for the case where indirect taxes are to be reformed is through

$$\lambda_i^v = -\frac{\partial V}{\partial t_i} \bigg/ \frac{\partial R_v}{\partial t_i} \tag{12.15}$$

where R_v is *shadow* revenue, i.e. government revenue where we treat $q - v$ as shadow consumption taxes and $(v - p)$ as shadow production taxes. When $v = p$, shadow and producer prices coincide, and we are back with λ_i and (12.6). One can also write

$$dV = \left\{\frac{\partial V}{\partial t} + \frac{\partial}{\partial t}(t \cdot X) + (p - v)\frac{\partial X}{\partial t}\right\} dt, \tag{12.16}$$

(where the derivatives are taken for constant p) so that in addition to the welfare and revenue effects (the first two terms on the right-hand side of (12.16), we have an additional shadow revenue term arising from the difference between shadow and producer prices.

13

Social Cost-Benefit Analysis

MAURICE FG. SCOTT

1. A Preliminary Outline

Social cost-benefit analysis (SCBA hereafter) is undertaken in order to improve investment decisions. An outline of what it involves helps to explain some terms commonly used, and this is followed, first, by a discussion of the inherent difficulties and of why, despite these, SCBA needs to be undertaken, and then a review of selected topics.

The analysis is from the point of view of a whole society, rather than that of a private individual or company, hence the '*social*' in the title. The decision-maker may be thought of as a government, a part of a government (e.g. a particular department), or the aid agency of a government or international organization. It makes a difference which of these is concerned, as we shall see.

The *investment project* is the action to be decided upon, and generally involves expenditure to change economic arrangements. Some have defined a project in terms of its quantitative effects (Drèze and Stern, 1987, p. 426), but I think it is more usual to distinguish the initial expenditure from its later effects. Little and Mirrlees

mean by a project any scheme, or part of a scheme, for investing resources which can reasonably be analysed and evaluated as an independent unit. The definition is thus arbitrary. . . . But it would not be sensible to consider separately two projects if they were so closely linked that one could not be operated, or fulfil its purpose, without the other. In such a case the two parts must be considered as a whole—that is, as one project (Little and Mirrlees, 1974, p. 3).

The projects may be in the *public or private sector*. Most SCBA is, for obvious reasons, concerned with public sector projects; but governmentally owned development banks lend to the private sector, as do international aid agencies, and governments often want to screen private investments by foreign companies. SCBA is relevant to all of these.

The decision-maker is credited with an *objective function*, generally with the desire to maximize the welfare of the citizens of the country concerned. This may be a burlesque of reality, but systems of project appraisal have yet to be devised which have Machiavelli rather than Bentham as their source of inspiration. Welfare may be thought of in cardinal utilitarian terms as being measured in 'utils', but more usually some measure in terms of the effects of the project on citizens' consumption is adopted. One controversial question, discussed below, is *whether consumption benefits should be weighted* so as to favour projects whose benefits flow more to the poor than to the rich. In any case, what SCBA seeks to do is to identify the effects of a project on citizens' consumption, these being related to the inputs and outputs, or costs and benefits, of the project, which can also be regarded as its disadvantages and advantages.

In order to set these off against each other, the inputs and outputs are valued in terms of a homogeneous *unit of accout* or *numéraire*. They actually consist of heterogeneous things: machinery, buildings, human effort, food, other consumer goods etc. Each must be multiplied by its *accounting price* or *shadow price* (the terms are used indifferently here) to express it in terms of the *numéraire*, and these prices, in turn, must measure the effects on citizens' consumption, where that is the objective. Since these effects can take place at any time in the future, and since a unit of consumption is generally deemed to be more valuable (i.e. has a greater effect in achieving the objective) the sooner it occurs, the timing of benefits (and costs) has to be allowed for. This is done by *discounting* benefits (and costs) by greater and greater amounts the further off in the future they come.

The rate of discount used for this purpose has been given many titles. If it is used to convert future units of the *numéraire* into units of equivalent value to a selected base year I shall refer to it as the *accounting rate of interest*[1] or ARI. In that case, it follows by definition that the ARI is the rate at which the *numéraire* falls in value through time. Other terms used for this are the *test discount rate*,[2] and the *shadow discount rate* (Drèze and Stern, 1987). It is useful also to have a term to describe the rate of discount which would be applied if the *numéraire* were marginal consumption benefits (which it need not be, see further below). Terms used for this are the *consumption rate of interest* (Little and Mirrlees, 1969, 1974) or CRI, and the *social time preference rate* or STP, or sometimes the *social discount rate* (United Nations, 1972). The STP was used in a prolonged controversy between those advocating its use and those advocating an alternative *social opportunity cost of capital* or SOC. In what follows, I ignore that controversy for lack of space (see, for example, Feldstein (1964), which also gives many references), but believe that its main lessons are duly taken into account.

Once they are all discounted and expressed in terms of the *numéraire*, the costs and benefits of a project can simply be added up, the costs being negative and the benefits positive. The sum is called the *net present value* or NPV, and the *decision criterion* is that projects with positive NPV should

---

[1] This term, like some others, originated with Little and Mirrlees (1969) and has become widely used since.

[2] This is used for the public sector in the United Kingdom. See e.g. UK Government (1967).

be implemented. However, this needs qualification because of the uncer-taintly of all such estimates, of the bias that can affect them, and of the existence in some cases of fixed investment budgets, which means that some projects with positive NPV cannot be done.[3]

Before filling in the above outline, a few more points may be mentioned here briefly, since there is no space to discuss them further below. Many public sector projects' outputs are not marketed. This is true, for example, of investments in education, health, public administration, defence, roads, and water supply. In principle one could measure their value to consumers in terms of willingness-to-pay for them, but in practice this is often very difficult, or impracticable, although in some cases (e.g. for roads) more or less satisfactory methods have been devised. *Cost-effectiveness* analysis may still be used in order to discover the least cost way of meeting a specific need, the latter being defined *ad hoc* (e.g. number of pupils or hospital beds). Shadow prices, the choice of *numéraire*, and discounting are just as relevant as in SCBA. Many projects are sufficiently large to affect the prices of relevant outputs or inputs. Where this is important, attempts must be made to measure the resulting changes in *consumers' or producers' sur-pluses. Linkage effects* of one project on others may be partly related to these. For example, by cheapening the supply of electricity a power project may encourage projects where electricity is an important input. Or it may involve building a dam which, as a by-product, supplies irrigation water cheaply to grow cotton. Linkage effects of a different kind may result from imitation,or training of workers who go off to other projects. These (and other effects, such as pollution) are also called *externalities*, and much has been written about them.[4] In principle, one should take them into account in SCBA. In practice they may have to be left among the unquantifiable costs and benefits which the decision-maker must allow for as best he may. He can draw comfort from the reflection that, where the choice is between investing much the same amount in different ways, it is the difference in their net external benefits which counts, and this may be small in relation to the more obvious costs and benefits.

2.   The Difficulty and Necessity of SCBA

Much of the literature on SCBA assumes that the inputs and outputs of a project are somehow known, and the problem to be discussed is how they should be valued, but this skips over many difficulties. Economists should

---

[3] The solution which is then usually recommended is to select those projects which satisfy the budget constraint and achieve maximum total NPV. This assumes that the shadow prices and rate (or rates) of discount should not be changed so as to eliminate the excess supply of projects.

[4] Hirschman (1958) drew everyone's attention to linkages. Two classic articles on externali-ties are Meade (1952) and Scitovsky (1954), and see also Little and Mirrlees (1974), ch. 16.

be familiar with the idea that everything affects everything else. How, then, can one identify all the quantitative changes which result from a particular project? Is it sufficient to describe these as the inputs and outputs and, even if it is, what precisely are they? Suppose, for example, that the project consists in building a bridge across a river at a point hitherto served by a ferry. The bridge will make the ferry redundant. Do we include as output the reduction in resources required to operate the ferry? Or, instead, the extra output elsewhere which those released resources will provide? How far along the chain of consequences do we proceed?

This question can only be answered at the same time as the shadow prices are defined. Thus, if we price the reduction in resources required to operate the ferry, that price must implicitly value the consequences of freeing them for use elsewhere, and the quantity change can be limited to the resources freed—boats, fuel, men etc. Alternatively, we could directly estimate the extra outputs produced elsewhere and multiply them by their shadow prices. Whichever we do the problem is the same, that is, we need to be able to trace the quantity changes which will result when the ferry becomes redundant. This looks like a formidable problem, and no less formidable when one remembers that the consequences cannot necessarily be assumed to be of a comparative static kind. Building the bridge does not just lead to a new configuration of outputs and inputs which persists for evermore, but in principle changes the whole future by amounts which vary through time. Thus the extra traffic generated may have consequences for future agricultural, industrial, or commercial development on both sides of the river, or even in more remote regions. How can anyone possibly estimate what all these effects will be?

Thus far we have mentioned consequences without specifying exactly what is being compared with what. It is usually said that the comparison should be between the situation with and without the project. This answer is insufficient. If the bridge is not built this year, will it be built next year? If it is not built at this site, will another bridge be built perhaps near by? Sometimes one is urged to compare the project with the next best alternative, but that is not useful if the 'next best' is an alternative differing in some trivial way from the one being considered (e.g. a pink bridge instead of an orange one, or one placed a yard further upstream, or completed one day later).

To answer these questions, we must recall the purpose of project appraisal, namely to improve investment decisions. In designing any particular project, many alternatives must be considered, including the colour, site, and date of completion of a bridge, for example. The choice between these alternatives can be guided by the same identification and evaluation of their differences in outputs and inputs as before. Once the best variant has been selected on this basis, it must be compared with other alternatives, such as maintaining or improving the ferry (this is the alternative of 'doing nothing' which,in reality, will usually involve further investment of some kind), or widening or building bridges much further away. There is no single one of these comparisons which is 'the' project, but cost and time will limit the alternatives which can be considered. The same procedure of identifying quantities and prices applies to each comparison, and the decision must be taken in the end in such a way that none of the alternatives considered is better than that finally selected.[5]

We must, then, limit the alternatives compared to those which we think important, but how do we deal with the problem of tracing the differences between them as they ramify through the economy and into the indefinite future?[6] If we could assume that the economy operated like the textbook models of perfect competition, with contingent markets for all goods in all states of the world, then we could safely ignore all these repercussions. The economy would then always be operating close to its optimum, and marginal *indirect* changes resulting from our project of any kind would have zero social value. Our problem would then be easy enough. We would merely need to multiply the *direct* inputs and outputs of the project by their actual money prices and add them up (suitably discounted). Thus, regarding the saving of the ferry's cost as a direct output of the bridge, there would be no need to trace the extra outputs produced by the boats, fuel, and men released, since they would be worth no more and no less than their cost. We could assume that there would be no social surplus (or deficit) obtaining if these resources shifted elsewhere. Likewise, future consequences could be ignored, since if subsequent investments were marginally changed, these changes would yield no net social gain (or loss).

It has been forcefully argued, however, that real developing countries are not like this textbook economy, and that it is precisely the distortions in their economies which require the use of shadow prices instead of actual prices (see, for example, Little and Mirrless (1974), ch. 2). It looks, therefore, as if we cannot escape from the difficulty by such a convenient assumption. Nevertheless, as we shall presently see, some part of the

---

[5] A distinction is sometimes drawn between *mutually exclusive* alternatives, and other alternatives. It is then pointed out that the use of the internal rate of return as a decision criterion can lead to mistakes with the former. In my view, and following the procedure in the text, one is *always* comparing mutually exclusive alternatives. Each 'with' is compared with some alternative 'without', and one cannot implement both together.

[6] Why the *indefinite* future? The repercussions of a project extend in principle for ever. It is often assumed that the changes resulting from a project, once made, persist unaltered for 10 or 20 years and then vanish. This is unrealistic, since many projects are not left unchanged, but will be more or less continually modified by subsequent investments. Even if the bridge, in my example, is not changed, its effects on traffic will change. In my view, most projects should be treated as if their effects were perpetual and associated future investments should be allowed for, if they are thought to differ between the alternatives being compared. Discounting will reduce the importance of effects in later years, but that should emerge from the calculations, and not be inserted at the beginning.

assumption survives. If it did not, the problem of estimating shadow prices would be insuperable.

Before getting to grips with it, let me remind the reader of what I regard (and he or she too, I hope) as the most important message of economics— the message for which *The Wealth of Nations* is justly famous. This is the idea that decentralized decisions, co-ordinated by a market system, are an efficient way of organizing an economy and, indeed, of developing it as well. *Laissez-faire* can doubtless be improved, but I do not think we have yet discovered a more efficient organization than the market. By comparison, the attempt to control a whole economy by a hierarchical system akin to that of a giant factory is a failure. Those at the centre lack the information available to those at the periphery, and cannot even digest and act on what information they have. Furthermore, the difficulties of motivating and monitoring the agents who must execute central decisions are severe. The one safe generalization to be made about the sources of worth-while innovations is that they are legion. Central planners cannot be expected to originate more than a few, and are likely to choke off the supply of many, thereby worsenig the quality of investment.

Nevertheless, those at the centre want to control public sector investment decisions to some extent. They will want to control, at the very least, the total amounts spent, and they will also want some control over the ways in which money is spent. Project appraisal and shadow-pricing can be regarded as one way of doing this which preserves some of the virtues of decentralization. The shadow prices and decision rules are known to those responsible for making investment proposals, who are free to put forward projects making use of their own ideas and local knowledge. The proposals, however, are scrutinized at the centre, which can check the plausibility of the estimates, ensure that the shadow prices used are consistent with (i.e. broadly speaking, are the same as) those used elsewhere in the public sector, and approve those satisfying the decision criteria to a total value decided in a way to be discussed below. This procedure of local design and proposal with central scrutiny and approval or rejection is almost inevitable in some form or other. The aim of shadow-pricing methodology is to secure greater efficiency than by alternative systems of control. In principle, the shadow prices include *all* relevant effects, properly weighted, so that simple addition is all that is needed to discover which projects are best, and should be approved. If, instead, market prices are used, or possibly no prices at all, then the centre has somehow to weigh up the advantages and disadvantages which have not been quantified commensurably. At worst, there is a jumble of physical outputs and inputs between which choices must be made. At best, there is a financial calculation, using market prices which are thought to misrepresent social costs and benefits to varying degrees. The scope for politicking, log-rolling, and 57 varieties of corruption is then well served. The puritanical self-restraint and austere efficiency of decisions based on a complete shadow-pricing system contrast sharply with that.

It would be a mistake, all the same, to conclude that shadow-pricing is an entirely satisfactory solution to the problems of public sector investment choice. There is, first, the already-mentioned difficulty of estimating the shadow prices themselves, including that of estimating future relative price changes, which could greatly affect profitability. However, one must not exaggerate. As Little (1987) points out 'the great bulk of the information "needs"—on physical inputs and outputs preferably for years ahead, and their prices, also for years ahead—are already required for a full finanacial analysis'. Secondly, there is the problem of probing the plausibility of the estimates submitted to the centre. In the competitive market system with private ownership, decisions are taken by those who stand to gain or lose by their outcome. In the public sector, officials and politicians have the pleasure of spending other people's money while promising popular benefits—and disappearing before an objective assessment of these becomes publicly available, if it ever does.

There is a well-known dilemma here. With decentralized decisions *and* decentralized responsiblity, as in the private market system, it is up to each decision-maker to make the best estimates he can of an uncertain future, knowing that he gains or loses by the outcome. But if he bears *all* the risks he may prudently avoid risky ventures whose expected returns are better than the safer ones chosen.[7] The average outcome for society as a whole will then be worse than if he were able to share at least some of the risks. For public sector projects, many, probably most,[8] of the risks are widely shared, so that higher expected returns can be sought despite the risks. But now the moral hazard appears: if the decision-makers bear no risk, their estimates may be over-optimistic. It is this which prevents any simple application of the NPV decision criterion. The centre has to probe the estimates and to correct for bias. This is sometimes done by using a higher rate of discount, but that could be inappropriate since it is often the initial capital costs which are underestimated rather than later operating profits over-

---

[7] This is not a straightforward matter. Individuals may undertake projects which, to an outsider, look very risky, but which they confidently expect to succeed. Thier knowledge of the projects, and of their own capabilities, is greater, which may explain the difference in perceptions, but there could be other explanations. Some individuals also enjoy taking risks. See Brook (1987), whose study of 20 very small 'high-technology' firms in the UK revealed that: 'With regard to the riskiness of their ventures, most founders emphasised that risk or uncertainty are largely matters of perspective, and that, given what they knew, the risk that they were taking . . . was not great . . . Few of the founders regarded themselves as having any particular preference for risk, though most considered themselves as more spirited or adventurous than their peers' (ch. 7).

[8] But not all. For example, those employed on the project will generally lose if it is a failure, and they are forced to look elsewhere for work.

estimated. A sensitivity analysis of particular estimates with *ad hoc* adjustments for suspected optimism might be better, except that those submitting projects for approval will soon learn to anticipate this. In the end, some devolution of responsiblity, with some, but incomplete, risk-sharing, may be the best compromise. In the private sector, the way in which risks are shared is intimately bound up with the way in which projects are financed. Economists should give more attention to the way in which public sector projects are financed—a topic frequently neglected in SCBA.

We come back, then, to the problems of motivation and monitoring. The logic of shadow-pricing requires that current operations, and not just investment decisions, should be monitored using shadow, rather than inappropriate actual, prices. Unless this is done, managers are provided with an organization ill-adapted to achieve the financial targets set, and they will inevitably seek to readapt it in ways which are inefficient if evaluated at shadow prices (see Heggie in Little and Scott (1976), ch. 8, and Lal (1980), p. 72).

There is much to be said, then, for adjusting actual market prices towards shadow prices as far as one can, and then using them both in evaluating investment proposals and in monitoring subsequent operations. In fact, the key to efficiency in the public sector may often lie in monitoring procedures rather than in investment appraisal procedures. A really satisfactory monitoring system should make central investment appraisal unnecessary, just as, in a large private enterprise, a system of decentralized profit centres, with monitoring based on profit performance, dispenses with the need to second-guess investment decisions at the centre. In effect, the centre becomes a source of finance and behaves more like a financier than a manager. There may be some decisions whose effects on other parts of the system are too big to neglect and which must be reviewed centrally, but most decisions can be left to those whose performance is judged by their outcome, and whose rewards depend upon it.

To set up this system in the public sector could, all the same, be difficult. Many outputs are not marketed at all, and yet would have to become so for the system to work. Where outputs or inputs already are marketed, the requirement is to make actual prices correspond more closely to shadow prices. There is little doubt that to do so would wonderfully concentrate the minds of those whose task this was. It is one thing to argue that a shadow wage equal to, say, half the actual wage is the best guess of the true social cost of labour for a particular project. It is another to pay the operators a subsidy at that rate. Yet if decision-makers cannot bring themselves to do that, are they serious about their estimate of the shadow wage?

Thus far we have been considering project appraisal from the point of view of those in control of the public sector in a developing country. Ideally, actual prices should be adjusted to shadow prices, and the problems are those of motivation and monitoring. There is, however, another point of view to consider where this ideal solution is unlikely to be found, that of the aid donor who wishes to give aid tied to projects. Aid is so tied, we may suppose, partly because the donor wants to satisfy himself (and his domestic critics) that it is being properly used, partly because he believes his objectives are not always the same as those of the government of the recipient country, and partly because he believes that he can thereby improve the methods of project appraisal and control used in that country—and there may be other reasons. The donor is probably well aware that the achievement of these objectives can be frustrated by the recipient government, at least to some extent. The latter may serve up projects which would have been implemented without aid, so that in truth the donor's funds are put to uses outside his control or even knowledge (the fungibility problem). Or projects may be implemented but then not properly operated, so that good roads degrade back to bad tracks, or schools and health centres are underutilized, or used for different purposes from those intended. The motivation and monitoring problems, in short, are as acute here as before. Nevertheless, the donor may be unable to persuade the recipient government to adjust actual prices to shadow prices, and may, as well, want to use a different set of shadow prices to those which would correctly reflect the recipient government's objectives. In these circumstances the donor could benefit from using shadow prices specially calculated by his own agents, and indeed, there are several large international and governmental organizations that have done that, including the World Bank, the European Development Fund, and the aid departments of the British, German, and United States governments. Perhaps this is the main way in which shadow prices are actually employed in project appraisal in developing countries.

One conclusion which emerges from the above is that the origination, design, selection, implementation, and subsequent operation of projects should ideally be guided by the same set of prices, which should reflect social costs and benefits. In the second-best (or n^{th}-best) economy of a developing country the problem of estimating these is appallingly difficult in *principle*. One can, nevertheless, attempt to improve decisions by some modifications of the actual price system. Even that is difficult, but the battle does not go to the faint-hearted. Only modifications which are substantial and relevant matter, and they are more important than modifications which are merely correct.

Within the government of a country, shadow-pricing is perhaps best regarded as a stage along the road to an improved actual price system. Even if actual prices can never be wholly satisfactory, a system of monitoring public sector projects which relies on them (improved as far as they can be) may be more efficient, all things considered, than one which attempts to combine two different sets of prices, shadow and actual.

For aid donors, shadow prices can also be used as guides to policies (concerning exchange rates, rationing, interest rates, taxes, and subsidies) designed to improve the actual price system. But for them it does seem likely that the use of shadow prices for project appraisal as well is likely to be needed for a long time to come.[9]

3. Some Problems of Shadow-Pricing: Unequal Weighting of Benefits

We turn now to a review of some of the problems of estimating shadow prices. In principle, as has already been pointed out, they are appallingly difficult. It is essential to cling fast to the main objective—the *improvement* of investment decisions. One is not looking for perfection, and the time and cost of taking (and failing to take) decisions are very relevant. Any system of shadow-pricing should be capable of simplification, with some short-cuts being used for smaller projects or where time is short.

The objective assumed in most systems is that of maximizing the weighted sum of consumption of the citizens of the country concerned. There has been much argument as to whether unequal weighting of consumption benefits should be used, and there are some who would like to maintain the simplicity of the view that a dollar is dollar is a dollar. What are the arguments on each side?

In favour of using unequal weights, with greater weight being given to a dollar benefiting a poor man than to one benefiting a rich man, one can argue that governments, aid donors, and the citizens of their countries all show by their actions (and rhetoric) that they approve of transfers from rich to poor. It is, indeed, one of the main motives for international aid. It is true that there are other ways of making transfers than project selection, such as luxury taxes, progressive systems of income tax, and the provision of free or subsidized goods and services to the poor. Nevertheless, there are limits to the amounts which can be transferred in such ways since incentives must be preserved and the political power of the well-to-do must be respected. Consequently, much inequality of consumption between rich and poor remains, and project appraisal can play some part in alleviating this. It can also be said that all practioners of social cost-benefit analysis discount future benefits, and hence give lower and lower weight to them the further off they are. One important reason for this is that future beneficiaries are expected to be richer than current ones, and, having granted

---

[9] See Little and Scott (1976) for examples of how shadow prices can be used to illuminate policy decisions.

the principle of unequal weighting here, it seems illogical to deny it for contemporary benefits to rich and poor.

Against unequal weighting one can argue that the use of project appraisal to improve distribution should take account of the effects on incentives and other factors which limit the use of taxes and subsidies as means of redistribution. A settled policy of favouring the poor through project appraisial, it could be argued, would also reduce incentives and come up against political resistance. If this were allowed for, a particular project's redistributive benefits could be partly or even wholly offset. Harberger has argued that the weights which have been suggested (e.g. in Little and Mirrlees, 1974, p. 240) imply that, for example, a marginal benefit of $1 to a poor man is worth the same as one of $4 (or even much more) to someone four times as rich. This implies that a project which benefited the poor man by $1 would be on balance worth while even if it cost the rich man a little less than $4. However, if one had to choose between two projects, each costing the same amount, with project P benefiting the poor man by $1 and project R benefiting the rich man by $4, one should definitely (in Harberger's view) prefer project R. This is because it should be possible to combine R with a transfer from the rich to the poor man which would involve a much smaller deadweight loss than three-quarters of the sum transferred. It would then be possible to benefit both the poor man by more than $1 and the rich man by more than zero. Harberber concludes that redistributive benefits should not be credited with more than saving the deadweight loss of achieving a similar transfer, and suspects that this would greatly reduce their importance.

He also speculates that societies in reality do not think along similar lines to utilitarian economists. They may favour the satisfaction of certain specific minimum needs in *kind* for all their members, such as some shelter, food, education, and medical care, but are not otherwise anxious to redistribute income, and are in particular uninterested in redistribution between those comfortably above some minimum poverty level. Economists may then be best advised to ignore redistribution and concentrate on efficiency (i.e. use equal weighting of dollar costs and benefits). Alternatively, if unequal weighting is to be employed, there is much to be said for a simplified system of estimating the net benefits accruing to those below some poverty line, and crediting projects with a redistributive gain in direct proportion to that.[10]

Lal (1987) has added another argument in support of Harberger's conclusion which goes back to the distinction between Benthamite and

---

[10] See Harberger (1978), which also provides a lucid analysis of the ways in which redistributive effects can be allowed for in setting taxes as well as in project appraisal. The argument in the text above is merely my paraphrase of part of this article. See also criticisms by Layard and Squire, and Harberger's reply in Layard *et al.* (1980).

Machiavellian decision-makers mentioned earlier (in Lal's terminology 'platonic guardians' and 'predators'). If SCBA is regarded as akin to auditing, a way of disciplining decision-makers by exposing their decisions to a more neutral and professional evaluation, then its methods have to be relatively simple and objective. Distributional weights can too easily be manipulated, and hence are best avoided. This type of argument is applicable to other shadow-pricing choices and, indeed, points to the use of market prices.

4. The Numéraire

The choice of *numéraire* is a matter of practical convenience. If errors are avoided, it makes no difference to investment decisions what it is —a positive NPV in one unit will be positive in any other. In the usual meaning of the term, a *numéraire* is homogeneous at a given point in time, but its value changes with time. In fact, the rate of discount is defined as the rate of fall in the value of the *numéraire*. Hence, at a given point in time all inputs and outputs must be expressed in terms of units of a homogeneous *numéraire*, say dollars, with each dollar being of equal value. Dollars next year, however, will (in general) be worth less than dollars now.

The word 'value' here means something like 'utils'. It is value in achieving whatever are the objectives of the decision-maker, say the government. If the government considers that a dollar benefit to a particular consumer A is worth, say, only half a dollar benefit to consumer B, then *both* of these dollar benefits cannot be a dollar in terms of the *numéraire*. If the *numéraire* is dollar benefits to A, then a dollar benefit to B must be two units of the *numéraire*. It should be clear, therefore, that to specify 'consumption benefits' as the *numéraire* is inadequate if differential weighting of benefits is being used. One should specify 'average consumption' (including how the average is determined), or else benefits to a particular consumption level, or group of consumers.

For a private decision-maker, the natural *numéraire* would be money. Since SCBA is for governments one might ask whether there is any obvious analogue, and the answer surely is foreign exchange. This can be spent in the international markets to obtain goods and services just like a private individual spends money in the local town. Furthermore, many developing countries rely heavily on foreign aid to finance projects, and they also borrow and lend foreign exchange. It therefore seems natural to use foreign exchange as the *numéraire*, although it can be expressed in terms of the country's own currency using any convenient exchange rate. As one needs to specify the date, it can be (uncommitted) foreign exchange in the hands of the government *today*, converted at today's exchange rate. For brevity, I refer to units of the *numéraire* at any date as 'current dollars', while a unit at the base date 'today' is 'base dollars'. This is, in fact, the Little–Mirrlees *numéraire*, and was their innovation. From what has already been said it should be clear that this choice of *numéraire* has no implications whatever for investment decisions, or any other policy decisions. It does not, in particular, imply that free trade is best, although some may have mistakenly thought so.

What is the relation between this *numéraire* and benefits to consumers? In general, one would expect that $1 of foreign exchange in the hands of the government would be valued more highly, by the government, than $1 of foreign exchange in the hands of the average consumer. Taxation, at the margin, imposes a deadweight loss since it distorts choices, imposes administrative burdens, and generally adds to discontent and unpopularity of the government. Hence it costs the average consumer more than $1 to provide the government $1 more through taxation. If the government equates the marginal social value of its current expenditure to the marginal social cost of financing it through taxation, as it should, then a marginal $1 of government expenditure (and so also income) should be more valuable than a marginal $1 of average private consumption.

This conclusion, it should be noted, is quite independent of whether consumption benefits are equally or unequally weighted. It reflects the *fiscal problem* which confronts all governments, and especially those of some developing countries. Of course, there are other ways in which they can obtain resources for current expenditure, notably by borrowing (whether domestically or from abroad) or by cutting investment expenditure or loans to the private sector. The social marginal costs of all these sources should be equated. The severity of the fiscal problem in some countries is attested by their high rates of inflation, as they desperately seek command over extra resources through the 'inflation tax' (see Chapter 2 in this volume), and as they borrow from abroad at high real rates of interest.

In earlier writings on SCBA there was a tendency to distinguish between 'consumption' and 'savings', but these are not homogeneous entities. There should be no difference between the marginal social benefits of a unit of resources devoted to government current expenditure and government investment, since one can always be substituted for the other.[11] On the other hand, marginal private investment could be less or more valuable than marginal government investment. Equally, and because of taxation for example, marginal private investment is likely to be more socially valuable than marginal private consumption. In my opinion, therefore, the

---

[11] It is sometimes argued that political constraints prevent governments cutting current expenditure in order to increase investment expenditure. In that case, however, one could say that the marginal social benefits can still be equated when the political effects are included in the benefits. An aid donor may want to brush these aside, but that could be dangerous.

important distinction in SCBA is between money in the hands of the government and that in private hands, with the latter further subdivided between consumption and savings. It is a mistake to lump public and private consumption together.

If unequal weighting of private consumption benefits is used, then there is likely to be a group of consumers so poor that benefits to them are considered by the government to be more valuable than its own current expenditure at the margin. The consumption level at which marginal benefits are equally valuable has been labelled *base-level consumption* (or 'critical consumption'). If the government could make transfers to such consumers, or those poorer still, without incurring other costs than the resources transferred, then it should be ready to do so, and some governments do. However, there could be 'side-effects' which inhibit these transfers, such as effects on incentives to work.[12]

5. The Accounting Rate of Interest (ARI)[13]

It is generally agreed that future benefits (and costs) should be given less weight than current ones, but the question of how much less is controversial, and has led to much confusion, not surprisingly as it is a difficult one to answer.

Let us first be clear that the appropriate rate of discount will, in general, differ according to the unit which is being discounted. We should all now be familiar with the fact that rates of interest on, say, equally safe bonds differ according to the currency in which they are denominated. In the past, sterling bonds have generally paid higher interest rates than US dollar bonds which in turn have paid more than Swiss franc bonds. This is because the price of pounds in terms of dollars has tended to fall, as has the price of dollars in terms of Swiss francs, and these falls have been anticipated. Hence the rate of discount has to be related to a specific *numéraire*.

Using the Little and Marrlees *numéraire* just described, it follows from what has already been said that the ARI should equal the rate of fall in the social value of current dollars of marginal government expenditure and of marginal expenditure by those with base-level consumption. Equally, the ARI should equal the rate of fall in the social cost of current dollars of marginal taxation. Current dollars could be measured at current prices (giving a nominal rate of discount) or at constant purchasing power in some

---

[12] For further discussion of base-level consumption, see Little and Mirrlees (1974), p. 238, Scott (1977) (where the concept is applied to the UK to estimate the ARI), and Scott in Little and Scott (1976), ch. V, 'Shadow Wages of "Surplus" Labour in Mauritius'. The work for the last was done in 1972 and, so far as I know, was the origin of the concept and use of base-level consumption in the context of SCBA.

[13] Rates of interest can vary through time, and the same is true of the ARI. For simplicity I assume in what follows that the ARI is constant.

sense (giving a real one). This is matter of practical convenience. Since cost-of-living index numbers are widely available, and are also often more carefully estimated than other price index numbers,[14] it is convenient to define the dollars as having constant purchasing power over base-level consumption (see Scott *et al.* (1976), ch. 2 for further discussion).

In principle, the government should bring the marginal social benefits and costs of all relevant margins (government current expenditure and taxation, public sector investment, and borrowing and lending, both domestically and abroad) into equality, since all are substitutes at the margin.[15] It has often been pointed out that marginal public sector investment projects should have zero NPV when discounted at the ARI, but this does not, unfortunately, provide a way of *determining* the ARI. One cannot, for example, find the ARI by trial and error as the rate of discount which ensures that the investment budget is just exhausted when all projects with positive NPV are implemented, unless, that is, one has some independent method of determining that budget. It could as well be argued that the budget should be determined by discovering the amount of investment achieving a positive NPV for an independently determined ARI. The same is true of all the other margins. For example, the marginal cost of borrowing from abroad (another popular candidate) must depend on the amount borrowed, which should depend on the ARI.

In principle, the ARI should emerge as the solution of a dynamic programming problem in which all of the above magnitudes (and others as well) would be simultaneously determined. It is doubtful whether this observation is of much practical value, however, any more than a similar observation sometimes made about the determination of shadow prices generally. No one knows the relevant parameters to set up the problem, even if one could then solve it. Instead, one must search for approximations and short cuts.

A convenient and simple formula in this context is

$$r = ng + p,$$

where *r* is the (real) ARI, *g* is the (real) rate of growth of benefits or costs to be discounted, *n* is an elasticity which measures the proportionate fall in

[14] There is, however, a danger that they may be manipulated by the government and so give a distorted measure of inflation.

[15] Governments may lend abroad at low rates of interest in order to have liquid foreign exchange reserves. In this case the apparent yield is not the true social yield, since the latter should include the social benefits resulting from the freedom for manoeurvre and smoothing out of fluctuations which result from the possession of such reserves. Extra reserves may cheapen borrowing costs. The latter are also not always what they seem. Not only may real rates of interest rise unexpectedly, but borrowing may lead to crises which impose heavy social costs. It is an implication of the statement in the text that the same ARI should be used to discount all public sector benefits and costs, once they are all expressed in the same *numéraire*. In practice, governments often resort to lower rates of discount for some types of project than for others, the rationale for which is unclear.

social value per unit proportionate increase in the relevant benefit or cost, when the proportionate changes are infinitesimally small, and p measures 'impatience' or pure time preference. p is then the rate of discount applied to 'utils', or is what the rate of discount would be under static conditions. In this formula, strictly speaking, r, g, and p are all measured in exponential terms, but the formula gives a reasonable approximation if they are expressed in percentage terms and the percentages are small.[16]

The formula could be applied, for example, to the rate of growth of base-level consumption and was so by the writer to supplementary benefit levels in the UK. To do this, I estimated n and p by reference to long-term yields on UK government bonds before 1914, concluding that n was between 1 and 2.5 and p between 0 and 1.5 per cent per annum (Scott, 1977). Later work has suggested some modification of these estimates. With supplementary benefit levels expected to grow more or less in line with average consumption per head at, say, 2 per cent per annum, the upshot was an estimated real rate of discount in the region of 5 per cent per annum.

This approach could be more widely used. In many developing countries there is nothing comparable to supplementary benefit level, and so base-level consumption is difficult to estimate. However, one can more easily estimate the rate of growth of government current expenditure or taxation per head. If one can assume that the benefits from the former, and the costs of the latter, are similar to those of private consumption (which seems reasonable), so that n should be at least roughly the same, then the formula can be applied. It seems likely that this would result in lower discount rates than, say 10 or 15 per cent per annum which have been suggested for some developing countries.[17] What is the reasoning behind these higher rates?

One powerful view has been that public sector investments ought to yield approximately the same at the margin as private sector investments, since they could be substituted for each other. Evidence is then produced of high *average* real rates of return in the private sector (before tax), and this is held to justify a high ARI.[18] A less extreme form of this view is that public borrowing, for example, increases private saving and reduces private investment. It is therefore only partially a substitute for the latter, and

---

[16] If $100i$ is the percentage rate of interest per annum, then the exponential rate which equals it is given by $e^r = 1 + i$, or $r = \ln(1 + i)$.

[17] See e.g. the estimates for different developing countries in UK Ministry of Overseas Development (1977), p. 57. These are (% p.a.): one rate of 6, six rates of 8, four rates of 10, one rate of 12, and one rate of 15.

[18] A more subtle version of this argument is that a government which taxes private investors should, if it is consistent, believe that the marginal social costs of $1 raised in this way are no more that the marginal social value of $1 to it. One can imagine the $1 of tax, if left in the hands of the private investor, yielding a stream of future social benefits (e.g. in the form of future tax receipts) which must e discounted at the ARI. The ARI must then be high enough to reduce their NPV to $1 or less. Newbery in Little and Scott (1976) used this approach for Kenya and concluded that the ARI was probably $12\frac{1}{2}$ to 15% p.a. However, some of the objections mentioned in the text apply.

for the rest it is compensated by a cut in private consumption. If private savers use a low rate of discount, say r_c, while private investors earn much higher marginal returns, say r_p, the difference being mainly explained by taxation of capital or saving, then the ARI should be a weighted average of r_c and r_p, the weights being proportionate to the amounts of private consumption and private investment crowded out per unit of public investment.

There are objections to this approach. In the first place, evidence of high *average* returns in the private sector is not necessarily evidence of high *marginal* returns. Secondly, both r_c and r_p should be social, not private, rates of return. This is why r_p is calculated before tax, but there could be other adjustments to be made which, admittedly, could go either way. Thirdly, the other relevant margins are ignored. Public sector investment can be financed by cutting public sector consumption, or by borrowing from abroad, or by taxation (which may impinge differently from public sector borrowing on private consumption and investment).

Can the available evidence there be reconciled with high rates of discount? If, on the contrary, the evidence points to lower rates, the conclusion should be that *both* public *and* private investment should be encouraged, rather than the status quo preserved. Thus a lower ARI should be used and private investment increased by lowering the tax on private saving so that r_p and r_c tend closer together.

This is an example of a more general point. It is tempting to *assume* that governmental policies are either optimal or at least given (determined by 'political' factors outside the concern of the project evaluator). However, shadow-pricing can be used to reveal mistakes and inconsistencies in economic policies just as in the choice of investments. We return to this point later.

To sum up, there is no way of estimating the ARI which is both practical and obviously correct. Guidance should be sought by considering all the relevant margins: government current expenditure and taxation, borrowing and lending, and public sector investment. Problems of risk and bias were discussed briefly earlier. Abstracting from them, my own belief is that rather low real rates of discount in the region of 5 per cent per annum are easier to justify in many developing countries than high ones in the region of 10–15 per cent per annum, although there are cases where growth is rapid and high rates apply. In most countries, investment is probably sub-optimal as well as being inefficient.

5. Shadow Prices for Commodities

In 1965 Ian Little was asked by the Bell Commission to make a report on a project to produce heavy electrical equipment at Bhopal in central India. A large British firm provided the consultants for the scheme, and he discovered that they had difficulty in estimating what the local prices of many of the outputs and inputs were or were likely to be. Instead, they used the prices they *did* know something about as a guide, namely international prices. Resisting the temptation to condemn this as inappropriate (and lazy), he reflected that the procedure had merit. If the main outputs and inputs were traded goods, as was the case, a project which was socially desirable should be able to make a profit at these prices. The fact that it could make a profit at local prices was a less reliable guide, since local prices could be manipulated by means of taxes and subsidies, or by outright prohibition of competitive imports, so as to make almost any project profitable. Thus was the idea of using world prices, or more strictly border prices, as a guide to shadow prices for traded goods born. In my judgement, and that of others,[19] it is the most significant contribution of the famous 'Little–Mirrlees' method of social cost-benefit analysis.[20]

It is, of course, necessary to complement this idea by estimating shadow prices for other inputs and outputs, in particular, non-tradable goods and labour. The importance of these will depend upon the project, but for a great many manufacturing projects in many countries tradable inputs and outputs are very important, and, where tariff or quota protection is strong (as it often is), the use of world prices instead of actual prices can make a very big difference to one's estimates of profitability. By contrast, for such projects it may generally make little difference whether one takes shadow wages equal to market wages or only half as great. It must be stressed that manufacturing projects' profitability is by no means always *reduced* by using world prices. For many the reverse is true, since protection may raise input prices by more than output prices, and generally discriminates against export industries (see Little *et al.* (1970), pp. 190–7).

The case for using world prices as a guide to the relative shadow prices of traded goods has frequently been challenged. Indeed, great ingenuity has been displayed in performing this task, and some wonderful and imaginative examples have been constructed to show how the use of world prices

---

[19] Thus the 'Guide' produced by UK's Ministry of Overseas Development singles out the use of world rather than domestic prices for tradable inputs and outputs as being 'far the most important' of the points basic to the 'Guide' (see UK Ministry of Overseas Development (1977), p. ix).

[20] In March 1965 (incorrectly stated to be March 1964 in Little (1969)) Ian Little gave a seminar at the Delhi School of Economics in which he outlined a system of shadow prices for use in public sector project selection in India, and which was subsequently published (Little, 1969). This included his suggestion of the use of border prices for traded goods and the drawing of a distinction between 'tradables' and 'non-tradables'. At the seminar, Jagdish Bhagwati pointed out that there was a close relation between Ian Little's criterion for project selection and Tinbergen's 'semi input-output method', in which the same tradables–non-tradables distinction was drawn (see Tinbergen, 1963). However, Tinbergen's proposals did not, it seems, relate directly to SCBA, and were not known to Ian Little when he first made his proposals. I believe that world prices have been used for some time as a guide in some East European countries where price controls have rendered domestic prices unreliable guides to social costs and benefits.

could lead to incorrect decisions. Those playing this game, however, have seldom tackled the problem of propounding a better guide to project appraisal in practice. World prices, in so far as they cannot appreciably be influenced by a particular small country's actions, are probably the best available measure of the marginal rates of substitution confronting that country. They are like the prices paid by any private consumer in the market. Another way of seeing their appropriateness is to consider the case where the domestic divergences between border prices and market prices for traded goods are entirely due to taxes and subsidies. The use of border prices then, in effect, gives recognition to this fact. An import bearing a high tariff, for example, does not really cost the public sector the tariff-inclusive price, but only the border price, the tariff being merely an internal transfer within the public sector.[21] Where protection is given by quota, however, this argument no longer applies, since then the premium of the domestic over the border price will accrue to a private importer, whose profits may be deemed to be less valuable than government revenue. Furthermore, if the quota is fixed, the good, although tradable, will in fact not be traded at the margin. Assuming it is not domestically produced, additional use of it by the public sector must then be at the expense of its use in the private sector.

This is an example of a more general point, already alluded to. Shadow prices can only be calculated on some assumptions about governmental as well as private behaviour. There is a whole host of governmental interventions in many developing countries: taxes, subsidies, quotas, planning controls etc. Governments have to finance themselves, but can choose between a variety of means. They may react to threats of inflation or depression, or of foreign exchange deficits, in different ways. What assumptions are appropriate about all these matters in social cost-benefit analysis? It is not very helpful to be told either that one must assume that the government (or decision-maker) will optimize within its field of control, or that one must make the best guess one can as to the policies which will be actually adopted. The second of these is correct, but gives insufficient guidance, while the first seems to beg too many questions, including knowledge by the evaluator of what optimization would imply. I cannot discuss this large question fully here (See Sen, 1972; Drèze and Stern, 1987), but the quota example is a good one to bring out a few points.

First, just because there is a fixed quota now, one cannot assume that there will be one for the future, and the future is relevant. Second, if one takes the point of view of an aid donor, it would surely be a mistake to finance a project whose social profitablity would disappear (let us suppose)

---

[21] Because it allows for indirect revenue gains or losses, an SCBA should commend itself to Ministries of Finance, a selling-point which should not be neglected.

if the recipient government were to relax a quota which, in the donor's view, should be relaxed. To do so would be a failure of project aid. Third, a similar argument applies within the public sector. If one accepts the case for using border prices when there is not a quota, then one will presumably want to argue against the use of a quota to convert a project from loss to profit. These arguments therefore lean towards the view that optimal policies should be assumed. But if the policy in question were less *ad hoc* and more long-standing—income taxation, for example—it would surely be more reasonable to assume its continued existence, even though one might take the view that a better policy was available—expenditure taxation, say. Here one leans more towards prediction of what is likely to happen.

For non-traded goods the only procedure of comparable simplicity to that of border prices for traded goods is the use of actual relative prices. This implicitly assumes that all the secondary repercussions of changing net demands or supplies cancel out. In a first-best economy they would be very small, tending to zero for small changes, but this *need* not be so in a real economy. Nevertheless, it may be more efficient to neglect them than to attempt to estimate and value these indirect effects. Attempts have been made, including some by the present writer (Scott *et al.*, 1976, pt. 1; also Lal, 1980), but their reliability is low. They usually proceed on the assumption of constant costs (so that one assumes that it is output, rather than consumption, which responds to changes in demand or supply), and they require estimates of cost structures or an input–output table which are assumed to remain constant through time. My own estimates for Kenya suggested that one would lose little accuracy by taking the same average ratio of shadow price to market price (this is called the *accounting ratio*) for all non-traded goods. The variance of this ratio was much less for non-traded than for traded goods, essentially because each was a weighted average of ratios for many traded goods, labour, and capital (Scott *et al.*, 1976, pp. 34–6). There are, of course, exceptions. A particular non-traded good may be of such importance to a project that an attempt at careful estimation is worth while. It may also be worth while estimating average accounting ratios for particular bundles of goods and services (both traded and non-traded) that frequently recur in different contexts, for example, transport and distribution costs, office costs, building costs etc. Such averages are termed *conversion factors*.

If actual prices are taken for a large group of non-traded goods and services they need to be adjusted by some uniform proportion (the *standard conversion factor*) to make them comparable to the border prices used for traded goods. The need for this adjustment, which is similar to that involved in using a shadow exchange rate, can be seen from the following example. Imagine a first-best economy in which, with no trade taxes or subsidies, shadow prices equal the prices of both traded and non-traded goods, and no adjustment is therefore required. Now suppose that a 10 per cent tariff on all imports together with a 10 per cent subsidy on all exports is imposed. To preserve the status quo the exchange rate must be appreciated by 10 per cent, and, if that is done, there will be no change in any internal prices. However, border prices will have fallen by 10 per cent in terms of domestic currency. Consequently, if they are used as shadow prices for traded goods, non-traded goods prices must be adjusted downwards by 10 per cent to obtain the correct set of relative shadow prices. One could describe the situation with the trade taxes and subsidies as being that of an overvalued currency. If all these taxes and subsidies were swept away, the exchange rate would have to be devalued to maintain equilibrium at the existing internal price level. More generally, in developing countries with overvalued currencies, non-traded goods prices need on average to be adjusted downwards probably rather more than in the same proportion as the exchange rate would need to be devalued if trade taxes and subsidies and other restrictions on trade were swept away. The adjustment required is more, since non-traded goods include labour costs and also some payments to capital, and their accounting ratios are likely to be lower than the average for traded goods.[22]

If accounting ratios are stable, this greatly simplifies matters, since the same set of estimates can serve many different SCBA. The ratios will be reasonably stable if *ad valorem* taxes and subsidies are reasonably stable and if they are the main reason why shadow prices diverge from actual prices. However, an economy permeated by quantitative controls destroys this convenient situation. Ratios of actual prices to border prices for traded goods will then vary with internal demand and the operation of the quotas, and this will impinge on accounting ratios for non-traded goods. In such an economy it may be necessary to rely on estimates of absolute traded-goods prices (instead of being able to multiply actual prices by standard accounting ratios), while for non-traded goods any estimates must be largely guesswork. If the price mechanism is badly disrupted, so will be the efficient selection of investment projects.

6. Shadow Wages for Unskilled Labour

Beliefs about shadow wages have ranged all the way from zero to actual wages (for unskilled labour). The argument for zero is that unemployment, both open and concealed, is heavy in many developing countries so that the alternative marginal product of labour employed in the public sector is

---

[22] Thus for Kenya, my estimates of accounting ratios for non-traded goods had a median of 0.77, that for exports was 0.995, and that for imports 0.855. See Scott, *et al.* (1976), p. 34. For a discussion of shadow exchange rates, see the Symposium on Shadow Exchange Rates (1974).

zero, or close to zero. Even were this true, it neglects the social cost involved in transferring resources from the government to the workers employed (and, indirectly, to those supporting the worker before he becomes
employed). As wages in the public sector are likely to be well above base-
level consumption, this transfer will be costly, and this will raise the shadow wage above zero. Furthermore, many would deny that the marginal
product of workers in agriculture in most developing countries is close to
zero.[23] Nevertheless, it could be argued that urban public sector wages are
typically far above rural wages, so that rural workers drawn into such
urban employment make a large gain. Even if this gain is given a lower
weight than the cost to the government of paying the higher wage, there is
still a sizeable net social benefit from employment which should be sub-
tracted from the actual wage to get the lower shadow wage.

A simple formula which takes account of the above points is

$$\text{SWR} = c' - \frac{1}{s}(c - m).$$

This is a formula given in Little and Mirrlees (1974, p. 270), but I shall
modify the terms slightly here. Let c' be the actual wage, and m be both the
wage and the marginal product of labour in the rural sector, from which it
is assumed that the worker is drawn. c is the urban wage expressed in a way
comparable, from the worker's point of view, with m, so that $c - m$ is the
benefit accruing to the worker from moving to the new urban public sector
job. The difference between c' and c is discussed below. Finally, s is the
ratio of the value of money in the hands of the government to that of
the extra money gained by the worker (i.e. $c - m$). c', c, and m are all expressed in terms of foreign exchange equivalents. The formula then says
that the shadow wage rate is the actual wage rate (adjusted by the
appropriate conversion factor) c', *less* the *social* value of the benefit
accruing to the worker from transferring to the urban public sector job.

It can be seen that the shadow wage rate is closer to the actual wage rate
the smaller is the benefit, $c - m$, and the less is the social weight given to it
(i.e. the greater is s). The shadow wage rate would equal the alternative
marginal product, m, if $c' = c$ and $s = 1$. However, in practice c' may be
appreciably greater than c because, for example, of the higher cost of living
in the town than in the countryside. A higher urban wage may do little
more than compensate the worker for higher urban rents, the additional
cost of travelling to work, the higher cost of food etc. This amounts to
saying that the actual wage rate is close to the supply price of labour, which

---

[23] See e.g. Harberger (1971) who quotes as evidence for India that 25% of the rural labour
force are landless workers, who on average work some 250 full-time equivalent man-days a
year, and whose average annual earnings are approximately equal to the per capita income of
the country (which, he points out, is similar to the position in US agriculture).

may be well above the rural wage rate. The supply price of labour, in turn, is measured by the actual wage in what Harberger has called the 'unprotected sector', i.e. where wages are free to respond to supply and demand. In that sector, $c - m$ would be small, and the SWR would be close to c'.[24] The same result would follow if s were much larger than one because the government's budgetary situation was very tight with a high marginal social benefit from current expenditure and a high marginal social cost of taxation.

There is another type of consideration which points to a shadow wage rate close to the actual one, even though the actual wage is fixed well above the supply price of labour, in what Harberger calls the 'protected sector', and even though s is close to one. If wages in the protected sector are regulated at a level well above the supply price of labour, this may result in a large number of unemployed workers in effect queuing up for these attractive jobs. The level of unemployment will act as an equilibrating mechanism to regulate the supply of would-be workers, and an increase in the number of protected jobs, by improving the chances of getting one of them, will induce an increase in the number unemployed. In these circumstances, the marginal social cost of employing an extra (protected) worker must include the costs of this additional unemployment. It is perfectly possible for these extra costs to equal the whole excess of the protected wage over the supply price of labour, so that the shadow wage rate equals the actual wage.[25]

While these considerations should make one cautious of assuming that shadow wage rates are well below actual wages, an assumption that earlier writers were perhaps too ready to make,[26] there are still circumstances in which this is so. My own estimates for Mauritius put the shadow wage for unskilled male workers, assumed to come out of the very numerous unemployed, at 40 per cent of the market wage, or at rather more than 50 per cent of the market wage adjusted by a factor similar to the standard conversion factor (Scott, in Little and Scott 1976). Estimates of the UK Minis-

---

[24] See Harberger (1971). See also Scott *et al.* (1976), pp. 173–8 for estimates of the difference between the rural and urban cost of living in Kenya in 1967/8. The latter was estimated to be roughly 60% greater than the former.

[25] The idea that unemployment acts as a regulator of migration to the towns in the hope of getting protected sector jobs was independently put forward by Todaro (1969) and Harberger (1971), and the implication that the shadow wage could then equal the protected sector wage was drawn by both Harberger and Harris and Todaro (1970). Heady (1981) generalized their models and showed that the conclusion held even though observed unemployment rates were well below the rates that were seemingly required to explain a sizeable wage gap between protected and unprotected wages.

[26] Ian Little himself argued for zero as a reasonable approximation to the shadow wage in Indian industrial projects in 1965 (see Little 1969, pp. 236–41), but he has changed his views since then.

try of Overseas Development for 11 developing countries also give SWR which are often low.[27] My own estimates for Kenya, and Lal's for India, however, are appreciably higher.[28]

As a final point it is worth noting that the use of SWR in SCBA allows for multiplier effects. The SWR allows for the increased consumption of additional workers employed, and also, when that extra consumption expenditure is incurred, it is costed at shadow prices. Those prices, in turn, allow for a labour element in which the SWR again appears, allowing for a second round of consumption benefits. . . . and so on.[29]

7. Conclusion: Suggestions for Further Reading

SCBA is applied welfare economics. Ian Little's first book, which made him famous, was his *Critique of Welfare Economics* first published in 1950. This was a mainly theoretical work, but it was very much theory with an eye to application in the real world. It must have been satisfying to have followed this up, some 20 years later, by launching with Jim Mirrlees a method of SCBA which has rapidly caught on, and is now used by major aid donors, as well as by India and some other developing countries.

In this essay I have tried to show the wide range of problems involved, their inherent difficulty, and the approaches which have been fruitful. The best single suggestion for further reading I can make is still Little and Mirrlees (1974). A shorter introduction is Squire and van der Tak (1975), and a more recent one, also commendably brief, Ray (1984). Two published attempts to estimate fairly comprehensive sets of shadow prices, as well as to make some applications of them, are (for Kenya) Scott *et al.* (1976) and (for India) Lal (1980). Little and Scott (1976) brings together a number of shorter studies of estimates and applications. A very useful practical guide which includes check lists for different types of project is UK Ministry of Overseas Development (1977). For those interested in more theoretical aspects, a comprehensive recent (but, for the non-mathematically proficient, rather tough) survey is by Drèze and Stern (1987), which contains an extensive bibliography, while another is by Hammond (1987).

[27] Six of the estimates of the ratio of the SWR to the actual wage rate given are 0.5, one is 0.25, and two are 0.6, see UK Ministry of Overseas Development (1977), p. 57.

[28] For unskilled labour, the ratio of the SWR to the actual wage rate in Kenya was estimated to be 0.7 for the urban formal sector, 0.8 for the urban informal sector, and 1.0 for the rural informal sector, see Scott *et al.* (1976), p. 32. Similar ratios for urban industrial labour in India are give by Lal for 15 states, and vary from 0.56 to 0.76. His comparable estimates for rural labour vary from 0.70 to 1.08. See Lal (1980), p. 203.

[29] For a formal demonstration, see Scott in Little and Scott (1976), pp. 149–52. My estimate of the multipier in Mauritius was quite small, 1.14, despite the existence of heavy unemployment. However, Mauritius is a very open economy, which reduced the multiplier through the marginal propensity to import.

References

Brook, P. J. (1987), *A Study of the Creation of Firms as Vehicles for Product Innovation*, D. Phil. thesis, Oxford.

Drèze, J. P., and Stern, N. H. (1987), 'The Theory of Cost-Benefit Analysis', in A. J. Auerbach and M. Feldstein (eds.), *Handbook of Public Economics*, (Amsterdam: North-Holland).

Feldstein, M. S. (1964), 'The Social Time Preference Discount Rate in Cost Benefit Analysis', *Economic Journal*, 74 (June).

Hammond, P. J. (1987), 'Shadow pricing in the public sector', in P. G. Hare (ed.), *Readings in Public Sector Economics* (Oxford: Blackwell).

Harberger, A. C. (1971), 'On Measuring the Social Opportunity Cost of Labour', *International Labour Review*, 103 (June).

——(1978), 'On the Use of Distributional Weights in Social Cost-Benefit Analysis, *Journal of Political Economy*, 86/2, pt. 2.

Harris, J. R., and Todaro, M. P. (1970), 'Migration, Unemployment and Development: A Two-Sector Analysis', *American Economic Review*, 60 (Mar.).

Heady, C. J. (1981), 'Shadow wages and induced migration', *Oxford Economic Papers*, 33 (Mar.).

Lal, D. (1980), *Prices for Planning* (London: Heinemann).

——(1987), 'Comment' in G. M. Meier (ed.), *Pioneers in Development*, 2nd Series, (Oxford: OUP for the World Bank).

Layard, R., Squire, L., and Harberger, A. C. (1980), 'On the Use of Distributional Weights in Social Cost-Benefit Analysis: Comments and Reply', *Journal of Political Economy*, 88/5.

Little, I. M. D. (1969), 'Public Sector Project Selection in Relation to Indian Development', *Indian Economic Thought and Development* (Bombay: Popular Prakashan).

——(1987), 'A Comment on Professor Toye's Paper', in L. Emmerij (ed.), *Development Policies and the Crisis of the 1980s* (Paris: OECD).

——and Mirrlees, J. A. M. (1969), *Manual of Industrial Project Analysis in Developing Countries:* Vol. II, *Social Cost Benefit Analysis* (Paris: Development Centre, OECD).

——(1974), *Project Appraisal and Planning for Developing Countries* (London: Heinemann Educational).

——Scitovsky, T., and Scott, M. FG. (1970), *Industry and Trade in Some Developing Countries* (London: OUP for OECD).

——and Scott, M. FG. (1976), *Using Shadow Prices* (London: Heinemann Educational).

Meade, J. E. (1952), 'External Economies and Diseconomies in a Competitive Situation', *Economic Journal*, 62 (Mar.).

Ray, A. (1984), *Cost-Benefit Analysis: Issues and Methodologies* (Baltimore, Md.: Johns Hopkins Univ. Press for the World Bank).

Scitovsky, T. (1954), 'Two Concepts of External Economies', *Journal of Political Economy*, 17.

Scott, M. FG. (1977), 'The Test Rate of Discount and Changes in Base-Level Income in the United Kingdom', *Ecoomic Journal*, 87 (June).

——MacArthur, J. D., and Newbery, D. M. G. (1976), *Project Appraisal in Practice* (London: Heinemann Educational).

Sen, A. K. (1972), 'Control Areas and Accounting Prices: An Approach to Economic Evaluation', *Economic Journal*, 82, Suppl. (Mar.).

Squire, L., and van der Tak, H. G. (1975), *Economic Analysis of Projects* (Baltimore, Md.: Johns Hopkins Univ. Press for the World Bank).

Symposium on Shadow Exchange Rates (1974), *Oxford Economic Papers*, 26 (Jul.).

Tinbergen, J. (1963). 'Projections of Economic Data in Development Planning', *Caribbean Organisation, Planning for Economic Development in the Caribbean*, Seminar on Planning Techniques and Methods (The Hague: Levisson Press).

Todaro, M. P. (1969), 'A Model of Labour Migration and Urban Unemployment in Less Developed Countries', *American Economic Review*, 59 (Mar.).

UK Government (1967), *Nationalised Industries: A Review of Economic and Financial Objectives*, Cmnd. 3437 (London: HMSO).

——(1977), *A Guide to the Economic Appraisal of Projects in Developing Countries* (London: HMSO).

United Nations (1972), *Guidelines for Project Evaluation* by P. Dasgupta, S. Marglin, and A. K. Sen (New York: United Nations).

14

The Population Enigma

GÖRAN OHLIN

THERE are two levels of discourse about population. The specialists, to whom I do not belong, are struggling to come to grips with a bewildering variety of evidence and theories. Economists tend to look for simple ideas that might be relevant to policy-making. I fall half-way between the two—impatient with some of the grossly simplified assertions about population that are so often encountered in the political arena, intrigued and disconcerted by the failure to make much headway in the interpretation of population changes.

The themes of this paper are very simple. First, to insist that we still do not understand very much about the dynamics of population. Many Western minds have long been locked into an unduly sterile position of viewing population as an adversary, at least when it occurs in developing countries. Second, the growth of population in developing countries is now slowing down, except in Africa, while populations in industrializing countries are not just stabilizing but declining. Third, these trends, combined with reduced costs of transportation, force attention to migration, which is perhaps a more important issue than the growth of world population.

1. Economists and Population

The first issue, then, is the relationship between population and the economy. Innumerable charts, for the most part with an alarmist intention, have illustrated the population explosion, in countries or regions and in the world as a whole. Some time in 1987 world population reached 5 billion, having doubled since 1950. If one takes a longer view, world population seems to have taken off in the eighteenth century after thousands of years of growth at a snail's pace.

This is obviously a staggeringly important aspect of the history of mankind, but it does not seem much better understood today than a century ago, in spite of all the attention that has been lavished on it.

It is a widespread attitude among economists that, although we might not know too much about other aspects of the future, at least population projections constitute a reasonably safe point of departure. The entrants to the labour force for the next 15 years are already born, and the parameters determining population growth are thought, especially by non-demographers, to be fairly steady. So why not simply regard population as an exogenous factor?

Some 50 years ago, Sir John Hicks, in *Value and Capital*, which was to have a great influence on economic theory, allowed himself the following reflexion *en passant*: One cannot repress the thought that perhaps the whole Industrial Revolution of the last two hundred years has been nothing else but a vast secular boom, largely induced by the unparalleled rise in population (Hicks, 1939, p. 302 n).

This readiness to regard population as an exogenous mystery does not seem very satisfactory. It is, after all, even more difficult to repress the thought that the population explosion of the last centuries must have been a response to vast economic and social progress.

2. Population Theory

Somewhere between economics and purely formal demography there is a rambling edifice called economic demography or population theory, or more modestly population thought. It is the place where speculations about the interrelationship between population growth and other kinds of social and economic change are stored. They go back a long time and have been meticulously catalogued: they include the reflections of Ibn Khaldun, the memoranda of Chinese civil servants hundreds of years ago, pamphlets and even tomes by clergymen reflecting on births and deaths and what they tell us about *die göttliche Ordnung*, the observations of Graunt and Petty, and a number of French students of the matter in the seventeenth and eighteenth centuries (see e.g. Graunt, 1662; Hull, 1899; Spengler, 1942).

But it was with Malthus that the discussion really took off. It was ignited by the controversy that still haunts it: was population growth good or bad? Malthus was provoked into the polemics about 'the principles of population' by his irritation with the simple-minded satisfaction of those who took the evidence of population growth to be evidence of progress. He saw it as the harbinger of misery. As he devoted his life to the collection of evidence to back up his original hypothesis about the pernicious effects of population growth, his *Essay on the Principles of Population* went into one edition after another and became a cornerstone of modern population theory. He absorbed the early advances in the analyses of human mortality and fertility, which have remained central to demographic analysis ever since. He wrote in the style of an educated man rather than that of the social sciences that had not yet been dreamed of, and perhaps because of that he brought to the study of population the virtues of the age of reason: detachment, objectivity, and a passion for facts.

Although Malthus was more of an economist than most of his successors in the study of demography, no historical experience could have prepared him or his contemporaries for the spurt of productivity which the Industrial Revolution was going to bring. It was impossible to know that his worries about over-population in Britain would prove unfounded. As it happened, population increase accelerated in the nineteenth century not only in England or the countries generally associated with the Industrial Revolution, but also in other parts of Europe where it was less clearly associated with major social change. There it took on a more Malthusian character and provoked a massive out-migration.

The recent volume on *The State of Population Theory: Forward from Malthus*, edited by Coleman and Schofield, was occasioned by the 150th anniversary of Malthus's death—'to take stock of developments in population theory' after Malthus. It documents in impressive detail the search for an approach to population regulation, including intriguing studies of animal populations, wild or in captivity, which seem to adjust rather differently from human ones to their environment. Coleman, in his encyclopaedic introduction, also makes the thought-provoking point that 'almost all populations and most species that have ever existed' have become extinct (Coleman and Schofield, 1986, p. 18).

There is no limit to the recondite areas of study into which students of population have been carried: the faunas of the Pleistocene, climatic change, the spread of infectious disease, the prevalence of war and violence, mathematical modelling, cultural systems, and so forth. This is an impressive testimony to the preoccupation with the population enigma, but it also suggests that for all the accumulation of evidence and sophisticated approaches there has not been much movement forward from Malthus. As the editors suggest, he sketched 'a total population system operating on specified, if elementary, rules relating population behaviour to the social, economic, and moral context' (Coleman and Schofield, 1986, p. 18).

Today the causes and consequences of population growth are often studied as separate issues which produce a confusing conception of social change. The most intriguing corner of economic demography today is in my view the one where attempts are made to put the pieces together and produce a 'total population system'. Ronald Lee, for instance, building on the work of others, has suggested a conceptual synthesis to illustrate the many ways in which the interaction between technology and population can explain the course of population growth (Lee, 1986, pp. 96–130). But so far such approaches remain on a very high level of abstraction and leave many black boxes to be filled.

3. The Present Concerns

For some time now, the growth of population has been viewed as a malevolent force threatening to engulf the efforts to promote the development of the Third World. Much of this concern has stemmed from a priori assumptions rather than hard evidence. The World Bank in 1984 devoted the *World Development Report* to the problem of population growth in developing countries. The report was aware that the evidence was not clear-cut but argued that for 'most countries, for any given amount of resources, a slower rate of population growth would help to promote economic and social development' (World Bank, 1984, p. 81).

Not long thereafter the US National Academy of Science published a report by a demographic working group on *Population Growth and Economic Development: Policy Questions* (National Research Council, 1986). On the basis of extensive review of the evidence and the literature, it found the negative impact of population growth on important development problems such as resource exhaustion, savings, urbanization, and unemployment to have been exaggerated.

This does not mean that population policy and family planning in developing countries are not important undertakings that deserve support and encouragement. Family planning is often seen as an essential ingredient in social policy. Population policy has many other objectives than to seek to reduce birth rates. A guarded position on the harmfulness of population growth would, however, seem to imply that aid-giving countries and institutions should not pontificate too much and not represent a swift reduction of birth rates as either a prerequisite for development or a short cut to it.

One thing that characterizes this neo-Malthusian debate is the focus on consequences of population growth and the neglect of its causes. Another is its lack of historical perspective. In earlier days, and for that matter even today, population growth has been seen as a sign of health. There is no reason to be upset by rates of population growth by themselves. They have to be interpreted in relation to the situations in which they occur and the reasons behind them. The present rates of rapid increase in developing countries are sometimes cited as if they are so monstrously large that it is self-evident that their consequences must be disastrous. Projections are cited for Third World countries which point to enormously large populations in the not so distant future—285 million for Nigeria in 2025, 174 million for Mexico, etc.—as if the figures by themselves would convince anyone of their absurdity.

But, to begin with, present growth rates in the Third World are not unprecedented. Already Malthus noted that the population of the United States, after allowing for immigration, seemed, in spite of unhealthy living conditions, to have had a natural increase in the late eighteenth century that made for a doubling in 25 years, which means an annual rate of close to 3 per cent.[1] The sensational rates of other settler populations, in par-

---

[1] E.g. Malthus (1803), pp. 338–40, or Glass (1953), where pp. 127–32 discuss the evidence of American censuses before 1820.

ticular French-Canadian ones, are also part of the lore of population history.

Secondly, it is not unfettered fertility that makes for growth in the Third World. The biological potential for population growth is far greater than the actual except in conditions of extremely high mortality. For all populations in the world today fertility is constrained by social forces rather than biological ones.

The real question is how the fertility transition will work out in the Third World, i.e. how long it will take for birth rates to follow death rates down, as they have done everywhere so far. Caldwell has argued that it might in some parts of the Third World be delayed for quite some time, chiefly because of the extraneous nature of the culture shock which has improved health conditions without fundamentally affecting value systems.[2]

The evidence so far suggests that, except in Africa, fertility is indeed declining, and natural increase too. Nevertheless for some time to come the number of young people and people of working age will be growing at a rate of 3 per cent. This is obviously going to put great pressure on the institutions in those countries, and not least on the system of international migration as populations in industrial countries show signs of declining.

4. The Depopulation of Industrial Countries

Those who have been concerned about excessive growth of population tended until recently to assume that, if it could be checked, the result would be a stabilization of population. There was no particular ground for this: it disregarded the evidence of long waves and the weakness of the mechanisms that relate fertility decisions to long-term economic trends. Today it is clear that the fertility decline in Europe is going well below reproduction levels.

The spectre of depopulation cropped up in industrial countries already in the 1930s when net reproduction rates fell below unity. It was later forgotten, as the postwar years produced a powerful resurgence of fertility, but it has now re-emerged, first in Eastern Europe and then in Western Europe as well. The impact of the decline in reproduction rates is only just beginning to be noticed. To some intellectuals it is not a problem at all—there are enough potential immigrants beating at the door to be let in. But that listless response does not try to explain why people in industrial countries do not want to have enough children to reproduce themselves.

Is the reason for that simply that the cost of children has become too high compared to the other ends which consumerist populations pursue? Or should it be sought in the reasons why such preferences have emerged at all? Are modern industrial societies organized in a manner that is basi-

---

[2] Caldwell (1982). Also a series of articles in *Population Studies* and elsewhere.

cally hostile to children, excluding them from its increasingly complex functions and fostering an international youth culture that constitutes a far more rebellious force than ever dreamed of by the theorists of the class struggle? Whatever the answer to such questions, it must be assumed that the combination of demographic trends, widening economic disparities, and lower travel costs will intensify migration from the Third World to the industrial countries in years to come.

5. International Migration

Prosperous communities have almost always tried to protect themselves against an onrush of migrants. In the Middle Ages European cities defended themselves by raising barriers against them similar to those of nation-states today.

But migration has also, quite obviously, been the essential element in the process of population growth and the settling of the earth. That process has had two principal and parallel themes—agglomeration and diffusion. Urbanization has sucked in rural populations, and the exploitation of new areas has created new urban systems and hinterlands. Migration has been the norm and not the exception. It has never been, nor is it now, the ultimate evidence of misery, although the students of it have difficulty in distinguishing between the pull and the push.

Present attitudes towards migration, whether internal or international, are profoundly political. Mobility inside nation-states provokes concerns about excessive concentration in urban areas and needs of expensive infrastructure. Even more important is the aggravation of ethnic conflicts that arises when suppressed majorities grow faster than the ruling racial or ethnic communities, which is in many developing countries a dominant issue of national political affairs.

International migration is held down by the policies of receiving countries, but it has taken on very substantial magnitudes. Very large amounts of money are being spent by people in developing countries to overcome the barriers to entry the other countries raise against them. There are great difficulties in measuring international migration, such as distinctions between permanent and non-permanent migrants, political and economic refugees, and so forth. Above all, it is obviously difficult to assess illegal migration, although in many parts of the world it is recognized to be very substantial. There are three great poles of attraction for migration, legal and illegal: the US, Western Europe, and the oil-rich countries in the Middle East, with the ebb and flow of economic fortunes giving rise to fluctuations and in some cases a reflux.[3] The number of migrant workers in West-

---

[3] In the early 1980s more than 300,000 Indian and Pakistani workers a year migrated to Saudi Arabia and other countries in the Middle East, see United Nations (forthcoming).

ern Europe increased from 2 million in the early 1960s to 6 million in the early 1970s and the trend has continued. The flow of illegal migrants into the US was in the early 1970s estimated by the Immigration and Nationalization Service to be a quarter of a million a year, and the total number of such migrants in the US was estimated to be between 7 and 12 million (Brandt Commission, 1981, p. 341). Migration among African countries is also a major phenomenon.

Population theory has so far been unreflectedly national, and demographers have indeed often focused on local communities. But international migration raises broader issues, especially at a time when it seems bound to be intensified.

As far as the economic consequences of migration are concerned, there is no reason to think that international migration would be very different from internal migration and mobility, and it is a reasonable assumption that it raises overall welfare, although the sharing of the gains might be a questionable point. And at first blush it would seem that the mutual benefits are obvious: labour-exporting countries have found their employment problem relieved and have received remittances. Labour-importing countries have benefited from a substantial import of human capital, and been able to increase their competitiveness while holding wages down.

But a vast social and cultural process of this kind is bound to raise many other problems, which I will only hint at. Too much attention may, for instance, have been given to workers' remittances, to the neglect of other important aspects. One of them is the brain drain, which Jagdish Bhagwati has tried to draw attention to. It means a huge loss of human capital to developing countries when intellectuals, sometimes educated at the expense of their own governments, are attracted by offers of well-paid posts in industrial countries. Another one is the financial capital flight which accompanies the resettlement of business men who flee from inhospitable investment climates.

The principal issue was raised a long time ago. It was echoed by Myrdal and later by Galbraith: migration from poor countries to rich ones is bound to be selective. It will drain the poor region or country of talent and enterprise, and correspondingly benefit the richer and more attractive country.

This has implications for the theory of international trade, which has been based on the comfortable idea that people should stay in their countries. Today, in the field of international finance, the implications of the radical integration of financial markets that has taken place in recent years are a major preoccupation. But the movements of people are not regarded in the same way, for obvious reasons. Their citizenship and the tax laws raise enormous barriers. In a number of regional contexts such as the European Community or the co-operation among Nordic countries, the principle of free migration of citizens has been adopted. While there is much talk about free trade and open markets for the world as a whole, there will not for a long time, given the income differentials, be much of a chance of free movement of people in the world, but the same income differentials will none the less ensure a significant flow of migrants. It is already apparent that migrants from the Third World have made a major impact on everyday life in the major cities of the industrial countries, not least in their universities.

6. Conclusion

Worries about population growth tend to be worries about the growth of others. The rich worry about the growth of the poor, but they are likely to worry as much about the decline of their own populations.

The increasingly accepted view of the world as a physical unit with a limited biosphere and other ecological limits raises serious issues of the pressure that the environment can take, and of the distribution of the carrying capacity of the world among nations and populations. Even if it is unwarranted to think that governments actually influence population growth very much, such issues are likely to become increasingly controversial.

The movement of people who respond to the opportunities that the world holds will test the patience of the officials whose task it will be to keep them out of their countries. It is a safe bet that those who overcome such hurdles will be resourceful enough to to succeed in their new countries, but their talents would have been needed in the countries from which they come. Governments should not create situations in which people of imagination and talent desert them.

References

Brandt Commission (1981), *The Brandt Commission Papers: Selected Background Papers Prepared for the Independent Commission on International Development Issues, 1978–1979* (Geneva and the Hague: Independent Bureau for International Development Issues).

Caldwell, John C. (1982), *Theory of Fertility Decline* (London: Academic Press).

Coleman, David, and Schofield, Roger (eds.) (1986), *The State of Population Theory: Forward from Malthus* (Oxford: Blackwell).

Glass, D. V. (ed.) (1953), *Introduction to Malthus* (London: Watts & Co.).

Graunt, John (1662), *Natural and Political Observations made upon the Bills of Mortality*, reprinted and ed. W. F. Willcox Baltimore, 1939.

Hicks, J. R. (1939), *Value and Capital* (Oxford: Clarendon Press).

Hull, C. H. (ed.) (1899), *The Economic Writing of Sir William Petty*, 2 vols. (Cambridge, Mass.).

Lee, Ronald Demos (1986), 'Malthus and Boserup: A Dynamic Synthesis', in Coleman and Schofield (1986).

Malthus, T. A. (1803), *An Essay on the Principle of Population*, A new edn. very much enlarged (London: J. Johnson).

National Research Council (1986), *Population Growth and Economic Development: Policy Questions*, Working Group on Population Growth and Economic Development, Committee on Population (Washington, DC: US National Academy of Science).

Spengler, Joseph J. (1942), *French Predecessors of Malthus* (Durham, NC: Duke Univ. Publications).

United Nations (forthcoming), *World Population Trends and Policies: 1987 Monitoring Report* (New York: United Nations).

World Bank (1984), *World Development Report 1984* (New York: Oxford University Press for the World Bank).

15

Government Intervention and Urban Labour Markets in LDCs

DIPAK MAZUMDAR

GOVERNMENT intervention in urban labour markets takes place either through labour legislation impinging directly on private firms or through wages and employment policies followed in the public sector, which accounts for a large part of the urban labour market in many LDCs. This chapter will deal with only the first of these two issues to keep it within manageable length.

The current paradigm of the private sector of the urban labour market has grown out of two pieces of observation. As household and earnings surveys have accumulated in LDCs many observers have been struck by differences in wage levels between the 'formal' and the 'informal' sectors of the market. At the same time there has been a proliferation of labour legislation in many LDCs since the end of the colonial era. Putting the two together many economists have been quick to conclude that government intervention has been responsible for creating a 'dual' labour market in the urban economy. In fact, the popular view is that the limits of the 'formal' sector are set by the ability of the government to enforce the legislative decrees. The 'informal' sector is the residual collection of widely dispersed firms, depending a great deal on self-employed labour, who provide insurmountable obstacles to the enforcement of labour laws.

In this view the state-created dual labour market is detrimental to economic welfare from several points of view. The size distribution of firms is distorted from its optimal (free market) pattern, leading to a loss in consumers' and producers' surpluses. The outcome worsens income distribution as a small portion of the labour force enjoys higher earnings at the expense of the majority of the workers whose earnings are lower than they would have been in a non-distorted labour market. From a dynamic point of view the growth in employment is dampened because of the higher capital intensity and lower competitiveness of the formal sector—which is presumably the 'leading' sector in employment generation.[1]

---

[1] Strictly speaking the argument is that the greater ability of the informal sector to contribute to employment growth (at an acceptable wage) does not compensate for the reduced performance of the formal sector in a dual labour market. The employment elasticity of the manufacturing sector in LDCs in recent years has been viewed by several economists as having been substantially less than in developed countries during their period of industrialization. Labour-market distortions could be one of the several major reasons for this outcome. Cf. Morawetz (1974) and Squire (1981).

When the research project on small scale enterprises was launched in the World Bank in the late 1970s, Ian Little, who was the major sponsor of the project, was very concerned about the role of distorted labour markets in the industrialization of developing countries.

1. The Evidence on Size-related Wage difference

Although casual empiricism as well as rather rough analysis based on gross average earnings abound in the literature, careful work on inter-firm wage differentials, controlling for measurable qualities of labour, is surprisingly rare. Perhaps the most detailed is the one done for Bombay city by the author in a research project conducted jointly by the World Bank and the University of Bombay. The results are discussed in Mazumdar (1984a) and Little *et al.* (1987). The analysis of monthly earnings of a sample of 5,000 manual workers employed in large factories, small establishments (both manufacturing and non-manufacturing), and casual day labour revealed that the size of the enterprise in which the worker was employed was the most important explanatory variable. The contrast with earnings functions fitted to data in developed countries is striking. In the latter, education and age (or experience) explain the largest share of the variance in earnings.

In the Bombay sample, the spread in earnings related to the size of enterprise was also seen to be enormous. Unskilled workers in the largest factories (with more than 1,000 employees) earned two and a half times the wages of casual workers—after controlling for all measured human capital factors.

There were, however, other results in the Bombay labour market which were not quite as expected. First, the analysis revealed a 'wage ladder' rather than a two-tier wage structure as suggested by dual labour-market theories. Earnings controlling for other factors increased steadily for casual labour through small establishments to factories of various size groups, reaching a peak for factories employing 500 or more workers. In fact, the 'net' earnings of workers in the largest-size group within the factory sector were 42 per cent higher than in the smallest-size group (employing 10–99 workers), while workers in the small factories earned 65 per cent more than casual workers.

The last point suggests an important question about institutional factors being primarily responsible for the observed wage difference. State-supported collective bargaining, generally taking the form of wage scales laid down by a tripartite body of employers, employees, and government, was common in this period in Bombay city. But the scope of these wage awards was limited to those establishments coming under the purview of the Factory Act. If this institutional influence were the major factor in wage differentials, then we would have observed a large wage gap between 'factories' of all sizes on the one hand, and other small establishments and casual labour on the other. Differences in wages by size of establishments within the factory sector would have been much smaller than were observed.

There is other evidence which suggests that institutional influence need not have been the major factor in creating wage differences within the same urban labour market. Historical studies by the author for Bombay have demonstrated that wages in the large textile factories have been established at a high level compared to alternative earnings of labour coming into town from the rural areas and to other non-factory labour in the city for a long time before the era of trade unions or government intervention (see Mazumdar, 1973). Secondly, large wage differences are found in urban labour markets in countries where institutional apparatus for wage determination is at a rudimentary level. An example in Indonesia has been documented in Lluch and Mazumdar (1983).

In fact economists should not be surprised at the existence of urban labour-markets with substantial intra-urban wage differentials since one of the most widely noted cases in labour history is the Japanese one. In Japan too segmented labour-markets (in terms of different wage levels) developed in an era in which the influence of trade unions or government in wage determination was minimal. It would be useful to reconsider the Japanese model in a little more detail.

1.1. The Japanese Case

Several studies have shown conclusively that wages in Japanese manufacturing industry increase significantly with the size of firms (see in particular Yasuba, 1976; Paine, 1971; Minami, 1972). In 1951 when the inter-firm differential was probably the widest the index of average wages (standardized for sex, age, and skill) was 41.7 in the establishment-size group of 4–9 workers with the index for the size group of 1,000 and more workers being 100 (Yasuba, 1976, Table 5, p. 258). We have also a fairly good idea of the historical evolution of the scale differential. The differential was fairly small before the First World War, when Japanese industry was dominated by textiles, and a majority of the factory workers was female. The scale differential became significant in the inter-war period and increased rapidly in the late 1920s and early 1930s. Great changes were taking place during this period with industrial diversification into heavy industries, and increasing use of male labour. But the important point to note is that this was a period of relatively plentiful supply of labour. Because of the impact of the depression on the rural sector of the Japanese economy, the supply price of migrants to urban industry was falling, as indicated by the declining trend in average real wages in industry. Since scale differentials were widening at the same time it is likely that the fall in wages was concentrated largely on small firms. Large firms found it to their advantage to follow a policy of relatively high wages. After the end of the Second World War surplus labour conditions in the Japanese economy continued for a decade or so. The data on scale differentials for 1951 show them to be wider than ever before (Yasuba, 1976). The 'turning-point' in the Japanese labour-market seems to have taken place in the next 10 years or so. Between 1951 and 1963, real daily wages for male workers in agriculture grew at 5 per cent per year, six times the rate of growth observed during the period 1854–1939 (which was 0.74 per cent per annum) (Hyami *et al.*, 1975, Table 2.10, p. 35). During the 1960s the Japanese agricultural sector responded to the growing scarcity of labour through increased mechanization. Real wages continued to grow at an even higher rate—at 7.2 per cent per year (Minami (1968, 1970*a*, *b*).) On the turning point in the Japanese economy see also Blumenthal (1980), p. 556; Ohkawa and Rosovsky, (1973), p. 42 and ch. 5; Lluch and Mazumdar (1983), p. 129–33). With the transformation of the Japanese labour-market sometime in the late 1950s or early 1960s, scale differentials in manufacturing industry have fallen steadily.

One writer has emphasized a major difference between the trends in the size-related differentials before and after the Second World War. In the pre-war years wage differentials increased during the depression years of 1929–32 and decreased during boom years after the war. But in the post-war years the wage differential has fallen persistently, even during the downward phase of large swings, viz. 1961–5. Minami ascribes this new development in the labour market to a structural change—'the disappearance of the surplus labour which had existed in traditional sectors like agriculture and small non-agriculture establishments' (Minami, 1972, p. 65).

The evolution of scale differentials under surplus labour conditions in Japanese history has parallels with the existence of scale differentials today in countries like India and Indonesia—economies also characterized by the availability of abundant labour.

It has been maintained in some discussions of Japanese labour history that although trade union or government could not be responsible for the maintenance of relatively high wages in large factories, other, more subtle, institutional factors might have been responsible for this phenomenon. The most widely discussed has been the the *Nenko Joretsu* system, under which the more established firms hired workers at a very early age and ensured virtually lifetime commitment of the workers to the firm through, among other things, guaranteed wage increases with length of service in the firm. The returns to training within the firm were retained by the firm because of the very low turnover rate and internal promotion to higher skilled jobs. Some sociologists, notably Abbeglen (1958), have developed the thesis that this system, which contributed to the scale differential in average wages, had roots in the 'paternalistic' elements of Japanese feudal culture. More recent writers, on the other hand, have stressed the similarity of the system with the internal labour-markets of large corporations in developed countries. In this view, substantial economic returns can accrue to the firm from lifetime commitment and internalized skill formation. (For a review of some of the relevant ideas by by a Japanese economist, see Arai 1982.)

The major problem with the system of lifetime commitment of workers is that it creates inflexibility in so far as labour becomes a virtually fixed factor of production. The Japanese factories dealt with this problem in two principal ways:

(i) A significant component of the workers were 'temporaries' who did not have the guarantee of employment like the permanent core. The wage cost was lower for the temporaries because they were hired at a lower rate and they did not generally enjoy the benefits (including wage increments related to seniority) to the extent granted to the permanents. Their number was also geared to the short-term requirements of the factory. At the same time working alongside permanents the productivity of temporaries would not be as low as they might have been if the entire factory were composed of temporaries. (The system is strikingly similar, in broad outline, to the one described in Mazumdar, 1973).

(ii) The second method was the complementary use of small establishments by the large factories. Japanese industry was able from very early stages to adapt the pre-industrial putting-out system to the requirements of modern factories. Subcontracting of many components of production to small firms with low wages and flexible labour contracts was very extensive.

Although this mixed labour system, with a combination of high-wage tenured workers and low-wage unstable labour, seems to have been a natural evolution in Japan, it was strengthened by plant-based unions. These unions were strongest in the larger factories, and managed to widen the scale differential (particularly if one included fringe benefits in wages).

1.2. The Economic Theory of Scale Differential

The Japanese experience suggests that scale differentials emerged independently of institutional factors. They became important in the period when industrial development in Japan led to a larger demand for male workers, in particular, who had to be attracted from rural areas to the newer industries. Furthermore, there was something in the economics of the system which resulted in scale differentials being wide while surplus labour market conditions existed in the rural areas. They tended to be reduced considerably when the transition to tight labour-markets occurred in the rural economy. Reflection on the Japanese case, and research in labour markets in several developing countries, has led me to suggest the following eclectic theory of scale differentials. (Earlier versions of the theory are in Mazumdar (1983), and Little *et al.* (1987), ch. 14.)

It contains three different elements: (*a*) the difference in supply prices of temporary (unstable) and permanent (stable) migrants from rural to urban areas; (*b*) the wage–efficiency relationship, and (*c*) internal labour-market theory. These elements are complementary not alternative explanations of the size-related wage differential. They could also describe a sequential process in the evolution of the wage differential.

An important element of labour markets under surplus labour conditions in LDCs is that rural-to-urban migrants are of two major types: individual migrants who come to the city for short periods, without their families, and more permanent ones who adopt the city as their normal residence for the greater part of their working life. The supply price of the individual migrant is very much lower than that of the permanents. The major reason is that the output forgone in the family farm due to the departure of one member for a short period is very low—and could, indeed, be negligible—while the migration of the entire family from the rural economy means the loss of the entire income of the farm. This difference in supply prices is exacerbated by the fact that the earner/dependent ratio for a typical family is significantly lower in the urban than in the rural economy—due to the more limited opportunity of female and child labour to participate in market activity in the former. Other factors working in the same direction include the higher cost of housing for families, and the cost of support during periods of sickness and unemployment which the rural family would provide for the individual migrant.

Given the large difference in supply prices, as long as a plentiful supply of temporary individual migrants exists, family migrants would not be utilized at all in the urban economy, if there were not a substantial difference in demand prices for the two types of migrants from the point of view of some employers. The demand price for family migrants would, indeed, be higher for firms which perceived a strong connection between productivity and stability of their labour force. Thus large, modern firms which could achieve high labour productivity with stable labour will have high wages to attract family migrants, while the informal sector is dominated by individual migrants who keep a downward pressure on wage levels in this sector. (Evidence from India is provided in Mazumdar (1984*a*) and from Indonesia in Hugo (1977).)

Temporary migrants are dominated by single males in most Asian and African countries. In Latin America they tend to be females.[2] There is in

[2] Research on this point is very inadequate in Latin America, but they do not return to the rural areas in the same way as single male migrants in Asia and Africa do. Cf. Nelson (1976) for some suggestive comments.

Japanese labour history a special twist to this problem. Before the First World War the large textile factories in fact made use of temporaries in the form of teenage girls who lived in factory dormitories and worked in the industry for 2–3 years before their marriage. Although their wages (related to their supply price) were low, their stability and productivity were not that low because of the rigid discipline of the dormitory system. Consequently the wage differentials did not develop until male labour came into the picture in a significant way in the 1920s.

The higher productivity of stable rural–urban migrants is not the only reason for the establishment of relatively high wages in some sectors of the urban economy. Labour which is stable from the point of view of urban residence could still have a high inter-firm turnover rate. Some firms, who are able to exploit the benefits of labour stability more efficiently, will offer higher wages to reduce inter-firm mobility. Once, however, a firm-specific labour force comes into existence, other economic forces come into play to increase wages still further. Since the firm is dealing with an exclusive body of workers, wage costs could be minimized by increasing wages as long as the efficiency of the work-force increases proportionately more. In early versions of the efficiency wage theory the physical effects of better nutrition were stressed (Leibenstein, 1957). But this hypothesis had limited empirical support and probably little validity for urban workers, whose wage levels are relatively high. In more recent work the incentive effect of high wages has been stressed. If information about the worker's potentiality were perfect, and monitoring of his performance were both possible and cost-effective, employment contracts could be written for individuals tying their work to productivity. With incomplete information, no general market for superior labour exists. Each firm is then faced with an inelastic supply of potentially productive workers who will be responsive to the incentives of high wages. Up to a point an increase in wage will increase the proportion of such workers in the enterprise and lead to a more than proportionate increase in labour efficiency (cf. Malcomson (1981), and also the literature there cited).

Finally, with a firm-specific labour force, the economics of internal labour-markets become strong. In such markets new workers are recruited principally to fill jobs at the bottom of the ladder, while vacancies at higher levels are filled as much as possible through promotion. This arrangement reduces screening and training costs, and increases worker incentives for skill formation. Internal labour-market theory suggests that large firms, which are able to benefit from arranging and filling jobs in a line of progression, will be characterized by a steep wage-experience profile for their workers, while the other two theories discussed earlier explain why entry wages are high for formal sector firms.

2. The Residual Influence of Institutions: Welfare Implications of the Wage Gap

The formation of a firm-specific and stable labour force encourages the unionization of the workers. In fact, in many instances unions are encouraged by management in the interests of peaceful industrial relations, with orderly procedures for employer–employee relations. Recognized unions and their officials often play a vital role in keeping out 'trouble-makers' from outside the work-force trying to ferment labour militancy. Unions, of course, can and do push up wages even higher than what has been established by economic forces in the large firms. Many of these firms which have adopted high wage policies have high labour productivity. They may also have significant oligopolistic power in the product market. Thus unions may find it easy to bargain for even higher wages based on the firms' 'ability to pay'. We have already noted above that plant unions in Japan increased scale differentials significantly.

In other countries, where state wage-setting machinery has been important wage boards have been known to take the 'natural' pattern of wage differences into account, and to widen the inter-firm differentials through their awards (cf.the discussion in Little *et al.* (1987), pp. 263–5 on the Indian experience).

It is not easy to estimate the residual influence of institutions on wage differentials. Regression analysis using, for example, dummy variables for union strength, is clearly unsuitable since the technique cannot apportion the wage differential between 'economic' and 'institutional' factors when both are present. Probably the best method is to identify the period of strong institutional impact, and to compare the wage differential before and after the event. Such detailed historical studies are rare in the literature, although much can be done with existing data sources if judiciously combined with information on wage awards, union contracts, etc. An attempt along these lines was made for the Bombay labour market. It showed that the strong institutional influences in the two decades after 1955 increased the wage premium in the factories relative to small units from 65 per cent to around 80 per cent.[3]

A conclusion of some importance follows if, in fact, a major part of observed wage differentials is seen to have developed due to economic factors not connected with institutions. The difference in efficiency wages (and hence of labour costs) between different size classes of enterprises could be much less than the observed differences in wages per worker. If this is the case, then the analysis of the problem caused by the 'wage gap'

---

[3] The comparison is between small units outside the jurisdiction of the Factory Act and the average of factories of all sizes (Little *et al.*, 1987).

within the urban labour market in terms of a welfare loss due to 'distortions' or inefficiency in the neo-classical sense is clearly overdone. In particular, one must have considerable doubts about the recommendation of a 'second best' policy of subsidy to the formal sector firms to offset the wage tax imposed on them. At the same time, if the above analysis is correct, the relatively low wages in the urban informal sector are not so much due to the monopsonistic exploitation of labour as to the low supply price of the relevant type of labour found in this sector. Thus any attempt to 'protect' these workers by extending the scope of minimum wage legislation could be counter-productive and lead to a loss in welfare.

The problem caused by the intra-urban wage gap has, however, another dimension to it. This is the implication for the distribution of income, and, in many cases, this might be a more relevant criterion for policy formulation than considerations of Pareto efficiency. Because of the higher efficiency of labour in the large-scale sector, the use of labour per unit of value added is substantially smaller in this sector compared to the small establishment. Thus the urban labour market tends to break up into a high wage–low employment segment coexisting with a low wage–high employment one. Workers in the former are generally a minority of the urban labour force. Furthermore, recruitment to the high wage sector rarely takes the form of graduation from the small-scale sector.[4] Because of the importance of kinship ties in the recruitment process, new workers, more often than not, are hired directly from the areas of origin of existing workers and foremen, at a young age. In his study of the Ahmedabad labour market (in Western India) Poppola found that the large factories operated a 'defacto closed-shop system' (Poppola, 1977). In another study Bannerji compared the proportion of new migrants who had entered the informal sector in a particular year but had moved to the formal sector within a 12-month period with the proportion of new arrivals who had found jobs in the formal sector directly. His figures showed, for example, 'that in 1967 new arrivals were at least four to six times more likely to get formal sector employment than those who had entered the informal sector in 1966' (Bannerji, 1983).

If there is limited upward mobility of labour from the low- to the high-wage sectors then over time the 'informal' urban labour market would tend to be dominated, not only by transient migrants from the rural areas, but also by members of the lower strata of the rural hierarchy. John Harris in his study of the Coimbatore labour market in India found that the dominant agricultural castes of the region were strongly represented in the regular work-force of large engineering firms, whereas general casual labour in

---

[4] This is, of course, in direct contrast to the labour-market process suggested in the Harris–Todaro model.

the town was dominated by members of the scheduled castes (who also constitute the bulk of landless agricultural labour).

The implications for policy of this model of urban labour markets suggested above are clear. There is a prima-facie case for promoting the small-scale or informal sector on grounds of equity. For the same volume of output, a larger share of small firms will, in general, mean not only a larger share of wages in value added, but also a larger share of low earners in the total wage bill.

An additional factor working in the same direction—which is quite important in many economies but often neglected—is related to the fact that there is a difference in product markets served by the formal and informal sectors. The informal sector typically produces goods and services which cater to the needs and tastes of poor consumers. This is even true of products ostensibly produced within the same narrowly defined industry. Large firms that make soap, for example, will place more emphasis on the product's 'luxury' attributes (scent, packaging, smoothness, etc.) while soap produced by small units will be chiefly designed and marketed for its basic cleaning property. In so far as this differentiation by product markets is important, an expansion in the supply of informal sector products tends, to some extent, to create its own demand. Encouragement of small-scale production shifts the distribution of factor income towards lower-income groups which, in its turn, augments the demand for products of small units.

We conclude that, as long as demand for labour in the large-scale sector of the urban economy in LDCs is not large enough to iron out the large wage differentials by size of firms, there is a case for some degree of subsidization and/or protection of the small-scale sector. This case is based more firmly on equity rather than static efficiency considerations.

This is not to deny in some economies there might be a case for intervention in *favour* of the small-scale sector on grounds of Pareto efficiency *as well*. We have argued that the apparent wage advantage enjoyed by small firms may not be as great in terms of labour cost. On the other hand, small firms sometimes face very real disadvantages in terms of access to the capital market. In economies with overvalued exchange rates and protection of domestic industry, large firms are also favoured with subsidized prices for imported intermediate goods.

2.1. Protection of the Small-Scale in Practice: The Indian Example

The case for some degree of subsidization for small firms can be established from the above considerations. It is, however, quite a different thing to endorse a policy of intervention as it has been implemented in practice. India, more than any other country, has pursued a policy of protection of the small-scale ever since independence. Our detailed study of this experience revealed serious problems in the conception and implementation of this policy. The results of this research are fully set out in Little *et al.* (1987). It might be worth while to underline a few of the more salient problems in the Indian case as an illustration of how a badly designed policy of intervention might succeed in achieving very nearly the opposite of what was intended.

In nearly all industries there is no simple choice between a modern (capital-intensive large-scale) and a traditional (labour-intensive, small-scale) technique. There is a spectrum of techniques producing products of different grades (or qualities). Before proceeding with interventionist policies, one needs detailed knowledge of cost-benefit ratios in the various alternative techniques. The Indian experience shows that this information base was singularly absent, and there seems to have been no attempt to develop it. Instead there was a fairly crude but widespread policy of protecting small establishments, principally by physical restriction on the capacity of large-scale units (defined either in terms of employment size or value of capital) but also by differential fiscal measures.

The bluntness of the policy instruments and the lack of monitoring of the results of the policy led to a series of developments which could hardly be justified either on grounds of efficiency or equity. First, in some cases there is evidence to suggest that support was given to the use of intermediate technologies which were, in fact, inefficient overall (i.e. at any factor/price ratios). This seems to have been the case in sugar, both because insufficient analysis was made of the economics of the large-scale sugar mills operating in an environment of controlled prices, and because the alternative of production of *gur* with non-mechanized techniques was ignored.[5] Secondly, in other cases a technology was promoted which was not the declared intention of the policy, and which could not be justified on social welfare grounds. This happened in the large textile industry in which the restriction on the large-scale factories led, not to the development of the handloom sector as envisaged, but to the creation and rapid growth of a sector making use of non-automatic looms in small units (called the 'powerloom' sector). Analysis, admittedly on the basis of limited data, has shown that under the tax-and-wage regime which is prevalent, the rapid growth of powerlooms was obviously very profitable for the private entrepreneur, but was inappropriate in a social sense. A peculiar twist in the Indian policy was the heavy taxation of man-made fibres, a policy partly inspired by the desire to protect small-scale growers of raw cotton. The powerloom sector increased its share of the mass market for low-grade cotton cloth dramatically. The increase in employment in the textile industry as a whole was more than if

---

[5] See Little, *et al.* (1987), pp. 41–3. The account is based largely on the research of Professor H. H. de Hahn of Erasmus University, Rotterdam.

the factory sector had not been restricted. But the growth of the power-loom sector produced very large profits (untaxed) for the owners who where not necessarily small entrepreneurs. The policy objective of providing more income for low-income earners' households operating handlooms was to a large extent vitiated. Furthermore, it is not clear that the growth in employment would not have been much larger if the factory sector had been better able to exploit the mass market for cloth at better prices which the new synthetics had made possible. (For more details see Little *et al.*, 1987, ch. 4, and Mazumdar, 1984*b*.)

This brings us to a major point about the promotion of small enterprises which the Indian experience brought out very strongly—and this is the implication of the policy for technological change and the quality of the products of the manufacturing sectors. The Indian policy for protection of the small scale sector might suggest to some that the large-scale factories were severely handicapped. This was not quite the case because the Indian policy of support for the small-scale sector took place in an environment of inward-looking development with heavy protection of industry (both large and small) from outside competition. Thus, large-scale manufacturing units in India could still find a lucrative domestic market, though admittedly more readily in intermediate rather than consumer goods. As far as the latter were concerned, the distinction in the domestic market between low-income and high-income products was accentuated, with the larger units concentrating more on the high-income market. The cost to consumers *qua consumers* in this system was, of course, substantial in terms of alternatives which might have been available. The impact on technological improvements was, perhaps, even more serious. India shared with other inward-looking economies the absence of incentives provided by foreign competition. But, in addition, the existence of a large market of low-grade products dominated by small units led to a perpetuation of stagnant technology. Even when the social case for protecting small establishments is strong, the damage to technological improvement could be reduced if opportunities exist for upward mobility of small units—in terms of size as well as technology. The Indian industrial policy as a whole, probably unintentionally, discouraged this type of mobility. The way the policies were administered ensured that as soon as a small enterprise grew beyond a threshold size, it was subject to the fiscal and labour laws pertaining to the large-scale sector, and it also lost the positive subsidies enjoyed by small units (cheap credit, absence of administrative control, etc.). Thus the size structure of Indian industry continued to exhibit a U-shaped pattern with a conspicuous paucity of middle-sized units.

We may return at this stage to the point made earlier that although wages are at different levels in the large- and small-scale sectors, the cost of an efficiency unit of labour is probably not that different. But this is true only for well-established firms in the large-scale sector who have success-fully adapted their labour processes to the high-wage scenario. Small firms which tend to grow into this sector will face prohibitively high labour costs unless they graduate slowly up the spectrum of technology, productivity, and wage levels. When the two sectors are separated by a large gap in technology, and markets, as seems to have happened in the Indian case, the possibility of successful 'graduation' is very much reduced.

There are two distinct effects of this type of industrial development which are detrimental to economic welfare. First, the economy gets bogged down in inefficient technologies along a broad spectrum of industries. Even when the necessity for opening up the economy is keenly felt at a subse-quent stage, the wide prevalence of inefficient firms effectively prevents any rapid move towards liberalization. The social costs of adjustment are simply too great.

Second, the Indian type of small-enterprise development seriously re-duces flexibility in the labour market. I have argued above that while trade unions or government regulations often provide for near-permanent em-ployment status to the labour force in the large factories by making costs of retrenchment very high, firms have ways of getting around such rigidities to some extent. After all, in the Japanese model, factories offered lifetime commitment to their workers from an early point without institutional in-tervention. One of the ways flexibility in the use of labour was achieved was the use of temporary workers along with the permanent core. An equally important method in the Japanese case was the use of small units as an integral part of the production process. The small establishments pro-duced a fair range of components used by the large factories. Since they did not have permanent employment of labour to the same extent as the large units, they had a vital role to play in accommodating the labour market to fluctuations in demand. But to be effective in this role the products of small units must have quality levels comparable with the products of the large units. The development of high-quality products in the small-scale sector is something which Japan succeeded in doing much better than India.

3. Conclusion

This chapter has confined itself to a single issue in the labour market literature—the wage gap for labour of apparently comparable skill be-tween sectors of the same urban labour market. The thrust of the argument has been that the role of institutional intervention in creating and maintain-ing this wage gap (and also differences in terms of employment) has been exaggerated. The popular view has also diverted attention from the real problem of urban labour markets in LDCs—that of distribution of labour earnings among manual workers.

The conclusion was reached that there is a case, on grounds of equity, for some government intervention in favour of small establishments in a dual labour market. This is the opposite of the view which has been advanced that large units need subsidies to offset the wage tax imposed on them by institutions.

However, a review of the Indian experience showed the extensive damage done to the economy by a policy of indiscriminate protection of small-scale enterprises. The lesson to be learned from this dismal case is that much more informed and selective support of small enterprises is needed even if we accept the general principle for such support. The Japanese model of the role of small units in the economy contrasts quite sharply with the Indian case.

Finally, I would like to stave off criticism of this chapter by recalling my initial statement that, because of limitations of space, government intervention in labour markets in developing countries in the form of public sector employment and wage policies has not been discussed. In many LDCs the public sector is a major source of employment. By the nature of things, efficiency wage considerations in the public sector play little role, partly because the product is generally ill-defined, and the firms are not profit-maximizing. Thus, the public sector is much more apt to produce distorted wage and employment structures in urban labour markets.

I have also not dealt with the impact of intervention in a dynamic-setting—what happens to employment and real wages due to the varying strength of institutional impact on the labour market over time. The principal way in which state intervention has produced wide swings in the urban labour market is again through employment and wage policies in the public sector which has alternated between booms and slumps in many economies in which the public sector is important. The stability which the real wage might enjoy in the private formal sector because of efficiency wage and similar considerations discussed above is, of course, not present in the public sector which does not pursue profit-maximization objectives. Another source of instability in urban labour markets in LDCs caused by institutions has been the administration of wage indexation policies, particularly in Latin America. Even private sector firms in the formal sector have been forced to adopt the guide-lines of the wage indexation formulae in periods of great macroeconomic instability. It is also well known that these indexation formulae have influence on wage levels outside the large firms. Thus even if wage indexation of shifting minimum wages over time may not have had a strong impact on *trends* in real wages in the relevant countries, it is clear that in many economies it has produced marked short-run changes in real wages.[6] This has been particularly true in countries and

---

[6] This seems to have been the case in Mexico as documented in the study by Gregory (1986).

periods experiencing sharp macroeconomic disturbances. Probably this is the area in which government intervention in urban labour markets has been most significant.

References

Abegglen, J. C. (1958), *The Japanese Factory* (Glencoe: Free Press).

Arai, K. (1982), 'Theories of the Seniority-Based Wage System', *Hitotsubashi Journal of Economics*, 23 (June), pp. 53–67.

Bannerji, Biswajit (1983), 'The Role of the Informal Sector in the Migration Process: A Test of Probabilistic Migration Models and Labour Market Segmentation for India', *Oxford Economic Papers*, 35, pp. 399–422.

Gregory, Peter (1986), *The Myth of Market Failure: Employment and the Labor Market in Mexico* (Baltimore, Md.: Johns-Hopkins Univ. Press for the World Bank).

Harris, J. R. (1984), 'Small-Scale Production and Labour Markets in Coimbatore', *Economic and Political Weekly* (June), pp. 993–1002.

Hugo, Graeme (1977), 'Circular Migration', *Bulletin of Indonesian Economic Studies*, 13/3.

Leibenstein, H. (1957), *Economic Backwardness and Economic Growth* (New York: Wiley & Sons).

Little, I. M. D., Mazumdar, D., and Page J. (1987), *Small Manufacturing Enterprises: A Comparative Analysis of India and Other Economies* (Oxford: OUP for the World Bank).

Lluch, Constantino, and Mazumdar, Dipak (1983), *Wages and Employment in Indonesia*, Country Economic Report (Washington, DC: World Bank).

Malcomson, J. M. (1981), 'Unemployment and the Efficiency Wage Hypothesis', *Economic Journal*, 91 (Dec.), pp. 848–66.

Mazumdar, Dipak (1973), 'Labor Supply in Early Industrialization', *Economic History Review*, 26/3, pp. 477–96.

——(1983), 'Segmented Labor Markets in LDCs', *American Economic Review*, 73/2, pp. 254–9.

——(1984a), 'The Rural-Urban Wage Gap, Migration and the Working of Urban Labor Markets: An Interpretation Based on a Study of the Workers of Bombay City', *Indian Economic Review*, 18/2, pp. 1969–98. Reprinted in the World Bank Reprint Series.

——(1984b), 'The Issue of Small versus Large in the Indian Textile Industry', *Staff Working Paper*, 645 (Washington, DC.: World Bank).

Minami, R. (1968), 'The Turning Point in the Japanese Economy', *Quarterly Journal of Economics*, 3, pp. 380–402.

——(1970a), 'Further Considerations on the Turning Point in the Japanese Economy (I)', *Hitotsubashi Journal of Economics*, 10/2.

——(1970b), 'Further Considerations on the Turning Point in the Japanese Economy (II)', *Hitotsubashi Journal of Economics*, 11/1.

——(1972), 'Transformations of the Labor Market in Postwar Japan', *Hitotsubashi Journal of Economics*, 13 (June), pp. 57–72.

Morawetz, David (1974), 'Employment Implications of Industrialization in Developing Countries: A Survey', *Economic Journal*. (Sept.), pp. 491–542.

Nelson, Joan M. (1976), 'Sojourners versus New Urbanites: Causes and Consequences of Temporary versus Permanent City-ward Migration in Developing Countries', *Economic Development and Cultural Change*, 24 (July), pp. 721–57.

Paine, Susanne H. (1971), 'Wage Differentials in the Japanese Manufacturing Sector', *Oxford Economic Papers*, 23/2 pp. 212–38.

Poppola, T. S. (1977), 'The Ahmedabad Labor Market', in Subbiah Kannappan (ed.), *Studies in Urban Labor Market Behavior in Developing Areas* (Geneva: International Institute of Labor Studies).

Squire, Lyn (1981), *Employment Policies in Developing Countries* (Oxford: OUP for the World Bank).

Yasuba, Yasukichi (1976), 'The Evolution of Dualistic Wage Structure', in Hugh Patrick (ed.), *Japanese Industrialization and Its Social Consequences* (Berkeley: Univ. of California Press).

16

The Colonial Burden:
A Comparative Perspective

ANGUS MADDISON

NOWADAYS, the colonial experience gets little attention in development literature and there is a tendency in some quarters to treat its economic impact as unimportant or even benign. This chapter is an attempt to survey its economic impact in the interwar period in Indonesia, which was an extreme case of colonial exploitation. It tries to put Dutch colonialism in comparative perspective. It considers (*a*) the scale of foreign presence and foreign income which accompanied colonial rule; (*b*) the payments 'drain' to the metropole; and (*c*) the policy response of the colonial authorities to world recession in the 1930s.

According to the 1930 population census, there were 240,000 Europeans living in Indonesia, roughly 0.4 per cent of the total population and 3.1 per cent of the population of The Netherlands. Of these 20,700 were Dutch officials or Dutch military personnel, 63,600 were working in plantations as professionals, traders, etc., and 156,400 were family dependents. On average for 1921–39, this group received 10.6 per cent of Indonesian net domestic product at factor cost. In addition, 5 per cent of national income in Indonesia accrued to non-residents (mainly Dutch) and to government entrepreneurship.

Over the 1921–39 period, Indonesian NDP (net domestic product at factor cost) averaged 82 per cent of Dutch NDP at current prices. As the income earned by the Dutch in Indonesia equalled 15.6 per cent of Indonesian NDP, these same incomes represented an 'augmentation' of income claims by metropolitan citizens of 12.8 per cent. The actual amount remitted to The Netherlands was less than this as the Dutch in Indonesia used some of their income for consumption and for asset accumulation in the colony. In 1921–39, total Dutch income from abroad from all sources averaged 9.4 per cent of Dutch NDP, and the bulk of this came from Indonesia. There seems to be general agreement that remittances from Indonesia amounted to about 8 per cent of Dutch NDP in this period, or nearly 10 per cent of Indonesian NDP. In addition there were remittances from Indonesia to some other countries, with around 0.5 per cent of Indonesian NDP going to China.[1]

---

[1] Estimates of the income and population of the Dutch in Indonesia and Indonesian NDP are from Polak (1943). Estimates of Dutch NDP and income from abroad are from Centraal Bureau voor de Statistiek (1979). These results are confirmed by the findings of Derksen and

From 1870 to 1930, the Dutch style of colonial rule could be described as 'free trade imperialism' more or less on the British model. In 1870 the Dutch had discarded the notorious *cultuurstelsel* which involved close bilateral ties with the metropole, compulsory levies of specific crops, or compulsory labour service with the proceeds remitted directly as tribute to the Dutch state (following more or less the early Spanish model in Latin America). The new policy was more acceptable to liberal opinion at home, more respectable internationally, led to more efficient resource allocation, and was also more profitable, if one considers the degree to which the two systems 'augmented' Dutch NDP.[2] In the 1930s, policy became more protectionist.

A striking feature of colonialism in Indonesia is that the Dutch presence encouraged the growth of the Chinese community and that of other Asiatics (Indians and Arabs), though these foreign Asiatic groups were present (in a somewhat smaller proportion) before the Dutch, and still remain in Indonesia. In 1930 there were 1,233,000 Chinese in Indonesia, 71,000 Arabs, and 45,000 other Asiatics, amounting to 2.22 per cent of the total population. On average for 1921–39, this group had 8.35 per cent of national income. The Chinese were not so unambiguously a product of colonialism as was the Dutch presence, but they did retain strong contacts with their ancestral home and seem to have remitted about 6 per cent of their income to China.[3]

In India, the British presence was relatively much smaller, more heavily concentrated on government pursuits, with a smaller resident dependency rate which indicated a lower proportion of permanent residents than in Indonesia. In 1931 there were 168,000 British living in India, amounting to 0.05 per cent of the population or about one-eighth the size of the foreign proportion of the population in Indonesia (Table 16.1).

About 60,000 of the British were in the army and police and 4,000 in civil

Tinbergen (1945, p. 213) that in 1925–34 income remitted from Indonesia was 8.3% of Dutch NDP, and Dutch income retained in Indonesia was 4.6% of Dutch NDP. For 1938 Derksen and Tinbergen show 7.6 and 3.2% respectively. Baudet and Wijers (1976) give a slightly revised figure for 1938 of 7.9% instead of 7.6% of Dutch NDP for remitted income.

[2] At its peak in the 1860s, the official revenue remittances (*batig slot*) to the Dutch exchequer averaged 32.4m. guilders per annum (*CEI*, Vol. ii, p. 18). In addition there were smaller remittances by the limited group then in private business in Indonesia. In 1860, I estimate that Dutch NDP was around 840m. guilders, so that the total remittances from Indonesia at that time were probably running about 5% of Dutch NDP. 1860 Dutch NDP estimates are interpolated from Maddison (1982) linked to the 1900 NDP level derived from Centraal Bureau voor de Statistiek (1979, p. 144) and using van Stuivenberg's price index (1860 prices 24% higher than 1900) cited by Griffiths and de Meere (1983).

[3] See Remer (1933, p. 185) who gives an estimate of the sources of Chinese emigrant remittances in 1930. Those from Indonesia came to about 25m. guilders or 5.8% of foreign Asiatic income in Indonesia as given by Polak (1943, in *CEI*, Vol. v, p. 70) for that year.

TABLE 16.1. Dimensions of foreign presence under colonialism

	'Europeans', metropolitan nationals, and those of assimilated status[a]	Pecentage of total population
Dutch Colony		
Indonesia (1930)	240,162	0.40
British Colonies		
Burma (1931)	34,000	0.23
Ceylon (1929)	7,500	0.15
India (1931)	168,134	0.05
Malaya (1931)	33,811	0.77
(inc. Singapore)		
French Colony		
Indo-China (1937)	42,345	0.18
Japanese Colonies		
Korea (1930–5)	573,000	2.62
Taiwan (1930)	228,000	4.96
US Colony		
Philippines (1939)	36,000	0.15
China[b]	267,000	0.06

[a] Includes Eurasians in Indonesia (134,000); in Malaya (16,043); and in Indo-China (approx. 14,000). The Philippines figure includes 10,500 Japanese, but excludes US military personnel and 200,000 Hispano-Filipino mestizos.

[b] China was not a colony in the sense in which the other countries were, but had surrendered national sovereignty in 'Treaty' ports to Japan, the USA, and European countries, as well as ceding territory to Japan and Russia and suzerainty over other areas to France, Japan, Russia, and the UK.

Sources: Burma: Hlaing (1964); the figure refers to foreign races other than Indian and Chinese. Ceylon: Snodgrass (1966, pp. 60, 306). China: Feuerwerker (1976, pp. 17–18); excludes some Russian and Japanese and all of the Korean population of Manchuria but includes 26,000 foreign military and police personnel. India: Hutton (1933). Indo-China: Robequain (1944). Indonesia: Central Bureau of Statistics (1941). Korea: Sang-Chul Suh (1978, p. 115). Malaya: Vlieland (1932). Philippines: Robequain (1948). Taiwan: Kuznets (1979, p. 18).

government. Only 26,000 British were engaged in private sector activities (0.008 per cent of population compared with 0.15 per cent for the corresponding group in Indonesia). According to my estimates, the British share of income in India of all kinds was around 5 per cent in the 1930s, only about a third of the Dutch (resident and non-resident) share in Indonesia. There were only 78,000 British family dependents in India, a dependency ratio of 87 per cent, whereas the Dutch had a 185 per cent dependency ratio. It should also be noted that 71 per cent of the Europeans living in Indonesia in 1930 were born there (Hugo, 1980, p. 119), whereas 60 per cent of the Europeans in India were born in the UK.[4]

In 1921–39, Indian net domestic product at current prices averaged 66.7 per cent of that in the United Kingdom. As British incomes in India were 5 per cent of Indian domestic product, we can see that the British in India 'augmented' British incomes by 3.3 per cent. About 1.5 per cent of Indian product was actually transferred to the UK, and this transferred part therefore augmented UK domestic product by about 1 per cent.[5]

It is clear therefore that the 'drain' from India which Indian nationalists assailed as the major burden of colonial rule was not as big as it was from Indonesia. This was partly due to a difference in colonial policy, but it also reflected a difference in economic potential. India was a land of ancient settlement, with a smaller potential vent-for-surplus than Indonesia, or other British colonies such as Burma, Ceylon, and Malaya.

In British Malaya where the economy was even more export-oriented than in Indonesia, the proportionate colonial commercial presence was bigger than in Indonesia; the 'European' population was 0.4 per cent of the total in 1931 and Eurasians with assimilated status formed another 0.37 per cent. In Burma, Europeans and assimilated were just half the Indonesian proportion, and in Ceylon they were somewhat less than half (Table 16.1). In all these colonies, the British encouraged the growth of ethnic minorities. In Malaya the nature of the Chinese role was similar to that of the Chinese in Indonesia, but in Burma and Ceylon the ethnic minorities were Indian and were used largely as labourers in plantations. All three of these British colonies were vent-for-surplus countries in Myint's sense (Myint, 1958), relying on plantation and smallholder agriculture to provide a high export ratio.

I have less evidence to compare Dutch with French colonialism in the 1930s but the French presence in Indo-China was relatively smaller than that of the Dutch in Indonesia (0.18 per cent of the population). I suspect that the commercial element was a smaller proportion than in Indonesia and the dependency ratio a good deal higher than in India, because the French established good secondary schools in their colonies, whereas Brit-

---

[4] The above description compares the 'European' population of India with that of Indonesia, using the census definitions. The Indian census included about 30,000 persons of mixed race as part of the 'European' total of 168,134, and noted that these were 'Anglo-Indians who are not handicapped by excessive pigmentation'. In addition, there were 138,395 persons who returned themselves as Anglo-Indians whom I have not treated as Europeans because, in British practice, they did not have 'assimilated status', see Hutton (1933).

[5] See Maddison (1971, pp. 63–7) for a discussion of the colonial burden in India and for net domestic product which was converted to current prices using the implicit deflator in Sivasubramonian (1965, pp. 337–8). UK national product is derived from Feinstein (1972, pp. T 5–6 and T 15–16). Total UK income received from abroad in 1921–39 averaged 4.9% of NDP at current prices.

ish colonials got subsidies to ship their children to boarding-schools in England.

In Japanese colonies, the colonial involvement was much bigger than in Indonesia. In Korea, the Japanese population was 573,000 in 1930–5, or 2.6 per cent of the total. This community had been there for centuries, although when Korea was annexed in 1910, the Japanese numbered only 172,000 so most of the Japanese there in 1930–5 were recent settlers. Japanese colonialism involved much stronger bilateral ties with Korea than those between the Dutch and Indonesia, whose exports went to world markets. The Japanese were innovative landlords spreading new techniques in agriculture, and they occupied skilled jobs in the rapidly growing Korean industry in which Japan had invested heavily. In 1935, 62,000 Japanese worked in administration and the professions in Korea. In Taiwan, the Japanese conquest (1895) was earlier than in Korea, and development efforts were more heavily concentrated in agriculture, particularly sugar. There was, in fact, a higher proportion of Japanese settlers in Taiwan than in Korea (about 5 per cent of the population).

Japanese colonialism was more developmental than that of other countries because it involved a greater effort to transfer and develop technology, higher physical investment, and better development of local education and human capital. Unlike most of Asia, Korea actually seems to have enjoyed a significant net inflow of Japanese capital as it had a trade deficit, whereas almost all the other colonies ran trade surpluses.

US colonialism in the Philippines dated from the Spanish-American war and was less exploitative than Dutch rule in Indonesia, with a smaller trade drain, and a bigger educational effort. The American presence in the Philippines (8,700) was proportionately as light as that of the British in India, but Americans were outnumbered by other foreign settlers, particularly by Japanese.

China, which was not the colony of any particular power, had been forced to cede territorial sovereignty to many foreign powers in the Treaty Ports. This foreign presence was relatively small by Asian standards and of about the same order of magnitude as the British presence in India. The peacetime economy of China was much less affected by the colonial presence than that of other Asian countries and the ratio of foreign trade to GDP was very low. Because of large remittances to China by emigrant Chinese communities, and because the foreign powers in China often spent more there on colonial-type purchases than they raised in local revenue, China ran a persistent trade deficit.

In default of complete balance-of-payments data for most of the countries, one crude clue to the size of the payments burden or 'drain' involved in colonial rule is the size of the commodity trade balance (see Table 16.2). It is quite clear that in the period when the Asian countries were colonies,

TABLE 16.2. Average ratio of exports (f.o.b.) to imports (c.i.f.)

	1840–69	1870–1912	1913–38	1950–9	1960–73
Developing Countries					
Indonesia	244.7	145.4[a]	175.0	139.1	112.2
Argentina	n.a	107.2	124.5	92.6	112.4
Brazil	97.9	126.3	127.0	100.6	97.8
Ceylon	86.0	96.4	122.8	109.1	97.8
China	n.a.	106.8	79.0	94.6	109.2
Egypt	155.3[b]	153.8	107.3	79.7	80.0
India	172.5	148.0	133.4	79.6	71.9
Indochina	n.a.	101.3[c]	122.9	26.8	13.7[d]
Korea	n.a.	47.5[e]	85.1	7.7[f]	34.1
Malaya	n.a.	n.a.	115.7	140.1	118.0
Mexico	n.a.	109.6[g]	131.6	78.0	67.8
Philippines	n.a.	118.3[h]	118.6	86.0	93.7
Thailand	n.a.	139.2	134.4	86.7	72.7
Average	n.a.	116.7	121.3	86.2	83.2
Developed Countries					
France	107.1	86.4	70.7	94.5	95.6
Germany	n.a.	85.6[i]	98.9[j]	107.5	114.9
Japan	n.a.	83.8	95.7	75.1	97.1
Netherlands	78.4[k]	80.1	70.1	83.2	88.8
UK	74.4	68.6	62.3	82.0	85.4
USA	92.3	125.2	140.0	136.4	118.7
Average	n.a.	88.3	89.6	96.5	100.1

[a] Excludes 1875
[b] 1850–69
[c] 1883–1912
[d] Excludes 1973; from 1955 the figures refer to South Vietnam
[e] 1886–1912
[f] Excludes 1950 and 1951
[g] 1881–9 and 1892–1910
[h] 1885–1912
[i] 1880–1912
[j] Excludes 1914–19
[k] 1846–69

Sources: 1950 onwards from UN, *Yearbook of International Trade Statistics*, except for China which is from US Congress (1978, p. 733). Earlier years for Developing Countries: Argentina: 1870–1910 from Ferns (1960, pp. 492–3); 1911–38 from Diaz-Alejandro (1970, pp. 461, 475–6). Brazil: 1840–1938 from IBGE (1960, p. 84). China: from Hsiao Liang-lin (1974, pp. 268–9) adjusted to a c.i.f./f.o.b. basis, and excluding re-exports (pp. 22–4). Mexico: 1881–1910 from Colegio de Mexico (1960, p. 175); 1913–38 from National Financiera (1966, pp. 243–4). 1913–38 imports adjusted upwards by 47.4% for undercounting of border trade; this is an

TABLE 16.2. (*cont.*)

average adjustment factor apparently applied by the Bank of Mexico in revaluing 1950–3 imports for this purpose. The previous figures for 1950–3 are in National Financiera (1963, p. 140). Thailand: 1870–1938 from Ingram (1971, pp. 333–4); includes trade in precious metals. Other Developing Countries from Mitchell (1982). Developed Countries: Earlier years for France, Germany, Netherlands and UK 1913–38 from Mitchell (1975); UK 1840–1913 from Imlah (1958, pp. 95–8) with re-exports excluded from imports. Japan: from Ohkawa and Shinohara (1979, pp. 332–5). USA: from US Dept. of Commerce (1975, pp. 884–6).

most of them had substantial export surpluses, and that since independence most of them have been able to run deficits. Trade accounts provide only a partial indicator of the balance-of-payments situation because part of the trade surplus was offset by service imports, or imports of precious metals.

In the 1913–38 period, the proportionate trade surplus of Indonesia was high with exports (f.o.b.) exceeding imports (c.i.f.) by an average of 75 per cent (Table 16.2). This is more than that of any of the other Asian countries and reflects the drain of The Netherlands on Dutch account (residents' home remittances, remittances to non-residential commercial interests, and government transfers) and much smaller remittances on Chinese account. In the period 1870–1912, the drain from Indonesia was smaller, but in the 1840–69 period of *cultuurstelsel* and primitive tribute, it was substantially higher.

In interpreting Table 16.2 it should be kept in mind that the ratio of trade to GDP varied a good deal between countries. For example, the average trade ratio in Indonesia was four times as high as in India (Table 16.3). If we combine this information with that in Table 16.2, it suggests that the unrequited export surplus was 2 per cent of Indian national income and 12.4 per cent of that of Indonesia, and therefore is a rough confirmation of our more direct estimates above.[6] In all the other Asian countries (with the probable exception of Burma)[7] the drain as measured in this proxy fashion was smaller than in Indonesia in 1913–38. However, the trade deficit overstates the payments drain for reasons already mentioned.

---

[6] The average trade surplus of Indonesia for 1913–38 equalled 75% of imports, or, alternatively stated, 43% of exports (75/175), and exports in 1929 (taken as a rough proxy for the 1913–38 ratio) were 29% GDP. Therefore the export surplus was 12.4% of GDP (i.e. 43 × 29).

[7] Hlaing (1964) estimates the share of exports in Burmese NDP at 38% in 1929 and 48% in 1938 and the Burmese export/import ratio at 142.3 in 1870–1915 and 193.0 in 1913–38. This would suggest that the trade surplus was 18.3% of NDP, i.e. bigger than the 12.4% found for Indonesia. However, Burma was part of the Indian customs area until 1937 and had official estimates only for seaborne trade. Hlaing used unpublished trade estimates of U Chit Maung.

TABLE 16.3. Ratio of merchandise exports to GDP at current prices

	1929	1950	1973	1986
Developing Countries				
Indonesia	29.0	7.7[a]	18.7	19.7
Argentina	26.7	8.4	8.6	8.7
Brazil	12.6	8.9	7.8	8.3
China	4.0	3.0	4.3	12.1
Egypt	n.a.	18.9	11.6	6.1
India	7.8	6.5	3.9	4.3
Korea	19.0	2.3	24.4	35.4
Malaya	n.a.	63.0	42.3	49.9
Mexico	12.4	10.9	4.1	12.5
Philippines	n.a.	9.5	17.6	15.5
Thailand	16.1	18.4	14.7	21.0
Average	n.a.	14.3	14.4	17.6
Developed Countries				
France	14.0	10.6	14.4	17.3
Germany	15.3	8.5	19.7	27.3
Japan	16.0	4.7	8.9	10.8
Netherlands	29.4	26.9	37.3	45.3
UK	15.5	14.4	16.4	19.5
USA	5.0	3.6	8.0	5.2
Average	15.9	11.5	17.5	20.9

[a] 1951

Sources: Developing Countries for pre-war years: Indonesia: CEI, Vol. II and Polak (1943); GDP in 1951 from Muljatno (1960). Argentina: Diaz-Alejandro (1970, pp. 14, 406, 461, 479). Brazil: Exports divided by current price GDP from Contador and Haddad (1975). China: Hsiao Liang-lin (1974, p. 280) and Liu and Yeh (1965, p. 66); post-war years: *An Economic Profile*, Vol. I (1967, pp. 73, 125), *Chinese Economy Post-Mao* (1978, pp. 231, 733) and World Bank data. Egypt: Hansen and Marzouk (1965, p. 174). India: *Cambridge Economic History of India*. Korea: Exports from Mitchell (1982); GDP from Sang-Chul Suh (1978). Malaya, Philippines, and Thailand in 1938 from Paauw (1963); Malayan GDP in 1950 and 1960 from Lim Chong-Yah (1967, p. 317). Mexico: GDP in current pesos from Fitzgerald (1984). Post-war years generally from *UN Yearbook of International Trade Statistics* and World Bank (1980). Developed Countries: Sources given in Maddison (1983).

A more accurate picture is given by the complete balance-of-payments data for Indonesia and India (see Maddison, 1985).

It is sometimes suggested that the apparent drain simply represents a normal and legitimate return of foreign investment in the colony, or on the entrepreneurship and skills furnished by the foreign settlers and adminis-

TABLE 16.4. Per capita net foreign capital position (portfolio and direct investments) of developing countries in 1938

	Foreign obligations ($m)	Foreign assets ($m)	Population (000s)	Net obligations per capita ($)
Burma	200	0	15,800	13
Ceylon	125	0	5,826	21
China				
(incl. Manchuria)	2,557	770	528,000	3
India	3,644	203	308,230	11
Indochina	391	0	23,000	17
Indonesia	2,378	7	68,409	35
Korea[a]	1,718	0	23,434	73
Malaya	696	1	4,235	164
Philippines	307	28	15,814	18
Taiwan	201	0	6,493	31
Thailand	200	0	14,755	14

[a] 1941.

Sources: Foreign obligations from Lewis (1948, pp. 321–41), except for India which is from Gurtoo, (1961, p. 69), and Korea which is from Sang-Chul Suh (1978, p. 129).

trators. It is true that there was a substantial foreign-owned capital stock in Indonesia, and it was bigger in per capita terms than in any other Asian country except Korea and Malaya (Table 16.4). However, in colonial situations such as in Indonesia where there had been a consistent and substantial trade surplus for 300 years, it is clear there was never any net transfer of funds from the metropole and that the foreign claims on Indonesia arose basically from reinvested earnings of the colonialists.[8]

Similarly, some of the earnings of foreigners derived not from the intrinsic worth of their entrepreneurial, administrative, and technical skills, but rather because they operated in a milieu which favoured them over the indigenous population who had little access to education or on-the-job methods of acquiring highly paid skills. The political system, too, systematically favoured expatriates. They had the dominant voice in the limited parliamentary body, and the higher levels of bureaucracy, which took orders from The Hague, were entirely Dutch. The banking, shipping, and insurance network was mainly in the hands of the Dutch, and so was estate management. Provision for indigenous education was weak, and the upper

---

[8] For trade balances from 1840 onwards see Table 16.2. For 1640–1840 see Prange (1935). There is an interesting article by Golay (1976) which reaches similar conclusions on the nature of the drain.

echelons of the old indigenous élite functioned mainly as instruments of the Dutch bureaucracy. Local entrepreneurs were almost entirely Chinese, not Indonesian. Colonialism skewed the 'human capital' situation against the locals.

On the other hand, it is only fair to note that the Indonesian trade balance continued to be positive after independence, presumably because of the continuance of substantial Chinese remittances, and the heavy dependence on expatriate skills and foreign capital.

Apart from the drain, and the handicap in developing indigenous human capital, the colonial tie also meant that Indonesia did not have autonomous macroeconomic policy weapons, as policy was dictated by the metropole's conception of its own interest. In the 1920s, this may not have been too harmful to Indonesia. Nationalists would have preferred tariff freedom to protect infant industry and provide revenue, but it is doubtful that this would have done much to improve welfare and growth in that period.

In the 1920s, the Dutch kept Indonesia out of the Stevenson scheme which the British devised to stabilize rubber prices, and this benefited In-

TABLE 16.5. Net domestic product deflators (1929 = 100)

	Netherlands	Indonesia	UK	India[a]
1921	114.3	132.8	138.0	126.1
1922	107.1	110.5	116.0	115.9
1923	100.0	108.8	106.6	109.6
1924	100.0	106.4	105.1	116.2
1925	100.0	104.5	105.5	113.6
1926	100.0	107.3	103.9	110.7
1927	100.0	100.2	101.4	108.2
1928	100.0	98.7	100.4	107.4
1929	100.0	100.0	100.0	100.0
1930	92.9	96.5	99.6	80.7
1931	85.7	73.1	97.2	71.9
1932	78.6	57.8	93.8	68.7
1933	78.6	47.6	92.6	65.0
1934	78.6	45.4	91.7	66.4
1935	78.6	45.8	92.7	66.9
1936	78.6	44.4	91.0	67.1
1937	78.6	48.6	96.6	68.9
1938	78.6	49.6	99.2	69.3
1939	85.7	48.1	101.7	74.1

[a] Indian figures are for fiscal years, 1921–2 *et seq.*

Sources: Netherlands from Central Bureau voor Statistiek (1979); Indonesia from Polak (1943); UK from Feinstein (1972); India from Sivasubramonian (1965).

TABLE 16.6. Foreign transfer burden of public debt service in NEI, 1921–1939 (% of NDP)

1921	1.39	1931	2.61
1922	1.62	1932	4.63
1923	1.77	1933	5.06
1924	1.81	1934	5.41
1925	1.68	1935	3.72
1926	1.62	1936	3.48
1927	1.74	1937	2.64
1928	2.01	1938	2.68
1929	1.74	1939	2.69
1930	1.94		

Sources: Debt service from P. Creutzberg, *Changing Economy in Indonesia*, Vol. II: *Public Finance 1816–1939*, 1976, pp. 82–3. NDP from Polak, 1943, p. 70.

donesia whose share of world markets grew. However, after 1929, one can argue that Dutch conjunctural policy damaged Indonesia.[9] In the first place, The Netherlands stayed in the gold bloc until 1936, long after British and US devaluations. This was not sensible from a metropolitan viewpoint in any case, but in Indonesia, which was competing on world markets with identical exports to those of neighbouring countries, it imposed deflationary hardships which could have been mitigated by simultaneous devaluation along with sterling (see Table 16.7 for exchange rates). The Japanese sensibly devalued by more than the British, which is one reason their exports did so well in the 1930s. In fact, Indonesian exports did not fall as much in volume as those of neighbouring countries because Dutch deflationary policy pushed prices and wages down very substantially.

As an independent country, Indonesia would probably not have pursued such a deflationary fiscal policy in the 1930s. It would certainly not have done so if it had been a Latin American country. By 1936, Indonesian prices had fallen to 44 per cent of their 1929 level, a much steeper decline than occurred in India, The Netherlands, or the UK (Table 16.5). Fiscal revenue fell considerably in money terms, although not in relation to the national income. Salaries were cut, but the public debt burden rose in real terms, even though the Dutch made a conversion issue which lowered the interest rate (Table 16.6). In addition, if Indonesia had been an independent country in the 1930s, it would probably have cut imports on a non-discriminatory basis by raising tariffs, whereas the Dutch used discriminatory quantitative restrictions, which favoured their exports rather than the cheaper ones available from Japan. This caused considerable dis-

---

[9] For an analysis of policy in the 1930s, see Prince and Baudet (1983, ch. 2).

TABLE 16.7. Exchange depreciation of other currencies against NEI guilder

	Malaya	India	Japan	UK	USA
1929	100.0	100.0	100.0	100.0	100.0
1930	99.3	98.9	106.0	99.8	99.6
1931	93.6	93.4	106.0	93.3	100.0
1932	73.0	73.6	62.1	72.6	100.0
1933	68.8	69.2	44.0	68.5	81.6
1934	62.4	61.5	37.9	61.7	59.6
1935	60.3	60.4	37.1	59.8	59.2
1936	64.5	64.8	38.8	63.8	62.4
1937	74.4	74.7	44.8	73.8	72.8
1938	73.8	73.6	44.8	73.2	72.8

Source: J. T. M. van Laanen, *Money and Banking 1816–1940*, Vol. VI of *Changing Economy in Indonesia* (The Hague: Nijhoff, 1980).

content, particularly as the restrictions mainly concerned cheap items of mass consumption (Ranneft, 1937).

In independent Latin American countries and China, the response to the crisis of the 1930s was debt default, but in Indonesia as in India and other colonies, the metropolitan power excluded such a solution. As a result the Indonesian depression was deeper than it need have been, though a considerable part of the deflation was absorbed by the very big fall in import volume. In 1929, Latin American countries were mostly without central banks, and their foreign transactions depended heavily on foreign banks as did those of Indonesia. However, in the 1930s they quickly acquired the instruments for autonomous economic policy. The exchange controls they imposed in those years increased their capacity to follow autonomous economic policy and the strengthening of indigenous banks also weakened the role of foreign commercial interests in their economies. This cathartic process did not occur in Indonesia until after independence.

References

Banerji, A. K. (1963), *India's Balance of Payments* (Bombay: Asia Publishing House).

Baudet, M. J., and Wijers, G. J. (1976), 'De Economische Betekenis van Nederlands-Indië voor Nederland, Oude en Nieuwe Berekeningen', *Economische en Statistische Berichten*, 15 Sept.

Centraal Bureau voor de Statistiek (1979), *Tachtig Jaren Statistiek in Tijdreeksen, 1899–1979* (The Hague: CBS).

Central Bureau of Statistics (1941), *Statistical Pocketbook of Indonesia* (Batavia: CBS).

CEI (1976), *Changing Economy in Indonesia*, Vol. ii: *Public Finance 1816–1939* (The Hague: Nijhoff).

Colegio de Mexico (1960), *Comercio Exterior de Mexico 1877–1911*, *Estadisticas Economicas del Porfiriato* (Mexico City: Colegio de Mexico).

Contador, C. R., and Haddad, C. L. (1975), 'Produto Real, Moeda e Precos: A Experiencia Brasileira no Periodo 1861–1970', *Revista Brasileira de Estatistica*, 36/143.

Derksen, J. B. D., and Tinbergen, J. (1945), 'Berekeningen over de Economische Betekenis van Nederlandsch-Indië voor Nederland', *Maandschrift* (The Hague: CBS).

Diaz-Alejandro, C. F. (1970), *Essays on the Economic History of the Argentine Republic* (New Haven: Yale Univ. Press).

Feinstein, C. H. (1972), *National Income, Expenditure and Output of the United Kingdom, 1855–1965* (Cambridge: CUP).

Ferns, H. S. (1960), *Britain and Argentina in the Nineteenth Century* (Oxford: OUP).

Feuerwerker, A. (1976), *The Foreign Establishment in China in the Early Twentieth Century* (Ann Arbor: Univ. of Michigan).

Fitzgerald, E. V. K. (1984), 'Restructuring through the Depression: The State and Capital Accumulation in Mexico, 1925–40', in R. Thorp (ed.), *Latin America in the 1930s: The Role of the Periphery in World Crisis* (London: Macmillan).

Golay, F. H. (1976), 'Southeast Asia: The "Colonial Drain" Revisited', in C. D. Cowan and O. W. Wolters (eds.), *Southeast Asian History and Historiography* (Ithaca: Cornell Univ. Press).

Griffiths, R. T., and de Meere, J. M. M. (1983), 'The Growth of the Dutch Economy in the Nineteenth Century—Back to Basics' (Amsterdam: Vrije Universiteit), mimeo.

Gurtoo, D. H. N. (1961), *India's Balance of Payments 1920–1960* (Delhi: Chand).

Hansen, B., and Marzouk, G. A. (1965), *Development and Economic Policy in the UAR (Egypt)* (Amsterdam: North-Holland).

Hlaing, A. (1964), 'Trends of Economic Growth and Income Distribution in Burma, 1870–1940', *Journal of the Burma Research Society*, 47/1.

Hsiao Liang-lin (1974), *China's Foreign Trade Statistics 1864–1949* (Cambridge, Mass: Harvard Univ. Press).

Hugo, G. J. (1980), 'Population Movements in Indonesia During the Colonial Period', in J. J. Fox (ed.), *Indonesia: Australian Perspectives*, Vol. i, *Indonesia: The Making of a Culture* (Canberra: Australian National University).

Hutton, J. H. (1933), *Census of India, 1931*, Vol. i, *India*, Pt. I, *Report* and Part II, *Imperial Tables*, (Delhi).

IBGE (1960). *O Brasil en Números*, Appendix to *Anuario Estatistico do Brasil 1960* (Rio de Janeiro: IBGE).

Imlah, A. H. (1958), *Economic Elements in the Pax Britannica* (Cambridge, Mass: Harvard University Press).

Ingram, J. C. (1971), *Economic Change in Thailand 1850–1970* (Stanford: Stanford Univ. Press).

Kuznets, S. (1979), 'Growth and Structural Shifts', in W. Galenson (ed.), *Economic Growth and Structural Change in Taiwan* (Ithaca: Cornell Univ. Press).

Lewis, C. (1948), *The United States and Foreign Investment Problems* (Washington, DC: Brookings Institution).

Lim Chong-Yah (1967), *Economic Development of Modern Malaya* (Kuala Lumpur: OUP).

Liu, T. C., and Yeh, K. C. (1965), *The Economy of the Chinese Mainland* (Princeton: Princeton Univ. Press).

Maddison, A. (1971), *Class Structure and Economic Growth: India and Pakistan since the Moghuls* (London: Allen & Unwin).

——(1982), *Phases of Capitalist Development* (Oxford: OUP).

——(1983), 'Economic Stagnation since 1973—Its Nature and Causes: A Six-Country Survey', *De Economist* 131/4.

——(1985), *Two Crises: Latin America and Asia 1929–38 and 1973–83* (Paris: OECD Development Centre).

Mitchell, B. R. (1975), *European Historical Statistics 1750–1970*, (London: Macmillan).

——(1982), *International Historial Statistics: Africa and Asia* (London: Macmillan).

Muljatno (1960), 'Perhitungan Pendapatan Nasional Indonesia untuk 1953 dan 1954', *Ekonomi dan Keuangan Indonesia*, 13 (Mar./Apr.).

Myint, H. (1958), 'The "Classical Theory" of International Trade and Underdeveloped Countries', *Economic Journal*, 68, pp. 317–37.

Nacional Financiera (1963), *50 Años de Revolucion Mexicana en Cifras* (Mexico City).

——(1966) *La Economia Mexicana en Cifras* (Mexico City).

Ohkawa, K., and Shinohara, M. (eds.) (1979), *Patterns of Japanese Economic Development: A Quantitative Appraisal* (New Haven: Yale Univ. Press).

Paauw, D. S. (1963), 'Economic Progress in Southeast Asia', *Journal of Asian Studies*, 23/1, pp. 69–92.

Polak, J. J. (1943), *The National Income of the Netherlands Indies, 1921–1939* (New York: Institute of Pacific Relations); reprinted in *Economy in Indonesia*, Vol. v: *National Income* (The Hague: Nijhoff, 1979).

Prange, A. J. A. (1935), *De Nederlandsch-Indische Betalingsbalans* (Leiden).

Prince, G. H. A., and Baudet, H. (1983), ch. 2 in H. Baudet and M. Fennema (eds.), *Het Nederlands Belang bij Indië* (Utrecht: Spectrum).

Ranneft, J. W. Meyer (1937), 'Hollands Fout in Indië', *De Gids*, 1.

Remer, C. F. (1933), *Foreign Investments in China* (New York: Macmillan).

Robequain, C. (1944), *The Economic Development of French Indo-China* (London: OUP).

——(1948), *Malaya, Indonesia, Borneo and the Philippines* (London: Longmans, Green & Co.).

Sang-Chul Suh (1978), *Growth and Structural Changes in the Korean Economy 1910–1940* (Cambridge, Mass.: Harvard Univ. Press).

Sivasubramonian, S. (1965), 'National Income of India 1900–01 to 1946–47', Ph.D thesis, Delhi School of Economics.

Snodgrass, D. R. (1966), *Ceylon: An Export Economy in Transition* (Homewood: Irwin).

US Congress (1967), *An Economic Profile of Mainland China*: *Studies Prepared for*

The Joint Economic Committe, US Congress, 2 vols. (Washington, DC: US Govt. Printing Office).

——(1978), *Chinese Economy Post-Mao: Studies Prepared for the Joint Economic Committee, US Congress* (Washington, DC: US Govt. Printing Office).

US Dept. of Commerce (1975), *Historical Statistics of the United States*, Vol. ii (Washington, DC: Bureau of the Census).

Vlieland, C. A. (1932), *British Malaya: A Report on the 1931 Census* (London: HMSO).

World Bank (1980), *World Tables* (Washington, DC: World Bank).

Bibliography of the Works of Ian Little

Books (in order of publication)

A Critique of Welfare Economics (Oxford, Clarendon Press, 1950; 2nd edn. 1957).

The Price of Fuel (Oxford, Clarendon Press, 1953).

Nuclear Power and Italy's Energy Position, with P. N. Rosenstein-Rodan (National Planning Association, Washington, DC, 1957).

Concentration in British Industry: an empirical study of the structure of industrial production 1935–51, with R. Evely (Cambridge: CUP, 1960).

Aid to Africa: An appraisal of U.K. policy for aid to Africa south of the Sahara (Overseas Development Institute, Pergamon Press, London, 1964).

International Aid: A discussion of the flow of public resources from rich to poor countries with particular reference to British policy, with J. M. Clifford (Allen & Unwin, London, 1965; reprint Aldine, Chicago, 1967).

Higgledy Piggledy Growth Again: An investigation of the predictability of company earnings and dividends in the UK 1951–61, with A. C. Rayner (Blackwell, Oxford 1966; reprint Augustus M. Kelley, New Jersey, 1971).

Towards a Strategy for Development Co-operation, with special reference to Asia, editor with H. B. Chenery, F. Baade, J. Kaufmann, L. H. Klaassen, and J. Tinbergen (Rotterdam University Press, 1967, and contributed chapter on 'Aid; project, programme, and procurement tying').

Manual of Industrial Project Analysis in Developing Countries: Vol. ii, *Social Cost-Benefit Analysis*, with J. A. Mirrlees (Development Centre, OECD, Paris, 1969; also French translation).

Industry and Trade in Some Developing Countries: A comparative study, with T. Scitovsky and M. FG. Scott (published for the Development Centre of the OECD by OUP, 1970; also French and Spanish translations).

A Social Cost-Benefit Analysis of the Kulai Oil Palm Estate West Malaysia with D. G. Tipping (Development Centre Studies: Series on Cost-Benefit Analysis, Case Study no. 3, OECD, Paris, 1972).

Estudio Social Del Costo-Beneficio en la Industria de Paises en Desarrollo: Manual de Evaluacion de Proyectos, con J. A. Mirrlees (trans. from Vol. ii, *Manual of Industrial Project Analysis*) (Centro de Estudios Monetarios Latinoamer, Mexico, 1973).

Project Appraisal and Planning for Developing Countries, with J. A. Mirrlees (Heinemann Educational, London, 1974).

Import Controls versus Devaluation and Britain's Economic Prospects, with W. M. Corden and M. FG. Scott (Guest Paper no. 2, Trade Policy Research Centre, London, 1975).

Using Shadow Prices, editor with M. FG. Scott (Heinemann Educational, London, 1976).

Una Critica dell' Economica del benessene, trs. Guido Tesarum (Instituto Editoriale Internatzionale, Milano, 1976, with new introduction by the author).

The Case against General Import Restrictions, with M. FG. Scott and W. M. Corden (Trade Policy Research, London, 1980).

Economic Development: theory, policy and international relations (Basic Books, New York, 1982).

Small Manufacturing Enterprises: A comparative study of India and other economies, with Dipak Mazumdar and John M. Page, Jr. (published for the World Bank by the OUP, 1987).

Contributions to Books (in order of publication)

'Fiscal Policy', in G. D. N. Worswick and P. H. Ady (eds.), *The British Economy 1945–50*, (OUP, 1952), ch. 8.

'Sources of Power: The Long-Term Outlook', in A. Shonfield (ed.), *The Chambers of Commerce Annual*, (London, 1958).

'Direct versus Indirect Taxes', in R. A. Musgrave and C. S. Shoup (eds.), *Readings in the Economics of Taxation*, (American Economic Association, Allen & Unwin, London, 1959), pp. 123–31.

(with R. R. Neild and C. R. Ross) 'The scope and limitations of monetary policy', in *Principal Memoranda of Evidence Submitted to the Committee on the Working of the Monetary System*, Vol. iii (HMSO, London, 1960).

'Fiscal Policy', in G. N. D. Worswick and P. H. Ady (eds.), *The British Economy in the 1950s* (OUP, 1962), ch. 8.

Comment on 'Evaluation of "Social Income": Capital Formation and Wealth by P. Samuelson', in D. C. Hague (ed.), *The Theory of Capital*, Conference held by IEA at Corfu (Macmillan, London, 1963), pp. 310–12.

'Tax Policy and the Third Plan' and 'The Real Cost of Labour and the Choice between Consumption and Investment', in P. N. Rosenstein-Rodan (ed.), *Pricing and Fiscal Policies* (Allen & Unwin, London, 1964), ch. 3, pp. 30–76 and ch. 4, pp. 77–91.

'Executive, Co-ordinating, Supervisory and Evaluation Machinery', in *Overcoming Obstacles to Development, Impressions and Papers of the Fourth Cambridge Conference on Development Problems*, 12–25 Sept. 1965 at Jesus College, Cambridge, ed. R. Robinson (Cambridge University Overseas Studies Committee, 18 Petty Cury, Cambridge, undated), pp. 135–9.

'Direct versus Indirect Taxes', in K. J. Arrow and T. Scitovsky (eds.), *Readings in Welfare Economics* (American Economic Association, Richard D. Irwin Inc., Homewood, 1969), pp. 608–15.

'Public Sector Project Selection in Relation to Indian Development', in A. V. Bhuleshkar (ed.), *Indian Economic Thought and Development* (C. Hurst, London, 1969), pp. 228–58.

'Regional International Companies as an Approach to Economic Intergration', in P. Robson (ed.), *International Economic Integration* (Penguin Books, Harmondsworth, 1971), pp. 304–10.

(with J. A. Mirrlees) 'Further Reflections on the O.E.C.D. Manual of Project Analysis in Developing Countries', in J. Bhagwati and R. S. Eckaus (eds.), *Development and Planning: Essays in honour of Paul Rosenstein-Rodan*, (Allen & Unwin, London, 1972), ch. 15, pp. 257–80.

'On Measuring the Value of Private Direct Overseas Investment', in G. Ranis (ed.), *The Gap Between Rich and Poor Nations*, Conference held by IEA at Bled, Yugoslavia (Macmillan, London, 1972), ch. 8.

'Social Choice and Individual Values', in E. S. Phelps (ed.), *Economic Justice* (Penguin Education, Baltimore, 1973), pp. 137–52.

'A Critical Examination of India's Third Five Year Plan', in C. D. Wadhva (ed.), *Some Problems of India's Economic Policy*, (Tata McGraw-Hill, New Delhi, 1973), pp. 116–36.

'The Economy of Poor Countries and their Population Stabilization: An Introduction', in H. B. Parry (ed.), *Population and its Problems: A plain man's guide* (OUP, 1974), pp. 213–16.

(with K. M. McLeod) 'The New Pricing Policy of the British Airports Authority', in G. P. Howard (ed.), *Airport Economic Planning* (MIT Press, Cambridge, Mass., 1974), pp. 445–66.

'The Use and Abuse of Capital in Developing Countries', in Y. Ramati (ed.), *Economic Growth in Developing Countries—Materials and Human Resources: Proceedings of the Seventh Rehovot Conference* (Praeger Publishers, New York, 1975), pp. 221–9.

'Bretton Woods'; 'Development Economics'; 'Necessary and Sufficient Conditions'; 'Take Off Point'; 'Under-development'; 'Welfare, Welfare Economics', in A. Bullock and O. Stallybrass (eds.), *The Fontana Dictionary of Modern Thought*, (Collins, London, 1977), pp. 77–8, 167–8, 413, 623, 652–53, 672.

'Welfare Criteria, Distribution and Cost-Benefit Analysis', in M. J. Boskin (ed.), *Economics and Human Welfare: Essays in honour of Tibor Scitovsky* (Academic Press, New York, 1979), pp. 125–31.

'An Economic Reconnaissance', in W. Galenson (ed.), *Economic Growth and Structural Change in Taiwan* (Cornell Univ. Press, Ithaca 1979), pp. 448–507.

'The Developing Countries and the International Order', in R. C. Amacher, G. Haberler, and T. D. Willett (eds.), *Challenges to a Liberal International Economic Order* (AEI Symposia, Washington, DC, 1979), pp. 259–78.

'Distributive Justice and the New International Order', in P. Oppenheimer (ed.), *Issues in International Economics* (Oriel Press, London, 1980), pp. 37–53.

'Social Democracy and the International Economy', in D. Lipsey and D. Leonard (eds.), *The Socialist Agenda: Crosland's Legacy* (Cape, London, 1981), pp. 63–74.

'The Experience and Causes of Rapid Labour Intensive Development in Korea, Taiwan Province, Hong Kong and Singapore and the Possibilities of Emulation' in E. Lee (ed.), *Export led Industrialization and Development* (Geneva, 1981), ch. 2, pp. 23–46.

Comment on S. Kuznets's 'Driving Forces of Economic Growth: what can we learn from history?' in H. Giersch (ed.), *Towards an Explanation of Economic Growth: Symposium 1980* (Institut für Weltwirtschaft an der Universität Kiel, 1981), pp. 65–9.

'Indian Industrialization before 1945', in M. Gersovitz *et al.* (eds.), *The Theory and Experience of Economic Development: Essays in Honour of Sir Arthur Lewis* (Allen & Unwin, London, 1982), pp. 356–71.

'Import Controls and Exports in Developing Countries', in R. K. Ghosh (ed.),

International Trade and Third World Development (International Development Resource Books, Westport, 1984), pp. 268–77.

'Discussion' in A. P. Thirlwall (ed.), *Keynes and Economic Development* (Macmillan, London, 1987), pp. 130–3.

'A Comment on Professor Toye's Paper', in L. Emmerij (ed.), *Development Policies and the Crisis of the 1980s* (Development Centre of the OECD, Paris, 1987).

'Crosland, Anthony', in J. Eatwell, M. Milgate, and P. Newman (eds.), *The New Palgrave: A Dictionary of Economics* (Macmillan, London, 1987), Vol. i, p. 728.

'Comments on Wolfram Fischer, "Swings between Protection and Free Trade in History"', in H. Giersch (ed.), *Free Trade in the World Economy: Towards an Opening of Markets* (Institut für Weltwirtschaft an der Universität Kiel, J. C. B. Mohr (Paul Siebeck), Tübingen, 1987).

'Resource Use Efficiency and the Small Scale Enterprise', in K. B. Suri (ed.), *Small Scale Enterprises in Industrial Development: The Indian Experience* (Sage Publications, New Delhi, 1988), pp. 118–28.

'Comment on Professor Findlay's Paper', in G. Ranis and T. P. Schultz (eds.), *The State of Development Economics: Progress and Prospects* (Blackwell, Oxford, 1988).

'The Macroeconomic Effects of Foreign Aid: Issues and Evidence—A Comment', in C. J. Jepma (ed.), *North-South Co-operation in Retrospect and Prospect* (Routledge, London, 1988).

Articles (in order of publication)

'A Reformulation of the Theory of Consumer's Behaviour' *Oxford Economic Papers*, NS 1 (Jan. 1949). pp. 90–9.

'The Valuation of Social Income', *Economica*, 16 (Feb. 1949), pp. 11–26.

'The Foundations of Welfare Economics', *Oxford Economic Papers*, NS 1 (June 1949), pp. 227–46.

'A Note on the Interpretation of Index Numbers', *Economica*, 16 (Nov. 1949), pp. 369–70.

'Welfare and Tariffs', *Review of Economic Studies*, 16/2 (1949), pp. 65–70.

'The Economist and the State', *Review of Economic Studies* 17 (1949), pp. 75–6.

'Economic Behaviour and Welfare', *Mind*, 1 (1949), pp. 195–209.

'The Theory of Consumer Behavior: A Comment', *Oxford Economic Papers*, NS 2, pp. 132–3.

'Direct versus Indirect Taxes', *Economic Journal*, 61 (Sept. 1951), pp. 577–84.

'Electricity Tariffs: A Comment', *Economic Journal*, 61 (Dec. 1951), pp. 875–82.

'Social Choice and Individual Values', *Journal of Political Economy*, 60 (Oct. 1952), pp. 422–32.

'L'advantage Collectif', *Economie Appliquee* (Paris) 5/4 (Oct.–Dec. 1952), pp. 455–68.

'Classical Growth', *Oxford Economic Papers*, NS 9 (Jan. 1957), pp. 152–77.

'The Economist in Whitehall', *Lloyds' Bank Review*, 44 (Apr. 1957), pp. 29–40.

'Die Rolle des Nationalokonomen in Whitehall', *Konjunkturpolitik*, Berlin (1957), pp. 129–42.

'The Aims of Monetary Policy', *Oxford Institute of Economics and Statistics Bulletin*, 19 (Nov. 1957), pp. 315–17.

'The Role of the Economist in Whitehall', *Administration*, Dublin, 6/2 (Summer 1958), pp. 151–65.

'Atomic Bombay?' *Economic and Political Weekly*, Bombay (29 Nov. 1958), pp. 1483–6.

'Some Aspects of the Structure of British Industry, 1935–1951', with R. Evely, *Trans. Manchester Statistical Society* (Session 1957–8), pp. 1–26.

'The Strategy of Indian Development', *National Institute Economic Review*, no. 9 (May 1960), pp. 20–9.

'The Third Five Year Plan and the Strategy of Indian Development', *Economic and Political Weekly*, Bombay, 12/23–5 (1960), pp. 885–91.

'The Real Cost of Labour and the Choice between Consumption and Investment', *Quarterly Journal of Economics*, 25 (Feb. 1961), pp. 1–15.

'A Critical Examination of India's Third Five Year Plan', *Oxford Economic Papers*, NS 14 (Feb. 1962), pp. 1–24.

'Welfare Criteria: a comment, a reply', *Economic Journal*, 72 (Mar. 1962), pp. 229–34.

'Higgledy Piggledy Growth', *Oxford Institute of Economics and Statistics Bulletin*, 24 (Nov. 1962), pp. 387–412.

'Two Comments', *Economic Journal*, 73 (Dec. 1963), pp. 778–9.

'Welfare Economics, Ethics and Essentialism: A Comment', *Economica*, 32 (May 1965), pp. 223–5.

'Regional International Companies as an Approach to Economic Integration', *Journal of Common Market Studies* 5/2 (1966), pp. 181–6.

'Direkte Gegen Indirekte Steurn', *Finanztheorie*, Cologne (1969), pp. 354–62.

'Symposium on Project Appraisal in Lesser Developed Countries', *Journal of Agricultural Economics*, 22/3 (1971), pp. 267–76.

'Trade and Public Finance', a memorial lecture for V. K. Ramaswami at the Delhi School of Economics, Nov. 1970, *Indian Economic Review*, NS 6/2 (1971), pp. 119–43.

'The New Pricing Policy of the British Airports Authority', with K. M. McLeod, *Journal of Transport Economics and Policy*, 6/2 (May 1972), pp. 101–15.

'A Reply to some Criticisms of the O.E.C.D. Manual', with J. A. Mirrlees, *Oxford Institute of Economics and Statistics Bulletin*, 34/1 (1972), pp. 153–68.

'Coping with the Arab Billions', with R. E. Mabro, *Financial Times*, 22 Dec. 1973.

'Economic Relations with the Third World—Old Myths and New Prospects', *Scottish Journal of Political Economy*, 22/3 (1975), pp. 223–35.

'Perspectives for the Second Half of the Second U. N. Development Decade', *Journal of Development Planning*, no. 9 (1976), pp. 19–51.

'Import Controls and Exports in Developing Countries', *Finance and Development*, 15/3 (1978), pp. 20–3.

'Robert Cooter and Peter Rappaport "Were the Ordinalists Wrong about Welfare Economics?": A Comment', *Journal of Economic Literature*, 23/3 (1985), pp. 1186–8.

'Small Manufacturing Enterprises in Developing Countries', *World Bank Economic Review*, 1 (Jan. 1987), 203–35.

(with V. R. Joshi) 'Indian Macroeconomics Policies', *Economic and Political Weekly*, Bombay, 28 Feb. 1987.

Reviews (in order of publication)

A la recherche d'une discipline economique by M. Allais, *Economic Journal*, Sept. 1950, pp. 558–60.

Income and Wealth: Series I, ed. E. Lundberg, *Journal of Political Economy* (1952), pp. 172–3.

Welfare and Competition by T. Scitovsky, *Economertrica* (1952), pp. 703–4.

Welfare Economics and the Theory of the State by W. J. Baumol, *Economica* (Feb. 1953), pp. 78–80.

Principles of Private and Public Planning by W. Keilhau, *Economic Journal* (Mar. 1953), pp. 133–5.

The History of Economic Analysis by J. A. Schumpeter, *Economic History Review* (1955), pp. 91–8.

An Expenditure Tax by N. Kaldor, *Economic Journal* (Mar. 1956), pp. 116–20.

The Role of the Economist as Official Adviser by W. A. Johr and H. W. Singer, trans. by J. Degras and S. Frowein, *Economic Journal* (Mar. 1956), pp. 133–5.

Theoretical Welfare Economics by J. de V. Graaff, *Economica* (Aug. 1957), pp. 262–4.

Some Economic Aspects of the Bhakra Nangal Project by K. N. Raj *Economic Journal* (June 1961), pp. 413–15.

Indian Economic Policy and Development by P. T. Bauer, *Economic Journal* (Dec. 1961), pp. 835–8.

Equilibrium and Growth in the World Economy by R. Nurkse, *Economic Journal* (Sept. 1962), pp. 688–9.

The Development of the Indian Economy by W. B. Reddaway, *Economic Journal* (Sept. 1962), pp. 722–3.

The Management of the British Economy by J. C. R. Dow, *Economic Journal* (Dec. 1964), pp. 983–85.

Project Selection for National Plans, Vol. i by A. Papandreou and U. Zohar, *Journal of Economic Literature* (1974), pp. 1336–7.

Economic Growth and Social Equity in Developing Countries by I. Adelman and C. T. Morris; and Redistribution with Growth by H. Chenery *et al.*, *Journal of Development Economics*, 3 (1976), pp. 99–106.

Pioneers in Development ed. G. M. Meier and D. Seers; and The Hobbled Giant: Essays on the World Bank by S. Please, *Finance and Development*, 22/1 (1985), pp. 47–8).

Forthcoming

(with V. R. Joshi) 'Indian Macroeconomic Policy', in R. Findlay, P. J. K. Kouri, and J. B. de Macedo (eds.), *Debt, Stabilization and Development: Proceedings of a Conference in Memory of Carlos Diaz-Alejandro* held at Helsinki, 1986.

Unpublished

Report on the Heavy Electrical Project at Bhopal, *Bell Mission Report*, IBRD, 1966.

Outline of Programme for Setting Up a System of Project Evaluation, Secretary of Planning Commission, New Delhi, 11 Nov. 1970.

External Post-Evaluation Report prepared for the Asian Development Bank: The First Loan to the Medium Industry Bank in the Republic of Korea, Feb. 1976.

I. Index of Subjects

II. Index of Countries

III. Index of Persons